KNOWLEDGE NEGOTIATION

KNOWLEDGE
NEGOTIATION

Edited by

Rod Moyse

Department of Educational Research
Lancaster University, Lancaster, UK

and

Mark Elsom-Cook

Institute of Educational Technology
The Open University
Milton Keynes, UK

ACADEMIC PRESS
Harcourt Brace Jovanovich, Publishers
London   San Diego   New York
Boston   Sydney   Tokyo   Toronto

ACADEMIC PRESS LIMITED
24–28 Oval Road
London NW1 7DX

United States Edition published by
ACADEMIC PRESS INC.
San Diego, CA 92101

This book is printed on acid-free paper

A catalogue record of this book is available from the British Library

ISBN 0–12–509378–0

Typeset by Columns Design and Production Services Ltd, Reading
Printed and bound in Great Britain by Hartnolls Ltd, Bodmin, Cornwall

Contents

Contributors

Laurence Alpay
Institute of Educational Technology
The Open University
Walton Hall
Milton Keynes MK7 6AA
UK

Michael Baker
Centre National de la Recherche Scientifique
Laboratoire IRPEACS
93 Chemin des Mouilles   BP 167
69131 Ecully Cedex
France

Mike Brayshaw
Human Cognition Research Laboratory
The Open University
Walton Hall
Milton Keynes MK7 6AA
UK

Roshni Devi
Institute of Educational Technology
The Open University
Walton Hall
Milton Keynes MK7 6AA
UK

Pierre Dillenbourg
Faculté de Psychologie et des Sciences de l'Education
Université de Genève
3 Place de l'Université
1211 Geneva 4
Switzerland

Mark Elsom-Cook
Institute of Educational Technology
The Open University
Walton Hall
Milton Keynes MK7 6AA
UK

Peter Goodyear
Department of Educational Research
University of Lancaster
Lancaster LA1 4YW
UK
Gordon McCalla
ARIES Laboratory
Department of Computational Science
University of Saskatchewan
Saskatoon, Saskatchewan S7N 0W0
Canada
Rod Moyse
Department of Educational Research
Lancaster University
Lancaster LA1 4YW
UK
Rachel Rimmershaw
Department of Educational Research
University of Lancaster
Lancaster LA1 4YW
UK
John Self
Department of Computing
University of Lancaster
Lancaster LA1 4YW
UK
Carolyn Stone
Department of Educational Research
University of Lancaster
Lancaster LA1 4YW
UK
Barbara Wasson
ARIES Laboratory
Department of Computational Science
University of Saskatchewan
Saskatoon, Saskatchewan S7N 0W0
Canada

Present address: Norwegian Telecom Research Department
                          Elverhøy N-9000, Tromsø, Norway

Acknowledgements

This book owes much to the unstinting help and encouragement given by many friends. In particular our thanks must go to Andrew Carrick and the people at Academic for making it all seem so simple, and to Karen Valley for knocking the references into shape. Colleagues and staff at the Open University provided the kind of supportive environment where things could get done, and library legwork was carried out by Ian Carr.

1 Knowledge Negotiation: An Introduction

ROD MOYSE[1] and MARK ELSOM-COOK[2]

[1] *Department of Educational Research,
Lancaster University, Lancaster, UK*
[2] *Institute of Educational Technology,
The Open University, Milton Keynes, UK*

1 THE IDEA

There has recently been a move in research on Intelligent Tutoring Systems (ITS) away from the idea that the tutor takes a directive role controlling the interaction. This view implied that the tutor had the *correct* knowledge about the subject area and was in a position of authority over the student. It has been realized that for many domains there is not a single correct representation, and that the interpretation of the domain, or 'viewpoint', must be jointly constructed between teacher and learner. This implies the need for representations and mechanisms to support negotiation. In this sense "Knowledge Negotiation" supports the direction established in an earlier book (Elsom-Cook 1990a) where an approach to less directive systems via Guided Discovery was presented. This approach required that the learner and tutor reach agreement about the locus of control of the interaction.

The new book examines some other implications of a less directive approach for ITS. In particular, it focusses on the model of tutoring as an exercise in 'negotiation' between the tutor and the student. This does not mean that knowledge negotiation is primarily concerned with specific techniques for dialogue between human and machine. Its main concern is with the interplay between such factors as the knowledge states, goals and experience of the student, and the reasoning capabilities and knowledge representations of the tutoring system. In this context, 'negotiation' refers to the general process by which the domain interpretation is constructed

KNOWLEDGE NEGOTIATION
ISBN 0–12–509378–0

or chosen, and to the set of techniques and design methods by which the desired adaptation to the student is achieved. The book introduces the idea of negotiated tutoring and examines its implications for knowledge representation, student modelling, interaction with the student and the design of the human–computer interface.

There are a number of main factors which are considered. The central issue is to decide what negotiation is, and what representations and mechanisms are required in order to support it. The representations required must get away from the idea of a single 'correct' representation, and in this book two approaches to this problem can be identified. One is the use of multiple viewpoints (see Chapter 5) and the other is the use of a single representation which permits uncertain knowledge (see Chapter 9). The mechanisms are discussed in terms of dialogue strategies, explanation generation and interpretation of the interface.

It is also important to note that the use of negotiation as a central component of interaction does not necessarily imply that that negotiation is explicit. As Rimmershaw illustrates (Chapter 10), there are many cases in human–human interaction where the negotiation is implicit in the communication. There is a need to make this negotiation explicit (as Baker attempts in Chapter 9) in order to understand the mechanisms, before it will be possible to utilize those mechanisms for implicit negotiation with the machine.

It can also be seen in this book that knowledge negotiation is sometimes treated as an engineering solution to the problems of tutoring, and sometimes as a theoretical issue. As attempts are made to make machines which can teach in domains that do not have clear or simple structures, it becomes apparent that the mechanisms which have often been used in ITS to date will not generalize to the new domains. Where new mechanisms are developed, they can also be applied to the more structured domains to give a wider variety of teaching styles. As a theoretical issue, it is clear that negotiation of the sort described here is a widely occuring phenomenon of interaction, and one for which computational models have not been developed. Work that treats negotiation as a theoretical issue is concerned with understanding human–human interaction as much as with the development of ITS.

In the remainder of this chapter we will provide further background to these ideas. Section 2 is concerned with the issues of knowledge representation. It reviews some of the more relevant approaches to representation that have been used in the ITS literature, and presents some of the reasons for using negotiation by contrast with a communication-based model. In Section 3 we present some design issues for a negotiation-based system, and guide the reader through the structure of the book in relation to those issues.

2   MULTIPLE VIEWPOINTS: THE NEED FOR KNOWLEDGE NEGOTIATION

2.1   Past work

"The multiple-viewpoint framework allows us to conceptualize the whole question of knowledge-driven CAI in a new way, in terms of how knowledge should be partitioned among different viewpoints" (Stevens et al. 1979. 1982 reprint, p. 23).

There are many references in the literature of ITS to the virtues of using multiple representations of the domain knowledge for a system, in order to express different viewpoints upon that domain. (These should not be confused with the 'viewpoints' of Lesgold (1988), which are primarily concerned with the issue of curriculum organization for tutoring systems.) From this literature we have identified four major reasons for incorporating multiple viewpoints into a teaching system. These issues are:

(a) The need to use multiple viewpoints in order to correctly carry out a single activity.
(b) The need to use different viewpoints in order to carry out different activities.
(c) The need to employ different viewpoints at different points along a learning path.
(d) The possibly contrasting needs for system efficiency in task execution, and clarity in explanations given to the student.

A possible fifth issue is the desire to promote meta-cognition and reflection in the student. These issues, and the influence that multiple viewpoints have had on system design, are discussed in the following sub-sections.

2.1.1   Different viewpoints required for the same activity

The earliest and most explicit statement of the need for multiple viewpoints in tutoring systems is found in the work of Stevens et al. (1979), when they discuss the limitations of the WHY system. In order to tutor the causes of heavy coastal rainfall, they implemented the domain representations of their system in the form of 'scriptal' knowledge, which defined the sequence of conditions leading to a downpour and described such entities as a warm airflow and warm water mass. This was found to be inadequate, however, as students' accounts of the process after tutoring contained a number of bugs representing the importation and incorrect use of concepts external to the intended domain. An example is the 'sponge' bug, which explains heavy rainfall in terms of the moist air mass being 'squeezed' against the coastal mountains. They concluded that it would also be necessary to represent and tutor 'functional' knowledge of particular processes, such as condensation, and of such generalized relationships as 'inverse processes' and 'feedback systems'. They also make the point that these differing viewpoints would have to be properly integrated and updated if other bugs were to be avoided. The argument here is that if students are to acquire knowledge about this domain without bugs or misconceptions, then different viewpoints on the domain will have to be tutored and integrated. (A means of implementing both viewpoints is described by Moyse in Chapter 5.)

Stevens and Collins (1980) discuss the issue of viewpoints (here 'views', or 'points of view') in a more general context. They discuss viewpoints in terms of alternative 'models' which can be applied to a given situation to form hypotheses and make predictions. They conclude that specific strategies must be available to determine when to use a given model, and also to determine how this model relates to the other models that might be used. This is seen as having major implications for education generally, and as necessitating a move away from 'static' or 'surface' forms of knowledge representation such as that used for WHY (Stevens et al. 1979).

A different combination of viewpoints is shown to be necessary by work on the successive versions of the SOPHIE system. This system was designed to train students in the repair of electronic circuits by having them find the faults in a simulated circuit. In SOPHIE I (Brown & Burton 1975) the student may advance a hypothesis and ask for feedback. This hypothesis is evaluated by comparing the current values it predicts with those found in the simulations of a working and a faulted circuit. (A numerical model of the circuit provides quantitative data about the various states within it). This data is interpreted by 'inference specialists' which embody the laws of electronics. This allows hypothesis generation and testing, but not causal explanation. The designers hoped to achieve such explanation by means of another module which contained qualitative knowledge, such as which components are most likely to fail, how power amplifiers may be stressed, and heuristics about how to combine this knowledge with the quantitative data.

Their ambitions were partly realized in SOPHIE II (Brown et al. 1976). Here, a troubleshooting expert demonstrated how it solved a problem by qualitative reasoning. It attempted to make its measurements causally meaningful, and to explain its strategy *en route* to a solution. In summary, both qualitative and quantitative analyses of the same electrical circuit were needed in order to provide a tutoring episode which contained both hypothesis testing and causal explanation. This may be described as a need for complementary modes of analysis or, more loosely, as a need for different viewpoints.

For SOPHIE III (Brown et al. 1982) it was intended that yet more viewpoints should be added, with the intention of providing active coaching in relation to the student's performance. The design called for an 'electronics expert' to draw on both the quantitative and qualitative knowledge of circuit behaviour so as to build up a database for a 'troubleshooting expert'. This troubleshooter was to have circuit-independent knowledge of how to manage a set of fault hypotheses, and how to propose new measurements to the electronics expert.

Yet other kinds of viewpoints may be found in NEOMYCIN (Clancey 1983). The ancestor of this system, MYCIN (Shortliffe 1976), was not a tutoring system, but an expert system designed to diagnose bacterial infections. It was, however, used as the basis (domain representation) of GUIDON (Clancey 1979), and it was this exercise which led directly to the development of NEOMYCIN. MYCIN attempted to formalize the knowledge of medical experts in a series of condition-action (if . . . then . . .) rules. The order of these rules, and the order of their subgoals, was critical to successful diagnosis. Each one that fired contributed to the database of evolving hypotheses. There was no explicit problem-solving strategy (beyond exhaustive search) built into the system. Rather, it ploughed through the same set of rules for each diagnosis. Although it was quite successful at problem-solving, its usefulness was limited by an inability to give convincing explanations of its conclusions.

Clancey (1983) describes how he and his colleagues at first saw themselves as 'applications engineers' whose task was to adapt MYCIN's explanation facility to a tutorial setting. It was, however ". . . surprising to find out how little the explanation facility could accomplish for a student" (*ibid*. p. 217). MYCIN did not solve problems in the same way as a human expert. Its production system rules were formulated to diagnose infections, which it did successfully by exhaustively searching the problem space. There was thus no explicit problem-solving strategy which could be taught to a student. As Clancey freely admits, "Focusing on a hypothesis and choosing a question to confirm a hypothesis are not necessarily arbitrary in human reasoning" (*ibid*. p. 220), thus raising serious questions about the usefulness of MYCIN as the basis of a system for tutoring students in diagnostic reasoning.

The relevance of this to the current discussion becomes clearer when one examines the ways in which Clancey tried to overcome this problem. The re-evaluation occasioned by GUIDON's failure led to the development of NEOMYCIN (Clancey 1983). After listing the kinds of knowledge used by human experts for diagnostic reasoning, a series of 'meta-rules' were developed to give meaningful access to the domain rules (i.e. to encode the notion of a hypothesis), and to manage and interpret a changing list of hypotheses. Similar structures were developed for GUIDON, known by such names as 'rule models' and 'rule schemas'. Their purpose was to make clear the relationships between the rules of a domain, so that a reasoning strategy could be learned. It can be argued that they still leave out a great deal of crucial procedural information, such as why the subgoals of each rule are considered in a particular order. The main point, however, is that the various meta-rules and their sub-structures may be seen as alternative viewpoints on the domain, without which any useful tutoring or explanation is not possible. This very point is made by Wenger (1987), who describes NEOMYCIN's substructures as 'orthogonal viewpoints', which ". . . act like windows, giving access to the knowledge base." He concludes that these ". . . access channels are crucial to support the variety of reasoning tasks and focusing strategies by which data and conclusions are connected." (Wenger, 1987, p. 276.)

2.1.2   Different viewpoints for different activities

The previous section described situations where a combination of different viewpoints was necessary for a given activity to be successful. The argument in this sub-section is that specific activities can strongly condition the way we need to perceive an object or system, and that this may imply the adoption of a specific viewpoint to support that activity. An everyday example could be the metallic body of a car being seen not in terms of its shape and mechanical functionality, but in electrical terms as an 'earth' connection. In short, the way we see things may depend on what we want to do with them.

A similar example exists in the ITS literature. Knowledge elicitation carried out in preparation for the construction of STEAMER (Hollan et al. 1984) showed that the way experts think about a particular machine does not necessarily depend on its physical components, but on the actions they wish to perform with it. Accordingly, the designers attempted to base the tutoring process on the conceptual abstractions (mental model) of the experts, rather than on the precise physical characteristics of the machines, and labelled their approach 'conceptual fidelity'. The system was built to tutor the operation and maintenance of steam propulsion plants, and was designed as a graphical interface to an interactive, inspectable simulation of such a plant. This core simulation had already been built. An example of the use of a function-specific viewpoint occurs when the complex assembly of parts which makes up a working turbine is labelled by experts simply as a 'steam chamber with drains'. The safe and efficient running of this 'abstract' machine requires some 'abstract' procedures, such as opening the drains before admitting steam to the chamber (Stevens & Roberts 1983). This example may be used to draw attention to the function-dependent or 'context oriented' aspect of viewpoints: their use may be dependent on a specific context or set of goals.

STEAMER makes use of this by offering over 100 different views of the plant in question, from abstractions such as 'the basic steam cycle', to control panels describing some specific state of an operating system. A pump may be seen as an instance of a 'positive displacement pump' or as a component of a 'pumping station'. The richness of the information provided by the simulation is exploited by a frame-based representation system which accesses the different combinations of data required to support different viewpoints. A specific object's relationship to the system may be described and explained in terms of its physical connections, energy connections, information connections, or perhaps in terms of the procedures which operate upon it. Trials with trainees have convinced the designers that the system's ability to change viewpoints is crucial to its effectiveness.

2.1.3 Different viewpoints from novice to expert

STEAMER (Hollan et al. 1984) showed a preoccupation with 'conceptual fidelity' in the interface used to access a pre-existent simulation. With QUEST, however (White & Frederiksen 1986), this concept was applied to the system's most basic domain representations. QUEST was designed to tutor the behaviour of electronic circuits. Like STEAMER it was conceived as an inspectable simulation with a graphical interface, but the underlying representations form a sequence of qualitative models based on a causal calculus. Rather than concentrating on a single device, QUEST's successive models corresponded to increasing levels of expertise in the principles of the domain.

The models differ along the dimensions of type, order, and degree. 'Type' describes such characteristics as 'qualitative', 'proportional' (e.g. descriptions such as 'less than' or 'equal to'), and quantitative, while 'order' deals with the derivatives that the model uses to define changes in a circuit. If one order describes any change of voltage, for example, the next may describe the rate of that change. The 'degree' dimension adds to the complexity of the model by taking additional constraints into consideration. The models are thus generic, each relating to a given level of complexity in the analysis of electronic circuits. A crucial connection between the models was 'upward compatibility', which ensures that a simpler model can be extended or refined so as to match the next more complex one with a minimum of effort. This system was quite successful in tutoring a small group of students in a restricted problem-solving area.

White and Frederiksen (1986) do not claim that the model structure they define provides an adequate model of expertise on its own, since they believe that this consists of much more than the ability to predict specific states. They regard it as crucially important that different models of various type and order be integrated into a coherent and effective understanding of the domain. This 'integration', and the question of precisely how particular models are related to the solution of particular problems, remain as topics for future research for them. These conclusions echo those of Stevens et al. (1979). If we regard the different model types as different viewpoints, we may conclude that such viewpoints may be implemented in a tutoring system, and that they may form a pedagogically useful progression from novice to some level of expertise.

2.1.4 Glass boxes and black boxes

The origin of the 'glass box' and 'black box' terminology may not be entirely clear, but an early manifestation can certainly be found in du Boulay et al. (1981). The point of the terminology is that different models of a system may be presented according to the needs or expertise of the user even when tutoring is not the immediate goal. The inner workings of, in this case, a computer language interpreter are not available for inspection and are regarded as a 'black box'. This may present little problem to an expert, but novices attempting to program in the language may soon find that their interactions with the system become unintelligible as they have no idea about what state the system is in. The problem may be alleviated by providing a 'notional machine' as an idealized model of the system which can describe the more important events occurring inside the 'black box' in terms familiar to the novice. Statements about 'stack overflow' for example, might be meaningless, while a statement concerning 'store size' might communicate usefully. This 'notional machine' is the glass box. Different models are thus provided for expert and novice. While du Boulay et al. are concerned primarily with programming languages, we may extend the idea to tutoring systems. The comments above in relation to GUIDON, SOPHIE and QUEST describe systems whose knowledge representations attempt to capture some degree of 'psychological validity' in the sense that they attempt to solve problems or make inferences in ways which are meaningful to humans. The meta-rules of GUIDON (Clancey 1983) are designed to encode the notion and form of hypotheses. The modules of SOPHIE (Brown et al. 1976) and the models of QUEST (White & Frederiksen 1986) are intended to exhibit qualitative reasoning. The point of this is that for tutoring purposes, the systems should be able to explain their inferencing in terms that humans might use or understand.

WEST (Burton & Brown 1982) shows that this and other pedagogical aims can be achieved without having the machine reason in those terms. Where the system presents the student with a task or problem, the system may solve that problem for itself by means of a 'black box', but, having found the solution, carry out its tutoring and explanation in terms of a 'glass box'. WEST is based on a game which exercises arithmetic skills. A player is given three numbers at random and has to compose an expression which is evaluated to give the number of moves towards the goal, their 'home town'. Players may also aim to 'bump off' other players or to take short cuts.

Tutoring is based on 'differential modelling'. The student's performance is compared to that of the system's expert, and diagnosis starts if the student's move is not optimal. This design strategy is necessary due to the random nature of the game, i.e. it is not possible to say in advance what skills will be required at any specific point in the game. The various possible moves are analysed in terms of 'issues' or strategies (e.g. trying for a 'bump') to identify those that the student is using and those that reveal weaknesses in their play. The system does not represent interactions between issues or erroneous issues.

Because the domain of the game is limited, the expert can work by exhaustively listing all possible expressions and simulating their application to the current state of play. This expert thus needs no representation of the issues. Its moves are analysed by the same diagnostic procedures that are applied to the student's moves. However, once the ideal move has been identified, it may be presented to the student in terms of the related issue. Two quite distinct representations (viewpoints) are thus exploited in conjunction so as to effectively tutor a single domain. As Wenger (1987) points out, the system expert has considerable performing power, but is not 'psychologically plausible'. The 'issue' recognisers have no performing power, but are able to justify the expert's moves in 'teachable' terms. Wenger also points out that in more complex domains, where the computational costs of analysing the expert's move may become prohibitive, the domain expertise would have once again to be implemented in terms of the pedagogical issues that the system was designed to address. Nevertheless, WEST shows that a 'black box' domain expert can be pedagogically useful if a suitable 'glass box' representation can be found to complement it.

2.1.5 Exploring the student's viewpoint

In the consideration of viewpoints and tutoring, it may be argued that we should encourage students to develop and explore their own views of a domain, and that tutoring should be adapted, where possible, to the student's view. The Alternate Reality Kit ('ARK', Smith 1986), while not strictly a tutoring system, does move in this direction. ARK is an environment designed to express physical laws (correct or otherwise). It contains a wide variety of objects, all of whose behaviours may be programmed or connected, and all of which obey the laws set for the environment as a whole. The intention is to allow students to appreciate why the laws of physics are as they are by seeing what happens when they are broken. Students may set the system up to reflect their own view of the behaviour of a physical process, and observe the consequences; (O'Shea & Smith 1987). While this system does allow students to express their own viewpoint on a domain, it does not carry out any active tutoring or student modelling, and is perhaps best characterized as a system which promotes the exploration of different viewpoints.

More generally, it may be claimed that learning environments, such as Logo (Papert 1980), are intended to enable students to construct their own view of a domain. This is a debateable issue, in that such environments are normally structured very carefully in order to lead the student to a particular viewpoint. They can reach that viewpoint by their own route, but the systems are intended to lead them to a particular model.

2.2   Design philosophies: the strategic necessity for knowledge negotiation

Why is 'knowledge negotiation' necessary? If we accept the need to represent multiple views of the domain to be tutored, then it is clear that any approach which emphasizes the acquisition of a single pre-existent account of the domain, is not adequate to our task. Self (1988a, 1988b, 1989) makes this point. He suggests that the reliance on a single representation of the domain can lead to an inappropriate 'trinity' model of ITS design (the student model, the domain representation, and the tutoring component), and that this may lead to a rather authoritarian style of tutoring with the assumption that the system embodies, in a Platonic sense, the one true representation of the domain. This being so, the approach may also lead one to assume that the student may be adequately represented as a 'subset' of the expert. Self (1989) indicates that 'education as transmission' is not an idea favoured by this century's educational philosophers and quotes Perkinson (1984) in saying that ". . . the transmission theory of education is both false and immoral."

While acknowledging the importance of the review of the field of artificial intelligence (AI) and education carried out by Wenger (1987), his proposals for 'knowledge communication' as a design philosophy are difficult to accept. Indeed, as we indicate below, it seems to us that what Wenger really intends is something closer to 'knowlege negotiation'. 'Knowledge communication' is initially defined as:

". . . the ability to cause, and/or support the acquisition of one's knowledge by someone else, via a restricted set of communication operations" (Wenger 1987, p. 7).

We argue that this approach has a number of conceptual limitations since it implies that some single, pre-existent mass of knowledge has to be carefully poured into a politely passive student. We maintain that the student is more properly conceptualized as an active participant who is engaged in the tutoring process, and whose learning involves the structuring and integration of the information with which they are presented, rather than its passive acceptance. This in turn implies that not all students may structure it in the same way. These points seem to be acknowledged later in Wenger's book. He stresses, with reference to Lave (1988), that the student must be actively engaged in problem solving, in order that they perceive specific problems, discover the limitations of their current view, and ". . . *demonstrate a new viewpoint's conceptual superiority.*" (Wenger's italics. Wenger *op. cit.*, p. 411.)

Several points can be made here. Firstly, while Wenger is happy to emphasize the importance of the student actively acquiring new viewpoints, this activity is not well described by the concept of 'knowledge communication' as defined above. Also, any system which was attempting to move the student from one viewpoint to another would have to have different accounts of the domain available to it, i.e. would have to have multiple viewpoints on that domain. This would require more than a 'communication' model as some decision processes for choosing, tutoring, and using the appropriate viewpoints would also have to be defined.

There are other indications that Wenger really intends his readers to see the student as a more active participant in learning. He proposes (p. 321) the notion of 'equivalence classes' of models of knowledge, ". . . within which communication is possible and useful." This sounds far more complicated than ". . . the acquisition of one's knowledge by someone else. . .", but we are not given any further information about how such equivalence classes might be derived, what they might look like, or how, precisely they might be used. Elsewhere we learn that:

". . . recipients must interpret communication by a process of reconstruction, and there is always some uncertainty about the similarity of the knowledge possessed by each participant." (Wenger *op. cit.*, p. 321).

We can only agree with this statement, but its implications for 'knowledge communication' are not made clear. On page 365, Wenger states that it is obvious that a 'model of communicable knowledge' need not be static, but could be modified by the communication process. Unfortunately, we are given no account of a model or mechanism to describe this process. In his Epilogue Wenger states that:

". . . both the knowledge states involved in knowledge communication are modified: knowledge communication is viewed as a dynamic interaction between intelligent agents by which knowledge states are engaged in a process of expansion and articulation" (Wenger *op. cit.*, p. 431).

This seems to bear little relation to the definition given earlier, which described the 'acquisition' by some other individual of one's pre-existent knowledge. While this latter statement does embody a more constructive view of the student, it comes late in the book and still leaves the reader with considerable doubt as to what 'knowledge communication' really entails, thus limiting its usefulness as a basis for design.

The knowledge negotiation approach is based on the assumption that there is not a single, correct model of a domain. It requires other representations: either an uncertain domain, or a range of viewpoints are available for tutoring the same topic. Using viewpoints, the approach advocates that account should be taken of the students' knowledge state, preferences, goals and experience in selecting from them (i.e. our systems should be properly adaptive). This means that decisions must be made about which viewpoint is to be tutored at a given point in the tutorial, how it is to be tutored, and why so tutored. We contend that, ideally, these decisions are best made through a process of negotiation between the system and the student, and should not be the result of some autocratic imposition by the system. We make this assertion partly in the light of the known difficulties of building systems which can infer such things as goals, experience, and preferences, and partly from the conviction that negotiation would increase the level of the student's 'engagement' with the system.

3 DESIGN REQUIREMENTS

If our systems are not to be based on a single representation of the domain to be tutored, then what should they be based on? Our general goal is to build adaptive systems where the current definition of the domain to be tutored, and the process of tutoring it, are determined by a repeated process of negotiation between system and student. It is necessary for us to determine the form that this adaptation might take. More specifically, we wish to identify the sorts of adaption and enhancements to the teaching and learning process which are only provided by a model based on negotiation. In the following sections we suggest an initial set of adaptations which are not facilitated by the idea of 'communicating' a single definition of the domain, and which could form the initial design goals of a knowledge negotiation system.

3.1 Adapting the domain representations and tutoring to the student's previous experience

The student may have a range of cognitive strategies and experience, and while it is very hard to infer these, we need to adjust our tutoring to them if it is to be successful. We may, for instance, wish to describe Prolog in terms of Logic, where we know that the student has previously studied predicate calculus. We may also consider here the notion of cognitive 'hooks' (e.g. Papert 1980). These 'hooks' are things with which the student is familiar, and upon which they can 'hang' new experiences so as to extend their knowledge. Elsom-Cook (1990a) discusses these 'transitional objects' and gives the example of using waves on water to introduce concepts relating to the nature of light. Problems seem to arise because of the personal nature of these cognitive links. There is little to indicate that what suits one individual will suit another, or even that a single one is sufficient in any particular case. Professionals maintain, however, that a good teacher will be able to identify what is likely to work. There is presumably an attempt to match an epistemological analysis of the domain to be taught against the structures which the student possesses, and to use the connections to identify appropriate hooks.

Some previous work in ITS is also relevant here. WUSOR-II (Carr 1977) has some representation of the student's need for repetition or tutoring, degree of forgetfulness, and receptivity to advice. The 'genetic graph' (Goldstein 1978, 1979), designed for WUSOR-III, would have allowed the system to model the evolution of the student's knowledge, and their level of belief or confidence in newly acquired knowledge. Tutoring could then have been adjusted to these models (although the system's domain models would not have been affected). QUEST (White & Frederiksen 1986) tutors different models of an electrical circuit depending on the student's level of expertise.

3.2 Adapting the domain representations and tutoring to the student's goals

Different accounts of a domain may be suited to different goals. A functional account of a mechanical system such as a car or an industrial plant may be quite adequate for routine operation such as driving. Efficient maintainance or repair may well require a structural account which details the causal relationships and dependencies.

The principle is neatly encapsulated in the concept of 'conceptual fidelity' developed by Hollan et al. (1984) through their work on STEAMER: the way experts thought about a particular machine did not necessarily depend on its physical components, but on the actions they wished to perform with it.

This form of adaption would enable us to broaden the scope of usage of a teaching system. At present, the learners are assumed to come to the system with a specific goal, and the representation is constructed from that point of view. A tutoring system such as Dominie (Elsom-Cook & Spensley 1988), for example, can be given a detailed representation of a telephone exchange suitable for training maintenance engineers, but if it is desired to train operators on the same exchange a different representation of the system is needed. The difference need not be one of experience or background knowledge. It is the difference in the goals of the students that is important: specifically, their educational objectives in coming to the system. It is clearly pointless to attempt to develop domain-independent tutors before we are able to support this level of adaption to student goals within one domain.

3.3 Combining different viewpoints on a domain so as to avoid misconceptions

Stevens et al. (1979) describe the need for both 'scriptal' and 'functional' models of heavy coastal rainfall in WHY, so as to avoid misconceptions such as the 'sponge' model of precipitation which visualizes an air mass being 'squeezed' against the mountains.

Since any model of a system is necessarily a simplification from reality (otherwise it would not be a model) there may be discrepancies between the system and model. These could either be due to limitations of the model, or errors in applying the model to describe the system. Since many of the models that are used (e.g. light behaving as a wave) can only describe part of a system, the use of a single model can lead to a flawed understanding of the way a system works. For this reason we can see that the ability to present different viewpoints can limit the development of misconceptions which arise from this type of over-generalization or faulty analogy.

3.4 Combining different viewpoints on a domain so as to improve the student's 'understanding' of that domain

Cowan (1986) criticizes engineering education which is based largely on the mastery of quantitative tasks, maintaining that knowing how to apply a particular algorithm does not necessarily provide any qualitative understanding of the problems involved. He describes an investigation which compares students' protocols recorded while solving either quantitative or qualitative problems. He maintains that the qualitative problems required an extra level of analysis, the purpose of which was to distinguish the significant features of the problem.

Laurillard (1990) makes a number of related points. She describes the 'technification' of knowledge, which separates, for example, the procedures for manipulating numbers from their real meaning in the world (or the formulae of classroom physics from the students own naive understanding). In other words, a child who can cope perfectly well with a supermarket and a budget may perform badly in arithmetic tests. Laurillard cites previous work to show that the outcome of problem-solving episodes depends crucially on the quality of reasoning that students apply in them. This is taken to indicate that we must go beyond the notion of 'misconceptions' in our analysis of students' performance, and instead consider that very quality of reasoning, and its social context. (Laurillard also raises the fascinating question of the extent to which it is legitimate to substitute a knowledge representation for the 'real' world upon which the student operates.)

Larkin et al. (1980) show that when experts indulge in problem solving, a phase of qualitative reasoning frequently precedes the application of quantitative methods.

In each of these cases, there is a claim that different perspectives on the domain lead to a different sort of understanding (or misunderstanding). In some sense, therefore, a learner who is able to take more than one perspective may be regarded as having a deeper understanding of the domain.

3.5 Tutoring when and how a particular model is best used

Teaching when to use a particular model may be seen as tutoring the efficient use of different problem spaces so as to reach a solution. It may also imply that we need to adjust our tutoring to the goals of the student, so that the kinds of problem space we address are meaningful to them. This in turn implies the need to diagnose what these goals might be, or to negotiate as to which ones are addressed, so that the system is not lead outside its area of competence. We must also consider the question of how and why we wish to teach the meta-skill of reflecting on our own problem-solving processes (see Self 1989).

This approach has been applied in Moyse (see Chapter 5) to the domain of learning to debug Prolog programs. The essence of this system is that there are several different models of Prolog, and that different ones lead to the detection of different sorts of bug. The system attempts to teach users how to use the appropriate model for finding a given bug.

3.6   Basing the tutoring on a process of negotiation

Negotiation is necessary as both the tutor and the student may have a range of goals which it is difficult to infer, and knowledge structures which may or may not be compatible. Elsom-Cook (1990a) sees negotiation as being necessary to the process of guided discovery tutoring for these reasons, and because tutor and student are both exploring and open-ended environment. Baker (1989d, this volume) describes a system intended to maintain a tutorial dialogue based on critical argument. This system can work with incomplete and uncertain domains, and has mechanisms to explicitly negotiate the goals of the dialogue. Crucial to this process is the concept of 'symmetry' between tutor and student, i.e. they must have the same dialogue moves available to them.

3.7   Encouraging students to develop their own view of a domain

There is considerable evidence that humans are active learners, continuously constructing hypotheses about the world around them. It seems inefficient to discard the learner's own constructions and attempt to totally replace them, since the personal view will be integrated with the learner's pre-existing cognitive structures. Instead, it is sensible to try and encourage the student to extenalize that view, such that it can become a focus for discussion and refinement. This approach was used in 'Shopping on Mars' which taught basic arithmetic to children. This system followed a trend in maths education towards encouraging children to extend their own informal arithmetic skills, rather than slavishly learning formal algorithms. To this end a graphical language, GADL (Evertsz et al., 1988) was developed which permitted children to externalize their own algorithms. A further positive aspect of encouraging learner's to develop their own view is the motivational argument that it facilitates appropriation of the learning experience, allowing the student to feel that the experience is her own. This is also useful from an engineering perspective, in that the more a learner can be encouraged to externalize her own model, the less 'magical inference' about the internal state of the learner must be done by the tutor.

A recent example of a system which supported the learner's exploration of her own view is the Alternate Reality Kit (O'Shea & Smith 1987). This system allows students to explore the implications of their own views of physics by violating the laws of nature. The intention is that this should help them to grasp why the laws must be as they are, and thus to debug their own models of physical laws.

While we would not claim that it is currently possible to represent or have a system learn any student's idiosyncratic view of the domain, we would regard progress in this area as a long-term goal of knowledge negotiation. Such progress is indeed implied in the investigation of 'beliefs' and 'local reasoning' as opposed to the more categorical 'knowledge'. An emphasis on beliefs and their revision also implies an emphasis on the justification and critiquing of those beliefs, through a process of critical dialogue. The importance of these processes is emphasized by Self (1989, this volume) and Baker (1989d, this volume).

4   OVERVIEW OF THE CHAPTERS

Self suggests that we should more properly represent the domains in terms of belief systems which may be reconceptualized and changed. In Chapter 2 of this book he provides us with a wide-ranging review of systems which attempt to model the holding and revision of sets of beliefs in an effort to list ways in which viewpoints might be structured and implemented. This review indicates that there are a number of serious problems to be overcome.

If we are to have negotiation, then we must have dialogue. The centrality of dialogue to ITS design has been stressed and explored by Elsom-Cook (e.g. 1984, 1991, 1990a), and a system designed to carry out tutorial negotiations described by Baker (1989d, this volume). Where a dialogue component is central to our systems, then we must face the issue of what planning or generative mechanism lies behind it. Possibilities range from the traditional view of planning caricatured by Suchman (1987), where a prior plan must be constructed at every level of detail as a prerequisite for action, to Suchman's own 'situated action', where uncertainty about shared context and intentions must be managed. The planning mechanism required as the foundation for a fully-developed knowledge negotiation system should ideally allow for the satisfaction of multiple goals, for plan monitoring and for opportunistic tutoring. A candidate is proposed in this volume by McCalla and Wasson (Chapter 3). Following their contribution, Goodyear and Stone (Chapter 4) discuss the degree of epistemological uncertainty that a system might have to deal with if a serious attempt was made to build one for an 'open' domain.

The second section of the book deals with specific techniques for building systems and for modelling students. Moyse (Chapter 5) describes a method for designing and implementing systems with multiple pre-defined viewpoints, while Devi (Chapter 6) reports on a formalism which could be used to both diagnose and model the multiple strategies used by children on simple arithmetic problems. Alpay (Chapter 7) describes a 'developmental student model' which details successive stages in a student's acquisition of clinical reasoning through multiple views of the diagnostic process. Dillenbourg (Chapter 8) discusses the design of tools and activities which would promote reflection and help the learner to internalize an active model of learning.

The third section is concerned with explanation and dialogue. Baker (Chapter 9) describes an approach to negotiated tutoring based on critical argument and a dialogue mechanism to support this. Rimmershaw (Chapter 10) presents an analysis of human dialogue aimed at determining the range of possible discourse moves by which explanations are negotiated, and presents these as a model for ITS designers.

The final part of the book confronts the issue of how the interface itself could be the subject of negotiation. It is clear that the development of the learner's models of system and domain are shaped by their interaction with the interface, and that the only information the system can acquire about the learner comes through that same interface. As O'Malley (1990) and Wenger (1987) point out, the interface and knowledge representations of a system can compete as representations of the domain being tutored. This indicates that interfaces can no longer be bolted on to a pre-existent system, but must be included as an integral part of the design process. Elsom-Cook (Chapter 11) investigates a formalism through which a shared model of the interface could be developed by two agents, the system and the learner. Brayshaw (Chapter 12) describes how multiple visualizations can be used to capture complex program behaviour at an appropriate level for a given student, and how the provision of a suitable toolkit can allow students to construct a visualization suited to their own needs.

5 CONCLUSIONS

In this chapter we have attempted to review some of the concerns about previous work in Intelligent Tutoring Systems which imply the need for an alternative to the knowledge communication approach. We have outlined the need for a negotiation-based approach, and for an alternative to the traditional methods of representing the domain. In particular, we have focussed on the possible use of multiple viewpoints for supporting negotiation. Subsequent chapters explore a number of aspects of the problem from a variety of perspectives. Each indicates issues where further exploration could be undertaken.

To re-iterate our original questions, in this book we are seeking to clarify what negotiation is and why it is of value in an educational interaction. Following from this, we are seeking to understand the mechanisms needed for negotiation, and the representations which are required to support those mechanisms.

2 Computational Viewpoints

JOHN SELF

Department of Computing, University of Lancaster, UK

1 INTRODUCTION

The aim of this chapter is to review various computational techniques for representing and processing 'viewpoints'. The informal notion of a 'viewpoint' as a position from which to look at things is hardly controversial: if we are asked to express a view on some matter (e.g. "how did Mrs. Thatcher treat her children?") then we are aware that we are able to summon up one or more viewpoints (e.g. Mrs. Thatcher as typical mother, as advocate of independent enterprise, as domineering leader, etc.) from which to derive such a view. Within intelligent tutoring systems (ITS) research, particularly, there has been an increasing recognition of the need to represent multiple viewpoints of a domain and the differing viewpoints of the agents involved, that is, the student and the tutoring system, in the simplest case. For example, Wenger's definitive review of ITS research includes a section arguing for the importance of the issue of 'viewpoints' for providing a context for diagnosis and for shifting the focus "from what is wrong to what is right in a statement" (Wenger 1987, pp. 355–361). He considers that "the topic seems ripe for more research."

However, despite a developing consensus on the need for representing viewpoints, we remain vague as to what precisely they are. If we are to use viewpoints within our ITSs then we need to develop some computational formalisms in which to express them. As we will see, the idea of a 'viewpoint' appears in various guises in many different fields of computer science and AI, in particular within distributed AI, belief systems, dialogue theories, database systems, and cooperative problem-solving, apart from ITS. The hope in carrying out this review of different 'viewpoints on viewpoints' is that we may move towards some computational precision in our discussions and implementations.

KNOWLEDGE NEGOTIATION
ISBN 0–12–509378–0

Our starting point will be to regard a *viewpoint* as a set of beliefs:

$$VP = \{B_1, B_2, \ldots\}$$

A *belief* is a dispositional state. A belief (and hence a viewpoint) is held by some *agent*. In the case of human agents, the *state* is a 'state of mind' (the philosophical analysis of which we will abort now): in the case of computer agents, the state is some propositional representation (which again we will not pursue further). A *view* is what results from applying a viewpoint. The word *dispositional* is intended to indicate that possession of the belief disposes the agent to behave in a certain manner but does not guarantee it. Consequently there is no straightforward mapping between beliefs (and hence viewpoints) and behaviour. We should also note that a belief is essentially 'passive' in that it may not be 'active' in the sense of influencing behaviour.

For the moment, we impose no conditions on the set of beliefs in *VP*. In a 'coherent' viewpoint we might expect the beliefs to all be relevant to the issue at hand, or perhaps to be structurally related to one other in some fashion. Unfortunately, we cannot give a precise definition of *coherence*: at this stage, therefore, we allow any set of beliefs as a viewpoint and leave its properties to emerge through its processing. We certainly cannot insist that a viewpoint possess the desirable properties of other computational representations, such as consistency and completeness.

Whether or not a viewpoint should (like a belief) be regarded as dispositional, or whether we would wish to include the operators which apply to the beliefs as an integral part of the viewpoint, is a matter for debate. As we will see, some writers define a viewpoint without any reference to how it may be applied; some use viewpoints that are so closely tied to operators that they appear inseparable. Perhaps we need to define an 'active viewpoint' as a 'passive viewpoint' plus 'operators'. However, the distinction is academic, since our 'beliefs' do not have to be simple declarative statements: we can allow a belief that "the use of this is that".

In reviewing the literature on viewpoints, a major distinction can be drawn between situations in which one or more viewpoints are held by a *single* agent and those in which they held by *two or more* agents. We will first review the former case, before considering the more complex latter case.

2   UNI-AGENT VIEWPOINTS

Sometimes we emphasize the similarity between two viewpoints, sometimes the difference. At the extremes, we have a second viewpoint which is a minor variation of the first (which we will call an **incremental** viewpoint) or a second viewpoint which radically opposes or conflicts with the first (which we will call a **disparate** viewpoint). Of course, in general, two viewpoints will share some beliefs but differ in others.

2.1 Incremental viewpoints

In 'classical AI' we have the idea of state-space problem-solving in which the transformation of some initial state (say, all the missionaries and cannibals on the left bank) to some goal state (all on the right bank) is to be achieved by applying a sequence of allowed operators (rowing certain people across). We could perhaps regard the **state** as a forerunner of a viewpoint: it represents a set of beliefs about the problem. Applying an operator moves us from one viewpoint of the problem to another, one closer to a solution, it is hoped. In this case, each successive viewpoint is an incremental viewpoint.

With simple problems such as the missionaries and cannibals problem the state can be represented by one term, such as *State(3,3,0,0,L)*, and the application of any operator can be represented by deriving a second term, such as *State(2,2,1,1,R)*. (Such state descriptions so strongly 'buy in' the operators that we may feel that the latter are an indissoluble part of the 'viewpoint': however, later viewpoints are more neutral in this respect.) With more realistic problems the state description will be a conjunction of a very large number of terms. Rather than defining an operator in terms of the consequent changes to all of these terms, it is usual to introduce a special object called a **situation** so that we can assert, say, *On(block_a, table, s23)* to mean that in situation *s23* the *block_a* is on the table, and then define axioms to say how situations change as we apply operators:

$$Ax \; On(x, \; table, \; s) \; \rightarrow \; Inhand(x, \; pickup(s))$$

that is, if a block *x* is on the table in situation *s* then in the situation *pickup(s)*, which we reach by applying the operator 'pickup' to the situation *s*, *x* will be in the robot's hand. The ramifications of this approach have remained a subject of research since it was introduced by McCarthy and Hayes in 1968. In particular, the 'frame problem', concerning how one defines what does *not* change from one situation to another, remains a problem (Shoham, 1988). Our point, however, is that the set of terms that hold in a situation can also be regarded as a viewpoint.

This approach to problem-solving in AI became sufficiently standard-ized that the new AI programming languages of the time included viewpoints as a data type. For example, QA4 (Rulifson, Derksen and Waldinger, 1972) provided *contexts* to represent hypothetical assumptions. However, this notion of context was limited by being tied to a stack-like control structure and associated inheritance mechanism. There was no general ability to transfer control and knowledge between contexts.

Contemporaneously and independently, philosophical logicians were developing the somewhat similar idea of a *possible world* in order to formalize the semantics of modal logics (Kripke 1963, 1971; Hintikka 1971). In this conceptualization, we may say that a particular expression is true in one possible world w_i but false in another w_j. An accessibility relation $R(w_i, w_j)$ is defined between possible worlds. An expression is true with respect to world w_i if and only if it is true in all the worlds accessible from w_i according to R. Specifying a semantics for such possible worlds enabled Kripke to develop modal logics of necessity and possibility, and others extended the idea to modal epistemic (knowledge), doxastic (belief), deontic (obligation) and temporal logics.

However, despite the wide scope of formal modal logics and the superficial similarity between 'possible world + accessibility relation' and 'state + operator', the preferred approach to formalizing belief in AI, as we need for our viewpoints, has been to adopt a *sentential logic* (Genesereth & Nilsson 1987). In such a logic, a wff is an ordinary wff in first-order predicate logic, or an expression $B(p)$ where p is a wff with (in the simplest case) no free variables, or is constructed from other wffs using connectives in the normal way. The expression $B(p)$ denotes that the proposition p is believed. Since this expression is itself a wff, it can be nested, so that $B(B(p))$ is also a wff. The semantics of such a sentential logic can then be described in terms of the wffs which are derivable using an agent's set of inference rules. The closure of an agent's base set of beliefs under the rules of inference is called a *belief set*. An agent is then said to believe p if and only if $B(p)$ is in its belief set.

AI programs which deal with belief sets often work with a 'belief base', performing reasoning from the propositions in the belief base, 'filtering' those propositions so that only part of the belief base is perceived, namely, the propositions that are under consideration (Martins & Shapiro 1988). At this point we begin to make contact with work on intelligent tutoring systems.

In the standard approach to ITS design, we have a *domain model*, which represents one (assumed correct) viewpoint on what is to be learned. The ITS also maintains a *student model*, which is usually an incremental viewpoint, being derived by 'perturbing' (i.e. introducing minor modifications to) the domain model. Sometimes the student model is a filtered version of the domain model (the overlay or subset model);

sometimes it is a variant of the domain model in which certain propositions have been replaced by other (deviant) propositions (the bug catalogue or mal-rule model). The student model is, of course, intended to represent the system's beliefs about the student's beliefs: by implication, then, in this approach to ITS design the student's viewpoint is considered to be commensurable with that of the system.

2.2 Disparate viewpoints

In the previous section, each successive viewpoint was derived by some systematic, small change to an existing viewpoint. Other researchers have emphasized the benefits and problems that may arise from maintaining alternative, radically different viewpoints on the same topic.

Even within the state-space problem-solving paradigm, there was much concern over the way the adopted state representation significantly influenced the ease with which a solution could be found. For example, Amarel (1968) considered different representations of the missionaries and cannibals problem. The 'normal' representation leads to a standard search tree; however, transposing the problem into one of moving about a two-dimensional grid leads to an algorithmic solution, almost by inspection, and to a general method applicable to more complex versions of the problem. There is no obvious relationship between these two representations, and it was, of course, a matter of some difficulty for AI researchers to determine how an appropriate representation could be specified.

Accordingly, an emphasis on *multiple representations* became common in the 1970s (Bobrow & Collins 1975). The idea (or hope) was that by providing an AI system with many representations it would be able to select an appropriate one to solve its problems. A 'representation' is not quite the same thing as our 'viewpoint': two different representations give the same solution; two different viewpoints may give different solutions. Two representations differ, then, in the form, but not the content, of what is represented.

As an example of the potential of maintaining different viewpoints, Costa et al. (1988) consider how a tutoring system might manage the following exchange:

> Tutor: *Why did Louis XIV wear a wig?*
> Student: *Because he liked having fun.*
> Tutor: . . .

There are many different possible viewpoints on the use of a wig: as a concealment for baldness, as an ornament for ladies, as part of a judge's costume, as a disguise, as a convention for noblemen of the seventeenth century, as a plaything, etc. Costa et al. define each viewpoint, which they call a *context*, as a set of Prolog axioms (in this case, then, the reasoning mechanism associated with a viewpoint is considered fixed and not part of the viewpoint itself). The viewpoints can share axioms and be organized into a hierarchical structure. Understanding the student's response involves finding a viewpoint within which the answer makes sense. This is implemented by using resolution to attempt to derive the answer from the viewpoint. If a viewpoint is incomplete, an interaction may be initiated to confirm propositions which, if added to the viewpoint, would enable a derivation to be completed.

As far as ITSs are concerned, there is the practical question of whether an exhaustive set of such viewpoints can be specified. In theory, no doubt, there are an infinity of viewpoints which a student might bring to bear, but in reality a usable system may be based on only a small number. It may also be possible, through some interaction with the student (as indicated by Costa et al.), to generate dynamically an appropriate viewpoint, by perhaps modifying an existing one.

Even if each viewpoint is consistent within itself, it seems reasonable to allow an agent to possess viewpoints which contradict one another, i.e. that $VP_i \rightarrow p$ *and* $VP_j \rightarrow \sim p$. For example, the viewpoints 'Reagan as Quaker' and 'Reagan as Republican' might lead to different conclusions regarding the proposition 'Reagan was a war-monger'. Fagin and Halpern (1987) have formalized this idea within a logic of *local reasoning*. They consider that an agent's beliefs may be partitioned into non-interacting clusters. An agent may believe something within one cluster (or *frame of mind*) but the opposite in another. The complete set of beliefs may be inconsistent but as long as reasoning is local, that is, within one frame of mind, then no inconsistency is apparent.

In summary, then, there is some agreement that agents need to adopt a viewpoint within which to reason. A viewpoint may be represented as a set of beliefs, with, in some cases, a reasoning mechanism considered to be intrinsic to the viewpoint. At any time, an agent may possess any number of viewpoints. Viewpoints may be simple variations of one another or radically different. They may be incomplete or inconsistent, within themselves or with each other. This implies that, while the syntactic definition of a viewpoint as a set of beliefs is straightforward, the actual reasoning within a viewpoint may be complicated.

2.3   Reasoning within a viewpoint

There is a preliminary question to consider, namely, how is an appropriate viewpoint to be selected? In the case of incremental viewpoints in state-space problem-solving, the selection of the next viewpoint was the main research question during the first decade of AI, and led to significant work in heuristic search, means-end analysis, etc. For disparate viewpoints, however, the problem of selecting the 'right' viewpoint has hardly been considered. Costa et al.'s system takes each viewpoint in turn until one works, which may indeed be adequate if, as we might expect, there is only a small number of potential viewpoints and it is possible to eliminate inappropriate viewpoints quickly. But the problem of identifying the student's viewpoint when using an ITS should not be over-emphasized: the question *"Why did Louis XIV wear a wig?"* would normally not be asked in a vacuum but only after one or a few potential viewpoints had been established. Costa et al. also suggest restricting the search to only those viewpoints which mention 'relevant' predicates, a suggestion which clearly needs to be made more precise and which is related to the general issue of the use of metaknowledge in AI systems. Perhaps we should insist that our representation of a viewpoint includes some explicit statement about its potential applicability.

Assuming that a viewpoint has been selected, the main controversy is over whether reasoning within that viewpoint should be logical or not. Hewitt (1985), for example, insists that only logical deduction should be used within a viewpoint (which he calls a **microtheory**). Since his work relates more to multi-agent systems it will be considered further below. Similarly, Martins and Shapiro (1988) consider that "it is advisable that contexts (their term for viewpoints) be not known to be inconsistent." In classical AI, with incremental viewpoints, the tradition has been to adopt logical methods such as resolution theorem-proving. Only recently have such logic-based methods been extended to handle non-monotonic reasoning (such as default reasoning) and reasoning under uncertainty. Since this field encompasses almost all of modern AI it will not be considered further here.

To reason within a sentential belief logic, we may modify the rule of resolution to state (in simplified form) a rule of **attachment**:

$$(B(p) \vee q) \mathrel{\&} (\sim B(r) \vee s) \mathrel{\&} (p \rightarrow r) \Rightarrow q \vee s$$

where $\rightarrow$ denotes the agent's inference rules, i.e. in the case where q and s are empty, if we can infer r from the propositions p believed by an agent then it is contradictory for the agent to believe p but not r. This rule has been proved sound and complete by Konolige (1984), although the extension to quantified beliefs is complicated.

Within the possible worlds model it is usual to define the accessibility relation in terms of a set of axioms, such as

$$B(p) \Rightarrow B(B(p))$$

i.e. if an agent believes p then he believes he believes it (the positive introspection axiom), and

$$B(p) \ \& \ B(p \rightarrow q) \ \Rightarrow \ B(q)$$

i.e. an agent believes anything implied by what he believes (logical omniscience). A large number of standard modal logics have been defined by adopting different sets of axioms. For example, logical omniscience seems unrealistic for finite agents and the corresponding axiom is omitted in some logics. In fact, almost without exception, the axioms specified in such logics seem appropriate for 'ideal believers' only, and it remains an open question whether such formalizations can be successfully adapted to model 'real believers' such as students using an ITS.

We might also wish to relate 'belief' to 'knowledge' through axioms such as

$$B(p) \ \& \ p \ \Rightarrow \ K(p)$$

i.e. if an agent believes something true then he knows it, and

$$K(p) \ \Rightarrow \ p$$

i.e. if an agent knows p then p must be true.

The idea of a 'viewpoint' has arisen in so many different forms because in many fields (including ITS research) it has been found necessary to take account of different ways of looking at some subject matter, to use non-deductive reasoning in order to improve problem-solving efficiency and to increase psychological plausibility. Unfortunately, processing mechanisms developed for viewpoints have been somewhat *ad hoc* because of the formidable fundamental technical difficulties. For example, unlike first-order predicate logic, modal logics using the belief operator B are referentially opaque, i.e. even if two expressions have been shown to be equivalent then we cannot in general substitute one for the other within the scope of B, so that from a student model containing *B("The composer of the New World Symphony was American")* and the fact that the composer was Dvorak we cannot conclude that the student model should also contain *B("Dvorak was American")*.

In order fully to understand the properties of viewpoint-reasoning mechanisms, abstract theoretical models will have to be developed, although it must be conceded that at the moment all practical systems use heuristic methods rather than precise propositional models. For example, we can identify in the literature four formal attempts to overcome the problem of logical omniscience, which is considered both psychologically implausible for human agents and technically undesirable for computer agents:

1. The distinction between *implicit belief* and *explicit belief* (Levesque 1984). An agent's implicit beliefs are considered to include all the consequences of his explicit beliefs. Thus implicit belief I corresponds to B with logical omniscience: explicit belief E is perhaps what an agent actually reasons with. Levesque formalizes this in terms of a possible worlds semantics with a three-valued truth function.

2. The idea of *awareness* (Fagin & Halpern 1987). The third value (in addition to true and false) is concerned with whether an agent is 'aware' of a belief, i.e. informally, whether an agent realizes that a belief is relevant. An 'aware operator' A might then be defined by

$$E(p \lor \sim p) \Rightarrow A(p)$$

and used in axioms such as

$$I(p) \ \& \ A(p) \Rightarrow E(p)$$
$$E(p) \ \& \ A(E(p)) \Rightarrow E(E(p))$$

Under some formalizations of awareness, the agent can hold inconsistent beliefs.

3. The use of local reasoning (as mentioned above). This might be related to the idea of explicit and implicit belief as follows: $E(p)$ means "p is believed in some frame of mind"; $I(p)$ means "p is believed if all the frames of mind are pooled".

4. The imposition of resource bounds. The limitation to propositions of which one is aware is one kind of resource bound. We can easily imagine other kinds of bounds, e.g. on the depth of reasoning or the time devoted to it, but formalizing them is not straightforward. Obviously, the psychological motivation for such bounds derives from limitations such as those on working memory.

While these formalizations have yet to be integrated into a comprehensive theoretical model of practical utility, it is clear that they all address issues which cannot be avoided by any ITS which aims to reason with viewpoints. For example, the Socratic method is essentially a dialogue about the distinction between implicit and explicit beliefs. In the meantime, ITS designers may, indeed have to, proceed without the underlying theory but at the cost of having no analytic explanation of the success or failure of resultant systems (as discussed in Self 1990).

2.4 Revising a viewpoint

A sizeable subfield of AI is concerned with the problem of revising a viewpoint that is deemed to be unsuitable, for example, it may have become inconsistent. This work goes under the heading of *reason maintenance* or **belief revision** (Martins & Shapiro 1988). For an incremental viewpoint (which is the case usually considered) the problem is relatively tractable, since it can presumably be attributed to the most recent small change through which the viewpoint was formed. If, for example, we have just added a belief to a viewpoint, $VP' = VP + p$, then the problem has arisen because of some kind of conflict between p and the members of VP. If p contradicts an element q of VP then there is, of course, no non-arbitrary way of choosing between them unless the 'supports' of p and q are known. Therefore, research in this field is concerned with reasoning about the propositions and hypotheses which have produced the contradiction.

For non-incremental viewpoints, the resolution of the conflict may be much harder. Since most of this work has been done with multi-agent systems it will be considered below, but we may briefly mention here the suggestion of Kornfeld and Hewitt (1981), since it is applicable to revising a single anomalous viewpoint rather than reconciling the disparity between two viewpoints. Influenced by philosophers of science such as Popper and Lakatos, they suggest the **adjustment** of a viewpoint to retain the 'core of fundamental concepts' within the viewpoint. Unfortunately, they do not give a precise definition of what such a 'core' might be and how the viewpoint should be adjusted, but the suggestion clearly implies (as does the work on reason maintenance) that a viewpoint should not be represented simply as an unstructured set.

The idea of a 'core' of a viewpoint accords with the suggestion of Wenger (1987) that a viewpoint consists of a 'kernel' and a 'scope'. The kernel, according to Wenger, consists not only of beliefs but also prior decisions, analogies and assumptions that explicitly belong to the viewpoint or must be inferred as underlying it. The scope 'delineates the foreseeable area of relevance' of the viewpoint. In general terms, the kernel contains what is needed to understand entities within the scope of a viewpoint. There is, however, a danger that, because of the apparent similarity to general AI notions such as frames and scripts, the essence of the concept of a viewpoint is evaporating. It appears, however, that a viewpoint is more than a set of atomic beliefs: certainly for ITS purposes we must expect to have to include:

(a) explicit links between beliefs, because it is often the case that if a
    student possesses one belief then he also possesses another,
(b) the origin or justification of a belief, because we often need to
    know why a student believes something before he can be induced to
    change his belief, and
(c) links to associated viewpoints, perhaps in terms of the beliefs that
    they share or disagree about, since an ITS must often seek not

merely to elaborate one viewpoint but to move to a different viewpoint altogether.

2.5   Reasoning between viewpoints

Wenger (1987) remarks that "the coexistence and interaction of viewpoints are fundamental epistemological issues that underlie the construction of warranted beliefs." One of the practical reasons for advocating that an agent should maintain multiple viewpoints is the hope that the agent may be able to integrate or coalesce the views provided by different viewpoints to obtain a more focused view than is possible with the viewpoints separately. However, this hope seems to lack any kind of computational realization, although some related ideas can be identified, for example:

1. *Analogy* can be considered to involve the mapping of a viewpoint (e.g. 'flowing water' or 'teeming crowd') from one domain to another (electricity) (Gentner 1983). Since all analogies provide only partial mappings, the eventual integration of such partial viewpoints would seem to be an important problem still to be satisfactorily addressed.

2. The field of *qualitative reasoning* (Cohn 1989) emphasizes that it aims to provide methods to be used with, not instead of, quantitative reasoning methods. However, so far, researchers have not really defined how such complementary methods may be used together.

The work on both analogy and qualitative reasoning provides a link to research on *mental models*, which are yet another manifestation of viewpoints, but one without computational precision. In fact, 'computational precision' is not really what mental models seek, since they tend to emphasize analogical representations akin to mental images rather than symbolic or propositional representations, and in so far as they 'run' they produce mainly qualitative inferences. However, mental models research is in sympathy with ITS work in emphasizing the role of an individual's beliefs and experiences, rather than the generalized theories of cognition more common in psychology. This work is reflected in the ITS field by, for example, the QUEST system (Frederiksen & White 1988), which provides a series of models along the qualitative/quantitative spectrum. But these models are pre-specified and adopted in turn (not together), and therefore do not address the problem of coalescing viewpoints.

3   MULTI-AGENT VIEWPOINTS

When multiple viewpoints are held by two or more agents then the main complication that arises over the uni-agent case is of course that any one agent will not in general have access to the viewpoints of the other agent(s). Indeed, a single agent may adopt a viewpoint about another agent's viewpoint, leading to nested viewpoints and complex interactions to reconcile apparent discrepancies. In simple cases, however, the viewpoints may be processed independently.

3.1 Independent viewpoints

Hewitt's microtheories, mentioned above, are intended to be small, idealized theories which are internally consistent and clearly demarcated from other microtheories. Each microtheory provides independent conclusions, which must then be reconciled in a separate process. His examples illustrate the idea of *open systems*, such as offices, where there are large quantities of diverse information being processed concurrently. For example, an advertising department might have a microtheory which says:

Increased advertising & Lower prices → Increased profitability

while the finance department might hold that:

Increased advertising & Lower prices → Decreased profitability

Such microtheories are formalized in first-order logic, permitting logical deduction.

The field of *distributed AI*, which includes the work on open systems, has been largely concerned with representing and managing such independent viewpoints. The two basic problems in distributed AI are to work out (1) how to divide a problem between nodes or agents, and (2) how to coordinate behaviour between agents. A common computational representation to adopt is the *blackboard system*, in which independent 'knowledge sources' monitor a shared blackboard and offer a contribution towards a problem solution when specified conditions are satisfied (Engelmore & Morgan 1988). Each knowledge source operates as an independent, autonomous expert offering a viewpoint on some problem. Knowledge sources do not, in general, reason about other knowledge sources. Indeed, it would be against the spirit of blackboard systems (and their simpler variation, production systems) to allow this, as the modularity of such systems, which is considered one of their main virtues, would be threatened by such inter-dependencies. A separate scheduler is responsible for coordinating the various contributions, and an overall problem solution is supposed to emerge from successive contributions, rather than from some meta-process.

3.2 Inter-dependent viewpoints

Cooperative problem-solving, as opposed to independent problem-solving by one or more agents, promises more effective solutions through the potential for integrating differing viewpoints. To permit cooperative problem-solving, an agent needs to represent and reason about other agents' viewpoints. Formally, therefore, we need to extend the notation to indicate which agent holds a viewpoint and a particular belief – so VP_a will denote that agent a holds the viewpoint VP and $B_a(p)$ will denote that agent a holds belief p. As before, we can nest beliefs, so that $B_b(B_a(p))$ denotes that agent b believes that agent a believes p (we will abbreviate this to $B_{ba}p$). By an obvious extension, we may write $B_b VP_a$ to denote that b believes that the viewpoint of a is VP.

Bruce and Newman (1978) considered how representations of the beliefs and plans of one agent are embedded within the beliefs and plans of another when attempting to formalize the plot of the Hansel and Gretel story. They define the **belief space** of agent a to contain all the propositions p such that $B_a p$. They describe a belief space as representing a 'point of view' (i.e. viewpoint). They also define a **mutual belief space** of a with respect to b to contain those propositions which a believes and which a believes b believes. The mutual belief space avoids the need to represent infinitely nested beliefs, for it contains those propositions p which satisfy $M_{ab}p$ where

$$M_{ab}p = B_a p \ \& \ B_{ab}p \ \& \ B_{aba}p \ \& \ \dots$$

The story involves three plans (the formalization of which is a separate issue): *abandon* – the mother's real plan to abandon the children in the wood; *walk* – the pretended plan to walk in the wood; *trail* – Hansel's plan to leave a trail to enable escape. The plot is:

$B_m abandon$	mother plans to abandon Hansel
$B_{mh} walk$	mother believes Hansel believes the *walk* plan
$B_m M_{hm} walk$	mother believes Hansel mutually believes *walk*

Then Hansel overhears the mother discussing the real plan, so:

$B_{hm} abandon$	Hansel believes mother plans to abandon him
$B_h trail$	Hansel plans to leave a trail

But he deceives the mother into believing the original pretended plan is still believed:

$B_{hmh} walk$	Hansel believes mother believes Hansel believes *walk*
$B_{hm} M_{hm} walk$	Hansel believes mother believes Hansel mutually believes *walk*

   As we can see, even simple stories may involve reasoning about deeply nested beliefs, in this case, perhaps not such a simple story because of the mutual deception.

   The use of viewpoints (or belief spaces) has been central to the development of dialogue theory in AI and computational linguistics, and the computational modelling of speech acts is now closely related to the modelling of beliefs of different agents (Allen 1987). An agent is considered to have a goal which is pursued through planning speech acts which are a function of other agents' beliefs and intentions. The hearer may reconstruct the speaker's goals in interpreting the intended speech acts. Moore (1977) based his approach on possible world semantics – to prove an assertion it would be translated into its equivalent statement in the possible worlds syntax and passed to a theorem-prover using that logic. Cohen (1978) created separate belief spaces using the partitioned semantic networks of Hendrix (1975). Interestingly, Hendrix's original motivation was to develop a representation suitable to support educational interactions. Recently, comprehensive formal theories of rational interaction have been developed (Cohen & Levesque 1987) in which speech acts are regarded not as primitive but as the consequences of principles of action.

   The idea of 'mutual belief spaces' reappears in different fields. In philosophy, Strawson (1971) has given a detailed discussion of the need for shared knowledge. In distributed AI, it has similarly been argued that multiagent cooperation is not possible without a base of common knowledge (Huhns et al. 1988). Formally, we may write $EB(p)$ to denote that 'everybody believes p', and $EB(EB(p))$ that 'everybody believes everybody believes p', and so on. Then we may define $CB(p)$ to denote that p is a common belief, by

$$CB(p) = EB(p) \ \& \ EB(EB(p)) \ \& \ EB(EB(EB(p))) \ \& \ldots$$

   It is convenient to imagine an agent which believes all and only common beliefs. In the case of the similarly defined 'common knowledge', this mythical agent is often called 'any fool'.

   If all the beliefs of all the agents are known then common beliefs can, of course, be determined. But in general they are not, and any individual agent needs to ascribe beliefs to other agents. How is this to be done?

   Ballim et al. (1988) propose a mechanism based on default reasoning. They first define a viewpoint to consist of a set of *environments*, each of which contains a set of propositions about some topic. (This is the same as our definition except that the propositions are partitioned, mainly for efficiency reasons.) A viewpoint is labelled with the name of the agent considered to believe the propositions in the set. They present this graphically as in Figure 2.1.

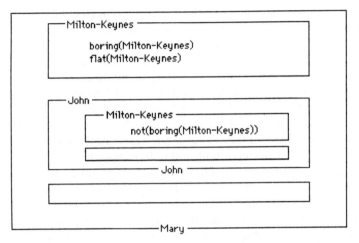

Fig. 2.1 Ballim, Wilks and Barnden's representation of viewpoints.

The agents' names are at the middle of the lower lines of the viewpoints, and the topic names are towards the left of the upper lines of the environments. Viewpoints may, of course, be nested. In our notation above, Figure 2.1 represents:

$B_{mary}(flat(Milton\text{-}Keynes))$
$B_{mary}(boring(Milton\text{-}Keynes))$
$B_{mary}(B_{john}(not(boring(Milton\text{-}Keynes))))$

Their basic belief ascription rule says that an agent a believes that an agent b believes what a does except where there is explicit evidence to the contrary. So, from Figure 2.1, we would add

$B_{mary}(B_{john}(flat(Milton\text{-}Keynes)))$

but not

$B_{mary}(B_{john}(boring(Milton\text{-}Keynes)))$.

Graphically, propositons in outer environments are 'pushed into' inner ones, unless blocked. Unfortunately, matters are more complicated, as Ballim et al. acknowledge: there are many 'atypical beliefs' (such as those deriving from expertise, self-knowledge and secrets) which are not normally ascribed to other agents unless there is reason to do so.

In case it should be thought that these intricacies are of little relevance to ITS, it may be pointed out that Ballim et al. (1988) go on to discuss how a medical expert (system) could discuss a case with two people, whom we may regard as students, with different medical knowledge. The conversation is manageable only if each agent is able to reason about his beliefs about what the second believes about the third's beliefs. Similarly, Douglas (1991) points out that human tutors (and we've little reason to expect computer tutors will do any better) spend up to 20% of their time repairing failures due to 'incongruent states of knowledge', that is, to mistaken assumptions about mutual beliefs.

The impossibility of reliably abscribing beliefs to other agents obviously presents a fundamental difficulty for multi-agent communication, but it is not necessarily an insurmountable one. It is not the case, as it might seem, *a priori*, that $B_b VP_a$ should be as close as possible to VP_a, or to be more concrete for ITSs, that $B_{system}VP_{student}$ (the 'student model') should be as close as possible to $VP_{student}$. There would be some computational redundancy in two agents maintaining identical viewpoints: it may be more efficient, and perhaps as reliable, for an agent to simply ask the other agent rather than to evaluate a model of that agent. Also, in an educational context, any discrepancies between $B_{system}VP_{student}$ and $VP_{student}$ may be the basis for fruitful discussions between the system and the student.

3.3 Incompatible viewpoints

In the previous section we have emphasized the need for some communality between viewpoints to permit effective problem-solving. However, viewpoints may sometimes provide such radically different views that there has to be some mechanism for resolving conflicts in order to permit some agreement about how to proceed.

The simplest solution is for one agent to have the authority to make over-riding unilateral decisions to select between the viewpoints offered. If this agent were to always select its own viewpoint then there would be no point in gathering alternative viewpoints. We therefore assume that the agent has some evaluation function for assessing viewpoints.

In most multi-agent problem-solving situations it is not acceptable for a single agent to take sole responsibility for decision-making. Often it is necessary for the decision-making agent to persuade the other agents to agree to the decision, to enable them to revise their viewpoints so that they may continue to be able to offer contributions and, in the case of human agents, perhaps for subjective reasons, to encourage future cooperation. This is often achieved by persuading an agent of a non-adopted viewpoint VP_b to adopt the desired viewpoint VP_a.

Teachers (and ITSs) possess a rich set of techniques for persuading students (possessors of VP_b) to adopt the 'required' viewpoint (the teacher's VP_a). The simplest technique is, of course, to transmit the required viewpoint, that is, to tell it to the student, and to assume that it will overwrite VP_b. The limitations of this technique hardly need elaborating here. More subtle are the various 'challenging' techniques (which are sometimes lumped under the label of Socratic tutoring) in which the student is led, by the use of counter-examples perhaps, to question the basis for his viewpoint and to revise it in the required direction, that is, towards VP_a.

In more egalitarian multi-agent systems, where there is no 'distinguished agent' responsible for resolving conflicts and making decisions, it may be possible to apply the technique of **mediation**, in which an independent, external agent, with no vested interest in outcomes, is brought in specifically to find some compromise between viewpoints.

Hewitt (1986) proposes such a technique for dealing with conflicts between his microtheories (mentioned above). The outcome from the microtheories (which, it will be recalled, are deductive theories) are passed to **metamicrotheories**, which contain axioms about microtheories and engage in extra-deductive techniques such as debate and negotiation to deal with inconsistencies and conflicts between microtheories. The metamicrotheories may themselves be inconsistent with one another. Unfortunately, the decision-making procedures of the metamicrotheories are not specified.

Metamicrotheories are regarded as one approach to formalizing the general (but even more elusive) concept of **due process**. Due process is proposed as a central activity in organizational information processing. In any large organization, a number of agents are concurrently developing beliefs, goals, plans, requests, etc. Gathering, analysing, debating and recording such objects is considered to be the activity of due process. Due process does not itself make decisions but informs the decision-making process. Due process is inherently self-reflective since it is concerned with the justifications and mechanisms for reaching decisions, rather than with the decisions themselves. Due process also 'specifically includes the social actions of computer systems' but how is again not made clear.

If two or more agents have conflicting views which have to be reconciled then, with or without a mediator, some **negotiation** is necessary. In distributed AI, particularly, there are many references to techniques which are considered to involve 'negotiations' among nodes of a system. Indeed, the centrality of the idea of negotiation was emphasised by Davis and Smith (1983) in an attempt to establish it as a dominant metaphor for distributed problem-solving. In a long, mainly discursive, paper they place negotiation within the mainstream of AI control structure development as a natural extension from the one-way information exchanges of then current AI programming systems.

Technically, their main contribution is the **contract net**, which provides opportunistic, adaptive task allocation among agents using a framework based on task announcements, bids and awarded 'contracts'. An agent can adopt both 'manager' and 'worker' roles, and a 'contract net protocol' enables the opportunistic communication between managers and workers. Since the contract net works through the mutual selection by both manager and worker processes, it differs from manager-centred invocations (e.g. procedure calls) and worker-centred invocations (e.g. data-driven computations). However, there is no mechanism for reasoning about the global effects of local decisions, nor any metalevel control, and consequently any global coherence emerges only incidentally.

Work on negotiation in distributed AI makes only token reference to studies of human-human negotiations, such as union-employer bargaining. Even in work that sets out explicitly to model human-human negotiations, such as that of Sycara (1989), which is concerned with adversarial conflicts in labour relations, it has been found (as usual) that sociological texts do not provide the required precision, and it has been necessary to devise new computational representations. In Sycara's system, called Persuader, negotiation is regarded as an iteration through three steps: generation of a compromise proposal by a mediator, generation of a counter-proposal based on feedback from a dissenting agent, and persuasive argumentation based largely on case-based reasoning (see Figure 2.2, which suggests that 'negotiation' is a rather complex process). Various argument types are defined, based on appeals to universal principle, a theme, authority, 'status quo', 'minor standards', 'prevailing practice', precedents as counterexamples, self-interest, self-protection, etc. – but this is clearly an area where further research is needed.

The large number of different techniques developed in distributed AI for dealing with different aspects of negotiation has led to "confusion and misunderstanding among researchers who are studying different aspects of the same phenomenon" (Durfee & Lesser 1989). For example, the contract net is concerned mainly with the allocation of tasks to agents, whereas Persuader emphasizes the iterative exchange of counter-proposals leading to compromise. In an attempt to impose some consensual basis, Durfee and Lesser propose a general definition of negotiation: "the process of improving agreement (reducing inconsistency and uncertainty) on common viewpoints or plans through the structured exchange of relevant information."

This definition has the virtue of distinguishing two aspects which have become intertwined in distributed AI and are in danger of becoming so in ITS research, namely, the distinction between negotiations aiming for shared plans and those seeking common viewpoints. For example, the

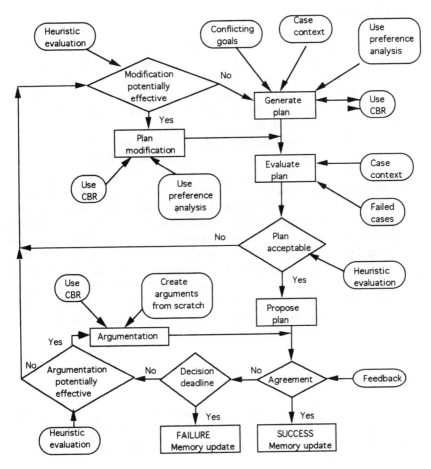

Fig. 2.2 The negotiation process (from Sycara, 1989).

KANT system (Baker 1989c) allows students to 'negotiate' both about the next concept to be discussed, and also about the concept itself. In ITS research generally, we find proposals emphasizing 'negotiation' for two main reasons: one to enable discussions about how to proceed, what strategy to follow, what example to look at, etc., in an attempt to loosen the tutorial control of standard ITSs; the other to permit discussions about the viewpoints (i.e. the beliefs or the knowledge) themselves, on the philosophical grounds that one agent (the tutor) should not be deemed to have infallible insight into the 'correct' viewpoint. If the experience of distributed AI is any guide, the former is rather more tractable than the latter.

4 SUMMARY

The concept of viewpoints has recently surfaced in ITS research in response to the facts that (a) it is rarely possible to define a unique 'correct' viewpoint to be communicated to a student, and often there are a number of (more or less) equally valid viewpoints, and (b) students have viewpoints too, and these need to be taken account of in any satisfactory tutorial interaction.

However, the general concept is not a new one: as we have seen, it has a long pedigree within mainstream AI, and a number of contemporary fields (including distributed AI, cooperative problem-solving, and dialogue theories) are grappling with aspects of the issue. As a common framework, we have tried to elaborate the definition of a 'viewpoint' as a set of beliefs. We have found that different writers have emphasized different aspects of viewpoints and proposed different extensions to the basic idea. We have not tried to impose a 'standard' view of what a viewpoint should be, as this would be premature. The aim of this review has been to put the ITS view of viewpoints into context and to give some idea of the various fields' different approaches and the progress they have made. We hope thereby to enable ITS researchers to base their own work on viewpoints on the experiences of others.

ACKNOWLEDGEMENTS

I am grateful for the viewpoints of Pierre Dillenbourg, Rod Moyse, David Nichols, Alan Parkes and Michael Twidale on a draft of this chapter. Needless to say, I take full responsibility for any failure to reconcile disparities.

3 Negotiated Tutoring Needs, Student Modelling and Instructional Planning

Arguments and Experiences from the Perspective of the SCENT Project

GORDON McCALLA[2] and BARBARA WASSON[1]

*ARIES Laboratory, Department of Computational
Science, University of Saskatchewan,
Saskatoon, Saskatchewan S7N 0W0, Canada
[1] Present address: Norwegian Telecom Research
Department, Tromsø, Norway*

ABSTRACT

In this chapter we argue that two critical requirements for negotiated tutoring are a good student model and the ability to flexibly plan instruction. We start by characterizing what negotiated tutoring is and what it isn't. Next, we show an extended interaction between a human tutor and a human student in order to illustrate the kinds of phenomena which occur during negotiated tutoring. We then discuss the design of an automated tutoring system which can undertake knowledge negotiation with a student. We focus particularly on the issue of how the tutoring system is able to determine its own bargaining position, and how it can plan instruction once an instructional goal has been mutually agreed upon by the student and the tutor. In the model proposed here, the tutoring system uses its knowledge of the student and its knowledge of the domain to choose instructional goals it feels are appropriate for the student. The student may, of course, disagree, in which case a negotiation between student and tutor over the most appropriate instructional goal to pursue

---

[2] This chapter was written while Gordon McCalla was a Visiting Scientist at the Centre for Systems Science at Simon Fraser University, Burnaby, British Columbia, Canada, under the sponsorship of the BC Advanced Systems Institute.

KNOWLEDGE NEGOTIATION
ISBN 0–12–509378–0

must take place. Once the instructional goal is decided upon, the tutoring system uses its knowledge of the domain as well as a wide variety of pedagogical and other planning rules to decide how best to plan out the instruction. Throughout the chapter, many distinctions are made to help clarify the negotiated learning paradigm, key among them the distinction between content and delivery, which allows the issue of *what* is to be learned to be separated from the issue of *how* it is to be learned. The system proposed here deals only in the content aspects of negotiated learning, not the delivery aspects. While there is still a long road to travel before tutoring systems with full knowledge negotiation capabilities can be built, we feel that the approach described in this chapter at least is a first step along that road.

1 INTRODUCTION

Moyse and Elsom-Cook (Chapter 1, this volume) characterize knowledge negotiation as follows: "knowledge negotiation implies that the current definition of the domain to be tutored, and the process of tutoring it, are determined by repeated negotiation between the system and the student." In other words, the tutoring system and the student engage in an extended bargaining session where the goals of the student have at least some role, probably a major role, to play in determining the kind of instructional interaction which occurs.

The partners to this knowledge negotiation do not have equal knowledge of the domain nor equal knowledge of how best to learn the domain. The fact that the student has agreed to the interaction with the tutor is implicit acknowledgement of the student's belief in the superior knowledge of the tutor in these matters. This unequal partnership has a number of implications. First, there will be times when the tutor must take control, due to superior knowledge of the domain being tutored as well as experience in what types of instructional interactions work best in various situations. This means that a knowledge negotiation approach does not necessarily result in a student controlled interaction. Second, the student will often have problems communicating with the tutor because of the mismatch in knowledge and terminology. This means that much of a knowledge negotiation session may involve knowledge elicitation, where the tutor is trying to figure out what a student knows and desires prior to figuring out how best to approach the instructional interaction. A third consequence of this unequal relationship is that the tutor has a role in reducing the cognitive load on the student. It is often unfair to burden the student with many details he/she is not yet ready to handle. Moreover, since the student does not have the experience to organize the new knowledge that he/she is acquiring, the tutor must help by providing cognitive hooks (e.g. Thomson 1989) to existing knowledge and by reiterating various concepts from multiple perspectives (Moyse 1989).

The important things that distinguish a knowledge negotiation approach from other approaches to tutoring are the explicit recognition of the student's goals and the value of these goals and the attempt to allow the student to carry out these goals wherever possible, given the constraints of the learning situation. The tutor is viewed as a partner in the learning process, not an information dispenser, albeit a very knowledgeable partner who must insist on control from time to time. If the instruction is moulded to the student's desires and tailored to the student's evolving knowledge, the student is able to more readily understand the domain being learned. The hope is that the student is highly motivated to learn, more capable of building new knowledge, and better able to integrate this knowledge with his/her existing knowledge.

In this chapter we would like to look at the problem of actually building a tutoring system with knowledge negotiation capabilities. In the next section, we will start by providing a portion of a negotiated interaction between a human tutor and a student. This interaction will be used to illustrate a number of features of knowledge negotiation. Then, the requirements for achieving a tutoring system based on knowledge negotiation will be discussed. In Section 3, we will outline some of our research into student modelling and instructional planning, and show how it could be useful to negotiated learning. A complete example will help to clarify our ideas. Crucial to this approach is having a solid student model. In fact, one of our main contentions in this paper is the central importance of student modelling to the knowledge negotiation enterprise. Section 4 concludes the chapter with a summary of the main contributions, and a brief synopsis of some important research directions which might be pursued in the quest for knowledge negotiation.

2   THE NATURE OF KNOWLEDGE NEGOTIATION

2.1   A sample knowledge negotiation session

What might a knowledge negotiation session be like? The following dialogue between a human tutor and a student involves many characteristics of knowledge negotiation.[1] The overall domain of the tutoring is

---

[1] The interactions occuring at the beginning of this dialogue (parts 1 and 2) are grammatically improved versions of actual student–tutor interactions recorded in an empirical study undertaken in the spring of 1989 – see Bhuiyan et al. (1989). The remaining interactions have been concocted as a natural follow-on to the first part of the dialogue to illustrate other aspects of knowledge negotiation. Those interactions are based on our tutoring experience, and had to be invented since the actual session had ended by then.

LISP programming. The student is a novice LISP programmer and wants to learn more; the tutor is an expert LISP programmer and experienced in helping students learn LISP. It is assumed that prior to the dialogue, the student has learned something about LISP control structures, in particular recursion and iteration, but is by no means accomplished in using these concepts. It is also assumed that the student has expressed an interest in consolidating her knowledge of LISP control structures.

Part 1:

T: How do you define the concept of recursion?

S: Recursion is a solution to a problem which uses itself to solve the problem. It calls itself in its own program to solve a smaller problem.

T: Could you explain a little bit more?

S: O.K. What it does is it solves the easiest problem and then it calls itself with the next smallest problem, and ultimately it solves the whole problem.

T: When it makes smaller and smaller problems it has to do something like...

S: Calling itself. It solves the problem by calling itself until it gets to what they call the base case, which stops the program. It's the end of the solution so that it can move back up.

T: When you move back up what do you do?

S: You insert the answer to the previous problem.

The first part of this dialogue is a necessary preliminary step undertaken so that the tutor can determine the student's knowledge of recursion. Without such knowledge the tutor will be unable to understand the student's needs, and will be unable to figure out what are appropriate goals to be negotiated for the upcoming instructional interaction. The tutor directs the dialogue, first asking a general question about the student's knowledge of recursion, then asking the student to try to specify this knowledge in more detail. The latter part of this dialogue segment is an attempt by the tutor to determine what parts of a recursive solution the student understands. In the tutor's second last utterance he is fishing for knowledge about the reduction step; in the tutor's last utterance he is trying to see if the student knows something about the composition step. There is some redundancy in this first part in order to reassure the tutor and the student that accurate information has been exchanged.

At the conclusion of part 1, the tutor has a good idea that the student knows the basic facts of recursion. However, her explanations of recursion are muddled enough that it seems clear she has not actually worked very much with recursive concepts. This knowledge pervades the remainder of the instructional interaction.

The dialogue enters part 2:

Part 2:

T: Would you prefer to work on an iterative or recursive problem this week?

S: I think I would probably prefer the recursion because it's a lot shorter. But it will also depend on what the problem is. Depending on the problem I will choose whether to use recursion or iteration.

T: What happens if you can solve the problem using both methods?

S: In a case like that I would probably use recursion.

T: Why?

S: Because you don't have to do it . . . {laughing} . . . the program does the work for you. You just have to solve the simplest part of the problem and let the recursion solve the rest.

In this part of the dialogue the tutor and the student negotiate over the nature of the high-level goals for the tutoring session. Dialogue part 1 has shown that the student has a basic knowledge of LISP recursion, but is by no means secure in this knowledge. Earlier tutoring sessions have shown that the student knows something about iteration, but her wish to learn more about control structures indicates some insecurity about this knowledge too. This implies that there are at least two possible general goals for the tutoring session: learning about recursion or learning about iteration. In the first utterance, the tutor suggests these two possible goals to the student. Note how this constrains the bargaining immediately: although it is still possible for the student to opt out of these choices, the tutor has set out an initial position which makes such opting out unlikely. We believe that imposing such constraints is one of the prime roles of the tutor in negotiated learning. Based on his knowledge of the domain and experience with students, the tutor can focus the instruction, label the goals, etc., thus reducing the need for the student to keep track of everything. Overall, the cognitive load on the student can be reduced by the imposition of appropriate constraints by the tutor.

In her first utterance, the student chooses a goal, namely learning about recursion, and explains some of her motivation for wanting to do recursion. The remainder of part 2 further explores the student's motivation for wanting to learn about recursion. For knowledge negotiation to work properly, understanding the motivation for an instructional goal is crucial to both parties: the student can gain insight by reflecting on these goals and can gain reassurance that her goals are important; the tutor can assess the seriousness of the student's intentions and can understand the bargaining position of the student much better in future negotiations.

Part 3:

T: O.K. We are going to work on recursion this session. There are different kinds of recursion. Do you know any of the types of recursion?

S: I think that in one type of recursion you want to look at each element of the list and if it meets a given condition then you do something with that element. In LISP you would cdr down the list.

In the third part of dialogue, the student and tutor attempt to further focus the instructional goal by choosing a specific type of recursion to discuss. The tutor suggests the need for such refinement; the student selects the particular refinement that she desires. Here we see a nice sharing of responsibility. The tutor's pedagogical experience suggests the necessity of making a refinement at this point, while the student is still allowed some latitude to determine which refinement would be most suitable. The student's response is a particularly good illustration of a communication problem caused by the student's naivety about the domain: the student does not have the terminology to label the kind of recursion she wants to study. Such terminological problems will occur over and over again until the student approaches the tutor's level of expertise, and will be a major source of difficulty in any kind of negotiated tutoring.

Part 4:

> T: Good. One kind of recursion is cdr recursion which, as you note involves reducing the problem to a simpler problem by cdring down the list. Since you have the basic idea about what cdr recursion is, lets see if you can show me in more detail how it works. Would you like an example that I ask you questions about, an example to trace, or a template to fill in?
> S: An example that you ask questions about.

Part 4 of the tutorial interaction is aimed at deciding how to carry out the specific instructional goal chosen in part 3. First, the tutor labels the instructional goal as learning about 'cdr recursion' so that the student's repertoire of terms is increased. Then a simple negotiated interchange happens where the tutor offers the student a selection of techniques specifically appropriate for carrying out the 'learn cdr recursion' goal and, in response, the student chooses one such technique. Once again the tutor is helping to focus the negotiation by suggesting things that have worked in the past with other students, thus reducing the student's need to synthesize goals from scratch. In Brecht et al.'s (1989) terms, the negotiation is happening over delivery aspects of the instruction. This points out that there are many different kinds of negotiation possible: negotiation over content goals, delivery aspects, level of instruction, etc.

In her response to the tutor, the student doesn't object to the tutor taking control of the tutorial interaction. Such relinquishing of control should happen frequently in negotiated learning, since not much learning is going to happen if every item, however small, is up for negotiation. In other situations, the tutor might extend control to the student so that she can embark on some sort of exploratory learning. This might happen in a consolidation phase of learning (where control by the tutor is no longer appropriate), or in an undirected phase of learning (where the student is trying to discover new goals for herself).

Part 5:

T: O.K. Here is a function:

```
(defun FindB (l)
(cond
    ((null l) nil)
    ((equal (car l) 'B) t)
    (t (FindB (cdr l)))))
```

Which line is the base case?

S: This line. {She points to ((null l) nil)}

T: Correct. Where is the recursive step?

S: {She points to (t (FindB (cdr l))}

T: Can you tell me what kind of answer the function will return?

S: {pause. . .} I think it will return either t or nil.

T: That's right. Now can you tell me what the function returns given the data:
    l = (A DOGS (ARE) WONDERFUL B (DOGS) ARE (WISE))

S: t

T: Yes, and with the data:
    l = (A C (B) DEVILISHLY (CLEVER) BOUNCE)?

S: nil

T: Great. You seem to understand what is going on. Now I am going to give you an
    example that may or may not work. Here it is, take your time and tell me if it works
    or not.

```
(defun FindB (l)
(cond
    ((not (atom (car l)) nil))
    ((equal (car l) 'B) t)
    (t (FindB (cdr l)))))
```

S: I think that it works.

T: Are you sure? Try tracing it with the data: l= (A (C) B D). Explain it out loud to me as
    you go along.

S: First it tests atom car l, l is (A (C) B D), this is true so now it applies the not, so not t
    is false so it drops to the next line equal car l 'B. Well, car l is A and that is not equal
    to B, so that is false, so it goes to the last line and calls itself again with the cdr of l
    which is ((C) B D). The first test is atom car l, which is false, not false is true, so it
    does the action so it returns nil and is finished. I guess it doesn't work because
    there is a B in that list and it stops before it gets to it. The base case line is wrong.

T: That is right. When you are writing a cdr recursion function, your base case needs to
    test explicitly for a null list, since this indicates the end of the list. Just checking that
    something isn't an atom won't do, as this example shows. It must check for nil
    explicitly.

Part 5 of the dialogue is a fairly standard tutor controlled session where
the student, having acceded control to the·tutor in part 4, is now led
through a couple of examples chosen by the tutor. If the tutor has
knowledge of the student's background and motivations, the examples
can be specially tailored to the student, although in this case they are not.
The interactions in part 5 show the tutor probing the student's
understanding, picking inputs that are particularly revealing so that the

student learns subtleties. For example, the choice of input (A C (B)
DEVILISHLY (CLEVER) BOUNCE) will reveal whether the student
recognizes the fact that a B nested inside a list should not be found by
FindB. The tutor is also reinforcing the student's knowledge of
terminology wherever possible (especially in the first part of the dialogue
and in the concluding comments). By suggesting to the student that she
trace the buggy function with a particular counter example, the tutor
helps the student learn this crucial debugging technique. Hopefully, in the
future the student will know better how to spot and then correct
misconceptions when they occur. Throughout, the student is treated with
dignity as a social equal who happens to be more ignorant than the tutor
about this subject, but is no less worthy for that. This is the ambience that
must pervade any negotiated tutoring, even in situations where a more
traditional tutor control is temporarily being enforced.

At the conclusion of part 5, the student is deemed by the tutor to have
a fairly solid grounding in the analysis of cdr recursive LISP programs.
This is a step forward for the student, who, after part 1, seemed to only
know the facts about recursion. But, it is unclear whether or not the
student can take the final step and actually synthesize this knowledge.

Part 6:

S: I'm getting tired of looking at examples of cdr recursion. Isn't there something else
we could do? Maybe do another type of recursion?

T: Maybe you'd like to try writing a program. You could learn about another type of
recursion, but you'll never be really sure of your knowledge of recursion until you
can create a recursive program yourself. Why don't we postpone other types of
recursion until you are actually able to build a cdr recursive solution?

S: O.K. I guess I'll try writing a program.

T: So, would you like to have me take you step by step through a solution or would
you like to try to write it on your own?

S: I think I could try one on my own.

T: O.K. Here is a problem. Take your time and write a program that finds the last
element in a list.

Thus, when part 6 of the dialogue commences, the tutor is not too
surprised by the student's desire to take control by requesting a change in
instructional goal. This illustrates the goal of allowing, wherever possible,
the student to take the initiative, essential if the bargaining is happening
between two social equals. In part 6, the student not only regains control,
but suggests a specific new instructional goal: learning about another type
of recursion. The tutor does not reject this goal out of hand, although he
would first prefer the student to work on synthesizing a cdr recursive
solution. This points out that even in a negotiated learning situation, the
tutor has instructional plans which he is trying to carry out, albeit with
flexibility and concern for the student's wishes. He thus offers the student

his own goal, synthesizing a cdr recursive program, as well as giving reasons why this is the most appropriate goal at this stage. Providing such motivation is important if the student is to be convinced that she has a real say in the selection of goals. It also provides a role model for the student about the need to justify goals should she wish to continue trying to persuade the tutor that her goal is suitable. Many students, through years of relatively docile compliance with standard tutoring methodologies, will not really have the negotiation skills necessary to argue for their points of view, and there is a role for the tutor in trying to help the student acquire the meta-skills underlying knowledge negotiation.

In part 6 the student is convinced by the tutor, and the goal becomes to synthesize a program. The tutor offers the student the choice between a strongly guided versus a weakly guided tutorial style as she creates her program solution. It should be noted that flexibility of tutorial style is basic to Elsom-Cook's (1990a) idea of guided discovery tutoring, although in guided discovery it would be largely a matter of tutor choice; in a negotiated learning context, even this is up for negotiation. However, as in earlier situations, the offering of a limited choice to the student reduces the need for unstructured bargaining.

In this case the student chooses to act with minimal guidance, and the tutor selects a problem for her to work on. The tutor and student need not bargain over what kind of problem to choose since the previous interaction determines that the student would only be able to work successfully on a problem requiring a cdr recursive solution. The tutor can always use his superior knowledge of the domain and his specific knowledge of the student to make many decisions of which the student is unaware. If he didn't do this, the student would be overwhelmed with details and would probably be unable to learn effectively. Thus, negotiated tutoring does not imply that everything is always up for negotiation.

This extended dialogue continues, but the essential idea of negotiated tutoring should now be clear. In the next section we will overview the basic requirements for a knowledge negotiation system.

2.2 Basic requirements for knowledge negotiation

One of the fundamental requirements of a knowledge negotiation system is that it be able to deal with the plethora of possible goals which the student might want to negotiate. There can be content goals (e.g. wanting to learn recursion) or delivery goals (e.g. wanting to work on a particular task). There can be deep goals (e.g. wanting to achieve a mental model of how recursion works) or shallow goals (e.g. wanting to learn the LISP function calling syntax). There can be a variety of goals for learning, ranging for example from learning the basic facts about an algorithm through learning how to analyse or ultimately to synthesize the algorithm. There can be primary goals (e.g. wanting to solve a particular programming task) or secondary goals (e.g. needing to learn about recursion in order to solve the programming task). There can be affective goals (e.g. wanting to please the tutor) or cognitive goals (e.g. wanting to learn about recursion). There can be goals to learn new things or to remediate (unlearn?) misconceptions. Many of these different goals are interdependent. For example, a student may want to learn about recursion in order to please the tutor, and may want to work on a particular task as a means of learning recursion. The tutoring system, of course, also has goals, although normally these would be suppressed or made secondary to the student's goals, at least if the negotiated learning is to have a student initiative flavour.

In order to deal with the variety of possible student goals, the tutoring system must incorporate knowledge of these different kinds of student goals and their relationship to one another, as well as the relationships of the goals to the domain knowledge the student should be learning. There is a topology to the domain knowledge space and the goal space that constrains the choice of goals in any given situation. Knowledge of this topology forms the basis for the tutor's pedagogical planning abilities. It is these pedagogical planning abilities that allow the tutor to take a negotiating stance and, when combined with an individualized student model, allows the tutoring system to suggest goals to a student, thus reducing the student's cognitive load. Consider the following example.

Assume the student has the goal of learning recursion. The tutor knows that one natural sequence of content goals needed to achieve this goal is to start by having the student learn the basic facts about recursion, then to follow by having her learn how to analyse recursive solutions, and finally to have the student learn how to synthesize recursive solutions. Moreover, each stage in this fact/analysis/synthesis sequence constrains the kinds of delivery goals which are appropriate. Thus, the basic facts phase might be achieved through examples, the analysis phase through tracing pre-existing recursive solutions, and the synthesis phase through solving programming tasks.

Still further constraints can be put on these goals, however, by the inherent structure of the knowledge to be learned. In this example, the knowledge space might define three different types of recursion: cdr recursion, car recursion, and car/cdr recursion. The knowledge space may also encode that cdr recursion and car recursion are natural prerequisites to car/cdr recursion. This type/subtype knowledge maps onto a goal/subgoal dimension in the goal space; that is, the student who wants to learn recursion may best be able to achieve this goal by first achieving the subgoals of learning the three types of recursion, with the goals of learning car recursion and cdr recursion preceding the goal of learning car/cdr recursion.

The fact/analysis/synthesis dimension and the goal/subgoal dimension can be interleaved in various ways. In one sequence, the student could learn the facts about cdr recursion, then the facts about car recursion, then the facts about car/cdr recursion, then the analysis of cdr recursion, then the analysis of car recursion, then the analysis of car/cdr recursion, then the synthesis of cdr recursion, then the synthesis of car recursion, and finally the synthesis of car/cdr recursion. There are many other possible sequences, but only some of them are appropriate given the constraints imposed by the knowledge and goal spaces. Thus, it may not be straightforward for a student to undertake a synthesis goal before the corresponding analysis goal has been achieved, and it would not be easy to achieve any kind of understanding (fact, analysis, or synthesis) of car/cdr recursion before achieving a corresponding understanding of both cdr recursion and car recursion.

Knowing these appropriate and inappropriate goal sequences, and understanding further constraints imposed by the other kinds of goals the student could have, the tutoring system has a responsibility to negotiate particular goals with the student that are compatible with these constraints. That is, it would be irresponsible of the tutor to allow the student to embark on goals which are clearly inappropriate. In this example, a total novice to recursion who wanted to carry out a task involving car/cdr recursion would have to be discouraged by the tutor. Similarly, for a task involving the synthesis of cdr recursion. The tutor would try to convince the student to look first at examples of either car recursion or cdr recursion, before proceeding to more advanced goals. Of course, if the student insists on following an inappropriate path, it may be useful to let her try something beyond her capabilities and fail (see Winne, forthcoming). This may be particularly important for motivating the student to pay more attention to the tutor's guidance in the future; essentially the student learns a lesson in the motivational domain, not the subject matter domain.

When there is a disagreement about goals during a knowledge negotiation session, a number of different resolution modes are possible, each reflecting a different tutorial style. We have emphasized student initiative which would resolve disputes about goals in favour of the student. In such a mode the tutor might point out goal conflicts, but would accede to the student in the end if persuasion couldn't change the student's mind. Such accession to the student may be necessary to achieve motivational goals. There are other possible modes. In a tutor-controlled

mode the student would be overruled by the tutor in cases where
unresolvable differences are found. Tutor-controlled mode will also
happen in situations where the student simply doesn't know what to do.
For example, in part 4 of the above dialogue the student asks the tutor to
enter something like this mode, and much of part 5 proceeds with the
tutor imposing goals on the student. There could be a mixed mode, as
well, where the tutor sometimes imposes its will (based on teaching
experience, perhaps), and other times accedes to student demands.
Hopefully, however, if the tutoring system explains to the student why
his/her goals are inappropriate (i.e. suggests the kinds of constraints it
knows about), then the student will feel more motivated to listen to the
tutor, and take advantage of the tutor's knowledge and experience.

It is not enough for the tutoring system to have lots of knowledge about
goals and their relationships, and to have available a variety of conflict
resolution techniques. The system must also have specific knowledge of
what the individual student knows, what goals the student has, etc. In
short, it must keep an individualized student model. Without this, it will
be impossible for the tutoring system to judge what is appropriate for a
particular student in a particular situation. For a student who already
understands the analysis of cdr recursion, for example, it would be
perfectly appropriate to have a goal of understanding the synthesis of cdr
recursion, whereas for a total novice this would, at least initially, be an
inappropriate goal.

It is this need to know specific attributes about the state of a student's
knowledge and goals that drives the knowledge elicitation phases of the
dialogue in Section 2.1. Such knowledge elicitation promises to be most
prevalent early in a tutorial interaction. As the instructional interaction
proceeds, the tutoring system must maintain its knowledge of the student.
It does this through its knowledge of expected outcomes of various
instructional actions. There is some redundancy in the tutoring, not only
because repetition helps the student reinforce concepts, but also to help
the tutor be certain that a student understands certain crucial concepts
before proceeding. Knowledge elicitation phases can be entered at any
time, of course, should the tutoring system be uncertain about a student's
knowledge or goals, or should the tutoring system want to help the
student recall information.

The model we will present in Section 3 below is able to deal with many
of the representation, pedagogical, and student modelling concerns
discussed so far in this section. However, there are two other main issues
which should be considered before proceeding to a detailed description of
our model.

First, the knowledge negotiation system should be able to deal with
multiple perspectives that the student may have about the domain

knowledge. While this issue is largely beyond the scope of our paper (but see Moyse 1989, Moyse & Elsom-Cook 1992), it does seem to us that there is some core knowledge that underlies all perspectives. Whether a student views recursion in terms of a template model, a problem reduction model, or some other model, he or she will still have to understand at a strategic level about base cases, reduction steps, composition steps, and how these are put together. Thus, a tutoring system which is able to grasp the student's ability (or inability) to understand and use strategies, however the strategies are really put together by the student, has a good chance of communicating with the student, at least at some level. It would be an interesting future research project to extend our knowledge representation system to handle multiple perspectives, and in fact one of the students in our laboratory is investigating this issue (see Bhuiyan et al. 1989).

A second important issue is tutor-student communication. In order to carry out knowledge negotiation, a tutoring system must have extensive communicative capabilities. We have assumed that this communication will be primarily linguistic, although in some limited domains it might be possible to enhance the communication with the student through non-linguistic graphical interface techniques. In linguistic communication, the mismatch in vocabulary about the domain is a critical problem requiring the tutoring system to understand circumlocutions, and requiring it to generate definitions and explanations to the student with great frequency. In our model, actual communication with the student is essentially ignored, even though it is an interesting and important issue. There is relevant research on this issue, however. Work by Baker (1989d) on tutorial dialogue and O'Malley (1989, 1990) on graphical interfaces for guided discovery learning provide two different perspectives on requirements for tutor-student interaction. This work might be readily adapted to a negotiated learning context, although much remains to be done, especially on the actual linguistic issues (as opposed to the interaction issues).

3 STUDENT MODELLING AND INSTRUCTIONAL PLANNING

3.1 Foundations

Figure 3.1 shows the architecture we envisage for a negotiated learning system. Central to our approach is the student knowledge analyst. Acting in parallel to the rest of the system as the instructional dialogue proceeds, the student knowledge analyst would be able to recognize at many levels (coarse grained and fine grained) the student's behaviour. The output from the student knowledge analyst would be a detailed student model showing, at many levels of detail, what the student knows and doesn't know about the instructional domain. It also would contain knowledge about the student's goals, similarly arrayed at various grain sizes. The student model would be created on the basis of the student's most recent actions, his or her earlier behaviour, and general knowledge of student behaviour. The student model would then be used by the content planner which would produce a plan outlining what concepts would be most appropriate for the student to learn, at what level of detail they should be presented, and in what order. This instructional plan would encode the tutor's instructional goals for the student, and would form the basis for the tutor's negotiating position. The plan would contain goals for the tutor itself as well as for the student, for example to enter into a knowledge elicitation interaction with the student in order to gain information with which to flesh out the student model. The content negotiation component would then bargain with the student over these instructional goals until an agreed upon set of content goals was reached. These would then be passed to the delivery planner to produce a set of delivery options for these goals. These options would then be forwarded to the delivery negotiation component which would bargain with the student over how the instruction could best be undertaken. Finally, the student would act upon the instructional goals. At any stage in interacting with the student, either during actual instructional activities or during negotiation, the student knowledge analyst could suggest changes to the student model which might percolate through the entire system and result in changes to instructional goals.

This architecture is an outgrowth of our research on the development of a programming advisor, SCENT, to aid novice LISP students (McCalla et al. 1986). The emphasis in the SCENT project has been on recognizing student strategies and planning instruction for the student. Knowledge negotiation *per se* has not been a major issue. However, we believe that much of what we have accomplished so far can be adapted to the broader goal of developing a negotiated tutoring system. In fact, Figure 3.1 is basically an extension of the SCENT-3 architecture (McCalla et al. 1990), with the negotiation components added on. We would also need a more sophisticated student knowledge analyst than so far developed, one that was able to recognize student goals in addition to student strategic thinking.

In the remainder of this chapter we will discuss our approach and show how it can provide some of the necessary elements of a negotiated tutoring system. We will emphasize the importance of student modelling to knowledge negotiation, in particular the importance of recognizing at many levels of detail what the student currently knows about the domain

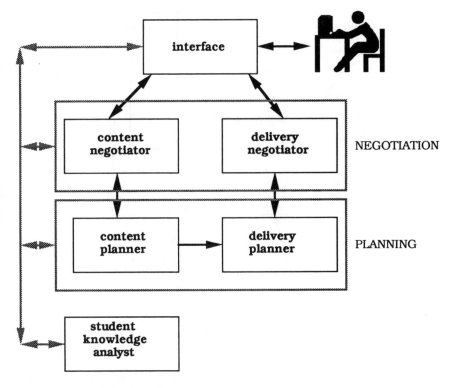

Fig. 3.1 An architecture for negotiated learning.

of instruction. We will also emphasize the importance of having a good understanding of the pedagogical constraints on learning goals, and will show how prerequisite information, granularity relationships, types of knowing such as fact/analysis/synthesis, can all be used to constrain the number of legitimate content goals. While the tutor can generate content goals, and can recognize the student's current knowledge state, it cannot yet recognize student content goals nor can it actually negotiate with the student over these goals. Delivery issues and interface issues have also been left on the back burner. Nevertheless, what has been done so far is a solid start towards the eventual goal of developing a negotiation-based tutoring system.

3.2 An approach to content planning

Content planning requires sophisticated reasoning about what content to focus on in light of the student's current knowledge state. Knowledge

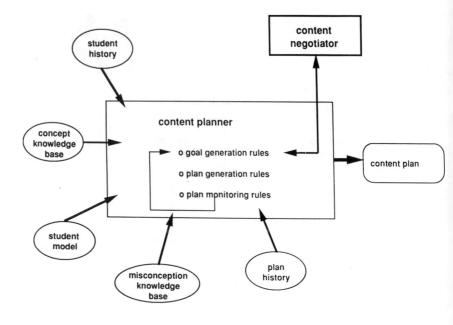

Fig. 3.2 The content planner.

about the concepts to be learned, relationships between these concepts, student abilities in using the concepts along with pedagogical information about typical misconceptions, standard sequences of learning, etc., are all necessary in order to make informed decisions that will tailor instruction to the individual student.[2] In addition, in a knowledge negotiation paradigm, where the content planner is responsible for constraining the content negotiation to concepts relevant to the student, pedagogical information about negotiation is necessary. Brecht (1990) presents an architecture for a competence-based content planner that uses explicit pedagogical knowledge to select an instructional content goal and plan to achieve it. Figure 3.2 presents this architecture (modified to allow for content negotiation between the system and the student) which takes into account the knowledge requirements cited above.

There are three phases to content planning: goal generation, plan generation and plan monitoring. A cyclic algorithm first negotiates a

---

[2] The content planner described here distinguishes between knowing about a concept (fact), being able to analyse a concept (analysis) and being able to synthesize a solution using a concept (synthesis). These distinctions have been adapted from Bloom's (1956) taxonomy of cognitive objectives.

content goal that is mutually agreeable to the student and tutor, and then plans to achieve the goal. This goal becomes, effectively, the *instructional point* of the student-tutor interaction. The content planner then monitors the execution of the content plan in order to determine when the current content plan has been carried out successfully, whether it needs to be interrupted or whether it has failed. Whichever of these cases actually arises, the content planner must potentially renegotiate the instructional goal, and the cycle begins again. In order to carry out this cycle, the content planner synthesizes information from the knowledge sources described below.

The concept knowledge base (CKB) identifies the concepts to be learned and the relationships between them. It constitutes the tutoring system's understanding of the domain. The CKB can represent various types of concepts such as domain-specific deep concepts (e.g. the programming concept recursion), domain-specific shallow concepts (e.g. the LISP language function append) or cognitive concepts (e.g. analogical reasoning). Figure 3.3 illustrates a portion of a domain specific CKB for recursion concepts. The concepts to be learned relate to one another in a variety of ways. For example **cdr recursion** is a **prerequisite** of **car/cdr recursion**, and **isa** specialization of **recursion**. Another kind of interaction is the **part_of** relationship. Concepts **car/cdr base case, car/cdr recursive call** and **car/cdr coordination** are all **part_of car/cdr recursion**.

The three different types of relationships in the CKB are highly important for the instructional interaction. The *prerequisite* relationship is crucial to negotiating an instructional point which is appropriate to the student's current background knowledge. The *isa* and *part_of* relationships allow the concepts in the knowledge base to be arrayed at many levels of granularity along the two orthogonal conceptual dimensions of generalization and aggregation. This is useful for negotiating an instructional point at an appropriate level of detail. It is also useful for recognizing what the student knows and doesn't know at an appropriate grain size.[3]

The student model (SM) keeps track of the system's beliefs about the the student's understanding (and misunderstanding) of the domain. The predicates **SK**(student knows), **~SK**(student does not know), **?SK**(it is questionable whether the student knows) and **MC**(misconception) are

---

[3] The granularity-based recognition system described in Greer and McCalla (1989) and Greer et al. (1989) is assumed to be available to the student knowledge analyst as it diagnoses a student's behaviour. Granularity-based recognition is extremely useful for educational diagnosis, in particular allowing a tutoring system to partially understand student behaviour without having to understand it in total. As Self (1988) has pointed out, it is extremely difficult to understand student behaviour, and granularity is one way to lessen the need for such full understanding.

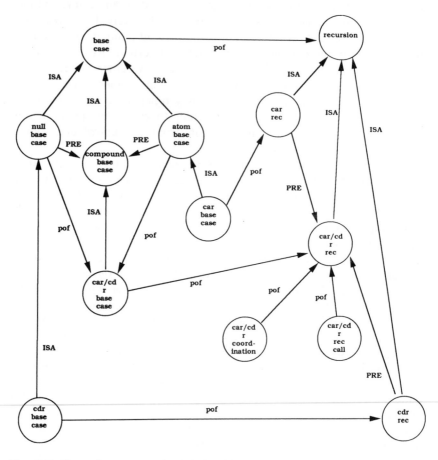

Fig. 3.3 Part of a concept knowledge base for recursion.

used to express these beliefs. The SM used by the content planner is an extremely simplified model where each entry corresponds to a concept in the CKB. For example, **SK(a, car rec)** indicates that the student knows analysis of car recursion, **~SK(s, car rec)** identifies that the student does not know how to synthesize car recursion, and **MC(cdr coord)** implies that the student has a misconception about cdr coordination. In the identification of the misconception **MC(cdr coord)**, it is not known what specific misconception the student holds, just that there is something wrong with the student's understanding of cdr coordination. In another case, for example **MC(x)** and **MC(missing x)**, there is more specific information available and the specific misconception **MC(missing x)** must be related to the more general **MC(x)**. This relationship is identified in the misconception knowledge base.

The misconception knowledge base (MKB) enumerates common misconceptions that occur in the domain and relates the misconceptions to the concepts in the CKB. For example, when a novice student is writing a car/cdr recursive function it is extremely common for the student to omit one of the two required base cases (an atom base case and a null base case). The misconception would be represented in the MKB as: **(missing car/cdr atom base case, car/cdr atom base case)** and **(missing car/cdr null base case, car/cdr null base case)**.

A history of the concepts that the system believes the student has learned is maintained in the student history (SH). This type of information is required because evidence may surface which indicates that a concept the student had supposedly learned has not actually been learned (or the student may have forgotten the concept). This situation requires the content planner to plan to reachieve the goal of having the student learn the concept, a different operation than planning to achieve the goal the first time.

The plan history (PH) keeps track of the goals that the content planner has planned to achieve. A goal that the delivery planner has already tried to achieve (but unsuccessfully) will require an alternate plan for the second attempt at achieving the goal. This information is also vital for identifying blocked learning paths.

The content planning rules utilize the information from these knowledge sources to produce a relevant content plan. There is an *implicit plan* inherent in the combination of the concept knowledge base and the pedagogical planning rules. It is unnecessary and inefficient to plan far beyond a current situation because of the unpredictability of the exact learning path an individual student will carve through the knowledge to be learned. Due to this dynamic paradigm, *explicit planning* only takes place as necessity dictates. A summary of the various modes of planning rules can be found in Table 3.1. Each of these modes will now be explained in more detail.

The content planner uses goal generation rules to negotiate an instructional point with the student. Negotiation prerequisite rules such as 'at the beginning of any session allow the student to choose to review any concept that has been covered in the past' or 'the student may choose to review any concept at any point in time' indicate points of content negotiation with the student. Other goal generation rules such as prerequisite rules 'achieve fact before analysis' and 'achieve analysis before synthesis' are not points for negotiation with the student. The designer of the content planning rules must specify which points are negotiable and which are not.

Table 3.1 Pedaogical planning rules for a content planner

---

1. Goal Generation
    - negotiation prerequisite rules (e.g the student may choose to review
        any prerequisite concept at any time)
    - prerequisite rules (e.g. achieve facts before analysis)
    - subgoal generation rules (e.g. when achieving analysis of a concept
        achieve analysis of one of its specializations)
    - subgoal selection rules
        – meta selection rules (e.g. use concept prerequisite rules
            before negotiation preference rules)
        – concept prerequisite rules (e.g. do iteration before
            recursion)
        – negotiation preference rules (e.g. use student preference
            to select a subgoal)
        – pedagogical preference rules (e.g. prefer cdr recursion
            before car recursion)
2. Plan Generation
    - operator assignment rules (e.g. if the student knows concept x
        then review x)
    - modifier assignment rules (e.g. when to plan to achieve
        fact, analysis or synthesis of a concept)
    - plan subgoal generation rules (e.g. if planning to achieve
        analysis of x then focus on analysis of x and then
        find out what the student learned about x)
3. Plan Monitoring
    - blocking rules (e.g. if the executor has tried twice in a row to
        satisfy a goal without success, assign the goal block-1 status)
    - plan adaption rules (e.g. if the currently planned for goal is not
        achieved and the current plan has been carried out, then
        the plan has failed)

Subgoal generation rules are used to generate subgoals. For example, when a goal of achieving analysis of a concept has been selected, then it is reasonable first to achieve analysis of one of its specializations. Subgoal selection rules are used to select among a number of possible subgoals. There are several types of subgoal selection rules, thus the need for meta selection rules to determine their interaction. The meta selection rule 'use concept prerequisite rules before negotiation preference rules' indicates that the prerequisite structure of the concept knowledge base must take precedence over student preferences, and the meta selection rule 'use negotiation preference rules before pedagogical preference rules' gives precedence to the student rather than predetermined pedagogical preferences.

Once an instructional point has been identified, the content planner uses plan generation rules to generate a content plan. An example of a content plan can be seen in Figure 3.4. Each node in the content plan

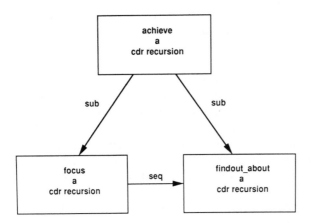

Fig. 3.4 A content plan for achieving analysis of Cdr recursion

consists of an operator, a modifier and a content. The operator suggests a reason for including the node in the plan. Possible operators include: *focus* (put in context); *refocus* (bring back into context); *review* (go back over already achieved material in the belief that concept is known to the student) ; *achieve* (plan to have the student learn a concept for the first time); *reachieve* (plan to have the student relearn a concept it is thought the student had achieved before); *remediate* (remedy an undesirable condition); *remove* (overcome a misconception by removing it); and *findout_about* (diagnose / obtain more information on a specified concept). The content of a plan node is the concept, from the content goal, that has been selected as a focal point, and the modifier indicates which kind of learning (f-fact; a-analysis; s-synthesis) of the concept is appropriate.

The goal selected by the goal generation phase identifies the concept to be planned for. Operator assignment rules, such as 'if the student knows concept x, then review x', determine which operator is appropriate to assign to the selected content. The modifier assignment rules indicate whether to have the student deal with facts, or with the analysis or with the synthesis of the content. Plan subgoal generation rules identify situations where a plan node has subgoals. The subgoals of plan node (**achieve a cdr rec**) (see Figure 3.4) were generated using the rule 'if planning to achieve analysis of x, then focus on analysis of x and then find out what the student has learned about x'. The rule results in the addition of the two subgoal nodes as **sub**s of the supergoal, appropriately sequenced.

The content plan is passed for delivery to the delivery planner which plans (through negotiation with the student) how to deliver the content. In order to take advantage of instructional opportunities as they arise, the content planner must be able to detect blocked learning paths, determine when prerequisite knowledge is missing, and recognize serendipitous gains in knowledge, all of which may render the current content plan inappropriate. This monitoring of the content plan will identify plan steps that are no longer required or must be added or must be altered, resulting in the plan being interrupted, patched or abandoned altogether.

The plan monitoring phase of the content planner is responsible for overseeing plan execution. Plan monitoring rules are used to analyse when these situations arise and control when the goal generation – plan generation – plan monitoring cycle repeats. Blocking rules are used to watch for blocked learning paths. A rule such as 'if the delivery planner has tried twice in a row to satisfy a goal without success, assign the goal block-1 status' is used to recognize when a particular goal (e.g. have the student learn analysis of cdr recursion) cannot be achieved by the system. These blocked situations force the system to negotiate other goals that might be achieved with the student. Another blocking rule might indicate that 'if the only goal left to achieve is a block-1 goal, then remove the block', or 'if the only goal left to achieve is a blocked goal then break the goal into its parts and try to achieve each of its parts individually'. The designer of the pedagogical rules has the flexibility to describe the actions that are to be taken in a blocked situation, again in accordance with whatever philosophy and insights he or she has about instruction.

Plan adaptation rules are required to deal with successful completion, failure, or inappropriateness of the content plan. A rule that recognizes that plan failure has occurred might be 'if the currently planned-for goal is not achieved and the current plan has been carried out, then the plan has failed'. This situation might call for replanning to achieve the goal (or if it has been planned for twice and not been achieved then the blocked goal rules would assign it blocked status). Another situation might be that the student has made some serendipitous gain in knowledge and the current plan is no longer valid, so the current plan is abandoned and a new goal negotiated. Finally, it might be the case that a situation arises that the current plan must be interrupted to deal with an important issue that has just been recognized (e.g. the student has a critical misconception that must be cleared up before the current plan can be continued).

These rules must be created to reflect the particular kind of instruction preferred by the designers of the tutoring system. Different styles of interaction can be achieved using different sets of rules. Presumably in a negotiated learning context, the rules would reflect the need for flexibility and student initiative. As in the design of any expert system, much help in the creation of these rules can come from a deep analysis of expert behaviour (in this case the behaviour of expert teachers and tutors). For example, pedagogical preference rules could be compiled from pedagogical experiences of instructors who have particular preferences in the order in which they present concepts.

3.3 The Content Planner In Action: An Example

The dialogue parts of Section 2.1 will be used to clarify how the content planner negotiates content goals and plans to achieve them. In order to describe the decisions made by the content planner, the following assumptions must be made:

1. It is assumed that the student knows how to write iterative LISP functions and has been introduced to recursion during a classroom session.
2. The **currentgoal** will indicate what content goal is currently the focus. It is expressed in terms of student model entries: **SK(modifier,concept)**. The **initialgoal** is the overall goal that we wish the student to achieve; in this example it is **SK(s, recursion)**, i.e. we wish the student to achieve knowledge of how to synthesize recursive solutions.
3. The student model has the initial entry: **?SK(f, recursion)**, i.e. it is questionable whether the student knows the facts about recursion.
4. The **goalstack** is a stack where goals to be planned for are pushed when another goal becomes the **currentgoal**.

The goal generation phase of the content planner takes the **currentgoal** and determines if it has been achieved. This is accomplished by checking for the presence of **initialgoal** in the student model. Since it is not in the student model, the goal generation rules, using the **initialgoal** as a starting point, generate a **currentgoal**. Using goal generation prerequisite rules 'analysis before synthesis' and 'fact before analysis', the **currentgoal SK(f, recursion)** is generated and a **goalstack** with goals (SK(a, recursion), SK(s, recursion)) is set up (note: the top of the stack is the first element of the list). If the student model had the entry **SK(f, recursion)** instead of **?SK(f, recursion)**, the **currentgoal** would be **SK(a, recursion)** and the **goalstack** would be (SK(s, recursion)). Once the **currentgoal SK(f, recursion)** has been generated, the plan generation phase will generate a plan to achieve the goal using the following rules:

Plan generation:

- operator assignment rule
  if **?SK(currentgoal modifier, currentgoal concept)** then operator is **findout_about**
- modifier assignment rule
  use modifier of the **currentgoal**

- content assignment rule
    use concept of the **currentgoal**

The result of this plan generation phase is the generation of the plan
(**findout_about f, recursion**), that is the system is to find out what the
student knows about the facts of recursion.

This content plan is passed to the delivery planner which would engage
the student in a dialogue similar to part 1 (see Section 2.1). Diagnosis
that takes place during the part 1 dialogue results in the student model
being updated to:

SK(f, recursion)
SK(f, base case)
SK(f, recursive case)

The plan monitoring rules recognize that the **currentgoal** has been
achieved (from the updated student model), and it passes control back to
the goal generation phase where the **currentgoal** is updated by popping a
goal off the **goalstack**. Thus, the **currentgoal** is **SK(a, recursion)** and the
goalstack is (**SK(s, recursion)**).

At this point, goal generation negotiation rule 'when a new concept or
ability in using the concept is judged to be the focal point, let the student
decide whether to review known concepts or learn the new concept',
would cause the content negotiator to carry out a dialogue with the
student similar to that in part 2 of the sample dialogue session. The
student indicates an interest in pursuing recursion so the **currentgoal**
remains **SK(a, recursion)**. If the student had expressed an interest in
iteration, then the **currentgoal** would become **SK(s,iteration)** (because
that is the highest level of iteration and the student has already achieved
it), and the **goalstack** would be (**SK(a,recursion)**, **SK(s,recursion)**). In any
event, here the **currentgoal** would be **SK(a,recursion)**, which would result
in the firing of subgoal generation rule 'when having the student learn
analysis of x, then have the student learn analysis of one of its
specializations'. Three possible specialized subgoals would be generated,
(**SK(a,car_rec)**, **SK(a,cdr_rec)** and **SK(a,car/cdr_rec)**), only one of which
will be selected (the **isa** links from recursion to its three specializations
are used to identify the subgoals). If this were not a knowledge
negotiation paradigm, the subgoal selection rules would select one of the
three subgoals to pursue (using, first, concept prerequisite rules and,
then, pedagogical preference rules, if necessary). However, in this
negotiation paradigm the meta selection rule 'use concept prerequisites
before negotiation preferences' would narrow the negotiation choice to
(**SK(a,car_rec)**, **SK(a,cdr_rec)**), and the meta selection rule 'use negotiation preference before pedagogical preference' signals the content

negotiator to negotiate which subgoal to pursue with the student. The content negotiator and the student would negotiate much as is done in dialogue part 3. During this exchange, the student indicates that he or she is aware of a type of recursion which the system recognizes as cdr recursion. This information is added to the student model as **SK(f,cdr_rec)**, and the **currentgoal** becomes **SK(a,cdr_rec)** with the **goalstack** now **(SK(a,recursion), SK(s,recursion))**.

At this time the plan generator phase takes the **currentgoal** and uses the following rules to generate a content plan:

Plan generation:

- operator assignment rule
  if ~**SK(currentgoal modifier, currentgoal concept)** or there is no entry in the SM about **(currentgoal modifier, currentgoal concept)** and the **currentgoal** is not in the student history then the operator is **achieve**
- modifier assignment rule
  use modifier of the **currentgoal**
- content assignment rule
  use concept of the **currentgoal**
- plan subgoal generation rule
  if plan node is **(achieve a x)** then subgoals are **((focus a x) sequence (findout_about a x))**

The resulting plan is shown graphically in Figure 3.4 (shown earlier).

This plan is then passed to the delivery planner, which executes the plan node **(focus a cdr_rec)**, negotiates the interaction style with the student in a manner similar to dialogue part 4, and executes the **findout_about** node in an interaction such as is shown in dialogue part 5. By the end of these interactions the system has enough evidence to update the student model to:

SK(f, recursion)	SK(f, cdr_rec)	SK(a, cdr_rec)
SK(f, base case)	SK(f, cdr_bc)	SK(a, cdr_bc)
SK(f, recursive case)	SK(f, cdr_rc)	SK(a, cdr_rc)
SK(f, coordination)	SK(f, cdr_coord)	SK(a, cdr_coord)

Dialogue part 6 begins with the student expressing a desire to switch the focus of the session to another type of recursion. While this is one possible action, the pedagogical preference rule 'prefer to complete all three of fact-analysis-synthesis for one concept before moving onto another' would have the content negotiator suggest to the student that she might like to try to synthesize cdr recursion (i.e. write a program) before moving on. The student agrees, so that, at the end of dialogue part 6, the **currentgoal** is **SK(s, cdr_rec)**.

This example of the content planner has been useful to illustrate the types of knowledge required by the content planner and the types of pedagogical rules that are necessary in order to make these types of decisions. The rules are by no means a definitive set, but rather have been chosen to show the flavour of the rules that are required. There are a wide variety of rules, ranging from rules about generating goals (such as fact before analysis before synthesis), producing subgoals (analysis of recursion can be broken down into analysis of one of the specializations of recursion), and selecting among subgoals (concept prerequisites should be dealt with before negotiated preferences), through rules for generating the content plan (assignment of operator, modifier and content), generating the subplan nodes, and monitoring the execution of the content plan (looking for blocked paths, serendipitous gains, failed plans). More detailed examples of the rules can be found in Brecht (1990).

4 CONCLUSION

A negotiated learning paradigm confronts a tutoring system with immense challenges. The system must be able to understand student goals and motivations, understand student knowledge states, understand the domain it is tutoring from many different perspectives, and have a subtle and sophisticated ability to interact with the student in pedagogically useful ways. What we have proposed in this chapter is an approach to negotiated tutoring which deals with some of these issues.

Central to our approach is the student model, which encodes all of the SK predicates which are so crucial to our planning algorithms. All else depends on the assumption that the student model reflects the student's knowledge and beliefs about the domain, at least at some level of detail. We also make a number of critical distinctions: content and delivery are considered to be separate issues in the planning of instruction; the process of negotiation is assumed to be different from the process of instructional planning; goals are assumed to be different from the plans for achieving these goals. It is suggested that a tutoring system will formulate content goals for an instructional interaction, negotiate these goals with the student, formulate a content plan for achieving these goals, and then pass this content plan on to a delivery planner. In the delivery planner, delivery goals will be formulated which are appropriate for the content plan, these goals will be negotiated with the student, and then a delivery plan will be formed to actually carry out the content plan. This is a competence-based model, of course, in that it describes an idealized negotiated learning interaction; negotiated learning between two people would proceed with many more fits and starts, and any model simulating real performance would have to be much more subtle, especially in its control structure.

In this chapter, we have sketched out an architecture for the content side of this process. The architecture is not fully fleshed out, and especially downplays the actual negotiation phase of the tutoring interaction, and the problem of inducing student goals (as opposed to student content knowledge, which is assumed to be induced). Nevertheless, we strongly believe that any negotiated learning system, whatever else it consists of, will have to have a solid student model. It will have to formulate content goals as the basis for its negotiation, will have to formulate content plans once this negotiation has settled on a particular instructional goal, and will have to monitor, and if necessary, change its goals and plans as the instructional interaction proceeds. To this extent, then, we have shed some light on the process of negotiated tutoring.

Much remains to be done, of course. Not only have we completely downplayed the delivery aspects of the interaction and the problem of inducing student goals, but we have also ignored the problem of multiple viewpoints on the same knowledge (a subject of keen interest to Moyse 1989, and Moyse & Elsom-Cook 1992, for example). Moreover, we have downplayed the actual process of negotiation, and the difficult problems in natural language understanding and dialogue modelling which naturally arise as a consequence of a negotiation between two partners with non-equivalent background knowledge. Notwithstanding the work of Baker (1989d), Petrie-Brown (1989a) and others on tutorial dialogue, much research is still needed on this aspect of negotiated tutoring. In fact, investigations in all areas of negotiated learning are still nascent.

One thing which we would like to see is the collection of more empirical data of actual knowledge negotiation sessions, and the correlation of this data with what is known in the literature about various teaching and learning styles. This process should result in a much clearer notion as to what knowledge negotiation is and isn't. Longer term investigations will have to create sophisticated planning rules, negotiation rules, and student modelling techniques in order that a computational model of negotiated learning can be developed. For the time being, we are hopeful that our semi-invented negotiated learning dialogue, our semi-complete analysis of this dialogue, and our semi-finished architecture for negotiated learning have at least begun to flesh out the negotiated learning paradigm. We are sure that the other chapters in this book will clarify many of the issues which are raised by the knowledge negotiation approach to learning, and will suggest techniques for dealing with these issues. Despite the difficulty of modelling a negotiated learning interaction, knowledge negotiation is a promising way of viewing instruction. Investigations on a broad front should continue.

ACKNOWLEDGEMENTS

We would like to thank the other members of the ARIES Laboratory for their input to the ideas in this chapter. In particular, Jim Greer and Marlene Jones have been instrumental in clarifying much of the content planning model which lies at the basis of our approach. We are also indebted to Phil Winne of Simon Fraser University for his thorough reading of an earlier draft of this paper, and his cogent comments from the instructional psychology perspective which helped to refine some of our arguments. We would like to acknowledge the financial support of the Natural Sciences and Engineering Research Council of Canada and the University of Saskatchewan. Finally, we would like to thank the British Columbia Advanced Systems Institute for providing the funds to support Gord McCalla's research leave at Simon Fraser University in the Fall of 1989 when this chapter was written, as well as the Centre for Systems Science at Simon Fraser for hosting him.

4 Domain Knowledge, Epistemology and Intelligent Tutoring in Social Science

PETER GOODYEAR and CAROLYN STONE

Department of Educational Research, Lancaster University, Lancaster, UK

1 INTRODUCTION

This chapter is intended as a contribution to a long-term programme of fundamental or 'ground-clearing' research stimulated by the goal of creating knowledge-based Intelligent Tutoring Systems (ITSs). We believe that much can be learned by active engagement in the task of ITS design, construction and evaluation, even if current implementation skills – and the pragmatic constraints imposed by hardware – mean that our ambitions far outstrip our capabilities. In this chapter, however, we stand back from the pragmatics of implementation and identify some problematic issues concerning the representation of domain knowledge in social science ITSs – issues that may be specific to social science domains and unaddressed by on-going ITS research. In the course of discussing these problematic issues, we make a preliminary attempt at describing some of the functional requirements for ITSs operating in social science domains and, in conclusion, suggest new items that must be posted on the ITS research agenda.

We illustrate some of the key issues with excerpts from a sociology tutorial. The excerpts have two functions. Firstly, they act as illustrations which may make some of our argument more accessible, particularly to those who have little familiarity with debates on epistemology and scientific method. Secondly, they demonstrate the existence, *in the*

KNOWLEDGE NEGOTIATION
ISBN 0–12–509378–0

practice of social scientists, of approaches to the use of knowledge which a sceptic might argue have no reality outside the literature of the philosophy of social science. These excerpts, and our commentary on them, have been placed in an appendix to avoid interrupting the flow of the argument.

In outline, our argument runs as follows. The possession of domain expertise is an important distinguishing characteristic of intelligent computer-based tutoring systems. Most tutoring systems implemented so far are concerned with domains in the physical sciences. Approaches to the representation of domain knowledge in the physical sciences may not be adequate for representing knowledge in social science domains. Since the ITS literature is chiefly concerned with extant physical science ITSs, the difficulties that may be associated with constructing an ITS in social science have not been made explicit. Our chapter represents a first attempt at giving recognition to this problem.

2   KNOWLEDGE FOR INTELLIGENT TUTORING

Our conception of an ITS is broader than that gaining currency through Etienne Wenger's (1987) review. We agree that an ITS will typically contain, and be able to reason with, explicit representations of knowledge of four kinds: subject-matter knowledge (otherwise known as domain knowledge), knowledge about teaching (tutoring or pedagogic knowledge), knowledge about the learner currently interacting with the system (encoded as a learner model), and knowledge enabling communication across the system-learner interface. The purpose of this explicitly represented knowledge is, of course, to permit dynamic adaptation of tuition through 'on-the-fly' decision making – the major intended advance of ITSs over conventional CAI systems.

However, we do not agree with the conventional view that these four components should (or can) always be clearly separate, or that each must be fully developed, or that the communication to the learner of the system's domain knowledge should always be regarded as the prime goal for an ITS (see, for example, Goodyear, 1991). On this last issue, as we argue in section 4.8 below, it may be that the prime goal should be the development of higher-level skills in the learner, through his or her active engagement with the ITS's domain knowledge, rather than that the learner should acquire the domain knowledge *per se*.

This may simply mean that a broader definition of domain knowledge is needed (one which also subsumes these higher level skills, such as the construction of sound arguments). It has become clear that the representation of domain knowledge has achieved a pivotal position in the ITS R&D paradigm, to the extent that domain analysis often closely determines the form and content of both learner model and pedagogical strategy (Goodyear, 1991). While we may regret the underdevelopment of work in these last two sectors of ITS research, it nevertheless remains the case that obtaining a clear understanding of domain knowledge and its computational representation will be a vital subgoal for most ITS projects. The concern which gives rise to this chapter is that current and recent work on problems of domain knowledge representation ignores some potentially serious issues, which may be unique to teaching in the social sciences, but which we suspect are merely more salient in those domains.

3 DOMAIN KNOWLEDGE REPRESENTATION IN A CONVENTIONAL ITS

A characteristic of an ITS, which distinguishes it from a conventional CAI system, is that it contains an explicit representation of domain knowledge about which (and with which) it can reason in order to solve a problem which has been set for or by a student. It should be able to solve such problems in a manner which sufficiently resembles human problem-solving methods that the system can display its working to the student or evaluate the student's attempted problem-solving. The system's expertise needs to be cognitively plausible and communicable (though see Section 8 below).

The most widely known ITSs cluster in the domains of physics (e.g. SOPHIE), mathematics (e.g. Anderson's GEOMETRY tutor) and computer programming (e.g. BIP, PROUST, MENO-II). There have also been influential systems in geography (SCHOLAR, WHY), medical diagnosis (the GUIDON family) and industrial plant control (STEAMER). These diverse systems need diverse knowledge, some of it general (e.g. a representation of causation or temporal order), some of it very specialised (e.g. about the symptoms associated with rare bacteriological infections). They are also characterized by diverse approaches to the representation of their domain knowledge: such as in the form of scripts (as in WHY), production rules (as in GUIDON/MYCIN), simulations expressed as systems of mathematical equations (as in early versions of SOPHIE), or as qualitative causal models. It has become apparent to many that effective support for tutoring can rarely, if ever, be provided by a single canonical domain representation – that multiple representational forms or multiple 'viewpoints' are necessary (Brown & Burton 1975, Moyse 1989).

We would argue that the knowledge representation methods used by the designers and builders of tutoring systems, as is the case with many other AI-based systems, were adopted on pragmatic grounds. Important considerations may have been computational efficiency (for knowledge retrieval and reasoning) and ease of modification (for maintenance or to support further knowledge acquisition). Epistemological considerations, such as issues to do with the assumptions underlying chosen representations, do not appear to have been salient.[1] For physical science domains this may not be of any great importance. But for social science ITSs it will be crucial, and since (to the best of our knowledge) there are no extant social science ITSs, there is a gap in the literature concerning epistemologically informed strategies for domain knowledge representation.

4   DIFFERENCES BETWEEN PHYSICAL AND SOCIAL SCIENCE KNOWLEDGE

Salient differences between physical and social science knowledge must clearly be an important focus for our discussion. It is not helpful to draw a sharp distinction between these two areas, since many of the epistemological issues which are problematic in the social sciences are similarly problematic in the physical sciences, and are acknowledged to be so by thoughtful physical scientists. However, one can argue that, for many purposes, it is possible within the physical sciences to act as if those problematic issues did not exist: in particular, the teaching and learning of facts, laws, explanations and techniques can proceed without the raising of epistemological issues. In the social sciences this is not possible: the disciplines of the social sciences are split into contending schools or traditions of thought with different conceptions of what is involved in

---

[1] In passing, we need to note that serious consideration *is* being given, in ITS design, to domain knowledge representation. Much of Clancey's work with GUIDON (Clancey 1987), for example, has been concerned with the nature of changes that must be made to the knowledge representation in a domain expert system in order to render that knowledge usable in a tutoring context. It is evident that issues concerned with 'meta-knowledge' (such as knowledge about how to use knowledge, e.g. in accounting for the use of a particular heuristic) are proving to be more important. We believe that this meta-knowledge will be crucially important in a social science ITS, and will need to have levels of sophistication not presently contemplated in physical science systems.

studying social phenomena. There is a lack of consensus about the proper objects of social study, about the appropriate methods of studying them, and about the form that descriptions and explanations of such phenomena should take.

Discussion of epistemological concerns is notably absent in the ITS literature. Consequently we provide, in the following section, a brief and selective outline of some of the contrasting epistemologies of social scientific knowledge. These entail different conceptions of the nature of scientific fact, explanation, theory, and so on. This general account is then made more specific with an example (Section 6): we show how the different conceptions of social scientific knowledge already described generate different approaches to the description and explanation of *human actions*. Sections 7–11 address some of the detailed implications of these epistemological points for the representation of domain knowledge in social science ITSs.

5 CONTRASTING EPISTEMOLOGIES OF THE SOCIAL SCIENCES

The major epistemological issue which is a matter of contention among social scientists and philosophers concerns the extent to which the social sciences are like and unlike the physical sciences. The two principal positions on this issue are often referred to as 'naturalist' and 'anti-naturalist'.

Naturalism is the view that there is no difference 'in principle' between the study of social and the study of physical phenomena; the same broad methodology is appropriate to both domains (although details of method may differ). Advocates of a naturalist conception of the social sciences see them as differing in degree, but not in kind, from the well-established physical sciences. Naturalism may admit that the social sciences have their problems (e.g. in practical and logical obstacles to the use of the experimental method; in that social phenomena are more 'complex' than physical phenomena; in that there are limitations on the possibility of prediction), but these are matters of detail. Naturalist criteria for a successful social scientific explanation would be those associated with the standards already established in the physical sciences. Hence, naturalists are sometimes described as being committed to 'the methodological unity of the physical and social sciences'.

In contrast, anti-naturalism (or humanism) contends that the phenomena of concern to social scientists are different not merely in degree of complexity but in kind from physical phenomena. Hence they require fundamentally different methods of study and forms of explanation and understanding. Human beings and their relationships have distinctive characteristics (e.g. human beings are 'free subjects', the agents of 'meaningful acts', the 'creators' of their social world) which demand an approach different from that in the physical sciences. Anti-naturalists would assert that there can be no such thing as a 'science' of society unless it is seen as an enterprise different in kind from the sciences of non-human nature. In fact, both 'naturalism' and 'anti-naturalism' stand for *clusters* of positions with certain claims (as indicated above) in common. It is not possible to discuss varieties of anti-naturalism within the scope of this chapter. Naturalist conceptions of the social sciences vary according to the conception of the physical sciences which they presuppose, and in terms of which the social sciences are understood. A useful classification of positions here is that provided by Keat and Urry (1975). They distinguish positivism, realism, and conventionalism. The following account is heavily indebted to their discussion.

Positivism and realism are often conflated under the general heading of 'positivism' or 'empiricism'. The two positions agree that science is an empirically-based rational enterprise, the aim of which is to generate true explanatory and predictive knowledge of nature.

According to positivism, prediction and explanation are similar in their logical structure and both depend on the discovery of laws (i.e. highly general statements expressing regular relationships which exist in nature). Laws are established on the basis of experiment and observation, which are the only reliable sources of empirical knowledge. Some of these laws describe causal relations between events, relations of regular temporal succession. To assert a causal connection is not to imply any necessary (i.e. non-contingent) link between cause and effect. It is not the purpose of science to get behind or beyond the phenomena accessible to sense experience – in order to provide knowledge of unobservable structures, mechanisms or essences. For positivism, a statement is only 'scientific' if it is possible to ascertain its truth or falsity by direct observation; thus any attempt to get 'beyond' observable regularities is ruled out as non-scientific. The use by scientists of 'theoretical terms' – that is, terms which (apparently) do not refer to what is observable – thus constitutes a problem for positivism.

Unlike positivism, realism claims an important difference between prediction and explanation. We can predict phenomena on the basis of knowledge of empirical regularities (plus knowledge of 'initial conditions'). But explanation of phenomena involves more than merely showing that they are instances of well-established regularities. Explanation of phenomena involves discovering necessary connections between them, by acquiring knowledge of the underlying structures and mechanisms in operation. That is, explanation involves reference to the existence of types of unobservable entities and processes which causally generate the observable phenomena. Thus realism differs from positivism in seeing causal relations as involving not merely relations of regular temporal succession between events, but also the existence of some kind of mechanism or process linking cause and effect. A scientific theory is a description of these mechanisms, processes, structures, entities, etc.

So for the realist (some) theoretical (i.e. not directly observable) entities really exist. A statement (e.g. about theoretical entities) is scientific if it is possible to make observations that would count in some way for or against its truth or falsity. (In contrast to the positivist position, it is not necessary that the meaning of each theoretical term be completely specifiable in observational terms.)

Conventionalism covers a diversity of opinions united by a rejection of the view that science is an empirically-based, rational and objective enterprise providing true descriptions and explanations of reality via theories which can be tested objectively by observation and experiment. Instead, the adoption of particular theories is seen as being, in some way, a matter of convention. In support of this type of view it may be claimed that observations cannot, by themselves, determine the truth or falsity of theories, and that no sharp distinction between theory and observation can be maintained. (There is no neutral observation language because all observation is 'theory-laden'.) Additionally, it may be argued that there are no universally acceptable criteria for choosing rationally between different theoretical frameworks – moral, aesthetic or instrumental values play an essential part in such choice.

This discussion of different conceptions of social science has necessarily been selective and incomplete, but it does highlight a crucial point. Given the epistemological disagreement that characterizes the social sciences, the representation of social science domain knowledge will have to support various functions not paralleled in a physical science ITS. In particular, we would expect a domain expert both to be able to present particular arguments in social science domains fairly – in the sense of being able to emulate the thinking, assumptions, knowledge, etc., of a social scientist adopting such an argument or position – and to be able to step outside such a framework in order to offer critiques comparable to those offered by other social scientists. An important practical, if not logically defensible, distinction between the kind of domain expertise we are describing here and that found in a conventional expert system is that the domain expert we need in a social science ITS will be capable of reasoning about facts, data, rules and theories, and about the epistemological (and other) assumptions within which such reasoning is set. It follows that some of the domain 'knowledge' required by a social science ITS should strictly be described in terms of 'beliefs' or 'knowledge claims' rather than 'knowledge'. What is 'knowledge' from the point of view of one conception of social science will not necessarily be so according to another.

6   IMPLICATIONS OF DIFFERENT CONCEPTIONS OF SOCIAL SCIENCE KNOWLEDGE: THE DESCRIPTION AND EXPLANATION OF ACTIONS

A central concern of some areas of the social sciences is the description and explanation of human actions and social practices. Thus a large part of the vocabulary of the social sciences is concerned with action concepts – that is, concepts used to characterize behaviour which is performed with a purpose, such that one can ask what was the aim or intent of the action. (Examples of action concepts are buying, bribing, promising, voting, declaring war.) Typically, actions are explained in terms of the actor's beliefs, goals, purposes, etc., in the context of particular sets of social rules which define social practices.

An important characteristic of actions, and the subjective states used to explain them, is that they are not straightforwardly observable. As indicated above, different epistemological traditions in science, for example positivism and realism, take different positions on the problem of the (apparently) non-observable.

A positivist approach (of which strict behaviourism in psychology is a good example) would be to exclude reference to the non-observable or to define all concepts referring to (apparently) non-observable entities in terms of what is observable. In this way it is not necessary to assume the (separate) existence of non-observable entities such as mental states. Reference to mental states is simply an economical and shorthand way of referring to observable behaviour. In contrast, a realist approach would be to regard mentalistic concepts as referring to structures, entities, processes etc., 'underlying', and causally responsible for, what is observable. For realists, subjective states stand in causal relations to observable behaviour.

The perceived limitations of empiricist treatments of actions and mental states have led to the development of a variety of anti-naturalist positions. Anti-naturalists argue, for example, that the identification of actions as being of a particular kind (e.g. this series of behaviours is a case of 'voting') involves a type of *interpretive understanding* with no parallel in the physical sciences. Again, the explanation of actions with reference to actors' beliefs, motives, etc., in the context of social rules defining social practices, is claimed by anti-naturalists to be non-causal.

The actors' subjective states constitute the *reasons* for their actions: these reasons *explain* the actions but do not *cause* them (in the way that the movement of one physical object can cause that of another, for example).

The process of understanding the 'meaning' of actions is said to be akin to generating a meaning from a text. In many contexts we read actions unproblematically. But sometimes we need to devote conscious attention to the process and the interpretive resources involved become explicit (for example, in the case of ambiguous actions or actions by a person whose culture or symbol system we do not share). Actions can be described at many different levels. For example, one and the same action may be described as a person 'writing her name', 'signing a death warrant', 'breaking a promise' and 'starting a war'. Sometimes, given a particular context, the identification of an action as being of a particular kind ('his waving his hand was a warning') is sufficient to explain it. Sometimes, explanation requires the further location of the action within a wider context of individual motives, systems of rules, social practices, social meanings, etc.

Moreover, anti-naturalists point to a distinctive feature of actions and social practices, namely that actors have their own accounts of what is going on in social life, their own sets of concepts for understanding themselves. It is claimed that this places constraints on the types of concepts that it is permissible for social scientists to use in their explanations of these actions and social practices. Thus several anti-naturalist writers (Schutz 1963, Winch 1958) have argued that the central aim of sociology, for example, should be the reconstruction of the ways in which actors themselves explain their actions. Consequently, the theoretical concepts used by social scientists must not radically depart from those used by the actors. The precise nature of the constraint that this places on social science concepts is a matter of debate and critics of anti-naturalism argue, in any case, that while the reconstruction of the actor's reasons for action may be an important level of analysis, it is not necessary to restrict social theorising to this level. Whatever the merits of the contending arguments, the important point here is that this is an issue which has no parallel in the physical sciences. The entities studied by physical scientists do not (yet?) have accounts of their own behaviour.[2]

---

[2] The issues raised by the description and explanation of actions have been highlighted by contrasting broadly empiricist approaches with anti-naturalism. But there is also the possibility of some kind of conventionalist naturalist position. The extent to which the (apparently) distinctive features of actions can in fact be accommodated within a conventionalist type of naturalism is a matter of debate. Typically, even writers who accept some features of conventionalism concede something to the anti-naturalist case (see, for example, Keat & Urry 1975, Thomas 1979).

7 PROBLEMS IN KNOWLEDGE REPRESENTATION FOR SOCIAL SCIENCE

In this section we draw on the preceding discussion of epistemological issues to identify four interlocking problem areas which need to be addressed if we are to construct workable ITSs in the social sciences. These are summarized below, elaborated in the next four sections and illustrated in the Appendix.

First, given the existence of competing conceptions of social science knowledge, it must be recognized that knowledge in this area is characterized by uncertainty and incompleteness.[3] Consequently, there are ethical and cognitive reasons for suggesting that it would be unhelpful to apply the conventional ITS model (Wenger's 'knowledge communication' model) in such situations. Instead, we should be aiming to develop systems which attempt to engage in critical argument with the student rather than to assert knowledge claims whose status is problematic.

Secondly, there is a problem concerning the formation and use of concepts in the social sciences. The semantic complexities entailed in representing social science knowledge are substantially greater than those faced in current ITSs in the physical sciences. Indeed, one can argue that debate about meaning and definition lies at the very centre of social science.

The third issue is that of explanation and causal modelling. Recent work on expert systems has revealed a need for systems to have a 'deep understanding' of their domain of expertise. This is often represented through a rule-based or qualitative causal model of the domain which the system can use to reason about processes and events (Hudlicka 1988). However, the nature of causal relationships is particularly problematic in the social sciences and, as indicated above, there are also problems concerning whether certain types of social phenomena are correctly to be explained in terms of *causes*. There is thus a need to confront some new and difficult questions concerned with non-causal reasoning and explanation and the ontology of domains.

Finally, it must be recognized that learners will have knowledge of the real world which is substantially richer than the 'real world' knowledge encoded in the machine. This is already recognized as an issue in the teaching of physical science (e.g. through research on 'naive' or

---

[3] Throughout this chapter we are reluctant to draw a hard and fast distinction between characteristics of the social and physical sciences. It can, of course, be argued that knowledge in many domains of physical science should also be viewed as uncertain and incomplete.

'alternative' conceptions in science (Gilbert & Watts 1983) and in the practical uses of mathematics (e.g. Lave 1988)). While there is no △comparable body of research on 'naive' conceptions in social science (Furnham, 1988), it is likely that the disparity of real world knowledge between system and learner will present some profound new problems for both domain representation and learner modelling (cf. Suchman 1987, Winograd & Flores 1986).

8 CRITICAL ARGUMENT

". . . knowledge communication is defined as the ability to cause and/or support the acquisition of one's knowledge by someone else, via a restricted set of communication operations . . . all the critical issues pertaining to ITS are issues involved in the intelligent communication of knowledge" (Wenger 1987).

Wenger's conception of teaching and intelligent tutoring is unduly narrow, in that it appears to be premised on a view of knowledge as something complete, certain and worthwhile enough to be a justifiable object of transfer from some knowledgeable tutor to some unknowing learner. While his view has some empirical support – his survey of ITSs depicts many systems whose designers would appear to accept this same premise – it places an unnecessary constraint on the space of tutoring possibilities open to ITSs. It is especially limiting for tutoring in the social sciences, given the points made earlier about different conceptions of social science knowledge.

A knowledge-based system which is to operate in a domain of social science will clearly need to be constrained by some explicit and principled epistemological underpinning. It will need to have some basis for making claims about the status of knowledge, whether its own, or the student's. It will need to be able to establish and challenge *warrants* for that knowledge. In so doing, it must be able to draw on rules of evidence that are founded in explicit epistemological positions – otherwise it will be unable to emulate the reasoning of a social scientist adopting that position.[4]

There is evidence of a recognition of this class of problem in current ITS work in domains such as music. Drawing on Reichman's notion of

---

[4] Note that we cannot reject this demand merely by refusing to accept the validity of the epistemology for ourselves: our systems (like our teachers) must be able to offer a fair presentation of even those positions with which they disagree.

'conversational moves' and more generally on game-playing models of dialogue (Levin & Moore 1977, Reichman 1985), Michael Baker (1992) has developed an ITS which will support a critical argument with the student. The approach stresses symmetricality, such that either participant can advance warrants for beliefs, or challenge those already advanced, or endeavour to redirect the argument. Dialogue goals in the system include the making of concrete and abstract claims, challenging claims, eliciting support for claims and making complementary claims.

The novel addition that would be needed to support similar critical argument within social science is a method for imposing epistemological constraints on the form of warrants. For example, a system operating from within a positivist position (such as one tutoring about certain strands of American post-war sociology) would need to be adept at distinguishing between empirically verifiable and supposedly 'metaphysical' (non-observable) concepts. Alternatively, a system working within a conventionalist framework and challenging the status of some empirical data offered by the student as warrant for a claim, would need to be able to steer the dialogue focus towards an examination of the theory- or value-ladenness of the proffered observations.

It can be argued that this suggestion can be rewritten as a request for a new kind of domain knowledge. Indeed, some attempts to de-emphasize the role of 'expert domain knowledge' in tutoring systems (e.g. Gilmore & Self 1988) have been criticised on this basis. We are accused of merely asking for conventional domain expertise to be replaced by content-free or domain independent expertise in argumentation, Socratic dialogue or inductive learning. Our response to this identifies the nub of what will prove to be an exceedingly hard problem, one which we do not believe current work is addressing. In effect, it will be necessary for an ITS in social science to be capable of engaging in epistemologically (and methodologically) sophisticated critical argument *and* to make use of domain knowledge in so doing. Moreover, it will need to have methods for coping with pre-stored representations of domain knowledge *and* new empirical knowledge developed in collaboration with the learner. We believe that the only current work addressing these issues (e.g. in machine learning or 'automated scientific discovery' (Gilmore & Self 1988, Langley et al. 1987, Lenat 1983)) operates within a primitive, loosely-empiricist, paradigm wherein questions of epistemology are not likely to become salient.

A second set of issues, arising from the emphasis on critical argument rather than the assertion of facts, touches on the problem of the representation of beliefs. The ITS and the learner each need to have a model of the other. An important part of the contents of these models will be beliefs about the beliefs of the modelled partner. AI research has some fairly well developed methods for handling reasoning with certain knowledge – for example, in those situations where the addition of a new piece of knowledge does not invalidate any elements of the existing knowledge base (Frost 1986). Working with beliefs, however, immediately requires a relaxation of this monotonicity assumption, such that the introduction of a new belief may require the re-examination of the whole knowledge/belief base in order to check its consistency. Recently there have been some impressive results in this area of 'truth maintenance' (de Kleer 1986) but our understanding is very far short of a point where we can routinely use such methods in ITS construction. Yet being able to decide what a partner in an argument could be intending to *mean* when using a particular sociological term will require quite sophisticated manipulation of alternative belief sets.

9 CONCEPT FORMATION AND USE IN THE SOCIAL SCIENCES

Knowledge-based systems operate by manipulating symbolic representations according to some set of defined rules. Many of the symbols will stand in some relation to things in the world – a symbol may represent an object, an attribute of an object, a class of objects, a relation, a concept, and so on. By manipulating symbols according to syntactic rules, a system may generate new knowledge – in the sense of constructing statements not previously explicitly contained in its knowledge base. It may do this to construct a proof, test a hypothesis, search a problem space: more generally, it will simulate reasoning by making explicit what is already implicitly encoded in its knowledge base, through employing processes of inference (Levesque 1986).

Symbolic representation requires abstraction and permits formalization and syntactic manipulation to create new statements. Much of the power of knowledge-based systems comes from this capability. What blunts the edge of this power, however, is the intrinsic difficulty of mapping symbols back onto the world – of *semantics* or the assignment of *meaning*. The construction of formal descriptions of the social world is a much more complex and problematic exercise than is its counterpart in physical science, and the maintenance of semantic consistency over time – during inferencing – is a non-trivial task. In general, the problem of *meaning* will be considerably more significant in social science ITSs than in the physical science ITSs which exist today. Some of these points concerning concepts and meaning can be illustrated with reference to the earlier discussion of actions and action concepts (see Section 6).

Firstly, straightforward AI approaches to concept representation will not be satisfactory. Most approaches to concept representation see it as adequate to equate the meaning of a concept with a trivially small region of a semantic net. In addition, they borrow heavily from the positivist assumption that simple observable attributes of an entity are sufficient to define it as an instance of a concept. (And work on concept learning does not seem to acknowledge that it might be significantly more difficult to handle a concept such as *Glasnost* than a concept such as 'Red Square'.) As we have seen, explanation by reference to things which are not straightforwardly observable (e.g. the subjective state of an actor or a social process such as *embourgeoisement*) is commonplace in social science. Yet current representational capabilities in AI do not offer methods whereby concepts of this kind could be the subject of critical argument between student and machine. Minimum requirements would include an ability to negotiate definitions of concepts, to maintain multiple definitions of concepts pending a resolution of conflicting definitions, and to be able to work with context-dependent definitions. Some of the more sophisticated work on belief systems and on 'Conceptual Dependency' (e.g. in the Yale natural language projects) suggests that progress may be possible on this problem, though the associated attempts at representing concepts in political ideology (Carbonell 1981) have not been convincing.

Secondly, it seems that the identification of, and reasoning about, action concepts will require sophisticated *classificatory* methods which are probably closer to those used in interpreting text than to those developed for simple concept learning.

Finally, acceptance of the view that reasoning may need to be done within a framework of actors' meanings (or rather, that some systems must have a capacity for accepting such a limitation) implies that methods will be needed for constraining the range of concepts about which it is permissible for the system to reason and speak. Computer science already possesses a good repertoire of techniques for handling modularity and the localization of knowledge (or data or 'methods'). We believe this may offer some unexpected assistance with the problem of constraining the range of 'messages' that objects in a system may send or respond to (Minsky 1987).

10   EXPLANATION AND CAUSAL MODELLING

There is considerable disagreement among the various conceptions of social science concerning the nature of causality and causal explanation, and also concerning the *scope* of causal explanation of social phenomena (Hage & Meeker 1988). For example, there is disagreement about whether explanations of actions in terms of the actors' subjective states are correctly represented as *causal*. In consequence, an epistemologically sophisticated ITS will need methods of reasoning about, and explaining, social phenomena without recourse to a *causal* model of its domain. Where causal models *are* used to explain particular types of social phenomena, there are reasons for thinking that types of domain knowledge representation familiar from physical science ITSs will not necessarily be generalizable to the social sciences.

ITSs in the physical sciences characteristically have a very narrow field of expertise. They tend to have knowledge about something as restricted as a particular physical device, or some methods for algebraic manipulation, or the epidemiology of a single disease, or the physics of light rays subjected to refraction. This narrowness of range is inherited from work on expert systems (more generally, from cognitive science research on the nature of certain kinds of expertise), and also from the 'microworlds' paradigm that underpins a number of recent 'guided discovery learning' environments (e.g. Kamsteeg & Bierman 1988, Reimann 1989).

So the domain knowledge incorporated into a conventional ITS can normally be characterized as a representation of a small, self contained, well-structured and relatively well-understood system. In some ITSs, the domain knowledge may only be available as a 'shallow' representation of the surface features of the domain, encoded in a rule-based formalism. More recent and more sophisticated systems may embody rather 'deeper' knowledge about the domain, expressed as a runnable (often qualitative) causal model.

Causal modelling offers a number of advantages over rule-based formalisms, particularly where an explicit representation of causal connections is important, and also where a highly interconnected knowledge base may need modification over time or be subjected to unanticipated uses (Hudlicka 1988). Causal modelling is probably best developed in work on the qualitative physics of simple devices – electric circuits or heating devices, for example (Bobrow 1984, Bourne et al. 1988, Iwasaki & Simon 1986, de Kleer & Brown 1984). Our concern at this point is to identify some assumptions made by work in this area which means that it is not offering solutions to domain representation that will be generalizable across social science.

A first problem arises from the way in which work in this area has grown out of (and still concentrates on) representing *devices*. We would argue that modelling causal relations that obtain in a device (such as a heat pump) gains unacknowledged leverage from characteristics peculiar to devices. For example, the seminal work of deKleer and Brown (1984) does not treat causal relations which are not embedded in, and intuitively derivable from, the *topology* of the device. ("Our basic intuition is that the behaviour of a system arises out of, and hence it is explained by, interactions among its constitutive components" (de Kleer & Brown 1986)).[5]

In thinking about generalization to social science, we must recognize:

(a) that most of the phenomena of interest to social science are not, in any straightforward sense, 'designed' – the scope for teleological explanation is radically different; and

(b) causal relations are not manifest in the physical appearance of social phenomena, but must be unearthed by more formal means than those of perception and intuition;

(c) much causal explanation in social science would seek to create explanations of component behaviour in terms of the structure in which components are set (rather than *vice versa*).[6]

Related to this is the issue of the genesis of causal models in social science, which do not so much 'emerge' (aided by intuition) from the structure of a system, but which are *constructed*. Most social science analysis confronts aspects of the social world that are amenable to an infinite number of representations – the construction of causal models entails explicit selection of some entities and relations, and deliberate decisions to ignore others. Claims that the process of system modelling are sufficiently well understood to be formalized and automated (de Kleer & Brown 1986) do not acknowledge the help obtained from system topology, and therefore do not obtain in modelling systems in social science domains.[7]

A third issue stems from assumptions about the boundedness of systems. It is possible, for many purposes, to treat physical devices as bounded systems and to ignore (or treat as 'black box inputs') factors exogenous to the system. Such a form of analysis is much less common, and more difficult to sustain, when working with phenomena of the social world.

---

[5] As Moyse (1989, p. 140) has pointed out, qualitative causal modelling in ITSs sometimes also uses a second level of interpretation: one which is task-dependent. His example comes from STEAMER, where the collection of components which constitutes a steam turbine becomes a 'steam chamber with drains'.

[6] Comte's phrase about "explaining men in terms of humanity, not humanity in terms of men" illustrates the point.

[7] We are convinced that this relates to a deep-seated problem in ITS research: that use of the term 'domain' is not seen as problematic. 'The domain' is believed to be something that exists out there in the world, whose characteristics can be transferred unproblematically to a domain representation. There is no sense of 'the domain' as a social and mental construct used to simplify and understand the world. This creates significant difficulties in those areas of science which do hold such a view.

Fourthly, in many social science studies, a major focus of attention is on the way in which the structure of a system changes through time. deKleer and Brown (1986) acknowledge that their approach to qualitative causal modelling is unable to cope with changing system topologies. Rival approaches to causal modelling (e.g. Iwasaki & Simon 1986) are equally unable to work with bi-directional causal relations. Despite significant interest, temporal logics (which enable reasoning about temporal relations) remain poorly understood. We are still a long way from the expert dialectician.

11   REAL-WORLD KNOWLEDGE

Finally, there are implications for successful tutoring that arise from the disparity between the real-world knowledge available to the learner and that available to the ITS.

Cognitive science research associated with the development of ITSs has told us a great deal about the range of misconceptions that students may bring to the learning encounter. There has been extensive, if not conclusive, work on the creation of 'bug catalogues' and on the analysis of more deeply seated misconceptions (Brown & Burton 1978, di Sessa 1982, Young & O'Shea 1981). In physical science domains it has become apparent that students (at all levels) have got rich assemblages of misconceptions – many of which derive from the 'naive physics' that they abstract from their direct experience of the physical world. Tackling such misconceptions through an ITS is not a trivial task. For example, a number of systems attempt to make students confront the apparent contradictions between their knowledge of physics operating on ideal objects (reproduced through the system's domain simulation) and their intuitive physics (derived from real-world experience). However sophisticated, such systems often founder through re-inforcing the student's belief that there is one (formal) physics for the laboratory/classroom and another physics for the real world. The two are perceived as separate domains of experience.

A serious problem arises here for social science ITSs, when the problematic status of misconceptions (or 'alternative conceptions' to use the more neutral term) is acknowledged. Apparent contradictions in physical science systems may be rationalized by the student, e.g. via recourse to the separate domains of experience model above. In social science, most (if not all) conceptions are provisional and contradictions may be attributable to intersubjective differences in 'world view'. If the system is to reason about an apparent misconception that it believes the student to have, it will need to pursue its diagnosis in a context which is informed by the set of assumptions about the world which is held by the student. This is likely to require a richness of real-world knowledge surpassing that currently contemplated in advanced Natural Language Understanding systems. While technical work on such systems is encouraging, it is clear that a number of very serious problems remain to be faced (Winograd & Flores 1986).

12 DIRECTIONS FOR FUTURE RESEARCH

In this short chapter, we have been able to present only the briefest of treatments of some of the epistemological complexities that need to be faced if one is to contemplate the construction of an ITS in a domain of social science. In the near future, we hope to be able to present an extended, and more satisfactory, account of the salient problems that emerge from the philosophy of social science, cast in a form which emphasizes the issues of knowledge representation and knowledge processing (whether in human or artificial social science experts or tutors).

It is already apparent, however, that a number of difficult research questions need to be added to the ITS agenda. Many of the computational issues identified are also keys to progress in AI generally (e.g. in natural language understanding, the representation of belief or modelling real world knowledge). It is probable that the necessary technical solutions will emerge from mainstream AI research, rather than from the narrow field of ITS, where resources are much more limited.[8]

Within ITS research, however, it would be possible to learn a good deal from empirically oriented studies. For example, we might attempt to learn more from professional social scientists, using knowledge engineering methods from expert systems R&D, or from cognitive science, to model the knowledge and problem-solving processes they (professional sociologists) use in tackling problems in their domain (cf. Voss et al. 1983, Voss 1988). It is also necessary to know much more about the knowledge that students bring to learning in social science – to engage in a social analogue of the 'alternative conceptions' work in physical science: a 'naive social science' (Furnham 1988).

It is probably too early to expect to learn very much from attempts to construct prototype social science ITSs, or even components of them. However, there may be more scope for extending our understanding of

---

[8] This may be another example where ITS research, necessitating as it does system interaction with real people in the real world, presses AI to face up to some hard problems.

the problems if we engage in the design and evaluation of qualitative modelling tools for learning in social science. (See, for example, the work of Bliss & Ogborne 1989.) It is clear that there are many open questions about appropriate representational forms for social scientific conceptual knowledge and reasoning mechanisms.

13 CONCLUSION

We have argued, in this chapter, that it will not be possible to regard work on ITSs in the physical sciences as readily generalizable to applications in the teaching of social science. At the centre of our concerns is a recognition of the problematic nature of knowledge in the social sciences. This shifts the emphasis away from the assertion of facts and towards critical argument. It also highlights such issues as the complexity of inter-subjective understanding, the difficulty of representing concepts and the questionable generality of causal modes of explanation. The difficulties to be faced in providing an ITS with the knowledge needed to tutor effectively and authentically in domains of social science are very great. However, it is clear that many of them will also need to be faced in building other kinds of AI systems that have knowledge of the social world – systems for counselling, advising, consultancy or collaborative research, for example. The scope for synergetic development in this area will be considerable.

ACKNOWLEDGEMENTS

We're very pleased to acknowledge the helpful comments of Rod Moyse on an earlier draft of this chapter. Colleagues involved with the Simulate project, at Lancaster and in the Netherlands, have also provided advice and encouragement. An early account of this work was offered at a Prolog Education Group Conference in Copenhagen (1988). The supportive response of that community came at a welcome time. Most important of all was the willing involvement of colleagues (staff and students) in the Sociology Department at Lancaster University who allowed us to observe their tutorial work.

APPENDIX

The following extracts are from a second year sociology tutorial for a 'Women in Society' course. The tutorial topic is 'Changes in housework during the twentieth century'. This is a tutorial which comes at a stage in the course where students are still in the process of acquiring relevant theoretical perspectives. Their theoretical knowledge is therefore patchy and explicit reference to epistemological issues is rare. Nevertheless, the extracts given below usefully illustrate some of the points made earlier concerning the complexities of representing social science knowledge with respect to ITS's.

Extract A comes from a part of the tutorial discussion in which the tutor is attempting to get the students to address the question of why it is *women* who have responsibility for childcare and housework. Extract B comes from an earlier part of the tutorial in which one of the students is presenting relevant themes and issues for discussion.

EXTRACT A

1. T . . . But it's still difficult to know why it is that it's the *woman* who is seen to have the responsibility in terms of being the key significant parent rather than the father.
2. A Maybe it's because it's seen as natural . . . Women have the babies . . . and should look after them. (*Mmmm.*)
3. T So that's the explanation that's used. *(Yes)* . . . is that somehow there's a link between having a baby and . . . doing the washing and the vacuuming and . . .
4. A But it isn't that. That's just the excuse, isn't it. *(Yes)* I mean it's capitalism, and paternalism, isn't it? It suits society to keep women in the home, or controlled, and to make them feel responsibility. . .
5. T But some people might argue that it's not necessarily in the interests of capitalism to keep women in the home, in the sense that, for example, it may suit capital to employ women as low paid workers *(Mmmm)*, and then to sell them the goods and services that they used to do for themselves, to sell them pre-prepared food or to sell them, whatever.
6. A But I just think that, by leaving the responsibility for housework with women, women are more likely to get part time jobs, so they're not doing a full day's work and going home doing all the housework. They're more likely to accept a low-paid part-time job, just to help out.
7. T So that you're saying women's responsibilities as mothers and housewives limit their access.
8. A *Mmmm.* Which suits the employer. They've always got a force, a workforce, that's ready to come in and do part time work on low pay *(Yes)* when they're needed *(Yes)*, and they can get rid of them when they're not needed and they can go back into the house and they're not going to cause problems. . . So that I think it really does suit them.
9. T I mean another argument would be to suggest that, in fact, it's the *exclusion* of women from better paid jobs in the labour market which forces them to do housework. . . It's because there are no alternatives . . . not no alternatives . . . because there are relatively few alternatives for women, that they're forced into economic dependency . . . on a man.
10. A But if they do get the well paid jobs and if they've got the money, they may employ women to do their housework for them. So women still get stuck with it. I

can't ever see the time coming where women get good jobs and employ men to do the housework. I think it's always going to be women. . . Even when the better paid women can afford help, they're using women's labour.

11. T But that's assuming that housework or childcare would never be shared between the man and woman, that it has to be one person in the well-paid full-time job and a dependent person. You see what I'm getting at . . . there are plenty of other ways in which you could organize childcare instead of employing women.

12. A If the state took responsibility?

13. T Yes.

14. A And I think it'd only do that if they needed more women in the labour force. . .

15 T I mean, because if what we're saying is that capital benefits from women doing the unpaid labour in the home (*Yes*), I mean why isn't it better for capital that the state should take collective responsibility for childcare? There'd be all the economies of scale in terms of looking after children collectively, doing housework collectively, whatever, and the possible benefits of employing women as well. . .

16. A I think that's supposing that . . .

17. B The state's not organized enough. . .

18. T Well, it's pretty organized about all sorts of things, isn't it?

19. B Only the things it wants to be organized about. . .

20. T Well, *precisely* but that's what you have to explain, isn't it?

21. A If you make women financially independent, that's great as long as you've got a stable labour market. . . If it's not stable then you're going to end up with twice as much unemployment when it hits, because you've got all these women that *are* financially independent all of a sudden losing their jobs and they're not going to be happy being packed off into the house. . .

22. T Yes, there would be those problems, but why should it be *women* that are the ones that are . . . who can be drawn in and out of the labour market? Why should capital mind whether it draws . . . I mean, obviously it wants to have . . . I mean, your argument is that it wants to have that kind of pool or reservoir . . . a reserve army of workers that it can draw in and out, but why does it matter to capital whether those workers are men or women? I mean one argument is that they've been doing this unpaid labour in the home and that's of benefit. . .

23. A I think they make an easier workforce to control. . .

24. T Why? Because women are naturally pliant and non-political? . . . Yes?

25. A No. If you've got women that are used to being oppressed in the home and that they come out six or eight weeks of the year, to work in the factories so that they can get the goods out at the end of the day and then they can get rid of them. . . These women are very very grateful to these wonderful bosses who are giving them a job and they're a lot easier to control, they're going to put up with a hell of a lot more than men will. . .

26. T Yes, but that already presumes that it's women who are the ones who have been made vulnerable or made pliant by their position of economic dependency. So that *presumes* what we're trying to explain in a sense, why it is that women have been, kind of, differentially treated. I mean I think it's a really, kind of, useful point about . . . that it may be in the interests of capital to divide its workers in systematic ways in order to get the benefits you were talking about. . .

27. B Yes. If you keep your unpaid women at home doing unpaid childcare and all the rest of it instead of . . . creches . . . I mean, economies of scale might not work, because childcare facilities being made available by the state and all the rest of it, you might save in terms of, during times of economic growth and all the rest of it. When you need to sort of dismantle it and all the rest of it . . . depression, you're

going to lose money. . . Because it's very inflexible, isn't it, if you've got to provide
. . . place and staff and food. . . As it's done now there's no childcare at all. With the
unpaid labour and all the rest of it, it's very . . . it's sort of responsive, if you see
what I mean.

28. T Yes, I see what you mean.

29. B And it's going to go to waste . . . [inaudible] . . . so it might be cheaper for the
state to keep its unpaid childcare and all the rest of it in the homes and for the state
to say we're not going to assume responsibility for that, even when capital could
benefit from it. So maybe that's the reason.

30. T So, you're saying it's in the interests (?) of capital to have one person in the
household who is in a vulnerable position in the home (*Yes*), able to do childcare and
housework when necessary, but able to cut down on it when necessary because
that's much more flexible, and can be much more flexible, to changes in the
economy?

31. B Yes also I don't think . . .

32. T But it still doesn't explain why it's *women* . . .

33. B I know it doesn't explain why it's women. It explains why it's economic, though.

34. C I just think that housework's been devalued, I think that's one of the biggest
problems, is that child rearing and everything else has just been devalued by society
. . . (inaudible) . . . that it doesn't account for . . .

35. T Well is it? I think maybe it is that question of valuing but it is also a question of
choice or obligation in the extent to which, if women still were confined to
housework, even though, say, it was paid or it was socially valued in some way,
could you, would you then still argue that women were still oppressed in some
ways, if it was still women's obligation or responsibility or whatever?

36. C Yes, because there'd still be a percentage that would prefer to go out and
work. . . But I don't think that would be all women. I think some women, if it was
valued, would be quite happy to stay at home.

37. T Yes but wouldn't some men as well then?

38. A Yes. . . But I don't think men will until it is valued. Not until it changes.

39. B . . . You hear lots in the media about there being more male househusbands, or
whatever, letting women go out to work . . . I'm not sure it's true, though. . .

40. T No, I don't think it's particularly true, I mean, even more recent studies than say
the Vannek suggest that men's participation in housework and childcare is still
minimal.

41. B Yes, but has the incidence of male . . . or whatever . . . homemakers gone up?

42. T I don't know the figures on that particularly, I wouldn't have thought much. I think
what *has* gone up is the number of single parent households and in particular the
number of women living independently of men. I think that's been one of the
significant changes. And I also think that the other aspect that you pulled out from
Vannek's figures, about the fact that women who are doing paid work do much less
housework is also significant, in terms of changing relations within the household. . .

43. A I think that part of the problem with, if you look at childcare, I mean I couldn't find
anything on Scandinavian countries and housework, but I think that would be
interesting, because their whole attitude towards childcare is totally different. It is
more . . . it is shared more. I mean men have paternity leave and it can be joint
maternity and paternity leave, you can share it and it's something like eighteen
months. Which is something they should look at, I mean men don't even get a
week's paternity leave here, they don't get anything.

44. T Yes. I mean that's possible . . . that doing that [providing paternity leave] would
make men more likely to take responsibility for childcare. However, some men,

even if it's available, are going to feel unwilling to take that for the reason that that
time out of work is going to seem to disadvantage them in terms of promotion or
career prospects or whatever like that.

45. A The way it does for women now.
46. T Yes. (*Laughs*) Yes. So that it wouldn't, I mean, that would be one step but in order
to build on it further, you would need to develop criteria for promotion which didn't
disadvantage people who had taken time out, perhaps for whatever reason, but
particularly for childcare.
47. B Yes, but how are you going to do that though. . . ? I mean the person who takes
time out from work for whatever reason is always going to be at a disadvantage in a
career . . . if they're being made to compete with someone else.
48. T Do you think that they are necessarily? Couldn't you argue that the particular kinds
of skills developed in childcare or housework are ones that can be useful for a lot of
jobs?
49. B Some jobs. (inaudible) . . . what if you're an accountant or managing a big firm.
50. T Well there are plenty of managerial skills in housework. I mean clearly you can't
then, . . . I mean the argument is whether you even come in at the same position or
whether taking that time out is seen to indicate that you're not taking your career
seriously, those kinds of things. . . Whether there are retraining courses that can
build on the skills that you've developed or allowed you to feed them through . . .
there are all sorts of ways in which it doesn't necessarily need to be a disadvantage.
51. B *Hmmm*. But I would assume that a company wants to employ someone who is
going to be there continuously . . . unless they found that . . .
52. C But if everybody was doing it, then it would be acceptable; it would have to be.
They'd have to accept it.
53. A If it was the norm that men took paternity. leave. . .
54. T And there are also . . . I mean that, I think that's a generalization and you can't say
that. . . I mean there are plenty of ways in which senior positions are filled by people
outside a company. That continuity isn't necessarily a criterion for promotion.
55. B It'll be a criterion for people in the company without sort of control over their
careers, but I mean, it's obviously, it's going to be a double standard whereby
obviously a lot of directors are brought in from the outside where this is completely
discontinuous. . .
56. T Well that happens a number of levels as well and not just at a senior level.
57. B Well, I've never worked in a company, so I just . . . (*Yes*) I've no idea. . . But that
impression is there, isn't it, that sort of it's one of the reasons . . .
58. T Yes but the argument in a sense is whether that really is a kind of efficiency
criteria or whether it's a definition which is biased in the interests of men. . .
59. B So what you're saying is that criteria might be there to . . . um . . . it's not because
it's to do with efficiency but it's to do with keeping women out of the labour force.
60. T Yes. Or keeping them in the low echelons of any particular career.
61. B Yes, it probably is. My mum reckons that she's been kept back.
62. T In what?
63. B She's a consultant now. But like . . . consultant anaesthetist but she says, when
you're a consultant anaesthetist, if you're a man, you get there half a dozen years
sooner than you do if you're a woman . . . for probably all kinds of reasons. She said
when she, I think she went for a job and she knew she was going to have me and
she said she always lied and said she was never going to have children.
64. T I mean because the argument is . . . I mean in some ways it might seem we've
got off the subject . . . the argument is that women's . . . that one of the difficulties
that we seem to have is explaining why it is that women are still doing housework

and what this argument suggests is that somehow it is related to paid work, it's not that who does what within the household is independent of what happens in paid work . . . and also to raise the question of whether it's simply in the interests of capital and, kind of, economic profit accumulation or whether it may also be in the interests of men, both in the home but also at work, because what we've said is that for instance criteria for promotion may use the fact that women are forced to take responsibility for childcare, and therefore take time out of work, to deny them promotion at work, if you see what I mean . . . so that not only is there the question of who benefits from housework in terms of men or capital or whatever, but also that men or capital can benefit in different ways. It may be that men benefit as husbands, but they can also benefit as workers.

65. C *Mmmm*. Because the key positions are left open for them, aren't they? . . . There's less competition.
66. A But how do we change it?
67. T How do we change it? This is a very good question. . .

EXTRACT B

If, as these studies suggest, domestic appliances do not save time and, given that they are expensive, the question is: then why do we still buy them? And there's several ideas about why we do this.

Some people say that even though there's no proof in our daily life that they save time, there's no actual . . . that it's going to save us lots of time, that it actually does, people still believe that it's going to save time.

Boyce (?) talked about the symbolic value of the equipment, that the housewife needs them to improve the quality of her work and thus her whole life. That's saying that, if she buys these devices, that she's going to be able to do her job better and improve the way that she can look after the family. Husbands who see themselves in the role as provider have the ability to give household gifts and that gives him symbolic power and reassures him of his dominance. He can go home and buy his nice little wife a new washing machine cos he's like, the breadwinner. . . Now they *were* considered as status symbols, that was another reason people bought them but I think that's changing because it's . . . everybody's got all these devices . . . I don't think that's really . . . they're really status symbols any more.

The other thing that I found interesting was that they're seen as a substitute for a more equal division of labour. Thrall (?) in 1970 studied this and found that men took responsibility for the garbage: they took it out to the bins, or whatever, and when the household had their own garbage disposal, the woman took responsibility for it. And one thing that I wondered about that was, whether it was because, we put the garbage disposal in the kitchen. What would have happened if we'd have put it in the garage, would the man have still taken responsibility? Because the kitchen's the woman's domain. And the same's said in the case of dishwashers. Husbands didn't help with the dishes because they bought their little wife a dishwasher, so she could do it all. So technology enables women to take over tasks previously done by other members of the family. . .

Note: Figures in brackets in the text below refer to paragraph numbers in extract A. In extract A, T is the tutor; students are denoted as A, B and C.

B1 Critical Argument

The whole of extract A illustrates the tutorial's focus on critical argument rather than on the transmission of factual knowledge. The tutor raises the key issue requiring explanation (1) and responds to the explanations offered in a variety of ways:
  (a) reformulating and thus checking out proffered explanations (for example, (3) (7) (30);
  (b) criticising explanations offered by querying the assumptions being made (5), (11) (15) (26);
  (c) suggesting alternative explanations (9);
  (d) returning the discussion to the key question (22) (32); and finally
  (e) offering an answer to that question (64).

What the tutor is patently *not* doing is telling the students lots of things about women and housework. But neither is she just using this topic to exercise their logical reasoning or argumentation skills. We are not witnessing the communication of a tutor's domain knowledge. Nor is this a conversation whose domain content is irrelevant. Both tutor and students are concerned with the truth value of the assertions that are made, but they are also concerned with the logic of the argument (e.g. 'that assumes. . .', 'that's what's to be explained. . .', etc).

Note also that there are very few occasions on which the tutor is directly asked a factual question (i.e. when she is asked to retrieve something from what might (naively) be thought to constitute her domain knowledge base). Her failure to provide 'the figures' (41,42) does not appear to be seen as a critical incident or weakness. Her primary role is conceived by the participants as being other than a source of factual information about the domain.

Finally, we should not lose sight of the fact that the tutor's role is not just as a facilitator of debate. She also chose the grounds for this argument. Her 'off-line' tutorial planning will have drawn on a rich store of 'pedagogical content knowledge' (Wilson et al. 1987, Goodyear 1990) which intimately combines pedagogical and domain knowledge.[9]

B2 Theoretical concepts in the social sciences

Extract A provides numerous examples of the use by the participants of theoretical terms (terms referring to what is not straightforwardly observable). Examples are:

---

[9] The tutorial discussion is amenable to much finer grained analysis than we need to present here. The recent work of Voss (e.g. 1988) and Resnick (1989) is of relevance.

'capitalism' and 'paternalism' (4)
'capital' (5)
'labour market' (9) (21)
'economic dependency' (9)
'the state' (12)
'collective responsibility' (15)
'economies of scale' (15) (27)
'reserve army of workers' (22)
'valuing' and 'devaluing' (35, 34)
'obligation' (35)
'choice' (35)
'changing relations' (42)
'disadvantage' (47)
'norm' (53)
'efficiency criterion' (58)
'echelon' (60)
'economic profit accumulation' (64).

The tutorial proceeds without any discussion of the meanings of these terms and, in particular, without any checking out by the participants that there is agreement amongst them as to the meanings of the terms. In order for the discussion to proceed succesfully, it must be assumed that all participants have some beliefs about other participants' understanding of the terms. Sets of beliefs of this kind (not all of which are necessarily true), need explicit representation in an ITS for the social sciences, and it is far from clear that the representational difficulties associated with concepts such as 'collective responsibility' are being addressed by current work in concept learning.

B3   Explanation in the social sciences

The two extracts given include a variety of different types of explanations. (These explanations are rarely given in full and explicit form.)

Extract B offers a number of different forms of explanation of why people buy domestic appliances.

(a) In terms of actors' perceptions of the situation: "people believe that domestic appliances are going to save time". Note that the speaker claims that there is no evidence that that this belief is true but this, of course, does not invalidate the explanation.
(b) In terms of sociological concepts (only indirectly related to actors' perceptions of the situation): people buy domestic appliances because of their 'symbolic value' or because they are 'status symbols'. (This latter explanation is immediately rejected.)
(c) In terms of actors' perceptions *and* sociological concepts: husbands who see themselves as 'providers' and 'breadwinners' demonstrate their capacities in these

respects by buying domestic appliances and this is then further explained in sociological terms with reference to 'symbolic power' and 'reassurance of dominance'.

The other extract (A) centrally involves an attempt to find an explanation of one aspect of the gender division of labour (why women have primary responsibility for housework and childcare) in terms of the functional requirements of a socio-economic system ('capitalism') of which this division of labour is one feature. The discussion eventually reaches a point where the tutor suggests that additional characteristics of the system need to be taken into account, i.e. not merely the fact that it is capitalist but also (in effect) that it is patriarchal.

B4   Real World Knowledge

It is notable that the students participating in the tutorial seem to find it very difficult to find an explanation of the fact that it is women who are responsible for housework and childcare. At several stages the tutor draws attention to the fact that the points made by the students show why it is useful (to capitalism) to have some group with this responsibility, but not why that group should be women. Apparently the students find it very difficult to envisage a different gender division of tasks (see (10) and (11)) and hence to keep the current gender division in focus as in need of explanation. The tutor's knowledge concerning the taken-for-granted assumptions about the world likely to be held by the students (for example, that women doing housework and childcare is somehow 'normal' and unchangeable) helps her to structure the search for an adequate explanation. In the extract given the search is not wholly successful, in that the tutor ultimately has to provide an answer herself (64), albeit an answer which draws on material provided by the students.

5 VIPER: The Design and Implementation of Multiple Viewpoints for Tutoring Systems

ROD MOYSE

*Department of Educational Research,
Lancaster University, Lancaster, UK*

1 INTRODUCTION

The literature of Intelligent Tutoring Systems (ITS) often refers to the virtues of using multiple representations of a domain, with the intention of describing different viewpoints upon it. A standard example is the WHY system described by Stevens et al. (1979). They concluded that to tutor the causes of heavy coastal rainfall properly it was necessary to represent 'functional' knowledge of particular processes, such as condensation, as well as 'scriptal' knowledge, i.e. knowledge about the sequence of conditions which leads to the downpour. Other examples include QUEST (White & Frederiksen 1986), which highlighted the differences between experts' and novices' views of electrical circuits, and the research conducted for STEAMER (Hollan et al. 1984) which showed that the way experts think about a particular machine does not necessarily depend on its physical components but on their intended actions.

There are, however, few attempts to deal with the general issues of how viewpoints are to be described, implemented and used in systems that are intended to be intelligent. Stevens et al. (1979) identify the need, but do not tell us how to satisfy it. White and Frederiksen (1986) are not concerned with viewpoints *per se*, but use different formulations of a specific domain to tutor at different skill levels. Hollan et al. (1984) are

KNOWLEDGE NEGOTIATION
ISBN 0–12–509378–0

concerned with the design of interfaces to previously-existing simulations rather than with the issues of how to design tutoring systems which can utilize different viewpoints on the domain in their tutoring.

This chapter reports work on a system whose development is intended to address the general issues. The work seeks to identify a suitable design method for the description, implementation and use of multiple viewpoints in tutoring systems. This method suggests that where multiple viewpoints are to be used, their use should be a central issue at every stage of system design.

2 POSSIBLE APPROACHES TO IMPLEMENTATION

In approaching the issue of system design, two questions arise. Firstly, what model of education is our use of multiple viewpoints intended to serve, and secondly, how are they to be implemented in our systems? Both questions are seen as being fundamental to the development of a design methodology related to the use of multiple viewpoints. The questions are also related, as the goals set by the model of education have to be realized by the implementation.

In a much-referenced review of the field, Wenger (1987) proposes the idea of 'knowledge communication' as a model of the educational process. This is defined initially as:

". . . the ability to cause, and/or support the acquisition of one's knowledge by someone else, via a restricted set of communication operations." (Wenger 1987, p. 7).

While we are happy to acknowledge our debt to Wenger for his review of the field, we must take issue with the notion of 'knowledge communication'. It may be argued that this approach has a number of conceptual limitations since it implies that some single, pre-existent mass of knowledge has to be carefully transmitted to a rather passive student. Others would argue that the student is more properly conceptualized as an active participant who is engaged in the tutoring process, and whose learning involves the structuring and integration of the information with which they are presented, rather than its passive acquisition. This in turn implies that not all students may structure it in the same way. In fairness we must say that these points seem to be acknowledged later in Wenger's book. He stresses, with reference to Lave (1988) that the student must be actively engaged in problem solving, in order that they perceive specific problems, discover the limitations of their current view, and ". . . *demonstrate a new viewpoint's conceptual superiority*". (Wenger's italics, *op. cit.*, p. 411).

Several points can be made here. Firstly, while Wenger is happy to emphasize the importance of the student actively acquiring new viewpoints, this activity is not well described by the concept of 'knowledge communication' as defined above. Also, any system which was attempting to move the student from one viewpoint to another would have to have different accounts of the domain available to it, i.e. would have to have multiple viewpoints on that domain. This would require more than a 'communication' model as some decision processes for choosing, tutoring, and using the appropriate viewpoints would also have to be defined.

There are other indications that Wenger ultimately intends his readers to see the student as a more active participant in learning. He proposes (*op. cit.*, p. 321) the notion of 'equivalence classes' of models of knowledge, ". . . within which communication is possible and useful." This sounds far more complicated than, (and quite distinct from), ". . . the acquisition of one's knowledge by someone else. . .", but he gives no further information about how such equivalence classes might be derived, what they might look like, or how, precisely they might be used. On page 365, Wenger states that it is obvious that a 'model of communicable knowledge' need not be static, but could be modified by the communication process. Unfortunately, he does not give any description of the mechanism by which this could take place. Other indications of a more constructive view of the student are found in the Epilogue (p. 431), where knowledge communication is described as a ". . . dynamic interaction between intelligent agents . . ." by which knowledge states can be modified.

While a welcome change of emphasis, these statements come late in the book and still leave the reader with considerable doubt as to what 'knowledge communication' really entails, thus limiting its usefulness as a basis for design. The issue is not clarified by Wenger's own brief definition of viewpoints as 'interpretive contexts' consisting of 'kernel', 'scope' and 'keys' (Wenger *op. cit.*, p. 355).

A quite different approach is taken by researchers such as Self (1988a, 1989) who conceptualizes viewpoints in terms of belief systems. If work based on this approach were able to achieve its goals, then the resulting systems would be able to generate and update representations of the student's viewpoints on-line. This offers much more than seems to be available in a 'knowledge communication' model of learning. This is no accident. Self (1988a, 1988b) argues that reliance on a single representation of the tutored domain has led to an inappropriate 'trinity' model of system design; (the student model, the domain representation, and the tutoring component). If this model leads designers to assume that the system has, in a Platonic sense, the 'one true' representation of the domain then they may also assume that the student may be adequately represented as a 'subset' of the expert, or domain representation. This easily leads to an authoritarian style of tutoring with an implicit 'transmission' theory of education being applied. Self (1989) indicates that 'education as transmission' is not an idea favoured by this century's educational philosophers and quotes Perkinson (1984) in saying that ". . . the transmission theory of education is both false and immoral."

There are, however, fundamental technical difficulties to be faced in applying the belief systems approach, as Self (this volume) indicates in a wide-ranging review. These difficulties involve such issues as the need to reconcile inconsistent and contradictory viewpoints, the use of non-deductive reasoning methods, the use of modal logics to process the belief systems, and the revision of the belief systems themselves. The application of the belief systems approach to tutoring system design may thus be characterized as highly problematic.

The design issue, as seen from the belief systems approach, may be loosely stated as follows: how may we overcome the problems involved in reasoning with belief systems to generate and update the representations of students' viewpoints in the required manner?

As Self makes clear, these difficulties will not be solved overnight. In the meantime, we may wish to see what can be achieved by re-defining the problem in less ambitious terms. From this perspective we may separate the issues surrounding the construction and use of viewpoints from those entailed in research upon belief systems. If we give up the demand for belief systems which can be generated and manipulated on line, then the problem can be framed in terms of what may be achieved by a tutoring system which utilizes a number of *pre-defined* viewpoints. This should allow a robust system to be built, thus allowing an investigation of the issues which arise when we attempt to progress beyond a 'knowledge communication' model of instruction and design. The research described here takes this approach. We argue that a great deal of flexibility and adaptability can be achieved by carefully pre-defining a range of different viewpoints as an integral part of the system design process. This approach to system design is referred to as 'knowledge negotiation' (Moyse 1989, Moyse 1991, Moyse & Elsom-Cook this volume) as an indication of the adaptability that it makes possible. The structure used to pre-define the viewpoints is described below.

3   DESIGN CONSIDERATIONS FOR MULTIPLE PRE-DEFINED VIEWPOINTS

What is required in this approach is a methodology for structuring viewpoints and for designing systems which utilize them, which takes account of all the relevant issues. Specifically, this means that the domain representations of the system being designed must be formulated in terms of the viewpoints that we wish to use and the way in which we wish to use them, and that the tutoring interactions that the system is designed to support must be oriented to the availability of multiple viewpoints on the domain.

The design methodology described here relates these factors, and specifies the particular kinds of adaptation to the student that can be achieved by the use of pre-defined viewpoints. The first step is to develop a single structure which can be used to represent various viewpoints on various domains. Once this has been done an example domain may be chosen and an example system implemented to investigate the kinds of adaptability that can be achieved. Our results indicate that if the viewpoints are carefully chosen and if the system is sufficiently developed, tutoring may be adapted to such factors as a student's goals, their previous experience of the chosen and other domains, and to any misconceptions that they may be harbouring. Also, since the structure for formulating viewpoints emphasizes the *use* or *application* of the knowledge being learned, tutoring may be conducted in terms of this meta-knowledge.

The paths of influence in the design process are thus circular or iterative: the viewpoints chosen for implementation in the system will depend on the kinds of goal, experience and misconception that are envisaged as being present in the target student population, and on the kind of tutoring that the designer wishes the system to carry out. At the same time, the kinds of tutoring dialogue and adaptation that are possible will depend on the specific viewpoints that can be represented and on the interactions that they will support. To the extent that viewpoints are chosen and structured, the design method *attributes* a structure to the domain. To the extent that the tutoring interaction is adapted to the viewpoints that the domain affords, the design method *exploits* the structures that are inherent in the domain. These two possible influences must be reconciled to produce an effective system.

4   THE STRUCTURE FOR REPRESENTING PRE-DEFINED VIEWPOINTS

The term 'viewpoints' as used here is intended to mean much more than just alternative representations. If the same information (e.g. the novice's view of an electrical circuit) were represented in two different formalisms, the information content would be the same in each case although the representations of that information would be different. What, then, does 'viewpoint' mean? We shall try to answer this firstly by exploring a specific example, and then by proposing a general structure for describing viewpoints. (This example has been given elsewhere but is reproduced here for the sake of clarity.)

The example is from Minsky (1981), who points out that for hard problems one 'problem space' (i.e. an initial state, a goal state, and a set of operators) is not usually enough. Troubleshooting the electrical system of a car, for example, may require that we use either an electrical or a mechanical viewpoint. Each has its own set of labels for the same set of objects (e.g. the car body as earth connection) and its own set of diagnostic questions. While electrical faults generally require mechanical manipulation in order to rectify them, the isolation of the fault may well require that both modes of analysis be used separately. This implies that there is some other form of knowledge involved, a 'control knowledge' which allows decisions to be made about when and how each mode of analysis is to be used.

The viewpoints described in the previous paragraph may be characterized in two ways. Firstly, they are complementary modes of analysis both of which may be required in a particular context. Secondly, they refer to the same set of objects, but identify and structure them in quite different ways. The value of this seems to be that each view brings out particular features of the domain in question.

With these points in mind the concept of a 'viewpoint' is proposed as a theoretical construct which is useful in ITS design. It is not proposed as a psychological reality. Viewpoints are initially conceptualized as being similar to the ". . .user's conceptual model. . ." described by Young (1983). While acknowledging a diversity of definitions for such models, Young sought to summarize a general agreement about their nature by describing them as:

". . . a more or less definite representation or metaphor that a user adopts to guide his actions and help him interpret the device's behaviour" (Young 1983, p. 35).

In order to describe viewpoints these models need to be augmented with a range of operators which can be used to infer different information from the model, or else transform it. This need can be illustrated by considering a model which describes some parts of a car alternator system and their relationships. Where the model describes a rotor, pulley wheels, wires and drive-belts and their correct relationships, it could be used to answer the two distinct questions: (a) 'does the system have a drive-belt?', and (b) 'Is this particular drive-belt in the correct condition?'. Each answer is obtained by performing a different operation on the model.

These inferential operators are seen as vital to the proper definition of a viewpoint for implementation. One reason for this lies in the belief that in order to tutor and explain a domain effectively a tutoring system must itself be able to perform the tutored tasks in the given domain. It must thus be able to draw the required inferences from a given model, and so must be equipped with suitable means of doing so. Also, as the Minsky example above indicates, we need some 'control knowledge' to decide when a particular model is applicable to a particular problem. Moyse (1989) suggests that this may be achieved by equipping each viewpoint with heuristics which describe the kinds of problems to which it may be applied. As mental models have to be applied to problems, and as we wish to describe this process, a viewpoint is seen as a description of the application of a mental model.

As described above, this structure for viewpoints was developed with the intention that it should be used as a basis for formalizing viewpoints which could then be implemented as the domain representations of a tutoring system. A study designed to test the structure's ability to formalize different viewpoints on a domain, and to develop it as necessary is described in Moyse (1991). It resulted in an extension and clarification of the proposed structure for implementing viewpoints. The study also allowed us to develop descriptions of three categories of operators which could be used to draw inferences from the models. These operator categories are described elsewhere (Moyse 1989, Moyse 1991). The use of heuristics to encode information detailing the *use* of each viewpoint was not tested in this study.

Our viewpoints are thus composed of three basic parts:

- The model, or set of descriptors, terms, and relationships which are used together in a particular mode of analysis in the domain.
- A set of inference mechanisms which are applied to the model in order to make the different inferences necessary in a given mode of analysis.
- A set of representations, heuristic or otherwise, which specify contexts in which the given mode of analysis may be used, and the goals which may be satisfied by doing so.

This is represented graphically in Figure 5.1 which is intended to convey the following: A solution to a given task or problem is produced by inference procedures acting on a model of the domain in question. Specific features of the problem will map onto specific elements of the model, and onto specific parts of the inference procedures. The choice of which model and set of inference procedures to apply to a given problem is controlled by a set of heuristics. A different formulation of these heuristics states the classes of goals (or contexts of use) which each

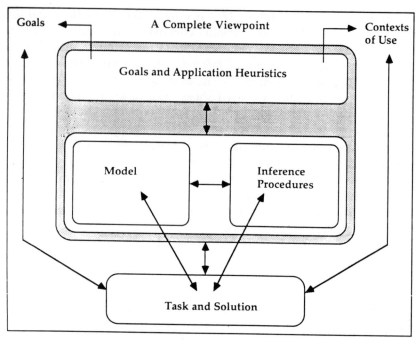

Fig. 5.1 The structure of a Viewpoint.

'model-and-set-of-inference-procedures' combination may serve. In combination, the heuristics, model, and inference procedures are referred to as a 'viewpoint'.

5 THE IMPLEMENTATION DOMAIN

The real test of this formulation for viewpoints was its use in the implementation of a tutoring system. A strong motivation while developing the system was that, as far as possible, a 'real' implementation domain should be chosen. By this we mean a domain where the actual viewpoints used by practitioners or students in that domain could be formalized and used, and some attempt made to deal with the real problems or misconceptions that they faced.[4] What was required was a domain of suitable size where the relevant viewpoints had at least been identified, where a definite educational need had been established, and where a sufficient number of users could be found to conduct an evaluation after the system had been implemented.

These needs were answered by the domain of Prolog, especially of Prolog for novices. The language is frequently a mystery to those who are encountering it for the first time, and sometimes even to those who are more experienced in its use. Attempts to alleviate this situation have included the description of a series of models (Bundy et al. 1985) which may be taught to novices so as to give them a more structured initial understanding of the language. We assumed that viewpoints based on these models could be developed. As the structure used to define viewpoints emphasizes the use of the knowledge involved, we wished to identify a domain where the different viewpoints could actually be applied, and where such application could be practised and critiqued as a part of the tutoring process. Models of execution are clearly necessary in the task of debugging. If students have problems understanding how Prolog works, then they will have even greater problems in debugging code. These considerations led to the choice of Prolog debugging for novices as the experimental application domain. The goal was to build a system which could tutor the skill of using different viewpoints to localize bugs in Prolog code.

6   DESIGNING THE SYSTEM AND FORMULATING THE DOMAIN

This section describes the domain formulations developed for VIPER (Viewpoint Based Instruction for Prolog Error Recognition). The structure of models, operators, and heuristics which is adopted to formalize and implement viewpoints is intended to be general and applicable to many domains, as is the basic system architecture. The domain formulation that results from applying the adopted viewpoint structure to Prolog debugging for novices is specific to this domain. A description of this formulation is included in order to support subsequent discussion of the system's tutorial interactions, and of the design process. We intend, however, that the emphasis of this discussion should be on the design and implementation methods by which viewpoint-based tutoring could be supported in many domains, rather than on the specific Prolog domain described here.

VIPER's formulations are described in terms of:

- The models of Prolog execution;
- A simplified debugging domain.

6.1   The models of Prolog execution

The first step was to define the necessary viewpoints on Prolog execution. Models were required to act as the core of each viewpoint. An initial set of models was defined based on those described in Bundy et al. (1985). Bundy et al. outline four complementary 'user's conceptual models' (Young 1983) of a Prolog interpreter which can be taught to novice students to help them understand Prolog execution. These are the Program Database, the Search Space, the Search Strategy, and the Resolution process. In various combinations, these four models can be used to comprehend the many different representations of Prolog execution such as Byrd Boxes, Arrow Diagrams, and And/Or Trees.

Three of the four models from Bundy et al. were formalized, and implemented (as sets of Prolog clauses). These models, when combined via a control structure, constituted an interpreter which exhibited a subset of Prolog behaviour, and which could be used to produce an execution history in the terms of the models defined. This 'history' could then be interpreted by a tutoring system, allowing it to describe or 're-play' the execution in terms of the relevant models. A range of tutorial actions can be based on this facility. The fourth model from Bundy et al. (1985) (the 'Program Database') was not used because the bugs it could localize were mainly concerned with syntax errors. It was assumed that syntax errors would be caught by the host environment of the completed tutoring system. The three models used were changed slightly to avoid duplicating descriptions of similar actions, and to suit the goals of the design and the needs of the domain formulation. (We are aware that this may be seen as serious liberty-taking, but claim a practical justification for the changes.)

Some changes were made to simplify the initial models used. It should be remembered that the purpose of the models was to tutor a set of viewpoints on (a subset of) Prolog execution which novice programmers could use to localize bugs in their code. These initial models were thus intended to be the first in an upwardly-compatible progression, and as such did not cater for backtracking or the use of the 'cut'. These aspects of Prolog were not seen as crucial to our preliminary goals for the prototype system, as we only intended to use problems which did not depend on backtracking for their solution. The intention was that more sophisticated execution models which described backtracking and its control should be developed when the initial system design had been proven.

The models actually presented to the student were cast in the form of a set of procedural 'if-then' rules to facilitate their use in the description of execution. The 'if' part specifies when a particular rule should be applied, while the 'then' part specifies what action should be taken. (This may be seen as unorthodox, if not heretical. It did, however, allow VIPER to explain why a particular part of a model was applicable at a given stage of the execution.)

As an example the simplified Search Strategy model is given in Table

Table 5.1 The Search Strategy Model as presented to the student

1. If there is a goal, try to resolve it with the head of the first/next database item.
2. If the head resolves consider subgoals.
3. If there are untried subgoals set the first as a goal with the full Search Space.
4. If there are no subgoals, or none left untried, the goal from the head resolution succeeds.
5. If a subgoal fails, or the head resolution fails, the whole resolution fails.
6. If a resolution fails, try to resolve the goal with the next item in the database.

5.1. This describes the search strategy of Prolog with the exclusion of backtracking. In order to develop a more sophisticated model, part 5 of Table 5.1 could be amended, and other clauses could be inserted to describe backtracking.

To be fully implemented as viewpoints, each model needed to be associated with a set of inference operators of the kind described in Moyse (1989, 1991) and an indication of each viewpoint's area of application. The operator sets specified the inference steps that, in combination, could localize bugs in a simplified domain. The 'area of application' in this case detailed the kinds of bug that could be localized using the given viewpoint. We will now describe the 'simplified domain' in which VIPER operated.

6.2 THE DEBUGGING DOMAIN

The operational goals of VIPER are that the student should be presented with standard novice-level programs which contain a single bug. The student's task is to learn how to localize the bugs. The system, if it is to tutor effectively, must also be able to locate the bugs. This does not mean that VIPER constitutes an intelligent debugger. Such systems have to deal with arbitrary code structures and multiple solutions to a single problem. VIPER utilizes an ideal solution to each problem set to the student and compares the execution history of this solution with the execution history of the bugged code in order to locate the bug. Our intention is thus not so much that the system should be able to find the bug, but that it should promote the skill of searching for it in terms of the tutored viewpoint. The use of an ideal version of the code allows us to concentrate on this pedagogical goal with the system determining which specific bugs may be dealt with in a given tutoring episode.

VIPER deals with a restricted category of bugs which are described in terms defined by Brna et al. (1987). This allows us to systematically describe the bugs that the system can handle and thus the classes of problems that may be incorporated as tutoring materials. The allowed bugs are described in terms of missing, extra, or wrong 'modules'. Depending on the level of description 'modules' may be such things as whole predicates, subgoals, or arguments. Bugs may be concerned with termination or with variable instantiation issues. Bugs concerned with variable instantiation may give rise to (a) the unexpected failure to instantiate a variable; (b) the unexpected instantiation of a variable; (c) a variable instantiated to an unexpected value.

The missing, extra, or wrong modules which may give rise to this behaviour may be listed. The search strategy of Prolog requires that we also add to the list the possibility of wrong order for clauses and subgoals. If our list of modules is complete then all possible (individual) bugs may be described in this way in relation to the ideal template code. Although this classification is 'syntactic' in that it does not include any of the procedural semantics of the programmer, it has the advantages of being simple, regular, and complete, while defining a finite number of bug types. The catalogue of bugs is related to the models of execution by a set of conventions which determine what is, for instance, a 'Resolution' bug, and what is a 'Search Strategy' bug. This 'mapping' from models to bugs allows us to state that certain bugs can be localized by using certain viewpoints, and thus allows us to formulate the heuristic which describes the area of application of each viewpoint.

Using Brna et al.'s (1987) classification we may define 'trees' of possible bugs for each of the three kinds of variable symptom (see Figure 5.2). The 'instantiation to an unexpected value' bug, for instance, implies that a goal containing variables succeeds in both the ideal and bugged code. Thus only bugs capable of yielding this result need to be considered. These 'trees' can also be used to specify the range of possible bugs which may be included in the problems set to the student if we stipulate that only a single bug may be present in each problem. For reasons of tractability and clarity, we also stipulate that the bugged code may only have one difference from the ideal code, that of the bug chosen.

6.3 DIALOGUES WITH VIPER

This section describes the dialogues conducted by VIPER based on the domain formulations described above. In order to clarify the nature of the dialogues, we first give a brief outline of VIPER's architecture.

The pedagogical goal of the system is that the student should develop

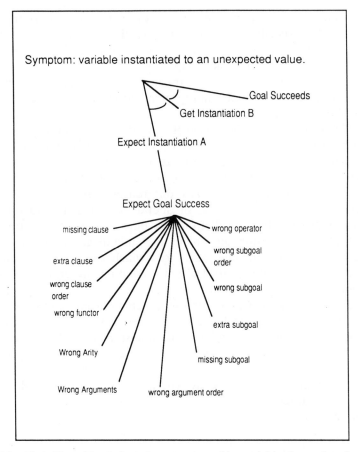

Fig. 5.2 The 'Bug Tree' for the symptom 'A variable instantiated to an unexpected value'.

the ability to describe Prolog execution in terms of the execution models so as to localize possible bugs. Where a student is asked to describe an execution, VIPER needs to check their input against its own description, or 'execution history'. This contains much more information than a normal trace would do, as each goal has to be shown being matched against all clauses in the program database, not just against those which share the same functor. If a given resolution attempt fails then the precise reasons for this must be reported so that the different types of failure can be made clear.

To this end, VIPER's meta-interpreter records each step of the execution as a series of asserted facts. These facts (the 'execution history') are labelled according to whether they relate to the ideal or bugged code, and are numbered in the order of their assertion. They contain symbols specifying the interpreter action which gave rise to the fact along with the current goal and clause whose resolution was being attempted. This method is an adaptation of that used by Eisenstadt (1985) to facilitate a form of tracing and debugging known as 'retrospective zooming'. Each interpreter action symbol is related to a specific part of a specific model.

In order to determine the effect of a particular bug in a given set of clauses both the ideal and the bugged code are run with the same initial query. The two outcomes and the two execution histories are then analysed to see firstly where (or if) they differ, and secondly which of the allowed bugs could account for any differences found. The analysis of differences is carried out by sets of operators designed to identify the specific conditions which result from the bugs of the relevant tree (see Figure 5.2). Each operator can explain the bug it diagnoses to the student by means of a text template with slots which can be instantiated to produce descriptions of the effect of the current bug in terms of VIPER's viewpoints.

If the correct operator succeeds the system will have available, for a given initial query, the ideal and the bugged outcome, a statement of what constitutes the bug, and execution histories for both ideal and bugged code. This information may be used as the basis for a range of tutorial activities.

The pedagogical goal of the system and the architecture described above suggest three essential tasks for the student.
These are:

- Correctly describe or predict the bugged execution in terms of the models of execution;
- Identify where the bugged execution diverges from what would be expected for a correct solution to the problem, and thus identify which clause contains the bug;
- Identify the bug and describe its effects.

These three tasks form the basis of three dialogues that VIPER uses to effect its tutoring.

For the first task the student is asked to describe each step of the bugged execution in terms of the appropriate models. If necessary VIPER can demonstrate this skill. (We use 'models' rather than 'viewpoints' here, as the description of execution is not carried out to achieve any particular purpose in the domain, such as the localization of bugs. This means that the full 'viewpoint' apparatus which includes heuristics determining the applicability of different models to a problem is not required.) The execution description exercise is carried out to check and rehearse a student's knowledge of the models before they are used to actually locate and describe bugs in the second and third dialogues.

The student describes the execution one step at a time by clicking on a button to indicate which model they think is currently applicable, and then making a selection from the menu which pops up as a result. Each menu option identifies a part of an execution model. The part chosen should correctly describe the relevant execution step. The screens used to take this input and to display the execution described so far are shown in Figures 5.3 and 5.4. (VIPER was squeezed onto a Macintosh SE 30 and the interface reflects the lack of available screen space.)

As may be seen in Figure 5.4, for example, a student might have chosen to apply the resolution model, and then might choose the option 'Functors Ok' to indicate that the resolution of a goal with a clause may be attempted. They may later choose the option 'Argument pair unify' to describe a specific step in that resolution.

The student's answers are checked against the system's execution history. The action symbol, goal, and clause contained in each line of the execution history allow VIPER to generate the correct answers and explanation. Explanation can be provided by expanding an asserted fact in the execution history to describe a specific execution step in terms of the models of execution (see Figures 5.5 and 5.6).

Partial descriptions of execution, relating to a specific model or combination of models, can be generated by successively expanding only those history facts which contain execution symbols relevant to the specified models.

When it is clear that the students can use the models to describe execution successfully, they are asked to choose which viewpoint they wish to concentrate on for the 'debugging' exercises proper. VIPER will then choose an example bug related to this viewpoint. The student can review their choice after each 'bugfinding' exercise is completed.

The second task for the student involves identifying where the bugged execution diverges from what would be expected for the ideal solution to the problem, and thus deciding which clause contains the bug. In the case of a variable being returned with the wrong value, this question breaks down into two others relating to separate events. If the bug causes the resolution which would give the correct value to fail, a second resolution has to succeed allowing the wrong value to be returned. The two questions are thus: (a) where does the correct value fail to get instantiated? and (b) where does the wrong value get instantiated? In each tutorial the system must make clear which question is being asked, as different descriptions and explanations are associated with each one.

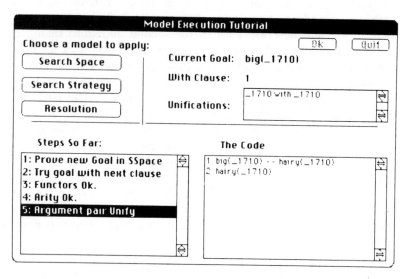

Fig. 5.3 The screen for describing code execution.

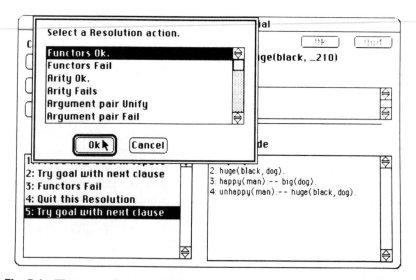

Fig. 5.4 The screen for describing code execution showing the Resolution model menu 'popped-up' to take student input.

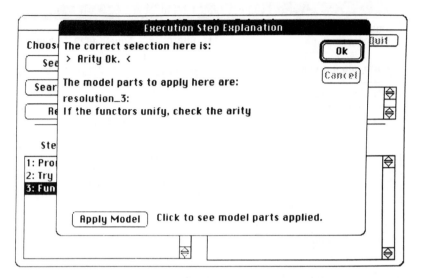

Fig. 5.5 An example of the explanations used in Dialogue 1.

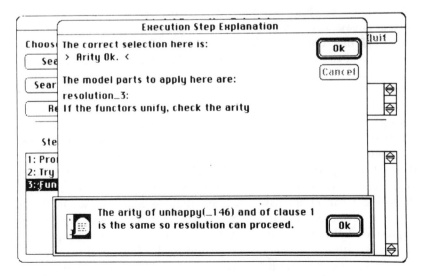

Fig. 5.6 The explanation of Figure 5.5 applied to the current execution.

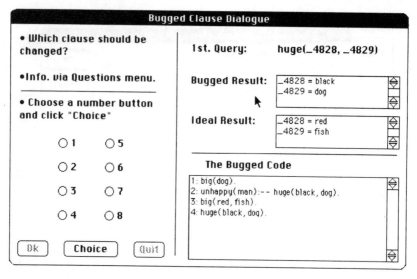

Fig. 5.7 The screen for identifying the bugged clause.

(Where the bug causes the 'wrong' resolution to succeed before the correct value could be instantiated, the two events described above are in fact the same single event and only one question may be posed.)

The students are shown the bugged code and are asked to indicate which clause contains the bug (see Figure 5.7). They are told that the correct answer is provided by an 'ideal' code solution (which they cannot see), and that only a single difference is allowed between this 'ideal' solution and the visible bugged code. (The need for these simplifications is discussed above.) This single difference must, of course, constitute the bug.

In order to check an hypothesis about this bug the students may ask questions about the 'ideal' code via a 'Questions' menu whose contents are given in Table 5.2. When one of the first six options (or questions) on this menu is highlighted a hierarchical sub-menu appears which lists, for the first five options, the numbers of clauses or, for the sixth option, the possible bug types. By choosing from both main and sub-menu options the student can either ask questions about specific clauses in the ideal code, or propose a candidate bug to the system. Where information is requested, VIPER supplies it. Where a candidate bug is proposed, this choice is either confirmed or disconfirmed. The seventh and eighth options on the 'Questions' menu have no sub-menus. They allow the student to ask how many clauses there are in the 'ideal' code, or to

Table 5.2 Options available on the 'Questions' menu

Menu Option	Contents of Hierarchical Menu
'What functor in clause. . .'	Numbers 1–9
'What arity in clause. . .'	Numbers 1–9
'What arguments in clause. . .'	Numbers 1–9
'What subgoals in clause. . .'	Numbers 1–9
'Show clause. . .'	Numbers 1–9
'Is the bug. . .'	List of legal Bugs.
'How many clauses in ideal'	None
'Give Explanation'	None

request a full explanation of the bug and its effect. This menu is also available in the third dialogue.

For the third task the student is asked to describe the effect of the bug in terms of the specific resolution of goal and clause that causes the 'bugged' variable binding to occur. They are then asked to state the implications of their description for the search and to choose the relevant bug from a list of candidates (see Figure 5.8). The student's input can then be checked against a template assembled by the relevant bug-finding operator. Variables in this template are instantiated to the appropriate clause and goal, and the description is given in terms of the relevant

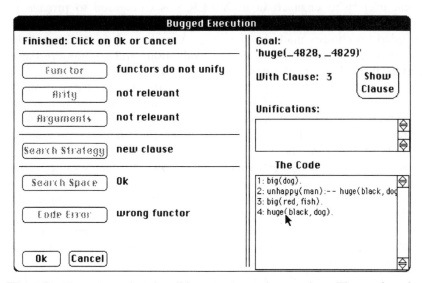

Fig. 5.8 The screen for describing the bugged execution. The student has described the resolution of a specific goal and clause and has stated the implications of this for their analysis of the bug.

models. These descriptions are given coherence by a set of explicit conventions which govern the mapping of the models onto VIPER's simplified bug catalogue. Where requested, an explanation of the current bug and its effect can be provided via the 'Questions' menu described above. This explanation is provided by operators which detail the inferences that can be made with each model in order to localize bugs.

In each dialogue there are thus correct and incorrect answers. This is not simply 'knowledge communication' in another guise, however. The system is adaptive even in its present underdeveloped form, as the student can choose which viewpoint they wish to work with. If the same techniques were used to implement a wider range of viewpoints, or if VIPER were extended to provide it with greater reactive or diagnostic capabilities, then the range and power of this adaptivity could be increased. As indicated below, these extensions could be achieved using well-documented techniques.

7 EVALUATION

In order to demonstrate the adaptivity of even this underdeveloped system, an evaluation of it by eight users was arranged. This was intended to demonstrate that the mechanisms as they stood could support a tutoring interaction that was deemed to be useful or effective by the human users who engaged in it. VIPER was configured to provide a tutorial based on the three dialogues. The exact progress of this tutorial depended on choices made by the user. A variety of printed materials were used to introduce users to the evaluation, and to support their progress through it. At the end of the tutorial, the users were asked to complete a questionnaire which enquired into their knowledge of Prolog, their experience of the interface, their views on the formalisms used in the system and the overall system design, and their views on the Prolog viewpoints in general. The group of users included both novices and more experienced Prolog users.

The results of this questionnaire were generally favourable. The formalisms used by the system were judged to be well-suited to the needs of novices. This was especially true of the description of execution which was judged to be rigorous and clear. In spite of some reservations expressed about the role of the Search Space viewpoint, the responses demonstrated that real learning had been achieved even with the system as it stood. This frequently involved the association of specific bugs with specific viewpoints. The strength of this mapping indicated that the viewpoints developed as the domain representations are well-suited to the tutoring of bug localization, at least in the limited domain that was implemented. Even one user who had described his Prolog ability as 'good' reported that his understanding of execution was clearer as a result of the tutorial. A number of specific proposals were made for the augmentation of the system with diagnostic mechanisms.

It was concluded that the research direction was a fruitful one, and that much could be gained by augmenting VIPER with diagnostic mechanisms whose potential and design have been demonstrated by other systems. Other possible developments, such as those which would allow the user to make limited changes to the code were also suggested.

8 DESIGN CONSIDERATIONS AND CLAIMS FOR VIPER

This section describes the design process that was followed, and indicates a number of ways in which the structuring and implementation of viewpoints is intimately bound up with the central issues of system design. The intended purpose of the discussion is to exemplify the design and implementation methods by which, we claim, viewpoint-based tutoring could be supported in many domains. The discussion deals firstly with VIPER as it was initially developed, and secondly with a number of extensions that would increase its adaptivity and power.

8.1 Design method

The method used to design VIPER can be summarized in the following steps:

- Specify a general structure for representing pre-defined viewpoints. (In our case models, inference operators, and heuristics detailing the viewpoint's area of application.)
- Specify Domain, Users, and possible Learning Goals.
- Jointly Specify
  - Models, inference operators and heuristics as used by the system.
  - Models, inference operators and heuristics as presented to the student.
  - Instructional strategies and tactics
  - The learner's modes of interaction with the system
  - Interface and tools used by the learner
  - Feedback and support methods and the representations required by them

- • Means of learner assessment and/or diagnosis
- • Implement the system in terms of an architecture which generates an execution history of the relevant process using the terms of the specified viewpoints. The required interactions are produced by interpreting the execution history in conjunction with the specified viewpoints.

The sequential presentation of these steps is not intended to indicate that earlier steps are necessarily independent of later ones. Evaluative stages should be inserted wherever these are thought appropriate.

The need to jointly specify a number of the system components arises from the need to cater to the 'circular or iterative' influences in the design process described earlier. The models, operators and heuristics chosen must be related to the target population, and must support the kind of tutoring interactions that are envisaged as appropriate. At the same time, the tutoring interactions that are possible will depend on the kind of viewpoints that can be represented. As described above, the choice of specific viewpoints *attributes* a structure to the domain, while the adaptation of the tutoring to available viewpoints *exploits* structures that are present in the domain. The design method outlined here is intended to promote the reconciliation of these two influences in the interests of producing an effective system.

In relation to our own use of this method, described above, we would make two claims. The first of these is that the viewpoint formalism of models and operators allows the implementation of pre-defined viewpoints in such a way that the resultant systems can perform the relevant tasks in the domain. A second claim is that the strategy of using a meta-interpreter or simulation to produce a history of some process which is sufficiently detailed and structured to support tutoring in terms of multiple viewpoints on the relevant domain, is a robust and flexible method of implementing systems which can tutor in terms of the multiple pre-defined viewpoints. The use of this method requires that the representational requirements of the different viewpoints, and of the tutoring mechanisms which are to exploit them, should be considered at all stages of the design process. We now discuss these claims in terms of the three dialogues described above.

8.2 Achievements of the design method

In the first, 'execution description' dialogue, the student merely has to select the appropriate part of each model to apply in order to describe each step. VIPER performs this task by retrieving data from the execution history. This action illustrates the use of the first class of operators defined (Moyse 1991), those which simply retrieve a specific explicit piece of information from a model or execution history. Simple as it is, this operator allows VIPER to check the student's prediction for an execution step; to provide the correct answer if this is required, or else an explanation in terms of the bound values at the relevant point in the execution; to demonstrate the skill of describing execution (when the operator is used repeatedly to describe a sequence of steps); and to describe the execution in terms of a single or of multiple viewpoints. This dialogue was praised by a majority of users in the evaluation, who reported that it gave them a rigorous and clear account of execution. We take this as confirmation that the use of an execution history interpreted by operators can support a powerful range of dialogues relating to pre-defined viewpoints.

The second dialogue asks the student to identify the bugged clause, and invites them to check their hypotheses about the difference between the ideal and bugged code by requesting information through the 'Questions' menu. This information is provided by other examples of the 'access' operator which simply retrieve stored values such as the functor of clause n , the number of clauses in the ideal code, or the name of the bug detected by VIPER. This facility was praised in the evaluation as an encouragement to exploration of possible structures in the 'ideal' code.

Where the student requests an explanation the second form of operator is brought into play. This operator relates two explicit statements via an inference procedure and thus makes explicit information which is otherwise only implicit.

An abstract example would be: $(A \to B, B \to C) \to (A \to C)$. There may be as many instances of this operator as there are inference procedures, and the inference procedure need not be logically correct. The operator seeks to define the bug by identifying a characteristic in the bugged code which is associated with the success or failure of a particular attempted resolution, and stating that this implies that the wrong result is obtained (first statement). The fact that the wrong result is obtained implies that the identified characteristic is different in the ideal code (second statement). Thus the presence of the bugged code characteristic coupled with the result of the specific resolution attempt implies that the characteristic is different in the 'ideal' code (conclusion). Operators of this kind are defined for each bug in such a way that only the correct one can succeed given the restrictions imposed on the domain. VIPER thus identifies the bug in terms of an inference procedure which is defined in response to observations of human reasoning, and which attempts, if inadequately, to have some relationship to that reasoning. The inferences made in the use of this operator are used to provide the explanation of the bug. The explanations that these provide, however, are not entirely satisfactory as they appear to combine disparate inferences in a rather arbitrary manner. In spite of this, some users described the explanation mechanism as a particularly useful facility, indicating again that the strategy of using an execution history interpreted by operators can provide effective tutorial dialogues.

In the third dialogue, the same information and explanation facilities are available from the 'Questions' menu. The dialogue itself describes the nature and effect of the bug, and is structured around a text template identified by the success of the relevant bugfinding operator. VIPER had very limited responses to student input in this dialogue. Nevertheless, several users reported that this the exercise was very effective in helping them to determine which bugs could be localized with which viewpoints.

These operator and model combinations thus allow even an un-developed VIPER to achieve a great deal in terms of performance by using pre-defined viewpoints. The study described in Moyse (1991) identified a third form of operator which added information to, or deleted information from, the models, so that different inferences could be made, or different information retrieved. VIPER was not developed to the point where this operator could be implemented although certain uses for it were envisaged, such as transforming the Search Strategy model to represent a more advanced description of Prolog's behaviour, or perturbing a model to represent a student's misconception.

While the precise value of these operators is a matter for further debate, we see no reason why the functionality that they provide could not be generalized to other domains where viewpoints were implemented in similar ways, and where the strategy of generating an execution history could also be adopted.

As has been stated above, the heuristics which would state a viewpoint's area of application are not implemented explicitly in VIPER, but are implicit in the structuring of the domain. As a result of this, we cannot show VIPER explicitly adapting to individual students' goals and experience. The system was not, in fact, equipped with the student models which such adaptation would require, although we indicate below that these models could be implemented using well-researched techniques. Rather than having the system decide, via some inferencing on a student model, which viewpoint a given student should study, we allowed the students to choose the viewpoint that they wished to work with for themselves. Our evaluation of the system shows that individual students would choose to work with a specific viewpoint in order to satisfy specific goals, such as improving their appreciation of the kinds of bug that can be trapped using the 'Search Strategy' viewpoint. This is taken to imply that, although the heuristics linking specific viewpoints with specific areas of application were not formalized explicitly for VIPER, the notion of linking viewpoints to goals and problems in this way is at least very useful in exploiting the adaptive potential provided by the use of multiple viewpoints on a domain. We see no reason why this kind of adaptivity should be limited to the domain explored by VIPER.

8.3 The viewpoint formalism as a factor in system design

The adoption of a structure of models, operators and heuristics to produce viewpoints on Prolog execution was central to VIPER's design. In terms of the design method outlined above the viewpoints were chosen or 'attributed' to the domain of Prolog debugging, as they facilitated the tutoring of novices, and gave an account of Prolog execution which was 'complete' in the sense that novices could use them to perform all the tasks with which they would be presented in the tutoring interaction. Conversely, the viewpoints 'exploited' structures present in the domain of Prolog debugging in the sense that they used such concepts as 'Search Space' and 'Search Strategy' which are widely used by Prolog practitioners, and which can be used (or frequently are used) to define sets of possible bugs. The point of attempting to 'exploit' the domain structure is that it should enable the system to perform the domain tasks in terms which are at least related to those used by human practitioners. If this can be achieved, the system should then be able to demonstrate and explain the tasks in similar terms. The models and operators that were finally implemented in VIPER were thus a result of an interaction between a pre-determined viewpoint structure and the structure of a specific domain.

A third factor in the design process was the consideration of educational strategies and tactics. The tutoring tactics and strategies adopted were based, in part, on the possibilities afforded by the domain formulations, while at the same time the domain formulations were chosen partly because of the tutoring strategies that they made possible. The educational philosophy which guided the design of VIPER's tutorial dialogues is that of Cognitive Apprenticeship (Brown et al. 1989, Brown 1990). This philosophy indicates that the purpose for which the knowledge being learned is to be used should be borne in mind at all stages of tutoring or system design. It indicates that the exercises and practice which a system requires of a student should be as 'authentic', or as close to those of real domain practitioners, as possible. (A weakness of VIPER in this context is the lack of any analysis of the social aspects of its domain knowledge.) VIPER uses the tutorial tactics of Cognitive Apprenticeship: modelling of the target skill, the provision of a 'scaffolding' of threadbare concepts, an emphasis on different possible problem decompositions, and extended general practice.

VIPER's domain formulations may be related to these demands. Our choice of models was intended to make the domain formulations as 'authentic' as possible, as described above, in spite of the simplifications necessary to make the debugging domain manageable. The 'modelling' of the target skill was provided by VIPER's ability to carry out, demonstrate, and explain the various tasks set to the student through the application of operators as described above. The models were intended to provide a 'scaffolding' while the viewpoints themselves were intended to emphasize alternative problem decompositions. It was intended that the 'purpose' of each viewpoint should be encoded in the heuristics which described its area of application. In fact, as described above, this information was encoded as an implicit part of the domain formulation. The space of possible bugs was thus divided into three sets, each of which related to a particular viewpoint in such a way that operators could be defined which allowed the relevant viewpoint in VIPER to identify the bug. The results of the evaluation indicate that students found this helpful in achieving an understanding of how each viewpoint could be used.

The use of viewpoints formalized in the way described influenced other parts of VIPER's architecture. The first of these is the use of an execution history. In order to determine the nature and effect of a specific bug VIPER compares the execution of the bugged code with that of an ideal version of the code. VIPER needs to know the results of the two executions to determine firstly whether a bug is present and, if so, what its exact nature may be. A history of each execution must thus be stored in order for VIPER to compare them. The use of viewpoints and of a specific viewpoint structure influences the *terms* in which this history is recorded. It is not sufficient to record the execution in terms of a single viewpoint. Instead the history must contain all the information required for an analysis in terms of any one of the implemented viewpoints (in VIPER's case there are three such viewpoints). The terms used to record this execution history must be recognizable by the viewpoints and their operators. This in turn implies that the interpreter which runs the code must be built so as to produce the kind of execution history which is required. The point to be made here is that the influence of particular viewpoints structured in a particular way extends to the very core of the system design.

Another feature of the architecture influenced by the viewpoint formalization and its implementation in the specific domain chosen, was the nature of the dialogues that the system would support. The viewpoint structure emphasizes the application of the knowledge involved. In this case this amounts to the localization of a bug. In order for the system to determine that the student has done this correctly, it must have positive evidence that two conditions are satisfied. Firstly, there must be evidence that the student has correctly identified the bug. However, correct answers here could be the result of guesses or random choice so a second condition must be satisfied: there must be evidence that the student correctly understands the effects on execution implied by the chosen bug. The investigation of each condition requires a separate dialogue. The point to be made is that the choice of a viewpoint structure which emphasises the application of the knowledge involved has implications for the kinds of tutorial dialogue that are deemed to be relevant and necessary.

8.4   Extending the basic VIPER mechanisms

The possibilities discussed in this section depend on further work being done to augment the basic VIPER mechanisms, but Moyse (1990) has demonstrated that these augmentations are quite feasible and only require the use of techniques which are well established in the literature. These possibilities will be referred to as 'weak' claims. VIPER in its present form thus does not constitute a complete ITS. Rather it is seen as an 'enabling technology' which could support the rapid implementation of an ITS.

Firstly, the basic VIPER system could be augmented to carry out some diagnosis in relation to inadequacies and misconceptions in the student's knowledge. This could be achieved in relation to each viewpoint by using unsophisticated student modelling techniques such as the use of a bug catalogue. This would allow specific patterns of execution description or of bug description input by the student to be interpreted as examples of bugs which had been previously observed in the relevant student populations. Alternatively, the students' use of the 'Questions' menu could be monitored to determine whether they were applying the appropriate viewpoint in an appropriate way, and appeared to be forming and testing hypotheses about the bug. An important development would be to increase the sophistication of VIPER's response to student's input describing the effect of a perceived bug on execution in the third dialogue of Section 5.6.3. The main issue here would be to determine whether students' input showed an accurate mapping from viewpoints to bugs.

A simple example of how some diagnosis could be performed may be given in relation to the 'Execution' dialogue (dialogue one) described in Section 5.6.3 above. A comparison of the correct execution step with the erroneous one actually chosen by the student may well yield information about misconceptions in the student's knowledge of the domain. The

efficacy of this technique has been demonstrated with such systems as
BUGGY (Brown & Burton 1978), although it does not attempt to deal
with the issue of *why* a student has a particular misconception, nor with
the issues of multiple interacting bugs or the inconsistent application of a
bugged procedure. What is proposed here is an enumeration of the well-
known bugs in describing Prolog execution, and an attempt to match
these to the student's input.

BUGGY attempts to achieve such a match by assembling fine-grained
sub-skills until a model which matches the student's performance is
achieved. An extended VIPER could attempt a similar matching by an
analysis of the sequences of execution steps that a student's input
described. A range of common bugs are defined for us by Fung et al.
(1987) and Taylor (1988), although the exploitation of these would
require a meta-interpreter and tutorial capability which reflected the full
functionality of Prolog. An example of a misconception which could be
detected in this way is the 'facts first' misconception detailed by Fung et
al. Students with this misconception assume that Prolog immediately
attempts to resolve a goal literal with a fact that could prove it, rather
than with any other clauses of compatible functor and arity that are prior
to the fact in the database. If, as suggested above, students were asked to
indicate which clause was next to be resolved with the current goal literal,
then the repeated skipping of intervening clauses could be interpreted as
an indication that this misconception was present.

Many of the misconceptions catalogued by Fung et al. relate to
backtracking and the use of the cut. If VIPER's models and mechanisms
were upgraded to describe these aspects of Prolog, then it is likely that
many more misconceptions could be 'caught' in the manner described
above. In fact, the current execution pattern described by VIPER would
then become a perfect specification of the 'try once and pass'
misconception which assumes that a resolution fails completely whenever
a subgoal first fails.

Another weak claim is that VIPER's domain could be extended to
include other pre-defined viewpoints on Prolog which could be implemented in the manner outlined above. This would not require any
changes to the basic architecture of VIPER, and would use the same
meta-interpreter and execution history.

Examples of such viewpoints could be:

- Prolog as a resolution theorem prover.
- The 'pointer' model from 'C' implementations of Prolog, where the
  pointers are changed to unify variables.
- Prolog as an object-oriented system where clauses are objects sending
  messages (Kahn 1989).

A third weak claim is that, since any different viewpoints that were implemented may be suited to different goals and experience, an augmented VIPER could adapt its tutoring to these factors (assuming it had some representation of them) by choosing an appropriate viewpoint. If, for example, we wished to introduce the student to the models of Prolog that *are* implemented in VIPER, it would seem pedagogically wise to begin with the model which is closest to something that the student already knows; i.e. the tutoring is related to their previous experience. The system could simply ask for information about this. Where the student has some knowledge of theorem proving we may decide to begin with the Search Space model, which has many similarities to traditional theorem proving. The complexities of the Search Strategy and Resolution models could then be approached later. Even where the student was familiar with all of the models the bugs and exercises chosen for tutoring could initially focus on search space issues. Our evaluation shows that novices may wish to concentrate on particular aspects of the language. They may, for example, wish to improve their understanding of resolution in Prolog. The goal may be satisfied by choosing problems and exercises which stress the use of the Resolution viewpoint. It is assumed that such adaptation would increase the student's engagement with the system, and would make the tutoring more meaningful to them. This desire to adapt to the goals of students means that the system design process must take account of the possible uses of the knowledge to be tutored from the earliest stages. In terms of the implementation described above, the area of application for each viewpoint would have to be explicitly encoded.

This kind of adaptation to the misconceptions, goals or experience of the students can be characterized as tutoring 'with' the viewpoints; i.e. particular tutorial strategies are realized through the use of different viewpoints. We can also describe a process of tutoring 'about' the viewpoints. The goal of such tutoring is that the student should appreciate that a given viewpoint is suited to the solution of particular classes of problems, and that it stands in a specific relationship to other viewpoints. If we again consider the electrical and mechanical views of a car ignition system, it is clear that they can both solve different classes of problems. They are, however, closely related, and there may be many situations which require their use in combination. Alternatively, it may be possible to say that if the possible causes of a fault implied by one view are excluded, then one of the causes implied by the other view must apply. This implies that the student must learn to think both 'with' and 'about' viewpoints and must, at least initially, engage in some meta-cognitive activities to consider whether they are applying the appropriate view to a particular problem.

The chosen structure for viewpoints can be related to these considerations. The use of an explicit model which is interrogated by sets of operators allows the system to tutor 'with' a given viewpoint; i.e. the system tutors, and can perform the tutored task, in terms of that viewpoint. This, in conjunction with the use of an execution history, allows the system to employ such tutorial tactics as demonstration, critiquing, and explaining. With further work, we claim that the system could also model student errors.

The inclusion of a set of heuristics in the viewpoint structure which detail its area of application allows the system to tutor 'about' the viewpoints in terms of their area of application and their relationship to other viewpoints. Such tutoring could be intended to remedy misconceptions in the student's knowledge of a viewpoint's applicability, or to promote some meta-cognitive appreciation of how the viewpoint is to be applied. These heuristics can be related to possible goals that a student may have, so that the system can adapt the viewpoint it uses for tutoring to those goals, where knowledge of those goals is available.

The adaptation of the tutoring to a student's previous experience is not dependent on any specific part of the structure described, but is a general form of adaptation implied by the use of multiple viewpoints. The system would require some specific knowledge relating its available viewpoints to other areas of study or other viewpoints. A specific viewpoint could then be selected as being appropriate to the tutoring of a given student in the light of this knowledge.

These 'weak' claims indicate that although the the VIPER dialogues described above are limited in their adaptability, the potential of the design and implementation method that underlies them goes well beyond that described by a 'knowledge communication' approach. As has been indicated above, tutoring could, with further work, be adapted to a student's goals and experience, while diagnosis could be carried out in terms of a range of possible viewpoints for a given domain. The relationships between these viewpoints could also be a topic for tutoring.

8.5 Using the VIPER architecture in a different domain

Another weak claim is that other, quite different, domains which require the use of multiple viewpoints can be implemented using the viewpoint formalism and system architecture described above. A detailed example of how this could be achieved is given here in relation to WHY (Stevens et al. 1979), which was one of the systems which first drew attention to the need for multiple viewpoints in tutoring system design. Essentially, the method involves building a simulation of the domain to be tutored and using this to produce an execution history for that domain. In this sense, VIPER's meta-interpreter is seen as a *simulation* of a subset of Prolog. For the new domain the execution history must be sufficiently well-structured and sufficiently rich to support the range of viewpoints that the tutoring demands. Each of these would be formulated in terms of the model, operators and application heuristics described above.

Stevens et al. (1979) built a tutoring system with a single, 'scriptal' view of its domain, which described the causes of heavy coastal rainfall. They described how a second 'functional' view of the domain would be required if the system was to cope with a number of the misconceptions that they subsequently detected in their students. One of these, the 'sponge' misconception, described rainfall as being a result of moist air being squeezed against mountains. Stevens et al. did not implement a system with this second viewpoint.

We now demonstrate how such a second view of the rainfall domain could be implemented, (along with the initial 'scriptal' view), using the design strategies developed in VIPER. Our demonstration requires that both scriptal and functional models of coastal rainfall be developed, along with the operators that draw inferences from them and, at some point, a statement of their area of application. Once this has been done, it is possible to specify the information that has to be available in the process histories to which the viewpoints would be applied. A suitable simulation can then be built which represents the crucial factors and their interactions, and which can generate a process history in the terms required. We show how such a system could support the distinction of the correct and bugged accounts of rainfall, i.e. the condensation as opposed to the 'sponge' account.

The viewpoints which utilize the process history

The model for the first kind of viewpoint, that describing the 'scriptal' account of rainfall, has been defined for us by Stevens et al. (1979). 'Scripts' are "...generic knowledge structures..." which represent knowledge about classes of phenomena, and "...a partially ordered sequence of events linked by temporal or causal connectors." The knowledge has a hierarchical structure where the detail of one script is expanded by a subscript. The scripts describe the relationships of sets of 'roles' such as AIR-MASS or BODY-OF-WATER which are bound to specific entities in the real world to describe a specific real-world process such as the evaporation of water over the Gulf Stream and is deposition as heavy rainfall on Ireland.

Examples of these scripts show a series of processes such as evaporation or movement due to wind pressure, linked by 'precedes' or 'causes' relations as in the following:

Heavy Rainfall
1. A warm air mass over a warm body of water absorbs a lot of moisture from the body of water.
Precedes:
2. Winds carry the warm moist air mass from over the body of water to over the land mass.
Precedes:
3. The moist air mass from over the body of water cools over the land area.
Causes:
4. The moisture in the air mass from over the body of water precipitates over the land area.
(Stevens et al. 1979, p. 14 of 1982 reprint).

These examples could be readily expressed in either procedural ('if there is a warm air mass over a warm body of water then the humidity increases over time.') or declarative ('A warm air mass over warm water gives an increase in humidity over time') form. The knowledge represented in each script could be represented by a series of such statements which together constitute a model, and inferences made on this model as described in Section 5.4. The hierarchical nature of the scripts could be represented by implementing each level as a different model, which, when combined with its own operator and heuristic set would constitute a viewpoint. The description of the evaporation process which Stevens et al. give as a sub-script of the 'Heavy Rainfall' representation, would thus be represented as a separate viewpoint, as Resolution is distinguished from Search Strategy in VIPER. A student's knowledge of such models could then be tested against the execution history stored for a given run of the simulation.

Other forms of viewpoint are necessary, however, as Stevens et al.'s (1979) paper argues forcefully. Our purpose here is to demonstrate that these too could be represented by the viewpoint formalism of Section 5.4. The main extra viewpoint discussed by Stevens et al. is the 'functional' viewpoint, which is required in order to combat a range of misconceptions such as the 'sponge' model of precipitation and the 'cooling by contact with mountains' bug. The functional viewpoint describes a number of factors which are not intended to be causally linked or temporally ordered, but which vary in relation to each other and which produce a specific result. Condensation is described in these terms. The description (see below) is in terms of ACTORS which have a ROLE in the process and are affected by a set of FACTORS. The RESULT is due to the FUNCTIONAL RELATIONSHIP that holds between the FACTORS and the ACTORS. These relationships are expressed in a

form which resembles predicate calculus. There is, for example, a positive
FUNCTIONAL RELATIONSHIP between the FACTOR of the temperature of the water source, and the RESULT of increased humidity in
the air mass. As it is stated by Stevens et al. (1979), this functional model
does not describe the degree or rate of change in the factors and the
result, although it may specify necessary conditions such as WARM for
the water source. Stevens et al. (1979) give the following example of a
functional model for evaporation:

```
Actors.
    Source: Large-body-of-water.
    Destination: Air-mass.

Factors.
    Temperature(Source).
    Temperature(Destination).
    Proximity(Source, Destination).

Functional-relationship.
    Positive(Temperature(Source)).
    Positive(Temperature(Destination)).
    Positive(Proximity(Source, Destination)).

Result.
    Increase(Humidity(Destination)).
        (Stevens et al. 1979, p. 16 of 1982 reprint)
```

The collection of statements which represent the functional knowledge
could be seen as a model which acts as the core of a viewpoint as
described in Section 4. This viewpoint is completed by providing the three
classes of operators to act on the model, and a set of heuristics which
govern its application.

The production of the process history

The ordered and causally-connected process described by the scriptal
model could be simulated in much the same way as the power station of
Moyse (1991) was simulated, if the crucial variables such as temperature
and humidity are defined for each of the 'roles' mentioned in the scripts.
In terms of Stevens et al.'s (1979) example, such a simulation would show
that the longer a warm air mass was above a warm body of water, then
the higher would be its humidity, and the longer it was subject to a wind
from a specific direction, the closer it would be to a given land mass. If
the simulation also caused the values associated with each 'role' to be
plotted against time (or against events), then this would provide the sort
of 'execution history' used in VIPER which could support a variety of

Table 5.3 Examples of possible execution history segments for a proposed 'Heavy Rainfall' tutor. (a) Elapsed time: 1; (b) elapsed time: 50.

Role	Instance	Factor	Value
Body of Water	Gulf Stream	Temperature	10
Wind	South-Westerlies	Strength	20 Knot
Land Mass	Ireland	Precipitation	0
Air Mass		Temperature	12
Air Mass		Moisture Content	30
Air Mass		Distance to Land	200 km
Air Mass		Volume	100%
Air Mass		Altitude	0 m

a

Role	Instance	Factor	Value
Body of Water	Gulf Stream	Temperature	10
Wind	South-westerlies	Strength	25 knots
Land Mass	Ireland	Precipitation	10
Air Mass		Temperature	2
Air Mass		Moisture content	15
Air Mass		Distance to Land	0 km
Air Mass		Volume	200%
Air Mass		Altitude	400 m

b

viewpoints if it were rich enough in information. Such an execution history could thus take the form of a series of values for the relevant factors calculated and recorded by the simulation against simulated elapsed time, i.e. each value would be calculated and recorded at the end of each simulated elapsed time interval. This could give an execution history of which the examples in Table 5.3 could be segments. An alternative way of structuring the process history would be to record the simulation data in segments which were related to *events* in the simulated system, rather than to the passing of simulated time.

These execution history segments are intended to represent two widely separated stages of a specific run of a heavy-rainfall simulation. At 'Elapsed time: 1' the air mass is over a warm water mass at sea level, and being driven towards a land mass by a twenty-knot wind. The precipitation over the land attributable to the current air mass is zero. The data recorded after the next time interval (not shown here), should show an increase in its moisture-content, with relatively constant temperature, altitude, and volume. The distance to the land mass should have decreased.

The data shown for 'Elapsed time: 50' indicates that the air mass is now over the land, and that its altitude and volume have increased, while its temperature and moisture content have fallen, and precipitation has occurred.

We assume that the starting values and data of the simulation could be set to represent conditions where rainfall would occur in varying degrees, or not at all.

The scriptal viewpoint could interpret this execution history through the application of operators such as those described in Sections 4 and 8.2, and in Moyse (1991). An example of an 'inference operator' would be one which interrogated the execution history to see if the following was true:

1. The arrival of a moisture-laden air mass at the land causes it to cool.
2. Cooling of a moisture-laden air mass causes precipitation.
Therefore the arrival of a moisture-laden air mass at the land causes precipitation.

What we also require is that the execution history produced by the simulation of evaporation and rainfall should be interpretable in terms of the functional model described above. This would be possible if the ACTORS and FACTORS could be mapped onto elements in that history. This mapping need not be direct, but could be the result of whatever inferencing or transformation is required. In fact, the ACTORS such as 'Large-body-of-water' and 'Air-mass' do map easily onto the 'roles' of the scriptal knowledge, as do the FACTORS such as their temperature and proximity. A functional interpretation of the execution history, then, would require that the values of the various FACTORS expressed in it should vary in a relationship which does not contradict the various FUNCTIONAL RELATIONSHIPS described by the functional model. If, for instance, the execution history of the simulation showed a rise in the temperature of the water source, then the functional model would predict a rise in the humidity of the air mass, but would not attempt to describe any causal connection between the two events. An 'inference operator' which could made this inference would test the execution history to see if the following was true:

1. Source temperature X at time 1 and source temperature X+ at time 2 indicates a rising source temperature.
2. A rising source temperature from time 1 to time 2 indicates an increase in destination's moisture content from time 1 to time 2.
Therefore source temperature X at time 1 and source temperature X+ at time 2 indicates an increase in destination's moisture content from time 1 to time 2.

As Stevens et al. (1979) describe, the usefulness of the functional viewpoint is shown by its use in combating misconceptions. A functional model of precipitation of the type described in the scripts would describe a relationship between the altitude of an air mass, its volume, its temperature, and its ability to support water vapour. As the air mass rises, it is forced to expand and thus its temperature drops causing the precipitation. If this functional model were applied to interpret a simulation's execution history for some precipitation of this kind, then, unless the functional model is to be violated, a fall in temperature must be accompanied by a rise in altitude and an increase in volume. An attempt to explain the precipitation in terms of a 'cooling by contact with the mountains' misconception would not give the expanded volume or the increased altitude. The 'sponge' misconception, which sees the air mass squeezed against the mountains and forced to drop its moisture would give a *reduced* volume and a stable altitude. A wide range of tutorial exercises could be based on these relationships.

Two of the factors discussed in the functional model, altitude and volume, have no place in the scriptal model. It is thus clear that they would have to be specially included in the simulation of the rainfall process if the functional viewpoint on precipitation is to be supported. The cost of this seems very small in terms of the possible benefits that could be gained. The point to be made is that an ITS can be built with multiple viewpoints available to it if these are defined beforehand, and if a sufficiently rich underlying representation is built to support them.

A domain that cannot be implemented using VIPER's architecture

Since the design and implementation strategy used in VIPER relies on interpreting the execution history of some process, then any purely declarative domain such as the geography domain of SCHOLAR (Carbonell 1970) cannot be implemented in this way. There is no process to be described and thus there is no execution history to be interpreted in terms of a model and operators. However, if we bear in mind the dictum from Cognitive Apprenticeship that the *use* of knowledge should always have a central place in the design of tutoring systems, then some possibilities for VIPER-like implementations do become apparent. The application of declarative knowledge to achieve some purpose must involve the execution of some procedure. The simulation of this procedure could give rise to an execution history which could be interpreted in the manner described above.

The design strategy of using a simulation to generate an execution history to support tutoring in terms of multiple viewpoints is thus seen as being suited to procedural domains, or to domains where processes are described and can be simulated. However, even purely declarative knowledge must be *applied* if it is to be used, and we would contend that the application of such knowledge could be tutored by systems based on the design method outlined above.

9 CONCLUSIONS

This chapter describes a design method for pre-defining and formulating viewpoints and for implementing systems that can tutor using multiples of such viewpoints. The method is discussed in terms of VIPER, a system implemented to tutor the localization of Prolog bugs to novices in terms of three viewpoints on Prolog execution. In VIPER a partial interpreter, or simulator of a subset of Prolog behaviour, is used to produce an execution history in terms which allow its interpretation through any of the required viewpoints. This strategy facilitates a range of tutorial interactions and adaptations which can be undertaken as a direct result of the availability of multiple pre-defined viewpoints on the domain. An indication is given of how other viewpoints on the example domain could be implemented, and of how the design method could be used in quite different domains. This method is seen as being best suited to procedural domains, and requires that the potential uses of the knowledge, the defined learning goals, the intended methods of tutoring, possible student goals and possible previous experience be taken into account at all stages of the design process.

The interplay between the adopted structure for viewpoints, the structure of the chosen domain, and the design of the system is described in some detail. The domain formulations of VIPER and the dialogues that they support are given in outline. The educational adaptations that the adopted structure for viewpoints makes possible are discussed, along with the need to tutor both 'with' and 'about' the viewpoints. The specific forms of adaptation which the design method described here makes possible are referred to as the adaptations of 'knowledge negotiation'.

During the work described in this chapter we found that a number of recurrent issues appeared to be central to the design of tutoring systems using multiple viewpoints. We state these issues as a conclusion in the hope that this may be of some use to others who are interested in the subject.

The issues identified were:

- The need to use multiple viewpoints to correctly carry out a single activity;
- The need to use different viewpoints to carry out different activities in a domain;

- The need to employ different viewpoints at different points along a learning path;
- The possibly contrasting needs for system efficiency in task execution, and for clarity in explanations given to the student;
- The desire to promote reflection and meta-cognition in the student;
- The desire to explore the student's own viewpoint;
- The adaptation of tutoring to a student's goals, experience or misconceptions;
- The need to formulate an adaptive and constructive philosophy of tutoring system design which does not rely on a 'transmission' theory of education;
- The identification of tutorial strategies and tactics which are appropriate to the use of multiple viewpoints;
- The need to formulate the tutored domain in a such a way that the different viewpoints are clearly stated and related.

ACKNOWLEDGEMENTS

This research was supported by a postgraduate award from the Science and Engineering Research Council of the United Kingdom.

This work owes much to the support of my supervisors, Dr. Mark Elsom-Cook and Dr. Diana Laurillard, and to all students and staff at the Centre for Information Technology in Education, of the Institute of Educational Technology, The Open University, U.K. Alternative views on Prolog were provided courtesy of Mike Brayshaw of HCRL, The Open University, UK.

6 Modelling Children's Arithmetic Strategies

ROSHNI DEVI

Institute of Educational Technology,
The Open University, Milton Keynes, UK

1 INTRODUCTION

The development of many arithmetical skills depends on basic concepts like commutativity[1], associativity[2], and distributivity[3]. However, little research exists on the acquisition of these concepts, their use and how they are related to other skills in arithmetic. The research described in this chapter examines children's acquisition of commutativity and associativity. Its main objective is to model the acquisition of associativity. An empirical study was carried out to identify the different strategies children use for solving problems and the conceptual knowledge associated with them. Models of the observed strategies for solving 2-term (e.g. 5 + 6) and 3-term problems (e.g. 5 + 6 + 5) have been implemented using production-rule formalism. The implementation, called PALM, (Production-rule Arithmetic Learning Modeller), is described in this chapter.

Having developed models that describe the 'space'[4] of strategies, a model of learning is currently being implemented to explain the transition from one of the observed performance levels to the next. The

---

[1] Commutativity (of addition): the order in which two numbers are added does not make a difference to their sum (a + b = b + a).

[2] Associativity: the order in which three numbers are added does not make a difference to their sum ((a + b) + c = a + (b + c)).

[3] Distributivity: a(b + c) = ab + ac.

[4] 'Space' of strategies refers to the set of strategies identified, by observing children at different performance levels.

KNOWLEDGE NEGOTIATION
ISBN 0–12–509378–0

computational model of the acquisition of associativity uses knowledge of commutativity as prerequisite knowledge. The model begins with basic rules representing the ability to solve 2-term problems. When presented with a 3-term problem, which is of a type that it has not encountered before, none of the rules are applicable and it fails. In this situation, PALM learns by generalizing its existing rules. Once it has learnt to solve 3-term problems, it learns more efficient strategies than those that it already knows.

The chapter is organized as follows. The first section of the chapter is an account of the empirical study. In the second section, the implementation of production-rule models of children's problem-solving strategies is discussed. The following section describes PALM's learning component, which models the application of 2-term rules to solving 3-term problems, and learning more efficient strategies. Finally, the implications of production-rule modelling and of computational models of learning for an intelligent tutoring system (ITS), that can be used to guide children towards more efficient strategies and to facilitate development of the conceptual knowledge associated with the strategies, are discussed.

2 EMPIRICAL WORK

The work described in this section builds on previous research on children's counting and addition strategies (e.g. Baroody & Gannon 1984, Resnick 1980, 1983, Gelman 1977, Carpenter & Moser 1983). Despite considerable research on addition, the relationship between counting strategies and the concept of commutativity has not been described in sufficient detail. Researchers, apart from Baroody and his colleagues, had assumed that children possessed knowledge of commutativity if their strategies logically implied the knowledge.

A study was carried out to investigate the development of the concepts of commutativity and associativity. The aims of the study were:

(i) to identify the stages that children go through in acquiring the concept of commutativity for addition of integers.
(ii) to gain insight into children's progression from commutativity to associativity.

2.1 Method

The subjects comprised 105 children (49 boys and 56 girls) between the ages of 5 and 12. They were given arithmetic problems (most of them being commuted pairs, i.e. $x + y$ followed by $y + x$) to solve. They were interviewed in order to obtain details of their skills and strategies, and to find out their levels of understanding of the concepts. To identify the different levels of understanding of the concept of commutativity, children at different performance levels were studied.

The procedure was as follows. After they had written down the answer for the first of a commuted pair of problems, they were asked 'Now, can you tell me if this will add up to x (where x is the child's answer) – the same as or different . . .', 'Why do you think it will be the same?' (or different, depending on their response). In addition, a pair of incorrectly-answered, large-numbered problems (like $1023 + 4970 = 5985$ for elder children, and $130 + 485 = 550$ for the younger ones) were written down, read out loud by the experimenter, and then the children were asked 'what will $4970 + 1023$ (with the appropriate numbers) be?' The children who demonstrated knowledge of the concept were tested to see if they generalized it to all numbers: 'If I swapped the two numbers around, will the answer always be the same?', 'Even for very large numbers? (If their answer to the previous question was "yes")', 'Do you know why that is?'. Furthermore, it was noted whether the subjects computed the sums for the second of the commuted pairs of problems, or whether they copied the answers from the previous problems. Finally, they were given a pair of subtraction problems to find out if they generalized the concept to subtraction.

Of the students studied for the stages of development of commutativity, 77 were tested for their performance on three-term problems. The sample size of 77 students was a result of ignoring those students (especially the younger ones) who were not competent enough for the study (i.e. those who did not know what to do or how to proceed on the 3-numbered problems).

2.2 Results and discussion

A 'space' of strategies was identified. For 2-term addition, the strategies included the following:

'count all starting from the first addend' (CAF)
'count all starting from the larger addend' (CAL)
'count on from the first addend' (COF)
'count on from the larger addend' (COL)

Children who use the CAF strategy start counting from 1, and the first

Table 6.1 Relationships between strategies for 3-numbered addition and knowledge of commutativity

	Strategy 1 (grouping)	Strategy 2 (linear)	Total
Knew commutativity	50	11	61
Did not know commutativity	0	16	16
Total	50	27	77

addend is always counted before the second. Hence, 3 + 4 will be counted as 1, 2, **3**, 4 (1), 5 (2), 6 (3), 7 (**4**). CAL is similar to CAF, except the larger addend is counted first. 3 + 5 solved using CAL is counted as: 1, 2, 3, 4, **5**, 6(1), 7(2), 8(**3**), where the numbers in brackets represent the smaller addend. COF and COL are counting on strategies. The counting begins with the first addend and the larger addend, respectively, hence saving the work involved in counting from 1 to the appropriate first count.

For solving 3-term problems (like 4 + 8 + 4), the *order* in which the subjects carried out the addition was noted. They used one of the following basic strategies:

(i) Performed the addition in any order. They *grouped* any two of the three numbers, and added them first. Hence, in a problem like $a + b + c$, they did either $a + b$ or $a + c$ or $b + c$ first.

(ii) Performed the operations from left to right (linear strategy).

Table 6.1 is a comparison of the above strategies used by children who used the concept of commutativity and those who did not. It indicates that knowledge of commutativity and use of grouping are strongly related. Not knowing commutativity implies not using grouping.

Table 6.1 shows that none of the subjects who did not know commutativity used grouping, and all the students who used grouping knew commutativity. This indicates that use of commutativity is a necessary condition for use of associativity. In addition, commutativity is not a sufficient condition for using grouping. The results show that of the 61 students who knew commutativity, 82% of them used grouping on the 3-numbered problems. The 11 students who knew commutativity, but did not extend it to 3-term problems suggest that there is a gap between knowledge of a concept, and its application. If it was not for this gap, commutativity would be a necessary *and sufficient* condition for grouping.

Furthermore, of these 11 children, there were three who did not use the grouping strategy, but showed explicit knowledge of the concept. Two of them revealed this by not computing the answer to the second of these problems again:

$$6 + 8 + 2 = 16 \ (8 + 6 = 14, + 2 = 16)$$
$$2 + 8 + 6 = 16$$

When asked how he had done this, one of them replied:

"You repeated the question".

The third subject solved $3 + 2 + 3$ using the linear strategy ($3 + 2 = 5$, $+ 3 = 8$). When asked for any other way of doing this problem, she replied:

"Can also do $3 + 3$ first and then add 2".

The performance of these three children shows that absence of a particular strategy does not imply absence of knowledge of that strategy. Gelman and Gallistel (1978) provided empirical evidence of children who appeared to lack understanding of a concept on one task and showed performance consistent with the concept on another task. This implies that children do not always use their conceptual knowledge. Some possible reasons for this are:

(i) they do not think of the concept at the time. For example, in case of commutativity:
"I knew it but I calculated it again because I didn't think of it".

(ii) even if they are aware that a particular concept is applicable, they know that they will get the same answer whether they use it or not. For example, there were a number of children in the commutativity tasks who knew the concept and were computing the answers to the second of the commutative pairs of problems. They were doing this so that they could check their answers to the first problem.

(iii) they have not reached the stage in the development of the concept where they can apply it.

The study indicated that the acquisition of associativity and commutativity are interrelated. Evidence for such indication was provided by children who were using commutativity for small numbers only (that is, their knowledge of the concept was not fully developed) and were using grouping on 3-term problems. There were also children who applied commutativity to 3-term problems partially – only to the first two addends. There was not a single child who was noted for using grouping (commutativity or associativity) on 3-term problems and not using commutativity on 2-term problems. This shows that a complete

understanding of associativity follows from understanding of commutativity. (A more detailed account of the study is presented in Devi
1990.)

Based on the results of the study reported above, production-rule
models of children's strategies for solving arithmetic problems like 5 + 6
and 8 + 5 + 9 have been implemented. The goals of the modelling are as
follows:

(i) to understand and clarify the details of children's performance.
(ii) the use of the models to support the implementation of an ITS.

The following section describes PALM, which simulates children's
strategies at different stages of development using production rules.

3   PRODUCTION-RULE MODELLING

PALM represents an individual's observed problem-solving strategies by
a set of fine-grained rules. A rule is of the form:

condition (s) → perform action (s)

where 'conditions' represent a specific state in the problem-solving
process and 'perform action' represents the step in the solution that is
carried out at that particular state. The results of the actions are stored in
working memory; the working memory is updated after each action. The
updated working memory shows the stage in the problem-solving process
that has been reached. The state of the memory is matched against the
condition sides of the production rules in order to select the next rule to
'fire'. At this stage, more than one rule could match the memory items.
To select one of the possible rules, PALM uses the following conflict
resolution strategies:

(i) Refraction – a rule cannot fire if its actions will produce results that
are already present in the working memory. Before a rule is selected
to 'fire', its actions are evaluated to check for this.
(ii) Recency – select a rule which matches to the most recent item in
working memory.
(iii) Rule ordering – if there are more than one applicable rules after
applying the first two resolution strategies, then select the first of
these rules.

In the process of solving a given problem, the interpreter performs the
cycle of matching rules against working memory items, selecting a rule
and 'firing' it, until either an answer is reached, or there are no more
rules to 'fire'.

The models are intended to be used for recognizing students' strategies in an ITS so that the ITS can then offer better alternative strategies. One of the reasons for choosing production-rule formalism is this application of the models. In an ITS, the tutorial goals can be represented as production rules as well, where the left hand sides of the rules would be the models representing students' strategies and the right hand sides would be the appropriate tutoring actions. The student's input is compared with the left hand sides of the rules. The implications of the models for ITS are discussed in Section 5.

Furthermore, this formalism was chosen because of the ability of production systems to learn new rules. The collection of papers in the book edited by Klahr et al. (1987) demonstrates this capability of production systems. PALM's attempt at modelling transition from one knowledge state to another is discussed in Section 4.

3.1 The representation

There are several possible ways of representing the example problems and the rules. The formal representation that is used in arithmetic is one example:

example problem: 4 + 5
example rule: A + B → ‹action›

The description language needed to be chosen carefully because PALM includes a learning component (see Section 4). We needed a representation language that describes the example problems, and has the potential of describing generalizations of examples. The descriptors chosen to describe problem states are *(number A X), (adjacent X Y)* and *(used A X)*, where *(number A X)* represents a number X, whose position in a given problem is represented by A; *(adjacent X Y)* refers to X and Y being next to each other, that is the difference between their positions, A and B, is 1; and *(used A X)* marks the numbers that have been added. For example, the problem 4 + 5 would be represented as:

(number 1 4) (number 2 5) (adjacent 4 5).

A rule for adding two numbers is represented as follows:

(number A X) (number B Y) (adjacent X Y) (not (used A X))
(not (used B Y)) → *(do addition)*

that is, add two numbers that are adjacent to each other, and that have not already been added. The 'do addition' part of each rule consists of a detailed addition strategy.

The above representation was chosen, especially the predicate 'adjacent', so that the models of problem-solving behaviour are restricted to solving 2-term problems only. They are not general enough to solve problems with more than two addends. In order to solve such problems, the program learns to construct new rules. To do this, it needs a representation that captures all the information required for solving 2-term problems, so that it can handle new problems with little restructuring of its existing knowledge.

In the following subsections, we discuss each component of the rules, and the students' performance that they simulate.

'Used'

When children count with concrete objects, they normally put to one side the set of numbers that they have finished counting, in order to distinguish it from the set(s) that remain to be counted, so that they do not count the items in a set more than once. The production-rule modelling needed a way to keep a record of this as well, in order to avoid the problem of the rules matching the same numbers. Hence, when numbers are added, one of the actions of the rules is to mark the numbers as they are used. This is done by adding to the working memory the facts that the numbers (on the condition side of the rule) that have just been added, are now used. For example:

$$(number\ A\ X)\ (number\ B\ Y) \ldots (not\ (used\ A\ X))\ (not\ (used\ B\ Y)) \rightarrow$$
$$\ldots (used\ A\ X)\ (used\ B\ Y).$$

On the condition side, the rule states: 'if there are two numbers that *have not* been used' and on the action side: 'do the addition and add to the working memory the facts that these numbers *have* been used'.

Furthermore, the 'used' clauses provide a means for deciding the state at which a problem has been solved. The rule interpreter, at each cycle of rule firing, checks whether the solution state has been reached. The addends in the given problem are compared with the addends that have been used. When all the addends have been used, and there is an additional (resulting) number, then the problem has been solved.

Indexing

Related to the problem of distinguishing the used and unused numbers, we also have to distinguish two or more addends that have the same value (e.g. 3 + 3). This, again, is a distinction that children (perhaps unconsciously) take into account. When counting 3 + 3, with concrete objects or using fingers, they count out *two* sets to represent each 3.

When using the 'counting on' strategy, one 3 is used as the number from which to start counting; the other 3 represents the number that is counted on. The two threes are somehow different. For making this type of distinction explicit in the modelling, each number in a problem is given a unique index (a place holder). Hence, 4 + 7 + 4 is represented as *(number 1 4) (number 2 7) (number 3 4)*. If the numbers are not given a unique index, then after doing 4 + 7, in 4 + 7 + 4, the first 4 is used, and the remaining 4 will never get matched, since the conditions in the rules specify that a number matches only if it is not used, and the two 4's are not distinguished. Indexing marks the 4's as two different ones.

Negation

The condition part of the rules may contain negated items. Negated items are those that are preceded by *'not'*s. Negation is used as a condition in rules to provide constraints for the items in working memory that can be matched. One such constraint is 'match a condition only to those working memory items to which it has not matched before'. This is achieved by adding a clause(s) which specifies the result of the condition(s) to the working memory and having the negation of the clause in the conditions. For example, adding the *used* clause to the working memory and adding the negated condition, *not used*, as a constraint to the rules. A negated condition is handled by matching the non-negated condition and adding the result of the match to a global variable (referred to from here-on as *nots*) and comparing it to the matches from the other condition-clauses (referred to as *previous_bindings*) of the rule. *Nots* contains a list of instantiations of items in working memory on which a rule is restricted to get instantiated. *Previous_bindings* is the list of successful bindings to which the rule can fire. After matching each clause, any item that exists in both *nots* and in *previous_bindings* is removed from *previous_bindings*, since it is not consistent with all the condition clauses. This is illustrated further with the following example, where the left-hand side of a rule has one negated condition and the working memory contains four elements:

conditions: *(number =I1 =X) (not (used =I1 =X))*
working memory: *(number 1 7) (number 2 7) (used 2 7) (used 3 14)*.

The first condition instantiates *previous_bindings'* to: $((=I1\ 1)\ (=X\ 7))$ and $((=I1\ 2)\ (=X\ 7))$. The second condition instantiates *nots'* to: $((=I1\ 2)\ (=X\ 7))$ and $((=I1\ 3)\ (=X\ 14))$, i.e. we wish to exclude numbers 7 and 14 as successful bindings of X. Comparing the two lists, $((=I1\ 2)\ (=X\ 7))$ is common and is removed from the *previous_bindings* list. Hence, at this stage the set of bindings that is consistent with the two condition clauses is $((=I1\ 1)\ (=X\ 7))$. (The conditions required a number that is not used.

There is one item in the working memory, *(number 1 7)*, that satisfies these conditions.)

3.2 Two-term problems

In this section, we describe simulations of children's strategies for solving problems like 4 + 5, that were observed in the empirical studies.

Strategies

The following is the basic rule template for all the strategies for 2-term addition:

> *(number a x) (number b y) (adjacent x y) (not (used a x))*
> *(not (used b y))* → *(do addition)*

where 'do addition' solves a given problem using one of the observed strategies.

For each strategy, the condition sides of the rules are the same. The 'do addition' part models the different strategies. These are CAF, CAL, COF, COL (discussed in Section 2). Note that all strategies are equally applicable – there is no attempt to model choice of strategy at this stage. Each of these strategies also has the alternative, 'copy the answer to the previous problem' (for the case of commuted pairs of problems). This is to model the strategies of those pupils who recognize the similarity of the sums in such pairs of problems and do not compute the answers to the second of the problems.

The following set of rules model the COL strategy:

> *(number i1 x) (number i2 y) (adjacent x y) (not (used i1 x)) (not (used i2 y))*
> → *(col i1 x i2 y)*
> *(col i1 x i2 y)* → *(fn coladd i1 x i2 y)*
> *(addd i1 x i2 y)* → *(fn addd x y) (used i1 x) (used i2 y)*

where function names are preceded by *fn*. Function *coladd* takes the two addends as arguments and returns *addd i1 x i2 y*, where *x* is the larger of the addends. This is because the aim of the COL strategy is to start from the larger addend. *Fn addd* computes the sum of the two addends. For example, for the problem 7 + 9 the first rule fires, and *col 1 7 2 9* is added to the working memory. This result matches the left-hand-side of the second rule, whose action evaluates *fn coladd* to *addd 2 9 1 7*. At this stage the third rule fires, evaluating fn addd which adds the 7 to the 9.

Efficiencies

Of the observed strategies, some are more efficient than others. One of the aims of an ITS in the domain of arithmetic is to help children make choices between the more and less efficient strategies. To be able to do this, the system needs to know which strategy is more efficient for a given problem. Thus, the production-system modelling includes a simulation of the efficiencies of the different strategies. The efficiencies are based on the amount of work involved in each strategy, and the demand on a child's memory. The amount of work depends on the number of counts, which depends on the size of the addends. The demand on memory is the effort required for keeping a record of the numbers that have been counted and that are left to be counted. The lower the efficiency value, the more efficient the strategy. For the problem, A + B, the amount of work involved in solving it using the CAF strategy is A + B (since all the numbers are counted, starting from 1). The demand on memory is a fraction (for example 1/10) of B. It is B because B is the addend that is counted second and as the counting proceeds, one needs to keep a record of how many of B is counted. Hence, for CAF, the efficiency value is A + B + a fraction of B. For CAL, the amount of work is the same as that of CAF, and the memory demand is a fraction (same as that for CAF) of the smaller one of the two numbers, A or B. For COF, the efficiency is the second addend, which is the number of counts. For the COL strategy, it is the smaller one of A and B.

The 'copy the answer to the previous problem' strategy is the most efficient (but can only be applied in special cases). Using these criteria for determining efficiencies, for a sample set of problems, the order of the strategies, from the most efficient to the least, is as follows:

> 'copy the answer to the previous problem'
> COL
> COF
> CAL
> CAF

3.3 Three-term problems

Strategies

From the empirical work, children's strategies for solving 3-term problems, based on the order in which the additions were carried out, can be categorized into either *grouping* or *linear* strategy (described in

Section 2). Each of these two general strategies includes other more specific strategies. For example, the linear strategy includes 'counting all' as well as 'counting on'. With the grouping strategy, once the two numbers to be added first are selected, the sum of these two numbers is recalled from memory if it is known as a number fact. The simulation of this part of the strategy is done by looking up a table which represents children's number facts. If the sum is known as a number fact, then this sum has to be added on to the third addend. This is done by using one of the two-term strategies described in Section 3.2 above. If the sum of these two addends is not known, then the problem is two 2-term additions. For our purposes, we only note whether a child solves the problem in the order in which it is written (i.e. linear strategy), or he or she ignores the order and uses the grouping strategy.

The following rule template models the linear strategy, where 'do addition' is one of the 2-term strategies:

(number A X) (number B Y) (not (used A X)) (not (used B Y))
$\rightarrow$ (do addition)

The rule instantiates to the first two numbers in the given problem, and the action part adds the two numbers giving another number as the result. The above rule fires again, this time instantiating to the resulting number and the third number in the problem, resulting in the solution to the problem. For example, for the problem 3 + 4 + 7, the rule fires on (number 1 3) and (number 2 4). The action of carrying out the addition is done by one of the 2-term strategies. Most of the children who used linear strategy used either CAF or COF strategy. Some used CAL or COL strategy. After performing the two-term addition, the result 7 is added to the working memory, with an arbitrary index 0 attached to it. The state of the working memory at this stage is:

(*(number 3 7) (number 0 7) (used 2 4) (used 1 3) (number 2 4)*
(number 1 3))

The above rule fires again, on *(number 0 7)* and *(number 3 7)*. The addition is performed using the same 2-term strategy as that used on the first two addends, resulting in *(number 14)* as the solution to the problem. This leaves the state of the working memory as follows:

(*(number 0 14) (used 3 7) (used 0 7) (number 3 7)*
(number 0 7) (used 2 4) (used 1 3) (number 2 4) (number 1 3))

For the grouping strategy, the left-hand side of the above rule requires three numbers, and the 'do addition' part involves trying out the different combinations of two numbers to find out if their sum is already known. The trace in Figure 6.1 shows the actions of a sequence of rules that 'fire'

---

1) Group-first 9 6 4

2) Lookup unsuccess 9 6

3) Group-second 9 6 4

4) Lookup success 10 9

5) Part-answer 10, Left-over 9

6) Count-on-from-larger 10 9

7) Answer 19

Fig. 6.1 Trace of 'actions' for grouping strategy on 9 + 6 + 5.

---

for solving the problem 9 + 6 + 4, using the grouping strategy. To decide which two of the three numbers to add first, the model tries all the three combinations (9 + 6, 6 + 4 and 9 + 4), looking up a working memory of known facts each time to find out if it knows the sum of the two numbers, until it succeeds. The second line of the trace, 'lookup unsuccess 9 6', means that the program does not have 9 + 6 as a prestored known fact. The result of a successful 'lookup' is 'part-answer' of the two addends and the 'left-over' addend. At step 4, 6 + 4 = 10 is known as a number fact. At this step, the interpreter records that 6 and 4 have been used. Step 5 tells us that there is a number left over (not used). Step 6 is the result of a rule which combines a 'part-answer' and a 'left-over' addend to make a 2-term problem. The two numbers are then added using the 'count-on from the larger addend' strategy to get the final answer. The 9 is used at this step. At step 7, the program halts, since the three addends have been used and there is a resulting number (19).

Efficiencies

The efficiencies determined for the strategies for solving 3-term problems are dependent on the problems concerned. One strategy might be more efficient than another for a particular problem, whereas the opposite might be true for another problem. For most problems, the grouping strategy is more efficient than the linear strategy. For the linear strategy, the efficiencies are calculated in a similar way to that for 2-term strategies. The grouping strategy requires grouping two of the three addends, for which the sum is either known (as a number fact), or is easier/faster to calculate. The amount of effort needed to group two numbers, and to lookup the known sum, is a fraction of that required to calculate the sum.

The empirically identified strategies for solving addition problems have been simulated using production rules. The models are descriptions of children's strategies. They do not explain where such models come from and how they got there. In the following section, our attempt to model the transition process from one model to another, is discussed. PALM goes through a learning phase in order to solve certain problems when it does not have the explicit rules for solving them.

PALM's cycle of matching rules to working memory items, conflict-resolution strategies, etc. remain the same with or without the learning component added to it. PALM uses the learning component when none of its current rules apply, and the solution to a given problem has not been reached.

4 LEARNING

We start with PALM being able to solve 2-term problems like 3 + 5, and not being able to solve 3-term problems. The ability to solve 2-term problems is represented as a set of production rules. When faced with a 3-term problem, like 3 + 4 + 5 (a problem which is of the type that it has not encountered before), none of its current rules are applicable. As a result of this failure, the program learns by generalizing its existing rules. It uses the rules for 2-term problems as prerequisite knowledge for solving 3-term problems. It also learns strategies that are more efficient than the ones that it already knows, by using the concept of minimizing the amount of work done. Figure 6.2 is an outline of the learning components of PALM. Sections 4.1 and 4.2 describe these learning.

4.1 Failure-driven learning

Learning in PALM is driven by failure when there are no rules that are applicable to its current problem-solving state. The program tries to adjust its existing knowledge to apply to the new situation. After solving 2-term problems, when faced with a 3-term problem, like 3 + 4 + 5, none of its current rules are applicable. The exisiting knowledge in this case is the rules for solving 2-term problems. An example of such a rule is:

(number a x) (number b y) (adjacent x y) (not (used a x)) (not (used b y))
$\rightarrow$ *(do addition)*

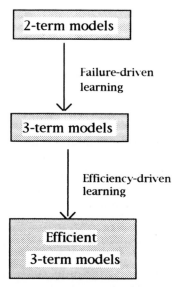

Fig. 6.2 The learning components of PALM.

The above rule adds two numbers that are adjacent to each other. It applies to 3-term problems to get only a partial solution. For example, for the problem 5 + 4 + 5 (represented as (number 1 5) (number 2 4) (number 3 5)), the rule applies to 5 + 4. The next step is to add the resulting 9 and the remaining 5. PALM is not able to do this because the two numbers are not adjacent to each other. At this stage, the program applies its learning mechanism. It uses one of the rules of generalization, called *dropping condition rule* (Michalski et al. 1983). The dropping condition rule makes a rule more general by deleting one or more of its conditions. For example, the following set of rules is a model for one of the strategies for solving 2-term problems:

(number i1 x) (number i2 y) (adjacent x y) (not(used i1 x)) (not(used i2 y))
  → *(col i1 x i2 y)*
(col i1 x i2 y) → *(fn coladd i1 x i2 y)*
(addd i1 x i2 y) → *(fn addd x y) (used i1 x) (used i2 y)*

Given the problem 7 + 15 + 6, PALM applies its 2-term rules in an attempt to solve it. The following is a trace of the actions after the above rules are executed. The function *SSTART* starts the execution of the program:

(SSTART '((number 1 7) (number 2 15) (number 3 6)))
(1) (adjacent 7 15)

(2) (col 1 7 2 15)
(3) (addd 2 15 1 7)
(4) (number 0 22) (used 2 15) (used 1 7)

The first step is a result of domain knowledge, which contains the definition of adjacency:

(number 1 x) (number 2 y) ⟶ *(adjacent x y)*

The program stops after the two-term rules solve 7 + 15. There are two reasons for the interpreter to come to a 'halt'. Firstly, if the problem has been solved, and secondly if there are no more applicable rules. In the example above, the program stops because of the latter. The working memory at this state is as follows:

((number 0 22) (used 2 15) (used 1 7) (addd 2 15 1 7) (col 1 7 2 15) (adjacent 7 15) (number 1 7) (number 2 15) (number 3 6))

In order to complete solving the problem, (number 3 6) and (number 0 22) need to be added. The first rule above should match to these two numbers, but it cannot since 22 and 6 are not adjacent to each other. PALM generalizes its rules by dropping one or more conditions of its rules. To choose a condition(s) to drop, the it assesses them to find the conditions that probably caused premature halt of the system. This is done by evaluating whether a condition matches the current state of the working memory or not. The preferred conditions to drop are those that do not match. In the above example, the process of finding out whether a condition matches or not returns:

((yes yes no yes yes) (no) (no))

The three lists correspond to the three rules listed above. The list shows that the third condition in the first rule, and the only conditions in the other two rules do not match. The first rule that has a 'no' is the rule that is selected to be amended. The 'no-conditions' of this rule are deleted one at a time, until the rule is applicable. If it is not applicable, then the next rule to generalize is chosen until an amendment of a rule leads to all its conditions being satisfied. If this does not succeed, then PALM is not able to complete solving the given problem. If it is successful at changing a rule(s) that becomes applicable, then the problem solving continues from the point where the program had 'halted'. In the above example, from the list of 'yes' and 'no', the preferred condition to drop is the third one in the first rule. The set of rules is reset with the first rule amended to:

(number i1 x) (number i2 y) (not (used i1 x)) (not (used i2 y))

$$\rightarrow (col\ i1\ x\ i2\ y)$$

The interpreter continues with the cycle of matching, selecting and 'firing' rules, producing the following output:

(col 0 22 3 6)
(addd 0 22 3 6)
(number 0 28) (used 0 22) (used 3 6)

The interpreter, at this stage works out that the problem has been solved, and hence comes to a halt. The final number, 28, is the solution to the problem.

Note that the rule that is chosen for deleting a condition is the first one that contains a 'no'. A more meaningful means of choosing this rule is rule specificity – select the rule that contains the most number of conditions. A second means is to select the rule that has the least proportion of 'no's, implying a higher chance of such a rule to be satisfied. In the example, demonstrated above, all these selection strategies produce the same result, but this will not be generalizable, and hence a number of selection strategies might be desired.

4.2 Efficiency-driven learning

After the failure-driven learning, PALM is able to add numbers that are not necessarily adjacent to each other. For example, for the problem above, it can now add the two 5's together first. Since the numbers do not have to be adjacent to each other, the system can learn specific conditions for which two of the three numbers to add first in order to get the most efficient strategy. To begin with, there is a set of initial problem solving strategies, a set of operators that represent children's known facts and a given 3-term problem. The goal is to combine the initial problem solving knowledge and the known facts to achieve a strategy that is more efficient than the initial ones. The following is an example of a rule representing an initial strategy:

$$(number\ i1\ x\ )\ (number\ i2\ y)\ (not\ (used\ i1\ x))\ (not\ (used\ i2\ y))$$
$$\rightarrow (fn\ col\ i1\ x\ i2\ y).$$

The condition sides for all the initial problem solving strategies are the same. The action sides include the two-term addition strategies, COL (rule above), COF, CAL CAF and 'lookup answer'. The operators representing known facts are as follows:

(equal x y) – two of the three numbers are the same.
(equal (x + y) 10) – two of the numbers that add to 10.

(equal (x or y) 1) – one (or more) of the numbers is '1'.
(equal (x + y) z) – the sum of two of the numbers equals the third.
(equal x (y + 1)) – one of the numbers is 1 more than another.

The operators represent features of problems that children use for 'shortcut' in their strategies. The above set is by no means complete.

Given an input problem, PALM's efficiency-driven learning algorithm works as follows. The operators are tested against the problem to select those that are applicable. The selected operators are added as additional conditions to the left hand sides of the rules for each strategy. The problem is then solved using each strategy, and their efficiencies are compared. The most efficient ones are added to the list of rules, and the inefficient ones are eliminated. For example, initially, the problem, 5 + 7 + 3 would be solved using the linear strategy, that is by adding the 5 and the 7 first. After testing each of the operators, **(equal (x + y) 10)** is the only one that is applicable. It is added as a condition to each of the strategies. Note that the initial, more general rule is not replaced, since the newly learned rule only applies in specific cases. The new rule for the 'lookup answer' strategy, for example, is:

(number i1 x) (number i2 y) (not (used i1 x)) (not (used i2 y)) **(equal (x + y) 10)** → (fn lookup i1 x i2 y)

The input problem is then solved using all possible combinations of two-term strategies. Some of the combinations for solving 5 + 7 + 3 are:

(i) lookup 7 + 3 followed by lookup 10 + 5
(ii) lookup 7 + 3 followed by COL 10 + 5
(iii) lookup 7 + 3 followed by CAL 10 + 5
(iv) COL 7 + 3 followed by COL 10 + 5

After trying out all combinations, 'lookup 7 + 3 followed by COL 10 + 5' is the most efficient combination of strategies. The two 2-term rules representing this combination are

(number i1 x) (number i2 y) (not (used i1 x)) (not (used i2 y))
    (equal (x + y) 10) → *(fn lookup i1 x i2 y)*
(number i3 x) (number i4 y) (not (used i3 x)) (not (used i4 y))
    → *(fn col i3x i4 y)*

4.3 Discussion

The empirical investigation in Section 6.2 did not resolve how the transition from 2-term to 3-term strategies takes place. In addition, it is not possible to investigate this transition empirically since children either know 3-term addition or they don't. There isn't anything like 'they know 2 and a 1/2 term. . .'. The computational model of learning by generalization is one hypothesis of the transition.

There are some similarities between the failure-driven learning in PALM and the impassse-driven learning proposed by VanLehn (1988). Firstly, both methods assume that learning occurs at 'impasses'. Learning occurs when the current knowledge base is insufficient. Moreover, it is not just any incompleteness that causes learning. A person's problem solving must require a piece of knowledge that isn't there (VanLehn 1988). In PALM, failure-driven learning occurs when there are no explicit rules for solving certain types of problems. Secondly, after learning, both in PALM and in the case of impasse-driven learning, the procedure continues from where it was stuck.

In the method for finding conditions for grouping two of the numbers in a 3-term problem, only one condition has been considered at a time. An obvious extension to this method is to allow the addition of more than one condition. For example, 6 + 4 + 4, satisfies two of the conditions, (equal 4 4) and (equal (6 + 4) 10). In this case, learning more than one condition provides a more specific description of this particular type of problems.

The idea of finding specific conditions is like that of ACM (Langley et al. 1984). ACM learns by discrimination because it has negative instances as well. In PALM's condition finding process, there are only positive instances, since its focus is on *different* strategies, and not incorrect ones. Furthermore, ACM learns by discriminating positive instances of an operator from its negative instances over a set of examples. PALM, on the other hand, considers only a positive instance of an operator and only over one example.

For a model of learning of the mechanisms for the transition from one snapshot of human behaviour to the next, it has to be psychologically valid. There is no claim that the models described in this chapter satisfy this criterion. However, an attempt has been made to make them as plausible as possible. The empirical work was used to guide the algorithms, and to match outputs of the models. The prerequisite or domain knowledge, for example, the operators for efficiency-driven learning, was compiled from children's protocols. The end products of the learning models are simulations of children's performance.

In the failure-driven case, the learning modelled a mechanism for the transition from ability to solve 2-term problems to that of 3-term problems. No explanation of this type of transition has been provided in the past. The generalization mechanism described above is one hypothesis for such a transition. For the efficiency-driven case, the end-product is consistent with the behaviour observed in children.

In summary, learning models based on existing ones (Michalski's learning by generalization and ACM's condition learning) have been constructed. The above section described a model of failure-driven learning that has been implemented as a candidate mechanism for children's transition from ability to solve 2-term problems to that of 3-term problems. It also described the implementation of an efficiency-driven model of learning that learns to apply children's number facts to problems in order to save work in computing a sum.

5   IMPLICATIONS FOR ITS

The production-rule models can be used in an ITS for student modelling. They can be used to diagnose student's strategies. For the diagnosis, an interface, like the Graphical Arithmetic Description Language (Evertsz et al. 1988) will be needed for students to simulate their arithmetic problem solving and to communicate it to the ITS. The information gathered from such an interface can be compared to the production-rule models. The production-rule models are then used as a basis for tutoring. The tutor could use its knowledge of the simulated, functional efficiencies of strategies to assess the efficiency of the student's strategies, and if necessary, guide its students to use more efficient ones.

Note that the production-rule models represent procedural knowledge only. Conceptual knowledge consists of facts and their relationships. Procedural knowledge consists of rules, algorithms and strategies for carrying out tasks, or for solving problems. Evidence from my empirical work and from other research (Hennessy 1986, Resnick 1983) strongly suggests the need to make a distinction between these two types of knowledge. For example, in solving $5 + 8$, a child's algorithm of starting from 8 and counting on 5 is a display of his/her procedural knowledge. The related conceptual knowledge would be the concept of commutativity, i.e. 'it does not matter whether one starts counting from the first addend or from the second, the sum is the same'. Self (1988c) highlights the need for student models to include descriptions of conceptual knowledge in addition to purely procedural knowledge. For an ITS to cope with this problem, it has the production-rule models to diagnose the procedural knowledge; it must have a separate machinery to diagnose the conceptual knowledge. This machinery could be based on the modelling of tasks that were presented to the students in the empirical work, and the measures that were used to categorize the different levels of the concept of commutativity (Devi 1990). For example, a child who generalizes commutativity to subtraction, indicates that he or she possesses some knowledge of the concept. Furthermore, whether a child copies the previous answer on a task like:

$$47 + 58 = 104$$
$$58 + 47 = ?$$

provides an indication of whether he or she possesses the knowledge of commutativity or not. The tutorial rules could be represented as production rules, where the left hand sides would contain conceptual as well as procedural knowledge, and the right hand sides would contain the appropriate tutoring actions. The analysis of the conceptual knowledge associated with each strategy would provide more information for the tutor's feedback to the student. In order for the tutor to suggest alternative strategies, it would need to analyse whether or not the student had the prerequisite knowledge necessary for mastery of the new strategy.

There is evidence from literature concerning domains in which procedural knowledge is acquired before conceptual knowledge (Fusion & Hall 1983, Briars & Sieglar 1984, Baroody & Gannon 1984), and domains where the reverse is true (Gelman & Gallistel 1978, Gelman & Meck 1983, 1987, Greeno et al. 1984). From my experience of the empirical work, in the domain of arithmetic, it is difficult to establish which comes first. Perhaps further research in the field will help us to solve this dilemma. From what is known so far, I conclude that the important thing is that children should know both, and know the relationship between the two. Hence, the separate diagnosis of conceptual and procedural knowledge could be used by the tutor to help students to link the two types of knowledge, and hence facilitate their understanding of their procedures.

In this chapter, we have demonstrated how our empirical work and computational modelling approach allow us to understand a task before we hypothesize ways of teaching it. The computational modelling process includes an attempt at modelling transition from one performance level to another. Understanding the transition process should help a tutor to facilitate this process. Hence, an ITS that has mechanisms for transitions to more efficient strategies, could use this knowledge to guide its student to progress from his/her current level (strategy use) to the desired level (a more efficient strategy) more efficiently. Previous student models (e.g. Langley et al. 1984) have the problem of not explaining how a student arrives at a particular knowledge state. This limitation has been noted by other researchers (Hennessy 1989, Laurillard 1989, Brown & Burton 1978, Wenger 1987). A tutoring system that has the potential of explaining how a student gets to a certain knowledge state, could focus its tutoring on the student's underlying learning and thus hope to gain more profound pedagogical effects.

ACKNOWLEDGEMENTS

I am grateful to Mark Elsom-Cook and Tim O'Shea for their support in the development of this work, and to Rod Moyse for his helpful comments on drafts of the chapter.

7 Alternate Approaches to Medical Reasoning and Diagnosis

LAURENCE ALPAY

*Institute of Educational Technology,
The Open University, Milton Keynes, UK*

1 INTRODUCTION

Medical diagnosis is a complex skill to teach. There is not always only one correct way to diagnose a patient, but there are better or worse ways of doing it. Medical students usually have to develop their medical skill with experienced physicians as models of reference. Modelling medical problem solving computionally has mainly been done from an expert point of view. The research problem addressed here is to model explicit levels of medical expertise, that is, the viewpoints applied to the diagnostic task, and to determine how to use these viewpoints for tutoring.

This chapter reports on a system DEMEREST (DEvelopment of MEdical REasoning STrategies), a *developmental* student model component which describes successive stages in the development of clinical reasoning using multiple views of the diagnostic process, and which could ultimately be part of a medical tutor. The focus is on the development of reasoning strategies of the medical diagnostic process in the domain of orthopaedics. A set of strategies has been identified in the medical problem solving literature. Development of these strategies has been determined through an empirical study, and protocol analysis has been used to analyse the data. DEMEREST can diagnose a medical student's reasoning strategies, determine the student's level of expertise, and

KNOWLEDGE NEGOTIATION
ISBN 0–12–509378–0

generate a plan corresponding to the application of these strategies. Planning in artificial intelligence was used as a means of decomposing medical problem solving into a set of goals; the goals being associated with the reasoning strategies. By taking this approach, medical reasoning is viewed as a planning process. Each level of expertise corresponds to a view of the medical diagnosis process, and at each level of expertise the application of reasoning strategies and interactions of strategies results in the production of a plan.

The chapter is organized as follows. The first section provides the background to the design of the system. It gives an overview of intelligent tutoring systems in medicine, and the student models used. It also reports on the domain of medical diagnosis, and the development of medical expertise. The second section describes the system DEMEREST. This section specifies the reasoning strategies used, reports on an empirical study which aimed to capture the development of these strategies, and details the planning approach taken to construct the developmental model. In the last section, research directions to generate additional viewpoints of the medical diagnostic task which could be taken for further work are proposed. The main result of the research reported here is that the design of the system DEMEREST demonstrates the feasibility of modelling the development of medical reasoning strategies and its usefulness for student modelling.

2 INTELLIGENT TUTORING SYSTEMS IN MEDICINE

The development of intelligent tutoring systems in medicine has been expert systems oriented' (Alpay 1988). Given the increased development of experts systems in medicine (Clancey & Shortliffe 1984), such systems have been the main resources to the development of intelligent tutoring systems in medicine. The system GUIDON (Clancey 1979) illustrates this situation. GUIDON, which represents a significant milestone in the design of intelligent tutoring systems for teaching medical diagnosis, is based on the expert system MYCIN. Using GUIDON for educational purposes was not entirely adequate; the main problem being that the knowledge base of MYCIN was used to embody domain knowledge as well as teaching knowledge. GUIDON incorporates a subset student model whereby the student's knowledge and understanding of the domain is entirely represented in terms of the expert physician. Such a model is not sufficient to explain the student's reasoning. Not only may the medical student take a different approach to the expert physician, but also her reasoning is not static and evolves over a period of time.

In contrast, the idea put forward in the developmental user model attempts to depart from the expert perspective taken in the overlay student model (Alpay 1989a). The user model aims to maintain a representation of the current state of the student from the student's point of view by incorporating the clinical reasoning process of the student (Figure 7.1). Thus, the student's knowledge is not represented in terms of the expert physician. The tasks of the user model are to analyse the medical student's actions in terms of her reasoning processes, and to determine the student's level of expertise. In the context of tutoring, it is important for an intelligent medical tutor to know how the student progresses and how her reasoning develops. More importantly, one should be aware that medical students have various needs in their learning phase. Firstly, they need to strengthen their medical knowledge. Medical students have to learn a vast amount of factual medical knowledge. Recently, a system called QMR has been developed (Miller & Massarie 1989) that offers medical students a means to explore medical knowledge in a flexible way. QMR can operate as an electronic text book; its knowlege base which is vast, describes the clinical manifestations of some 600 diseases in the domain of internal medicine. Secondly, and more importantly to this research, students need to get feedback on their strategic knowledge. Students usually have access to feedback on their performance rather than their reasoning processes which are not taught as part of their preparation for clinical practice. Moreover, medical students are expected to learn increasing amounts of knowledge in ways that favour passive receptive learning instead of stimulating strategic methods or manipulating what they have learned.

3   MEDICAL PROBLEM SOLVING

Medical diagnosis has been studied from different approaches. Numerical models have provided ways in which medical information can be manipulated to reach the most likely diagnosis. In contrast, psychological models have provided a better way to understand and describe the medical diagnosis process. Within the psychological approach, medical problem solving has been studied from four perspectives (Alpay 1988), outlined below.

3.1   Generic form of medical problem solving

The generic form of medical reasoning corresponds to the hypothesis generation and testing model (Elstein et al. 1978). In this model it is

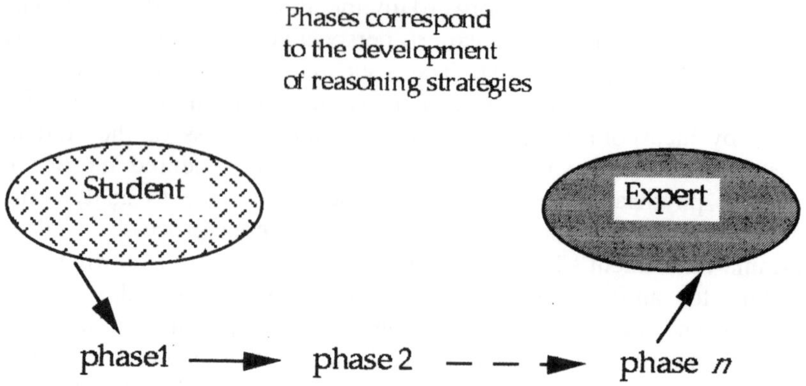

Phases correspond
to the development
of reasoning strategies

Fig. 7.1 Developmental user model.

suggested that clinicians use early cues to generate sets of tentative hypotheses for the patient's condition. These hypotheses are then used to structure and guide further interrogation of the case. Hypotheses provide expectations for additional clinical manifestations that should be present if a hypothesis is true for the patient case, and the findings of the patient are compared to expectations to select among the alternatives. Hypotheses can be restructured or changed as the diagnosis progresses.

3.2 Contents of medical problem solving

The study of the contents of medical reasoning (e.g. disease categories) has complemented the generic form by providing a model of the effects of medical knowledge on the diagnosis and the changes in such knowledge as individuals gain experience (Feltovitch 1980).

3.3 Medical problem solving as a process

A shift from the first perspective has been to study medical reasoning as a process. Three stages of the diagnostic thinking process were identified (Gale 1983). Stage 1, called 'initiation', refers to the interpretation of clinical information; stage 2, 'progress', corresponds to the progress of these interpretations, and stage 3, 'resolution', constitutes the final selection, rejection or not of the interpretations and re-interpretations of the first two stages. Medical problem solving has also been viewed as an interactive process of case understanding (Patel 1984), whereby the physician constructs a case representation from patient data, and then uses the case representation to access disease frames, narrowing down the range of possibilities and generating hypotheses.

3.4 Development of medical problem solving

A more recent approach has focussed on representing the development of an individual's medical diagnostic skill. The acquisition of medical diagnosis (in the field of radiology) has been represented as changes in the rules of interpretation used to interpret X-rays (Lesgold 1984). Another study related to that issue has characterized some phenomena of medical students' reasoning processes (Ramsden et al. 1988), and showed two categories of description, i.e. structuring and ordering that portray the different ways in which the information in diagnostic problems is handled by students.

3.5 Discussion

From this variety of models, a number of conclusions can be drawn. Firstly, there is a lack of uniformity in the methodologies, subjects and medical domains used to derive these models. Hence, there is no existing formal framework within which researchers agree to work. This also means that there is no formal paradigm of medical diagnosis, and no consensus on the exact nature of medical reasoning. Underlying each approach to medical diagnosis, researchers have taken different orientations (e.g. information processing, problem-solving, propositional analysis). Moreover, models of clinical reasoning have been *expert based*. That is, the models have been constructed from the expert physician's behaviour and then compared with less experienced clinicians. Although the literature describes differences between novices and experienced physicians, and reports on medical student's behaviours (e.g. Ramsden et al.), descriptions of the development of medical reasoning are lacking.

Various methods to teach medical diagnosis (e.g. problem-based learning, integrated curriculum, cognitive skills training) are practiced. However, there is little evidence of the teaching of *the models* of clinical cognition described above. In fact, medical students are rarely presented explicitly with any of these models of clinical reasoning. Rather, in most cases, medical students build their own models of clinical reasoning in an implicit way from comments and questions to and from the medical teachers.

For the research discussed here, the domain of orthopaedics was selected, principally for its characteristics. It is a difficult and vague domain, which is important in the medical curriculum but which is not taught well. In Great Britain, back pain affects a large number of the people; it is a symptom with a large number of different causes and various forms of management. Hence, in diagnosing a back pain problem the physician will be subject to apply a variety of reasoning strategies.

4   THE DEVELOPMENT OF MEDICAL EXPERTISE

In the past years, research in the area of 'expertise' has been studied in terms of three research directions: expert behaviour, novice behaviour, and differences between experts and novices, in various domains. Although research in this area indicates differences between novices and experts, it does not provide a clear account of the process of becoming an expert (Leventhal & Instone 1988).

The evolution from novice to expert is a developmental process. It occurs in stages and over a period of time. The concept of developmental models is not new and has been examined in different ways in the literature (see Alpay 1989b for a review). However, its application to medicine has been restricted to the development of medical expertise in radiology. Lesgold (1984) found that the differences between novices, intermediates and expert radiologists lie in the rules of film interpretations. At the novice level, the film analysis is bound to physical features captured by the image without context in which it appears. At the intermediate level, the radiologist can perceive complex anatomical details, and the constraints imposed by the film context. The intermediate radiologist can also construct a global model of the patient's medical conditions and conditions of the film production. At the expert level, the film interpretations tend be direct like the novices, but the interpretations contain contextual factors (e.g. chest form) with recognition interpretation and evaluation rules for each of these forms (e.g. over exposed chest). The investigation of the developmental process of medical expertise is not only limited to medical perceptual skill in the diagnosis of X-rays, but has also remained at a theoretical level. No attempt has been made to embody this concept within a medical tutoring system. Moreover, the work has not focussed on the development of reasoning strategies, and the changes of strategy over time.

5 REASONING STRATEGIES

Medical problem solving literature does not provide substantial information about the kinds of reasoning strategies medical students possess. Most of the research on medical reasoning has studied what expert physicians do (see Alpay 1988 for a review). The presumption has usually been that students use the same general form of reasoning as experts but with less powerful and organized domain knowledge (Gale & Marsden 1983, Feltovich 1980). From some observations of how medical students reason, seven reasoning strategies were identified and refined. Each strategy is defined as follows (the examples are from the domain of back pain):

- Generalization (GEN): generating a general hypothesis from a specific one (e.g. *mechanical cause of back pain* from *prolapsed intervertebral disc*).
- Specialization (SPEC): generating a specific hypothesis from a general one (e.g. *disc prolapsed* from *mechanical cause*).
- Confirmation (CONF): validating a hypothesis based on evidence and including it in the differential diagnosis (e.g. confirming *disc prolasped* if there is *tenderness*).
- Elimination (ELIM): ruling out an hypothesis based on evidence, and removing it from the differential diagnosis (e.g. eliminating *disc prolasped* if there is *no bony tenderness*).
- Problem refinement (PREF): refining the problem presented by the patient by gathering more details (e.g. refine *pain* to a*cute pain* or, refine patient case by asking about *social history*).
- Hypothesis generation (HGN): generating one hypothesis from a symptom, signs or test results (e.g. *disc prolapsed* from *pain in lower back*).
- Anatomically based (ANAT): generating an explanation (which may or may not contain an hypothesis) using anatomical knowledge (e.g. explaining pain in the leg by relating it to the activity of the sciatic nerve).

6 DEVELOPMENT OF REASONING STRATEGIES

Having identified a set of reasoning strategies from the literature, developmental stages of medical reasoning were examined from an empirical perspective. The aims were to (1) identify the reasoning strategies gathered from the literature which are applied during the medical diagnostic process, and (2) analyse the development of these strategies from novice to expert clinicians. Subjects ($n=10$) ranged from medical students to expert consultant in the domain of orthopaedics. The task of the subjects was to diagnose a patient. Although the setting was a simulated consultation, details of the patient case were extracted from a real case. Subjects' protocols were recorded, transcribed and analysed. The analysis of the protocols was done at two levels of coding.

The first level of coding (called low level coding) looked at medical categories (e.g. diseases of back pain, symptoms) and a planning category (i.e. goal such as check location of the pain) made during the consultation.The second level of coding (called high level coding) looked at the reasoning strategies. Each reasoning strategy was defined in terms of the low level categories. For example, a specific instance of specialization was defined in terms of the low level categories: hypothesis (e.g. *mechanical cause*, and *disc prolapsed*), and the decision (e.g. *check palpate the back*). The validity of the low level categories was assessed by a non-medically trained independent judge. The agreement of encoding with the independent judge of 71% was taken as a validation of the reliability of the low level coding.

Interactions between reasoning strategies at different levels of expertise reflect developmental stages of medical reasoning. We report here some of these interactions which are used to construct the model of developmental stages of the reasoning strategies. A more detailed analysis of the study can be found in Alpay (1990). One kind of interactions between strategies was found, referred to as *direct interaction*. In a direct interaction, one strategy is first applied and its result is then used to apply a subsequent strategy. An example of a direct interaction between HGN and SPEC is found in the 5th year student's protocol: the student generated the hypothesis *abnormality of the urinary tract* given the evidence that *a kidney was missing*, and then specialized into the kinds of abnormalities such as *double ureters*, *ectopic ureter*, and *kidney material lower down*.

Some of the interactions of strategies which were identified are:

- Interaction between HGN and SPEC which implies generating an hypothesis and then generating a more specific one, occurred at various levels of expertise, i.e. 3rd and 5th year students, senior house officer (SHO), general practitioner (GP), trainee in general practice (GP-T) and expert consultant.
- Interaction between HGN and ELIM which implies generating and hypothesis and then eliminating that hypothesis, was found from the level of 5th year student.
- Interaction between CONF and ELIM which implies trying to confirm

or eliminate an hypothesis was also found at the 5th year student level as well as the expert level.

- Interaction between PREF and HGN implies that the subject has generated from observation obs1 another observation obs2, which is then used to generate an hypothesis h. This interaction was found from the level of the 3rd year student.

At the level of the house officer, further developmental features have appeared: the interaction with the same strategy, that is, the repetition of the same strategy. Two interactions of this kind were found.

- In the first interaction, a repetition with PREF involves generating from an observation obs1 another observation obs2, and then uses obs2 to generate obs3, and so on. For example, the house officer generated from the observation *aggravating factor*, the observation *movements limited*, and then used *movements limited* to generate *bony pain*.
- In the second interaction, a repetition with HGN involves generating a hypothesis h1 from some observation ob1, and then using ob1 with some other observation ob2 to generate h2, and so on. For example, the HO generated the hypothesis *kidney infection* from the observations *feeling hot sweaty and sick* and *pain in the back*. The observation pain in the back was collected ealier in the consultation and before *feeling hot sweaty and sick*.

In the process of examining direct interactions of strategies, another kind of interaction was found, referred to here as indirect interaction. In an indirect interaction, the link between two strategies is at the immediate higher level of abstraction. For example, the 5th year student applied a protocol based refinement strategy to refine aggravating factors of the pain and then a hypothesis generation strategy to generate the hypothesis sciatica from radiation of the pain. These two strategies are linked at the abstract level of the characteristics of the pain because they include information about the characteristics of the pain, i.e. its aggravating factors and its radiation. In the case of an indirect interaction, the strategies will be applied from two different goals, but each will have in common a goal at an immediate higher level of abstraction. Indirect interactions have not been fully examined in the current research work.

It should be pointed out that at all levels of expertise, the beginning of the diagnostic reasoning process started with HGN and PREF, whereas at the more novice level (3rd and 4th year students) ANAT was applied at the beginning of the consultation. In summary, the results of the study give evidence that this set of strategies form a coherent system of reasoning processes for medical diagnosis: all the defined strategies have been applied, and the interactions connect and hold the strategies together to form the diagnostic process. Although some changes of strategy were reported, no evidence of monotonic development of reasoning strategies was found. By monotonic development, we mean an evolution of the strategies applied at each level of expertise. It should be stressed that with a limited number of subjects, this study has reported on some aspects of the development of the reasoning strategies, and has provided a conceptual basis for the developmental picture, rather than a full descriptive model of the development of these reasoning strategies.

7 MODELS OF DEVELOPMENT OF REASONING STRATEGIES

Following the results of the empirical work, the modelling of the development of strategy consists of building not one model but a number of models that show how medical diagnosis varies at different level of expertise. Each level of expertise incorporates a model of the reasoning strategies interactions constructed from the empirical study discussed in the previous section[1]. The models for novices (medical students at different levels of clinical training), an intermediate (HO), and an experienced physician (GP) are shown in Figures 7.2 and 7.3. The process of building these models is incremental, that is, each model is built as an extension of the model at the level below. By doing so, the changes that have occured from one level of expertise to another are made explicit. Changes can either be addition (e.g. level 3 – HGN ELIM) or modification (e.g. level 4 – HGN SPEC ELIM) of strategies and interactions of strategies. At the level of the 3rd and 4th year medical students the models are fairly simple; from the next level onwards, models become more and more complex.

7.1 Model of level 1

There were three direct interactions used to build up this model. The model shows that PREF is between ANAT and HGN. This representation was chosen because in most of the protocols, the beginning of the diagnostic process started with PREF and HGN. ANAT is the first

---

[1] Half of the protocols were used to build the model of changes of reasoning strategies; the other half was used to test it.

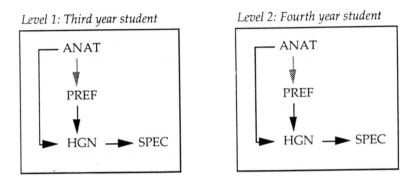

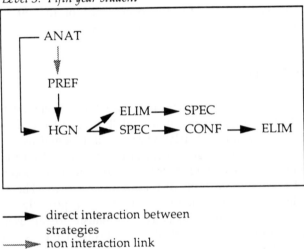

Fig. 7.2 Models of changes of reasoning strategies at various levels of expertise (Levels 1 to 3).

strategy in the model, since the level is the most novice one, and ANAT is a strategy that students used more than experienced physicians (even if not significantly). A consequence of building the model in that way was an extra link created between ANAT and PREF.

7.2 Model of level 2

This model contains fewer kinds interactions of strategies than the previous model as the student did not apply as many kinds of interactions as the 3rd year student. Since each model is constructed from the previous one this means that the level of the 3rd year is the same as the level of the 4th year. In other words, the interactions used by the 4th year student are already included in the model of the 3rd year student.

7.3   Models of levels 3, 4 and 5

These models contain additional interactions of strategies. In particular, one may notice, at level 4, the interaction of two similar strategies and the way in which two interactions of strategies from different levels can integrate. For example, one interaction found at level 3 is SPEC CONF ELIM, and another interaction found at level 4 is SPEC ELIM GEN. The former interaction includes the latter and is extended by one strategy (GEN). When the system tests for the occurrence of the interaction SPEC ELIM GEN, it will skip the strategy CONF.

ARCHITECTURE OF DEMEREST

The model of interactions of the reasoning strategies discussed in the previous section forms the developmental modeller part of DEMEREST (see Figure 7.4). The system DEMEREST, a developmental user model component of an intended intelligent medical tutor, is based on the idea of the developmental process, and is designed to model developmental phases of clinical reasoning in terms of reasoning processes. The system analyses the student's diagnostic actions, determines a possible level of expertise of the student and uses plans as a formalism to represent the student's reasoning processes. In particular, the tasks of the user model are (1) to diagnose the reasoning strategies that the student has used, (2) to identify development of these strategies that will help the system in determining the student's level of expertise, and (3) to produce a plan corresponding to the application of these strategies.

8.1   DEMEREST in context

The tasks of the user model could be supported by the other parts of an intelligent medical tutor. For the purpose of discussion, we assume that several main components of the tutor are available.

These are:

- the teaching module which determines what to teach, when to teach and how to teach the student;

Level 4: House Officer

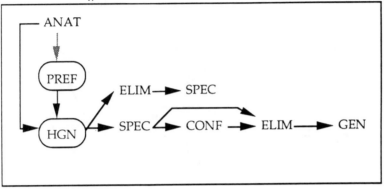

Level 5: General Practitioner

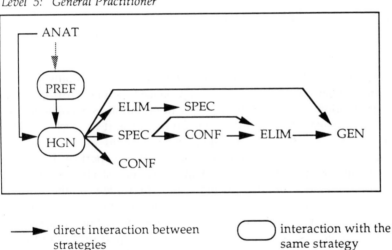

⟶ direct interaction between strategies
⟶ non interaction link
◯ interaction with the same strategy

Fig. 7.3 Models of changes of reasoning strategies at various levels of expertise (Levels 4 and 5).

- the domain module which contains the domain-specific knowledge, e.g. back pain knowledge;
- the user model which represents the student's understanding of the domain, i.e. in this research the student's diagnostic process;
- the interface which facilitates communications between the student and the tutor.

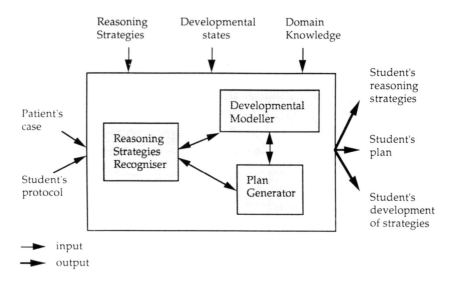

Fig. 7.4 Overview of the system DEMEREST

Once DEMEREST has identified the student's reasoning processes, determined her level of expertise and produced the plan corresponding to the application of the strategies, this information is passed on to the teaching module which will determine how to use it to teach the student further. In particular, the teaching module could propose alternative strategies and plans giving the student's level of expertise; it could also use the information about the student's reasoning strategies and level of expertise as a basis for advising and testing the student on the application of medical reasoning strategies. The student not only has the chance to reflect and get feedback on the performance of her medical reasoning, but also has access to various levels of medical expertise. For instance, let assume that the user model has diagnosed a fifth year student at level of expertise 2 and not 3 as expected since the student did not apply particular patterns of reasoning strategies specific to level 3. The teaching module may then gather the patterns of level 3 and presents them to the student through examples. A particular pattern can be generating an hypothesis (HGN) and then generating a more specific hypothesis (SPEC).

Given the nature of the task to teach (i.e. medical diagnosis), and the kinds of users that would be tutored (i.e. medical students), the role of the medical tutor should be to aid and advise the medical student, and let the student have control of the interaction, rather than forcing the student into a socratic tutoring session. Moreover, there is a time factor to take into account: from their third year, medical students spend a certain amount of time with patients, and may not always be able to sit in front of a computer screen for a long time. Hence, sessions between the tutor and the student should be flexible in length to allow the student to decide how long she wants to work with the tutor. In addition, as the student starts to see patients, she may want to go back to a particular patient case and get feedback on her diagnosis process. The tutor could help the student do so by making explicit the strategies that she has been applying. It should be pointed out that the domain module of the medical tutor contains back pain knowledge for each level of expertise, and not just for the expert's level as in other tutors. There is of course knowledge common to all levels since some pieces of information are used not just at one level of expertise, e.g. onset of the pain is considered at all levels of expertise.

8.2 Hand analysis of protocols for input to DEMEREST

Let us assume that the student has been interviewed and her protocol recorded and analysed manually by method of protocol analysis (rather than by machine). The student's protocol is thus transformed by hand analysis into a plan that can be understood by the system. The plan is made up of a set of goals of the student's diagnostic process. The input of this hand analysis is the student's protocol and the output is the student's plan in terms of goals. This hand analysis is done in the following manner: an interaction between the physician and the patient is selected, that is, a question/answer or a set of questions/answers (e.g. about the location of the pain) and a goal which can be associated with it is being defined (e.g. the goal is *check location of the pain*). The process of the interpretations of the protocols is related to the issue of plan recognition. The problem of plan recognition is:

"to take as input a sequence of actions performed by an actor, and to infer the goal pursued by the actor, and also to organise the action sequence in terms of a plan structure" (Schmidt et al. 1978, p.52).

Plan recognition is an ongoing research problem, a detailed discussion of which is beyond the scope of the research work reported here.

The results of the hand analysis of the student's protocol, that is, the goals of the student's plan serve as input data to the system. DEMEREST has three components, each described in the following sections: (1) the reasoning strategies recogniser, (2) the plan generator, and (3) the developmental modeller.

8.3 Reasoning strategies recogniser

Given a goal, the reasoning strategy recognizer identifies the strategy associated with it. Its inputs are a goal from the student's plan which was generated through hand analysis, and the set of reasoning strategies. The output is an *instantiation* of one of these reasoning strategies, that is, the context in which the strategy has been applied (e.g. the goal, the hypotheses generated, etc.). It should be pointed out that there may be more than one strategy associated with a goal. A strategy is instantiated by accessing from a given goal the necessary medical knowledge in the medical database that characterizes that strategy. An example of an instantiation of the hypothesis generation strategy applied by the 4th year student is showed below:

Strategy applied: HGN
Goal: check location of the pain
Observation: right sided back pain
Hypothesis: kidney problem

The student asked about the location of the pain, and being told by the patient that the pain is on the right side of the back, the student concludes that there may be a kidney problem.

8.4 Plan generator

The role of this component is to generate the student's plan. The inputs are the student's goals and the reasoning strategies she has applied, and the output is the student's plan. The plan contains the goals and their associated strategies in the order which corresponds to the student's diagnostic process during a consultation with a patient. By having different accounts of the clinical reasoning, that is, alternate plans of expertise, the appropriate information to bring the student from one level of expertise to another is made explicit. Moreover, by modelling the reasoning processes of the student, the student's own view of the problem is represented.

8.5 Developmental modeller

The role of this module is to identify the student's interactions of strategies, and determine her level of expertise. Given the student's goals, the developmental modeller not only generates the student's reasoning strategies (using the reasoning strategies recogniser), but also determines the student's level of development. The inputs are the student's set of goals, the set of reasoning strategies, the expected development of reasoning strategies (derived from the empirical study). The outputs are the reasoning strategies applied by the student along with their interaction and a possible level of expertise of the student. Since the developmental modeller contains models of clinical reasoning at different levels of expertise, it can match the student's reasoning with these models and determine the student's level of expertise.

9   AN A.I. PLANNING APPROACH

Planning in artificial intelligence was used as a means of decomposing medical problem solving into a set of goals; the goals being associated with the reasoning strategies. By taking this approach, medical reasoning is viewed as a planning process. In this planning approach, plans correspond to multiple views of the diagnostic process; each view being associated with a level of medical expertise. That is, for each level of expertise, different strategies and interactions of strategies have been applied. Hence by mapping the reasoning strategies and their interactions into plans, the system generates alternate plans.

9.1   Planning in medical diagnosis: related research

A number of studies have examined the issue of planning in the context of medical diagnosis. Kuipers et al. (1988) have shown that expert physicians make an initial decision at an abstract level, and go on to specify it more precisely. Miller (1975) has suggested that there are two distinct but closely related planning activities involved in taking a present illness[2]: data acquisition and diagnosis. Data acquisition planning specifies what data to look for next, whereas diagnosis planning specifies what to do with each piece of data once it has been obtained. Langoltz et al. (1987) have considered treatments of the patient management as a planning activity. Although the results of planning in medical diagnosis corroborate Kuipers's work on the use of planning by expert physicians,

---

[2] A present illness corresponds to a description of the patient's presenting problem. Taking a present illness is different from performing a complete diagnosis, in that it is the typical consultation a patient has with a general practitioner. The patient usually presents a 'chief complaint' that becomes the initial focus of the consultation, and diagnosis is based on only very low cost sources of information (such as patient history, physical examination and routine laboratory tests). High cost or high risk procedures that may be necessary for a complete diagnosis are not used.

the research reported in this chapter differs from Kuipers's and other studies for the following reasons: (1) it is concerned with the planning approach taken not only by experts but also by less experienced physicians including medical students, and (2) it focusses on the reasoning strategies that the physician has applied during her diagnostic process.

9.2   Representation of plans and planning process

A plan consists of a hierarchy of goals designed to achieve the desired goal, i.e diagnosis of the patient case. The goals represent the operators of the planner.

The structure of a goal is as follows:

- Name of the goal
- Preconditions of the goal
- Subgoals of the goal
- Action of the goal
- Effects of the goal

The name of the goal indicates what the goal to be achieved is. A precondition is a specification of the state of the goal that has occurred before the goal can be applied. A goal may be decomposed into a set of subgoals. An action is an action in the world which carries out a goal. An effect is a state of the world after an action has been performed. The effect of an action corresponds to some observations (signs, symptoms and test results). Attached to each name of a goal is the prefix check and to each action of a goal the prefix ask to distinguish between the composants of the goal. The prefix check is taken in a broad sense – check if the pain radiates, check if there is tenderness in the back, check for an X-ray of the back. The prefix ask is also taken in wide sense – asking the patient a question, asking for a test to be done.

As an example of these points, the decision to gather some information about the onset of the pain is represented as the goal below.

GOAL:
Name of the goal: check onset of the pain
Precursors of the goal: no radiation
Subgoals of the goal: none
Action of the goal: ask about the onset of the pain
Effects of the goal: onset of the pain this morning

A typical plan contains one or more goals to achieve (see Figure 7.5). The main goal is the diagnosis of a patient. Figure 7.5a shows an example of a plan. DEMEREST may be viewed as a non-hierarchical type of

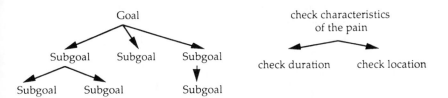

Fig. 7.5 The structure of a typical plan (Left). Right: An example of a plan.

planner. Unlike hierarchical planners, it does not generate a hierarchy of representations of plans in which the highest is a simplification of abstraction of the plan and the lowest is a detailed plan, sufficient to solve the problem. Instead, in DEMEREST all the goals are at the same level of abstraction, and the assumption made is that all goals are important to the diagnostic problem solving task.

The set of information present in a plan does not convey all the necessary knowledge to diagnose medical problems in general, and back problems in particular. There is a large body of medical knowledge that the plan representation cannot handle in a flexible way. Hence, in order to reduce this limitation, the goals of the plan are extended and complemented by two knowledge bases which form the medical knowledge of orthopaedics. The knowledge base of observations contains knowledge about signs, symptoms and test results of back pain. The knowledge base of diseases contains knowledge about diseases and clinical states of back problems. An example of how knowledge in these knowledge bases is encoded is given below: a symptom is of the form kinds(symptom, Symptom_name), e.g. kinds(symptom, right_sided_pain); an hypothesis is represented as kinds(hypothesis, Hypothesis_name), e.g. kinds(hypothesis, kidney_problem). The two knowledge bases are linked together with causes(observation, hypothesis), e.g. causes(right_sided_pain, kidney_problem).

The goals of the plan are linked to the knowledge bases of diseases and observations in the following way (see Figure 7.6 for example). An effect of a goal contains either a sign, a symptom or a test result. The effect is connected to the knowledge base of observations which contains also signs, symptoms and test results. These elements of the knowledge base are in turn linked to their associated diseases and thus linked to the knowledge base of diseases. For example, the effect *right_sided_pain* is a symptom found in the knowledge base of observations which is caused by the hypothesis *kidney infection* in the knowledge base of diseases. One advantage of this structure is that the goals and the medical knowledge applied are represented separately.

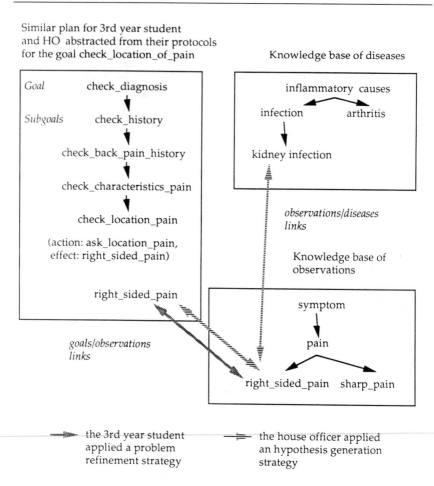

Similar plan for 3rd year student
and HO abstracted from their protocols
for the goal check_location_of_pain   Knowledge base of diseases

Fig. 7.6 Examples of plans and reasoning strategies.

The way a plan is processed is driven by the reasoning strategies that have produced it. In other words, associated with each goal of the plan are one or more strategies. Unlike the usual approach in AI planning, the building of the plan and its execution are intertwined: a reasoning strategy not only produces a plan, but also reflects the execution of the plan. Medical students as well as expert physicians apply different reasoning strategies which produce different kinds of plans. The presence of different reasoning strategies used either by the student or the physician mirrors the fact that goals of the plan have been manipulated in different ways.

For example (Figure 7.6), in the study reported earlier on, both the 3rd year student and the house officer had the same goal *check location of the pain* in their plans. However, the student applied a problem refinement strategy with that goal by considering location as part of a characteristics of the pain, while the HO applied an hypothesis generation strategy by generating the possible hypothesis *kidney infection*. In other words, in this particular case, the student was non-hypothesis directed, whereas the HO was hypothesis directed.

9.3 Interactions of goals

Goals rarely occur in isolation. In most cases, a problem is solved using a conjunction of goals. The interactions of goals are directly associated with the reasoning strategies applied to produce the plan, and represent the order in which the plan is being carried out. The kind of goal interactions modelled in the system are 'effect/precondition' interactions, that is, the effect of one goal is a precondition of another goal. In this kind of goal interaction, the achievement of one goal allows another goal to be carried out (Wilensky 1983). For example, consider the case of the 4th year student whose plan contained the following goals:

Goal 1 (4th year student):
    Name of goal 1: check radiation of the pain
    Precondition of goal 1: none
    Subgoal of goal 1: radiation of the previous pain
    Action of goal 1: ask about radiation of the pain
    Effect of goal 1: no radiation of the pain
Goal 5 (4th year student):
    Name of goal 5: check location of the pain
    Precondition of goal 5: no radiation of the pain
    Subgoal of goal 5: none
    Action of goal 5: ask about the location of the pain
    Effect of goal 5: right sided back pain

The student had asked the patient about radiation of the pain, and was told that there was no radiation (goal 1). Then the student asked the patient about the location of the pain, and was told that the pain is on the right side (goal 5). Once goal 1 had been ·activated and its associated reasoning strategy generated, the system is looking for a next goal to achieve to pursue the plan. To do so, the system takes the effect of goal 1 and searches for a goal (in this case goal 5) whose precondition slot is the same as the effect. Goal 5 can only be achieved if its precondition *no radiation of the pain* exists, that is, if goal 1 has already been achieved.

9.4   DEMEREST and planning for tutoring

By having a plan of the student's protocol, the tutor is given the appropriate information to help the student understand her plan. The decomposition of the student's reasoning strategies into a set of goals (associated with their corresponding strategies) that form a plan provides a representation of the student's view of the clinical problem. The student is able to reflect on her current plan and the tutor could assist her in manipulating and adjusting goals of her plan in various ways. Since a plan is a product of applying one or more strategies, the tutor could present the student with the instantiation of a strategy that has been applied, that is, the goal upon which the student was focussing, the hypothesis generated, the symptom or sign considered. Teaching what is a strategy is not enough. What is also important to the student is to understand the context in which a strategy was applied.

In addition, by combining different viewpoints of the diagnostic process (for a given patient case), that is, different levels of expertise, the student's understanding of that process might be improved. The tutor could help the student compare her plan with other plans from different levels of expertise. The tutoring system could decide to do this in the following cases:

Upon the student's request

For example, the student might want to view how the history taking was conducted at the GP level and relate her plan with the GP's plan.

Low expertise level

The student's level of expertise, determined by the tutor, is lower than the level that was expected. The tutor could show the student goals and interactions of strategies that can be applied at the student's expected level. This situation was illustrated earlier in the chapter.

Demonstrate higher level of expertise

The teaching strategy of the tutor might be to enhance the student's diagnostic processes by exposing the student to higher levels of expertise. Hewson (1986) has showed that medical students who were instructed to think like experts demonstrated an improvement in their diagnostic thinking. It might also be useful to expose students not only to expert level, but also to various levels of expertise that would to help them understanding the diagnostic task.

The tutor might not teach planning to the student, but rather might use planning as a way to analyse and decompose the diagnostic process and discuss it with the student. For example, there are a number of goals that can be applied for determining the characteristics of the pain, e.g. *check location of the pain, check radiation of the pain, check severity of the pain.* There are also a number of strategies that can be applied with these goals, e.g. hypothesis generation by generating from the observation *radiation of the pain* the hypothesis *sciatica*. The student will have applied some of these goals. The student may have done so in a routine manner, and the tutor may then examine with the student the goals for determining the characteristics of the pain and the strategies that can be applied with these goals which depart from the way the student applied them.

10 FURTHER RESEARCH DIRECTIONS

As mentioned in this chapter, each level of expertise provides a viewpoint of the medical diagnostic task. Additional viewpoints of the plan at each level of expertise could be achieved by classifying the physician's plan. The system could be extended to include a plan classifier. Plans could be classified in three dimensions of choice, each having two states: (1) global versus local, (2) abstract versus concrete, and (3) complete versus partial[3]. As the names of the plans suggest, each class of plans offers a different perception about the plans: a global plan contains the main goal, and its subsequent goals. A local plan relates to subgoals and actions at a certain position of the plan. An abstract plan involves only subgoals, whereas a concrete plan involves only actions. Finally, a complete plan includes all subgoals and actions, while a partial plan includes some subgoals and some actions. The classification of the student's plan would allow us to have different views of the student's reasoning. For instance, the student may have started her reasoning at a local level, and then progressed to other local plans. The student can also learn how complete or partial was her plan, what levels of abstractions her plan contained and the reasoning strategies she applied in the local plans.

With a classification of the student's plan, the tutor could help the student compares parts of her plan (and not just the whole plan) with other levels of expertise. For example, the student may view how the history taking (a part of the plan) was conducted at the house officer level

---

[3] This classification results from a combination of ideas in different literature sources; i.e. planning in medical diagnosis; planning in HCI (Human Computer Interaction) and AI planning.

and compare her plan with that of the HO. The student's protocol as well as the house officer's contain the goals *check characteristics of the pain* and *check previous back pain history*. On one hand, the student first has focussed on the first plan using goals *check duration of the pain* and *check severity of the pain* and then moved on to the second one. On the other hand, the HO has focussed on both local plans at the same time, applying a goal from one plan, e.g. *check duration of the pain*, and then another goal from the other plan, e.g. *check previous accident back*.

A preliminary analysis of the protocols collected in the empirical study showed the following plans classification: at all levels of expertise, each subject's protocol includes all the kinds of plans from the classification. Moreover, each subject's protocol contains the same global abstract plan which corresponds to the phases of the consultation (i.e. history, physical examination, investigation and treatment).

The differences of plans appear within each phase of the consultation. For example, in the history phase, the 3rd year student and the house officer have a similar abstract plan which contains the goals (*check back pain history, check past medical history, check social history, check medicines taken*). This similarity of plans at that level may be explained by the context in which both subjects work, namely the emergency room in the hospital. However, at a subsequent levels of the plan, this similarity disappears. The house officer has different partial plans (e.g. in goal *check past medical history*), and the ordering of the goals are also different (e.g. in goal *check characteristics of the pain*).

At the most novice level, the use of local plans is more emphasized than at other levels of expertise. For example, the 3rd year student's protocol contains a local plan with as its top goal *check back pain history*. The student reasoning focussed on that part of the global plan, and once that local plan was achieved went on to another local plan *check past medical history*. In contrast, other subjects reasoned with more than one local plan active at the same time, going back and forth to these plans. For example, the house officer started her reasoning by asking to the patient about characteristics of the pain (one local plan with its top goal *check characteristics of the pain*), then asked about previous back pain (another local plan with its top goal *check previous back pain*), and then went back to the previous local plan of *check characteristics of the pain*.

Completeness of the plans is not only related to how much knowledge one possesses, but also to how one selects this knowledge. Medical students in their 3rd and 4th years do not have much knowledge about back pain or about the procedures to carry out a back pain physical examination, whereas 5th year students already have some training in that area. The plans for physical examination of the 3rd and 4th year students are partial, while the ones of the 5th year students become more complete. Both the house officer and the GP know how to conduct the physical examination. Still the local plan for physical examination of the HO is more complete than the local plan of the GP. Surely, the local plan for physical examination of the GP is in reality complete (or almost so), but the active part of the local plan is only partial given the circumstances of the patient case. Thus, in the context of medical reasoning, producing a complete plan is not always desirable.

Reasons for applying partial plans in the context of Human Computer Interaction (Young & Simon 1987) can also be applied in the context of medical reasoning. One reason is related to the limitations of the problem solver's memory. Even if a physician knows about all she could do during a physical examination, she does not necessarily have to recall all of them in her working memory, or at least does not recall each detail for each physical examination action. The same is true for less experienced physicians. The difference may be in the way each chunk of information recalled is compiled in the long term memory. Another reason is that the physician may not know exactly what will happen as a result of a course of action. This is especially true of less experienced physicians.

11   CONCLUSIONS

This chapter has reported on an innovative approach to modelling the development of expertise for teaching in medical diagnosis, and has described a system DEMEREST that diagnoses medical students' reasoning strategies and determines their level of expertise. Given the small number of subjects upon which the development of reasoning strategies was built, the research has not offered a complete descriptive model of the development of these strategies, but rather has brought to highlight several aspects of this developmental process. Moreover, it has showed the feasibility and the usefulness for ITS of developmental user models. Planning in artificial intelligence was used as a means of decomposing medical problem solving into a set of goals; the goals being associated with the reasoning strategies. By taking this approach, medical reasoning is viewed as a planning process. The research has taken advantage of already existing planning techniques to build the model, and no new planning mechanism has been proposed. Adopting a planning approach to model medical reasoning has provided a means to investigate further the issue of planning in the context of medical diagnosis.

Tutoring in terms of the developmental process has several implications for tutoring systems: firstly the developmental user model provides the tutoring system with a decomposition of student's clinical reasoning into a set of goals that form a plan and which contained the reasoning strategies and interactions of strategies applied by the student. Secondly, by having different accounts of clinical reasoning, that is, alternate plans for different levels of expertise, the tutoring system has appropriate information to bring the student from one developmental stage to a next one. Furthermore, since the developmental user model is able to diagnose the reasoning strategies applied by the student, the tutoring system is given appropriate information to teach the student from the student's view point on the domain.

Medical students are mainly taught medical knowledge, and little about medical problem solving methods. The developmental user model offers the possibilities to tutor the student with more than one view point of the clinical reasoning, and to improve the student's understanding of medicine by combining different representations of clinical reasoning. Furthermore, by making explicit and available developmental stages of the student's reasoning, the system gives the student a means to reflect on her own medical diagnostic processes.

Previous work using other domains than Medicine has been also taken a developmental approach to tutoring. For instance, QUEST (White & Frederiksen 1986) contains successions of mental models that correspond to increasing levels of expertise about the principles of the domain (electrical circuits) rather than a given device. These causal model progressions serve as a basis for an intelligent learning environment that helps students learn to predict and explain circuit behaviours. Although we share with White and Frederiksen the view that models that capture some of the progressions from novice to expert can play a valuable role in the design of educational systems, we have addressed that issue in a different way. We have presented DEMEREST as a student model component of a medical tutor, whereas QUEST is a system in which the student model, the tutor and the domain simulation are incorporated within the single model that is active at any point of learning. Moreover, the nature of the domains differ greatly: unlike diagnosing an electrical circuit, diagnosing a medical patient involves using incomplete and uncertain knowledge. The focus of the development also differs: DEMEREST models changes of medical reasoning strategies over time, while QUEST models principles of circuits behaviors as they become more complex.

The research work in progress with DEMEREST has demonstrated the importance and potential of designing intelligent tutoring systems based upon development of expertise and its acquisition. In that respect, it supports the research work accomplished with QUEST. An adequate representation of the domain to be learnt can not only improve the student's understanding but also prevent misconceptions (White & Frederiksen 1986). Moreover, such systems enhance the learning environment for the students by providing them with multiple views of the domain, reflection and feedback on their reasoning processes, and allow instructional strategies to be investigated.

8 The Computer as a Constructorium: Tools for Observing One's Own Learning

PIERRE DILLENBOURG

Faculté de Psychologie et des Sciences de l'Education, Université de Genève, Switzerland

1 THE PEDAGOGIC FACET OF KNOWLEDGE NEGOTIATION

Knowledge negotiation (KN) defines a particular style of interaction between a learner and an educational computing system (ECS). The choice of a particular type of interaction is a complex decision process based on knowledge about the domain, the learner and the pedagogical methods. The KN approach has its specificity with respect to each of these three components. We briefly describe the two first, the domain and student models, and develop this chapter around the third one, the pedagogical approach.

If we consider the domain model, KN tackles philosophical issues about the very nature of knowledge: the Platonic view of knowledge, that underlies the widespread idea of expertise, is progressively abandoned for a view of knowledge as the temporary product of social processes (Carley 1986).

Concerning the student model, KN addresses some major criticisms made against current cognitive diagnosis techniques. It especially questions the possibility of representing the student knowledge as a perturbed copy of the expert's knowledge. Representing the learner's knowledge as a collection of partial models, potentially completely

KNOWLEDGE NEGOTIATION
ISBN 0–12–509378–0

different from the expert's model, sometimes incompatible, selected and applied according to the context, finds instead a growing support in human psychology and artificial intelligence (Richard 1990).

This chapter will concentrate on the third facet of KN, i.e. the relationship between the KN style of interaction and the pedagogical decisions. The pedagogical approach determines the features of the learning interaction. In the particular case, the KN style is based on a constructivist view of learning, which implies that the learner tests her own representations in the learning environment. These statements reflect the designer's view: pedagogical decisions lead to some particular design. The learner observes indeed this relationship from the opposite point of view: *the interaction reifies the underlying pedagogical approach and hence conveys the designer's theory of learning.* This speculative chapter investigates a copernician move towards the learner's position. We explore a particular form of the 'transparency' concept (Wenger 1987, Brown 1990): designing styles of interaction that explicitly reveal the pedagogical foundations of the ECS.

2   THE LEARNER'S MODEL OF LEARNING

Children elaborate concepts that describe mental activities, such as knowing or remembering. For early children, these concepts often do not correctly match our understanding of these words (Wellman 1985). For instance, pre-school children seem to consider that they 'know' something when they give a correct answer, even if this answer results from guessing right (Misciones et al., quoted by Wellman 1985). More globally, children tend to define mental activities by some associated external behaviour; they understand mental verbs as referring to observable behaviours. We are concerned by a particular mental activity concept: learning.

Learners have some representation of the meaning of 'learning', here referred to as a 'model of learning'. Like other similar concepts, the childs representation of learning finds its roots in the observable activities labelled or considered as learning activities, i.e. mainly in school activities. Therefore, we must compare it with the representations that students elaborate from educational interactions. By the terms 'model of educational interaction', we refer to the student's representation of any interaction which explicitly aims to promote learning for at least one of the subjects in interaction. The role of this model appeared in educational literature under the concept of 'didactic contract' (Brousseau 1980): students and teachers tend to behave according to implicit rules they induced from previous classroom experiences.

The important assumption here is that these interactions are internalized into some representation of learning: "The representations constructed by pupils of knowledge and the causes of success and failure in obtaining this knowledge are determined by the interactional and didactic context of the classroom" (Schubaueur-Leoni & Bell 1987, p.6). As Lochhead pointed out, passive school experiences potentially generate a baneful representation of learning: "Students tend to view learning as a passive experience in which one absorbs knowledge or copies fact into memory. Little of what they do in schools leads them to question that perspective" (Lochhead 1985, p.109). University teachers may confirm this statement for students that have spent around 12 years in schools. The mechanisms by which educational interactions are internalized into some model of learning will be described in Section 3.3.

The relationship between the learning model and the educational interactions model is not straightforward. Our representation of any event is closely associated with the context in which the event occurred (Tiberghien 1986). Learners probably have context-related sub-models of learning interactions, and subsequently, contex-related models of learning. Research on mental models confirms this complexity. Humans do not handle a simple unitary model of the task performed, but instead some 'distributed' model, i.e. a complex structure of partial models (DiSessa 1986). In 'learning a poem', 'learning to drive a car', 'learning a foreign language', 'learning to be happy', the word 'learning' refers indeed to processes we perceive as quite different to each other. These differences result from the object learned (data, a complex skill, . . .), the domain (biology, mathematics, sport, . . .), the context (in/out school, with/ without adults, . . .) and the learner.

3 THE 'ICONOCLASTIC' PRINCIPLE

The adjective 'iconoclastic' describes actions that lead to breaking an image. In our case, this image is the student's representation of learning. Our iconoclastic goal is to break the learner's passive model of learning. *The iconoclastic principle is articulated around the link between the interaction model and the learning model: if this link has been used for creating some model of learning, it can be reused in order to break this model.*

The rest of this chapter investigates how to implement this principle in an educational computing system.

This implementation is articulated around four stages:

- the transfer: the iconoclastic principle is only applicable if there exists a transfer mechanism from classroom situations to learner-computer settings; this transfer mechanism generates the learner's expectation towards the educational interaction she will participate in;

- the conflict: in order to deserve its iconoclastic title, an ECS must contradict these expectations by proposing a different interaction style;
- the constructorium: the ECS must offer activities that will lead the learner to internalize a better model of learning;
- the reverse transfer: if learners would bring their new model back in the classroom, then ECSs would get some potential to modify school practices, i.e. ECS would be considered as agents of innovation.

These four stages form a continuous and recurrent process, but they are now described separately and sequentially for didactic purposes.

3.1   The transfer from classroom to computer contexts

There is an apparent contradiction in our discourse. We described mental models as partitioned in context-related subsets, and we now postulate that students transfer the classroom-made model to settings where they engage in a dialogue with a computer. This contradiction may be overcome by analysing more closely the differences between the two contexts, the classroom and the workstation, and between the respective sub-models of learning. The context of learning activity is defined by various factors. Replacing the blackboard by a keyboard modifies one of these factors. Replacing the teacher by a computer and suppressing the other learners constitute more important changes. But on the other hand, some factors do not change. The 'scholastic' label of the activity often remains. Many scholastic concepts contribute to make the two contexts closer: exercises, errors, scores, tests, definitions, . . . And finally, the distribution of educational roles is not modified: with most ECSs, there is still an ignorant agent that has to learn and a knowledgeable agent that has to 'communicate' (in Wenger's sense) its knowledge.

These similarities between learning in a classroom and learning with a computerized teacher (sometimes in a classroom) mean that there is some overlap between the learner's respective models of learning interaction. The extent of this overlap determines the transfer process. For instance, device-dependent features of behaviour will probably not be transferred : most learners know for instance that they cannot communicate with a computer by using the same language as they use with a teacher. But they may transfer more device-independent pieces of knowledge such as the necessity of systematic practice to reinforce newly acquired skills. Such transferable rules are more related to how knowledge is acquired, i.e. to the student's model of learning.

We believe that the standard ITS architecture facilitates this transfer process: in learning with an ITS, there is still an expert which knows what the student has to learn, and there is still a tutor which knows what is the most suitable treatment for the student and which takes decisions about their learning. This architecture is in agreement with the role generally allocated to learners in the classroom. The presence of the expert component may reinforce the undesirable 'copy' model of learning: if knowledge may be copied inside the computer memory, why not into the student memory? Learners would be right to wonder why they must reconstruct some knowledge which exists inside the computer in some inspectable form?

Moreover, the probability of observing such a transfer process is increased by the general tendency to attribute a 'mental life' to computers. This has been examplified in another domain by systems like Weizenbaum's ELIZA program, or by Carfinkel's counselling system (Suchman 1987). The latter produced randomly 'yes' and 'no' answers to the users that believed however that the system performed some complex and intentional reasoning. A similar attribution process may be hypothesized about how students imagine the tutor's reasoning. This reinforces the hypothesis that learners transfer classroom-made models to the workstation context.

The Logo debate should be reconsidered in the light of this transfer process. Researchers have implicitly attributed the failure of free exploratory systems to the intrinsic limitations of learner's cognition. More precisely, these limitations concern the metacognitive skills involved in driving one's own learning. Learners do obviously have some limitations. However, we should take into account the fact that their attitude also reflects the effects of several years of passive schooling or, in our terms, that the attitude results from transferring to a new learning environment an inadequate model of learning acquired in the school environment. This complementary explanation is important for the design of systems. Instead of designing systems that compensate for metacognitive deficiencies by becoming increasingly directive, we should develop systems that support the learner's metacognitive activities (or, even better, that develop their metacognitive skills).

3.2 Creating a conflict

Didacticians have studied the (naive) representations that learners bring into learning, and showed the necessity to jeopardize these pre-representations before trying to install new ones, otherwise the pre-representations reappear shortly after the lesson (Jonnaert 1985). In order to encourage the abandonment of these pre-representations, the constructivist approach suggests that we should design activities which will reveal their inaccuracy The usual methodology attempts to generate an explicit conflict by asking the learner to produce predictions of some phenomena, and then running (or simulating) the phenomena and comparing the predictions to the actual results.

The student's model of learning may be viewed as a particular type of representation. Its specificity is that it does not concern the content of learning but the learning process itself. In order to jeopardize the learning-level pre-representations, ECSs should present a style of interaction which clearly contradicts the student's expectations, based on their passive learning models.

The idea of knowledge negotiation has some potential for creating a conflict with respect to the student's representations of learning. Usually, classroom interactions do not show knowledge as something which can be negotiated (except in a few domains where the importance of personal judgment is well accepted). Another potential surprise is the fact that the system ignores what it is teaching. This is one of the hypotheses we explore through the design of a collaborative learning system (Dillenbourg & Self in press). At the outset, the computerized co-learner is a novice in the domain (electoral systems). It has some naive model of elections as its disposal and tries to learn by interacting with the real learner within a micro-world where electoral experiments may be performed.

Given the current state of the art we cannot generalize these features to determine some general technique for creating such conflicts. Designing iconoclastic styles of interaction is indeed a challenge for the creativity of the system designers. This challenge is made more difficult by the fact that these designers have themselves grown up inside traditional classrooms! Moreover, we have to be modest about the effects expected from of these conflicts. No system will in one hour destroy a model that learners have built and consolidated during thousands of hours. As a former teacher of nine years old pupils, I remember how some of these implicit behavioural rules were already very solidly anchored. Conflicts alone do not have the power to simply destroy the existent model of learning in a moment of miraculous insight. The complexity of the model itself makes it very resistant to change. It is more accurate to say that these experiences may extend the student's model of interaction, and progressively move its centre of gravity towards a point where the student's active role in knowledge acquisition appears to be crucial.

In spite of the resistance to change, the disproportion between thousands of hours of classroom presence and a few hours with an ECS is somewhat reduced by two factors. Firstly, not all classroom experiences reinforce the learner's passivity. Good teachers take care to vary the kind of didactic strategies they use, even for the same content. Secondly, in classrooms, the learning model is implicit, and it is only its daily repetition that allows students to progressively induce some patterns. ECSs may counterbalance their brevity of use by focussing on the learner's awareness of the activated models. This is the object of the next section.

3.3 The constructorium: integrating a new model of learning

An ECS must include functionalities to promote the learner's awareness of its learning interaction characteristics and the internalization of these features into some (better) model of learning. We called such a system a constructorium (Dillenbourg & Self in press). We have introduced this concept in our work on collaborative learning. In a collaborative situation, the communication between learners makes the learning process observable. A pair of collaborative learners constitutes a micro-society where one can observe the construction of knowledge, hence the name constructorium. In this sense psychologists create a constructorium when they observe peer interaction for collecting think-aloud protocols. The educational interest is that learners are also inside this construc-torium, and in some way may also observe the construction of knowledge.

In this kind of constructorium, learning as an intra-individual process is made observable by transposing it as an inter-individual process. It corresponds in some way to a reversal of Vygotsky's internalisation process (Vygotsky 1978).We want here to extend the constructorium idea to situations where the learner is alone. In this case, making learning observable means showing to the learner some representation of how they have learned.

The process of becoming aware of one's own knowledge or one's own cognitive processes, i.e. the 'reflection' process, is a topic growing interest among the researchers on metacognition and among ECS designers. The use of computers for promoting reflection has been advocated by Brown (Brown 1985, Collins & Brown 1988). There are several techniques for promoting reflection. They have in common the technique of presenting some trace of the learner's activities and of the environment's responses. Systems such as Algebraland (Collins & Brown 1988) or the Geometry Tutor (Anderson et al. 1985) facilitate the learner's reflection by displaying the learner's solution path as a tree structure. This representa-tion is not neutral, but emphasizes some aspects of the learner behaviour.

In these two systems, the heuristic aspect of the solution process is made apparent by the structure of the tree. We may describe this by saying that the interface reifies some abstract features of the learner's cognition. *Reification* means making concrete abstract aspects of behaviour, or, in Wenger's terms (1987), creating a written notation for a process. This practice is based on the assumption that metacognitive regulation is easier when it manipulates concrete objects instead of the abstract represented properties.

The design of tools for reflection is still an item on the research agenda for ECS building. If we want to build tools that reify the learning process, we need to represent visually how knowledge structures have evolved through experience and communication. Figure 8.1 shows a very simple example of representation that reifies the concept learning process (in the simple case of learning non-natural concepts such as quadrilaterals). This figure represents a learning session where the successive hypotheses expressed by the learner are noted in the columns, and the various instances against which the learner tested the hypotheses are shown in the rows.

This representation is arbitrary, but reifies a simple principle of concept learning (and several other kinds of learning): each hypothesis must be tested and rejected if it mis-predicts the concept to which each instance belongs. A mis-prediction is represented by a small rectangle. Learning a concept does not any more appear as the memorizing of some definition, but as the process of actively testing one's hypothesis against a set of instances. Other features of concept learning can be reified in this simple representation; for instance, the relative usefulness of instances, i.e. their capability to break an hypothesis, can be read in the columns.

Figure 8.1 is not presented as an universal solution but simply as an illustration of our ideas. Most important concepts such as 'democracy', 'insect' or 'sentence' are more complex; their definition includes fuzzy attributes and some exceptions. In the systems quoted above, Algebraland and Geometry Tutor, the designers represented the problem solving process by a tree. We do not make a real distinction between learning and problem solving, and hence think that trees structure are particularly suited to illustrate the heuristic aspects of learning.

In his work on metacognition, Schoenfeld (1987) uses a graphical representation of problem solving processes that adds a temporal dimension to simple trees (but loses some other information). The purpose of this representation is to emphasize the active aspects of a mathematical problem solving process. Figures 8.2 and 8.3 show a representation of the actions of two problem solvers (or the actions of the same learner at different levels of expertise in problem solving). These representations are slightly simplified with respect to Schoenfeld's one. Each figure

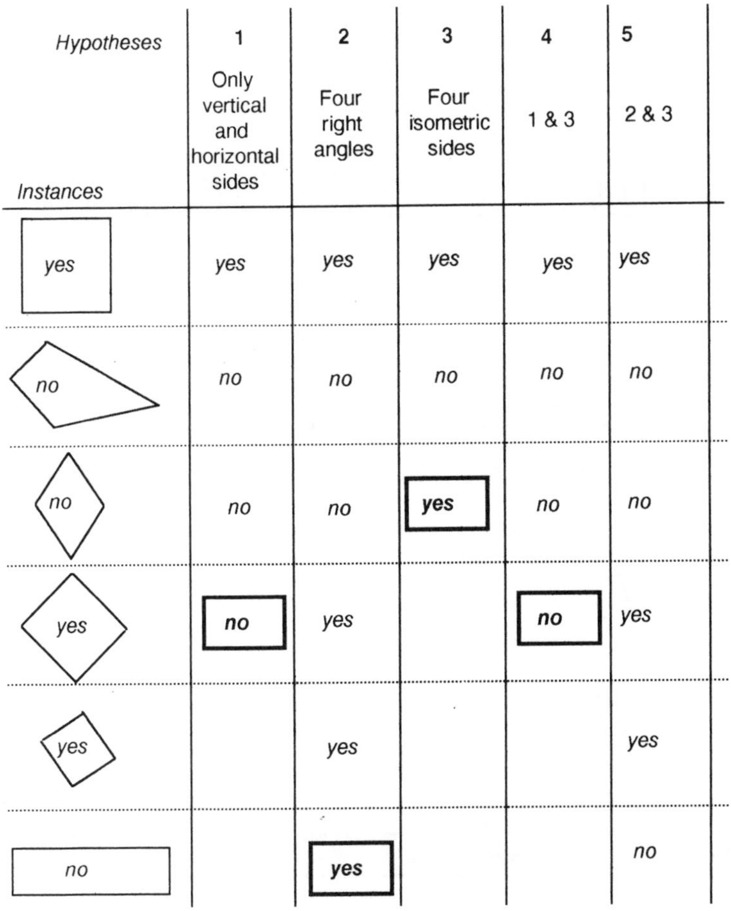

Instances / Hypotheses	1 Only vertical and horizontal sides	2 Four right angles	3 Four isometric sides	4 1 & 3	5 2 & 3
[square] yes	yes	yes	yes	yes	yes
[quadrilateral] no	no	no	no	no	no
[kite] no	no	no	**yes**	no	no
[diamond] yes	**no**	yes		**no**	yes
[small diamond] yes		yes			yes
[rectangle] no		**yes**			no

Fig. 8.1 A simple representation of a concept learning process. (Bold rectangles indicate a mis-prediction.)

represents the time spent by the subject on the various stages of the solution process. The time is represented on the horizontal axis (20 minutes) and the solution stages on the vertical axis. Shaded areas indicate the time spent by the subject at some stage of the solution process. The subject represented in Figure 8.2 is typically a passive problem solver. She decided to explore one direction and, during nearly 20 minutes, continued in that direction without ever considering another solution.

The subject represented in Figure 8.3 explores a solution (stage 'implement') but, after some time, she starts to feel that her solution will

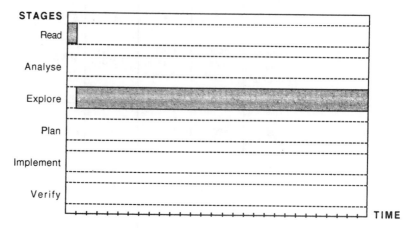

Fig. 8.2   Schoenfeld's representation of problem solving, the trace of a passive
subject.

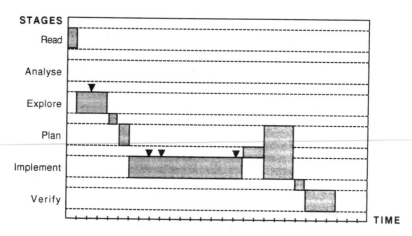

Fig. 8.3   Schoenfeld's representation of problem solving, the case of an active
subject.

probably not be successful and decides to tackle the problem in another
way (back to the 'plan' stage). Each small triangle, absent from the
previous figure, indicates a time when the subject said something like
"How am I doing?" and decided what to do next.

These figures are only examples. It is difficult to express in a general
way what characteristics of learning have to be reified because they are
largely context dependent. Moreover, this approach, although very
promising, raises some complex issues.

The first issue concerns the *epistemic fidelity* of such representations (Wenger 1987), i.e. the degree of consistency between the physical representation of some phenomena and the expert's mental representation of this phenomena. Assessing this epistemic fidelity is very difficult when the object represented is a concept as controversial as 'learning'. Moreover, we believe with Roschelle (1990) that representations should rather be assessed on their *symbolic mediation* qualities, i.e. their abilitiy to

". . .bridge the gap between commonsense and scientific interpretations of the world by providing an enriched physical situation to act in and talk about" (Roschelle 1990, p.1).

The scientific validity or completeness of the constructorium is indeed less important than its ability to conduct an interaction on metacognitive aspects of the learner's behaviour.

The second issue concerns the adequacy of the displayed representation to the actual learner's cognition, i.e. the *psychological validity* of the representation. Does the representation correspond to the way the learner is actually learning? This psychological validity differs from the concept of epistemic fidelity. The former refers to the learner's knowledge while the latter refers to the scientific knowledge.

We here meet a dilemna frequent to ECS designers. At the outset, the learner is probably not able to build this kind of representation. If the system builds it for them, then it may build something that does not correspond to the learning strategy used by the learner. This point becomes more forceful when we consider that a representation based on some virtual average learner probably does not cover a large variety of learning styles. This bias is not totally negative. It can be considered as a way of inducing a new learning strategy. The size of this bias depends on the validity of the cognitive diagnosis process implemented. It will be somewhat reduced by giving the advanced learner some tools to build her own representation. We imagine these tools as some kind of 'cognitive MacPaint'. In the case where the learner has to build a representation of her own learning, there is still a bias although it is indirect. The tools restrict the range of descriptions that the user can draw. The availability of these tools should increase proportionally to the learner's task level skills because a more skilled learner can free cognitive resources in order to pay more attention to meta-cognitive reasoning. If the learner does not fully master the basic operations, we can speed up the process by adding system functionalities that perform these computations instead of the learner (as in Algebraland).

These statements lead us to the third issue: the learner's activities on the given representation. Does the display initiate any kind of metacognitive activities? This basic question should be answered experimentally. However, we may unfortunately expect a negative answer. The availability of reflection tools does not guarantee that users do indeed reflect on their learning experiences. We can only claim that the learner reflects if they perform some activities on the representation of their problem-solving. This issue is very important since the symbolic mediation function relates the display qualities to the activities performed on it. By comparing a few ECSs (quoted below), we have defined five levels of activities:

- *observing;* the learner just looks at the description;
- *editing*; the learner has some tools to edit the description;
- *orienting*; the learner uses the description to select a problem state;
- *composing*; the learner creates the description by combining items;
- *creating*; the learner builds the description from scratch.

If the interaction description is a tree, the levels of activities might be:

- *observing;* looking at the tree;
- *editing*; annotating nodes by justifications;
- *orienting*; selects a node for backtracking or ask for replay;
- *composing;* builds the tree from a bank of parts;
- *creating*; drawing the tree with lines and boxes.

Editing activities are for example offered by Algebraland, while composing activities exist in TAPSII (Derry 1990). In this system on algebra word problems, the learners are invited to build a representation of the problem to be solved (and of the solution process itself). They build this representation by selecting problem schemas in a bank that includes a few schemas, and instantiating the schema components with the data of the word problem. When designing the learner's activity space, we have to keep in mind the global framework of this chapter. The challenge is to lead the learners to internalize some new model of learning. This process of internalization has been defined by Vygotsky:

"Every function in the child's development appears twice : first, on the social level, and later on the individual level; first, between people (inter-psychological) and then inside the child (intra-psychological)" (Vygotsky 1978, p.57).

In the current case, the social level is the interaction with the ECS. Unfortunately, psychological theories fail to give much detail about the mechanisms of internalization. Vygotsky outlined the linguistic nature of these mechanisms when he declared that "...*verbal thought is the transferral of speech to an internal level...*" and that "...*reflection is the transferral of argumentation to an internal level...*"(Vygotsky 1981, quoted by Wertsch 1985, p.73). This linguistic dimension is important for our purpose since it emphasizes the relationship between the model of interaction and the model of learning.

Some precision about these linguistic aspects of internalization has been proposed by Wertsch (1985). He suggested that intra-psychological processes are sketched out at some stage of the inter-psychological level. By zooming on the semiotic processes of the inter-individual communication (including its non-verbal aspects), he reduced the discontinuity of the internalization process. Wertsch observed mothers monitoring their children solving a puzzle. He found that mothers change their referential perspective according to the child's skills. When identifying a piece of the puzzle, beginner's mothers refer to piece attributes that both agents can observe (e.g. 'a green piece'), while later, mothers tend to refer to the strategical role of the piece (e.g. 'a piece with the same texture as one you have already put'). Wertsch claims that the cognitive processes necessary for understanding the second type of communication are "... *virtually identical with the cognitive processes required to carry out strategic activities independently...*" (p.94)

These findings correspond to the principle that underlies this chapter: the tutorial dialogue must refer to objects with respect to their role in the learning process. Figure 8.1, for instance, emphasizes the role of positive and negative examples in rejecting wrong hypotheses. In this case the reference to the learning strategy was represented by graphics, but in more complex examples a short text could fulfill the same role.

3.4   The inverse transfer: from computers to the classroom

Until now, the success condition for most computer based learning (CBL) material has been its adequacy with respect to teachers' habits, to their curricula and to their teaching styles. In other words, CBL has been generally accepted when it did not promote innovation. For instance, many teachers do not accept the loss of their central role within the classroom, and hence use courseware as an electronic blackboard (that they can control themselves).

Some ECSs have the potential to break this loop. By temporarily changing teachers into advisers or collaborators, a system can sightly modify the classroom structure (Schofield et al. in press). This is a small but real change in the relationship between the teacher and the students. We speculate that an ECS used as a constructorium might have some innovative power. If learners can internalize a better model of learning and transfer it to classroom situations, then ECSs will bring with them some potential for improving classroom practice. The question remains of how teachers will exploit this potential.

4 CONCLUSIONS

This chapter does not summarize long empirical studies. Instead, it raises questions concerning the acquisition and transfer of learning models and argues in favor of the following hypothesis: under some circumstances, the computer can promote the acquisition of some model of learning. The empirical validation of this hypothesis remains to be done. However, our speculative investigation of this idea raises interesting issues related to the concepts of reflection and transparency.

Brown (1990) pointed out that the learners should be provided tools to build a model of the expert's reasoning and named this property 'internal transparency'. This chapter described a particular kind of internal transparency, some 'pedagogical' transparency, that should give access to the model of learning (Wenger 1987) that underlies the system design. In our large understanding of the word learning, the expert's reasoning may constitute a form of learning. Since an ECS is supposed to be based on some theory of learning, let the learner discover this model by transparency. However, this model cannot be accessed in an abstract way. It must be instantiated by the learner's behaviour. This raises the issue of knowing to what extent the instantiation of the system's model by the learner's behaviour corresponds to the learner's actual learning strategy. Transparency and psychological validity are closely related concepts (Wenger 1987).

In this chapter, we also described the use of reflection tools for helping the learners to observe some model of learning through their own behaviour. The objects manipulated by the learner should be described by reference to their role in the learning strategy. By comparing these two last paragraphs, it seems to us that transparency and reflection are non-exclusive properties of glass boxes or, in other words, that an ECS can be compared to a plate-mirror.

ACKNOWLEDGEMENTS

Thanks to R. Moyse, D. Schneider and J. Self for their long comments on previous drafts of this chapter.

9 Modelling Negotiation in Intelligent Teaching Dialogues

MICHAEL BAKER

*Centre National de la Recherche Scientifique,
Laboratoire IRPEACS, 93 chemin des Mouilles,
BP167, 69131 Ecully Cedex, France*

1 INTRODUCTION: NEGOTIATION IN TUTORIAL DIALOGUES

In this chapter we describe how a computational model for generating intelligent tutoring dialogues may be developed which incorporates mechanisms for *negotiation*. As a preliminary, we need to describe what we mean by negotiation, and why it is important that tutorial dialogue models should incorporate it. Beginning with the second question, the argument is essentially that negotiation fulfills some *function* which must be fulfilled in computational tutorial dialogue models. We also argue that tutorial dialogue models which have previously been developed within the framework of intelligent tutoring systems (ITS) do not already fulfill this function. Consider first a larger question : what is the function of a tutorial dialogue? If we could decide this, then the function of negotiation might be described relative to a specific view of the function of tutorial dialogues. An immediate and trivial response is: 'that the student should learn'. There is more to the story, however, since we are also concerned with *how* this learning takes place – teaching and learning styles – and with the related degree of learner autonomy. 'Student autonomy' does not mean 'complete student freedom', but rather the flexible possibility of sharing control throughout the learning process. The role of negotiation becomes apparent when we clearly state that the function of tutorial dialogues should be that the student learns within a *cooperative* interaction. Now, this is partly an educational philosophy, and partly a theoretical point of view in the educational psychology of learning. The

KNOWLEDGE NEGOTIATION
ISBN 0–12–509378–0

educational philosophy is what Bennett (1976) termed 'progressive teaching', elements of which are also present in the situated learning approach (Lave 1988). The psychology of learning is one of 'learning by being told', or more generally, 'by engaging in dialogue', and one where the autonomous engagement of an individual in his own learning is viewed as an important determinant of the extent to which he will be willing and able to integrate new knowledge. On this point, we pass also to an *epistemology of learning*, associated with our view of cooperation in tutorial dialogues – that the 'knowledge' communicated in educational interactions is not a static thing to be transmitted, but is rather an emergent property of negotiation. In other words, that nature of what is mutually agreed to be 'knowledge' is not predetermined but is rather *negotiated* in interaction. Thus, as part of his 'new epistemology of learning', Brown states that:

"Good learning situations and successful ITS are successful not because they enable a learner to ingest preformed knowledge in some optimal way, but because they provide initially underdetermined threadbare concepts to which, through conversation, negotiation and authentic activity, a learner adds texture" (Brown 1990).

We have now described *one particular* point of view on the function of tutorial dialogues. Within this framework we therefore argue that the functions of negotiation in tutorial dialogues are essentially twofold: firstly, to maintain cooperation and a flexible degree of joint control over the interaction, and secondly, to permit *knowledge negotiation*. Since negotiation of knowledge depends on the freedom to do so, the first may be viewed as a precondition for the second. Knowledge negotiation in the context of tutorial interactions presupposes the willingness and freedom to arrive at *mutually agreed belief* on what counts as knowledge in a given domain.

We can now pass to the question of what we mean by 'negotiation', the answer to which we propose clearly relates to our point of view on its function. As well as the function of negotiation, we need to consider the terms within which our definition is stated – linguistic, cognitivist, or other. Essentially, we claim that *negotiation is a sequence of dialogue exchanges whose function is that of securing cooperation with respect to some set of propositions*. The definition is stated in both dialogue and mentalistic terms:

Negotiation (definition)

'Negotiation' is the term for a sequence of dialogue exchanges between agents capable of generating and understanding them, during which the

mental states of interlocutors are transformed from the propositional postures of indifference (absence of cooperation or conflict) or of conflict with respect to one or more propositions, to one of cooperation with respect to one or more propositions, and where one or more agent possesses the goal that this posture should be achieved.

Negotiation is therefore defined in terms of sequences of dialogue exchanges and changes in complex mental states of negotiating agents. Galliers (1989) has produced a number of definitions for the complex propositional postures of COOPERATION, CONFLICT and INDIFFERENCE, in terms of the logic of intention of Cohen and Levesque (1990). It is of course possible that negotiation takes place in which neither speaker has the goal that cooperation be achieved – such as 'arguing for the sake of it'. We therefore make a minimal assumption of cooperativity. As a first approximation, propositions include reference to states of affairs and the attitudes of speakers towards them – such as that they want or believe a given state of affairs. States of affairs may themselves be complex attitudes. In the domain which we consider, propositions concerning the domain (and concerning the attitudes of other agents), are modelled as *justified beliefs*. Our view of what beliefs are is intimately linked to the idea of negotiation: beliefs are dispositions towards generating dialogue actions whose content is negotiable in the sense that it is not assumed to communicate 'certain' knowledge. In this chapter we restrict our discussion to negotiation of one specific kind of proposition: *negotiation of dialogue goals*. We need to say what is meant by 'dialogue goals' rather than other kinds of goals. A dialogue goal is here defined in terms of three kinds of *parameters*: (1) an utterance type, (2) the conceptual content of the utterance, and (3) dialogue roles. This corresponds loosely to an utterance analysed by speech act category with propositional content, and definition of speaker roles. Within speaker roles, the speaker who initiates the negotiation is distinguished from the speaker who will perform the cooperatively agreed goal. For example, in the situation where 'the teacher asks the student to give an answer to a question about PROLOG variables in a predicate PR1', this is represented as follows :

negotiator = teacher
speaker = student
concept = PROLOG(variables)
instance = PR1
utterance type = INFORM.

That is to say, 'the teacher negotiates that the student should make an INFORM utterance about the concept "variables", instance "PR1"'. This is not to say that negotiation of *beliefs* is not important – we have analysed this in the context of cooperative explanation generation in Baker (1991) – but rather that negotiation of this type of goal does occur in tutorial dialogues, and thus needs to be modelled. In a later section of the chapter the role of such a representation in a more general dialogue model is discussed in more detail. In the next section we compare this way of posing the problem of negotiation with other definitions derived from existing work, most of which associate negotiation exclusively with the incidence and resolution of *conflict*.

Finally, we claimed earlier that existing models for dialogue in intelligent tutoring systems have not included functionalities for negotiation. This is not surprising since, given that negotiation is a phenomenon which occurs in *dialogue*, little previous work has included a model of dialogue *per se*. 'Dialogue' may be defined initially by comparison with 'discourse' and 'conversation'. Discourse is written or spoken communication, with no interaction with the hearer(s). It may be more or less adapted to the discourse generator's knowledge of the hearer(s) knowledge, and more or less coherent. A conversation is a sequence of exchanges, each of which may be a discourse, between two or more agents, generally occurring in everyday life with no fixed topic or goals. A dialogue is a conversation in a specific setting, with specific goals or objectives. For example, consider the dialogues of Plato, or film dialogues, or again, a tutorial dialogue, occurring in an educational setting, with the objective that the student learns something within a specific domain. Dialogues may be more or less 'rich' in dialogic characteristics. Consider the case where the student only responds 'yes' or 'no' to a teacher's utterances. If these are the only possibilities *available* to the student, then this is not a dialogue. If, however, the student *could* interact otherwise (but in fact did not) – proposing his own point of view, etc. – then this is simply an impoverished dialogue. We therefore need to introduce the idea of 'symmetrical interactional possibilities' into the definition of dialogue. In terms of this discussion, the early work of Carbonell (1970), and Collins and Stevens (1983) concerned minimal dialogue – the student had the possibility to respond 'yes' or 'no', or to ask certain questions, but the system had greater interactional possibilities. In Elsom-Cook's earlier (1984) work, a model for extended discourse was developed which included many of the aspects (focus model, goal and topical elements, dialogue moves) to be included in a model for symmetrical dialogue, in later work (Elsom-Cook 1990b). The work of Brown and Burton (1982) and of Clancey (1987) was conceived as providing 'coaching rules' and 'dialogue rules', respectively. This research resulted in the generation of non-continuous discourse, within the context of computer-based learning environments, and did not attempt to incorporate models for phenomena described in human dialogues (coherence, relevance, focussing, etc.). More recently, the work of Petrie-Brown (1989b, 1990) and of Blandford (1990, 1991) has provided some of the theoretical and formal underpinnings of tutorial dialogue models, which could contribute to models for negotiation, but which do not explicitly address this issue.

In our own research (Baker 1989c) we have developed a computational model for sustaining tutorial dialogues which aimed to incorporate some aspects of negotiation observed in human dialogues. The model is called 'KANT' – Kritical Argument Negotiated Tutoring system. After describing the model, we describe an agenda for future work by comparing its performance with the structure of negotiation phases analysed in a set of computer-mediated teaching dialogues.

We focus our analysis on the following questions which may be asked in connection with negotiation :

Q1: What is negotiated in tutorial dialogue?
Q2: When does negotiation occur, and why?
Q3: What interaction structures occur in negotiation?
Q4: When negotiation occurs, why does it occur explicity or implicity?
Q5: When and why is negotiation successful?

KANT incorporated specific preliminary responses to some of these questions as follows:

Q1: Speaker and negotiator roles, utterance types and associated conceptual content are negotiated, as described above.

Q2: Negotiation occurs at the beginning of the dialogue when there are no cooperatively agreed goals, by speaker_2 when a goal negotiated by speaker_1 is rejected, or when speaker_1 has completed a negotiated dialogue action.

Q3: Negotiation proceeeds hierarchically, from general to specific utterance goals, and with increasing concreteness with respect to speaker and topic parameters.

Q4: In KANT, all negotiation is explicit – no goals are assumed agreed, and hence subgoals are negotiated explicitly.

Q5: Negotiation succeeds when the composite goal negotiated is viewed as *relevant* by a speaker, otherwise not. Determining relevance involves evaluating a complex set of *preconditions* with respect to a *dialogue state*.

As we describe later, not all of these responses are supported by dialogue analysis, and they are all a very partial view of what happens in negotiation.

2 EXISTING WORK ON NEGOTIATION

Most existing work on modelling negotiation has been carried out within
the framework of Distributed Artificial Intelligence (DAI) research
(Bond & Gasser 1988). Here the problem addressed is usually that of
resolving conflicts in resource allocation and in bids for problem solving
subtasks between distributed agents. For example, Adler et al. (1988)
define negotiation as ". . . a process of exchange of conflict information
and tentative committments of resources to plans" which is done through
the exchange of problem-solving plans (p. 141). Conflict which gives rise
to negotiation is itself viewed as being caused by *resource limitations*:
"Generally speaking, resources needed to solve a problem are the
physical sources of conflict : there aren't enough or they are in the wrong
place or they aren't the right kind" (*op. cit.*, p.146). If we count
knowledge of how to solve a problem as a 'resource', then this way of
defining negotiation may be applicable to some tutorial dialogues, given
the assumption that the teacher does not possess complete and infallible
information or 'knowledge'. However, in the tutorial dialogues we
consider here, conflicts may also occur concerning the problem to be
solved – the learning goal – itself, rather than with respect to the
information resources required to achieve it. *Adler* et al. (*op. cit.*) also
propose a useful classification of negotiation styles along three axes:

(1) the degree to which goals are expanded before negotiation begins ;
(2) the complexity of information exchanged and of models agents build
    of others;
(3) the degree of control the agent has over the negotiation process.

In terms of these axes, KANT begins with high-level dialogue goals
which are successively expanded, the dialogue participants exchange
information about their beliefs and justifications, including those about
the other's stated beliefs, and each has the same degree of control over a
fixed negotiation procedure.

The work of Sycara (1988, 1989) is also concerned with negotiation
from conflict, in the specific case of *goals* of participants in labour
disputes. Due to the relevance of this work for negotiation in tutorial
dialogues, it merits discussion in some detail. Previous DAI work on
negotiation had considered the case of single negotiations ; thus an
important part of Sycara's work was on defining more extended
negotiation sequences, leading to a *compromise* which satisfies all (both)
parties. Compromises are found by searching a database of previous cases
and the associated compromises reached, in order to find a *successful* one
which is most *similar* to the present case – Schank's (1982) method of

'case-based reasoning'. This involves using ". . . a set of salient features of the domain (e.g. industry, geographical location) as memory probes" (p. 247). An 'evaluation function' is used to select the 'best' case, which is then adjusted to fit the present conflict situation. A final check on the suitability of the case is then performed by selecting its features, and searching memory to check whether there are cases with these characteristics which previously *failed*, in accordance with Schank's (1982) 'intentional reminding' theory. Once found by a 'mediator' program, compromises are presented to each participating agent. If they agree, then the program reports success, otherwise the PERSUADER program attempts to *convince* agents by generating *arguments*. "Convincing someone can be modelled as increasing the payoff that the compromise gives him" (Sycara 1988, p. 248). An agent's payoff is respresented as a linear combination of coefficients for the *importance* an agent attaches to an issue, and its *utility value*. The PERSUADER attempts to generate statements which would change these parameters for an agent towards those associated with the compromise solution. For example, an increase in wages represents an increase in company labour cost. The argument addressed to a union that has refused a proposed wage increase 'IF the company is forced to grant higher wage increases, then it will decrease employment' is meant to decrease the importance the union attaches to wage increases by pointing out unpleasant consequences for the union of forcing a wage increase, not wanted by the company. The PERSUADER's strategy for repair is 'explanation-based' where the reason for rejection is supplied by the rejecting agent. The method used is again to search for cases where there was a similar 'impasse', and use its associated *repair method*.

Some aspects of Sycara's work are clearly relevant to negotiation in tutorial dialogues, although there are many dialogue features which need to be modelled with which her work is not concerned. As will be described in the next section, there are some kinds of negotiation in tutorial dialogues which involve arguments where one speaker attempts to convince the other to accept a learning goal. This is done, however, by appealing to their abilities rather than interests. It is not clear to what extent speakers have memories for success and failure of past cases of negotiation in a dialogue, although they may have a more general conception of what kinds of negotiated goals are likely to be acceptable to another or not. In terms of dialogue modelling, it is important to note that Sycara does not consider the structure of turn-taking in negotiation, nor its relationship with focus constraints, since negotiation is managed by a third party (the 'mediator'). Finally, our analyses show that the incidence of negotiation in tutorial dialogues is not restricted to *conflict* situations, this being the case in Sycara's work.

There is presently relatively little work within Intelligent Tutoring Systems research which deals with negotiation in dialogue. One example is the work of McCalla and Wasson (this volume). Within the SCENT project, they presently consider the problem of negotiating the *domain content* of tutorial interactions rather than their delivery style. From analyses of Lisp teaching dialogues, they identify different kinds of goals which may be negotiated (content, delivery, cognitive, affective, deep and shallow). They also make the important point that ". . . negotiated tutoring does not imply that everything is always up for negotiation", and stress the importance of the student understanding the motivation for negotiated instructional goals.

In summary, existing work on negotiation has almost exclusively been concerned with negotiation from goal conflicts in distributed problem-solving. A number of mechanisms for resolving conflicts and managing the ensuing negotiation have been described which may be applicable in some kinds of tutorial dialogues, notably those concerned with problem solving domains. However, the questions which we pose here are somewhat wider : we want to establish the range of things which are and which should be negotiable in tutorial dialogues, to describe attendant dialogue structures, and to relate these to fundamental aspects of protracted dialogues. We describe the role of a number of these features by analysing negotiation phases from human–human computer-mediated teaching dialogues in the next section.

3 NEGOTIATION EXAMPLES AND ANALYSES

For purposes of illustration, here are two examples of negotiation taken from computer-mediated tutorial dialogues in the domain of teaching Prolog. These dialogues will be used as examples throughout this chapter. We use the following notation :

T = teacher
L = learner
<<. . .{comment}>> = omitted section from dialogue

The following are communication clichés developed by T and L themselves :

? = asynchronous interrupt
'. . .' = I am thinking

The dialogues were collected over a period of two years, and were conducted via electronic mail at a distance of over 200 miles. The teacher was a university lecturer in artificial intelligence, and the learner a masters student in the same subject. We shall discuss short extracts from a single dialogue, in terms of our research questions stated above. In the first, the two speakers attempt to achieve cooperation from a position where there were no explicitly agreed goals. In the second, conflict occurs, and is resolved (or 'removed') essentially by *persuasion*.

Negotiation Example 1

T1: I would greatly enjoy doing some Prolog. Did you have something in mind?
L2: No, not really. Like I said I haven't really looked at your program with the idea of extending it yet. Could we do something simplish, just to make me feel good?!
T3: Certainly. You have a choice of something simple and interactive now, or something fairly simple with an interactive session later on today.
L4: Um. I'd like to do something now, cos I really should do the vp stuff later on . . . is that ok?
T5: Fine. Ummm. . . How about writing a predicate called second_word, which takes as its argument a string, and instantiates its second argument to be the ATOM corresponding to the second word of that string eg
      second_word("fish and chips",M).
      M=and
yes. How does that seem?
L6: Ok I think. um can you do something else in another window while I think about it?
T7: Certainly . . .
<<continues>>

To clarify our discussion, we use the following predicates to analyse negotiation structure and content, which relate to primitives of our model:

negotiates(n s p) – 'n negotiates proposition p to be pursued or stated by speaker s'
responds(s r p) – 'speaker s responds r <n=negative,a=affirmative> to proposition p'.
    _ – variable
    <> – proposition value
    U1 . . . Un – utterance names
    &,OR – logical connectives

Aspects of the dialogues which are not negotiations – 'dialogue actions' – will be left in the analysis.
A general analysis of example 1 is therefore :

T1: U1(negotiates(T _ prolog)).
    U2(negotiates(T L negotiates(L _ prolog))
L2: U3(responds(L n U2)).
    U4(negotiates(L _ <something simple>))
T3: U5(responds(T a U4))
    U6(negotiates(T L < <simple & interactive & now> OR <fairly simple &

```
         interactive & later>>))
    L4:  U7(responds(L a U6))
         U8(negotiates(L L <<U6<simple & interactive & now>> &
         <vp & later>>)
    T5:  U9(responds(T a U8)
         U10(negotiates(T L <probem to solve – predicate,argument,string,atom>))
    L6:  U11(responds(L a U10)
         U12(negotiates(L T <do something else to allow L to think>))
    T7:  U13(responds(T a U12).
```

We now attempt to respond to our five general questions with respect
to this extract.

Q1: What is negotiated in tutorial dialogue?

A wide range of phenomena are negotiated, all of which are negotiated
goals for one or both speakers, rather than *beliefs*. These include :

- proposed topics for future problems to work on (Prolog, strings,
  arguments)
- specific problems to work on ('write a predicate called second_word')
- interaction style of problem-solving (interactive)
- future planning of joint problem-solving goals (now, later)
- level of difficulty of problems (simple, fairly simple)
- that the other speaker should negotiate a goal for a given topic (U2)
- 'time to think' (U12)

Q2: When does negotiation occur, and why?

It is clear that negotiation occurs here because it is the beginning of the
dialogue, and no joint goals have been decided, rather than because of
conflict. In Gallier's (1989) terms, this is negotiation from a posture of
INDIFFERENCE to one of COOPERATION, where 'indifference' here
is understood as lack of a common goal. What is important to note, is
that the negotiation moves from non-specificity to specificity in terms of
the values of negotiator, speaker and topic parameters.

Q3: What interaction structures occur in negotiation?

Interaction structures are of the socially expected form, according to the
Schegloff and Sacks (1973) turn-taking rules:

```
speaker1:            negotiation
speaker2: response, negotiation
speaker1: response . . . .
```

The fact that this exists shows a high level of social cooperation. In terms of topic and speaker role parameters, the negotiation begins with the general topic of 'Prolog', and ends with a specific problem to work on. The general topic is discussed before that of the speaker role – that the student should solve the problem for the teacher to criticize.

Q4: When negotiation occurs, why does it occur explicity or implicity?

Negotiation is all more or less explicit here – presumably because in a situation where the general goal is clearly understood to be achievement of cooperativity in defining a problem-solving goal, neither speaker needs indirect speech in order to interrupt that process, or negotiate a goal which may be not accepted by the other. These matters may be more clear in examining cases where goals were negotiated implicitly.

Q5: What makes negotiation succeed or fail?

In this extract all negotiated goals succeed except for U3, where the learner says that she does not have a specific problem to suggest to be worked on. This is understandable given that it is the very beginning of the dialogue, and that the teacher will not yet have been able to model the learner's goals and beliefs adequately in order to propose only goals which have a likelihood of receiving an affirmative response. In all other cases, negotiated goals are approached by successive levels of generality to specificity, which minimizes the chances of conflict. Since no goals have yet been pursued, the learner is not yet sufficiently aware of her own problem-solving abilities in order to be able to definitely refuse a proposed goal (U10).

This relatively crude analysis does not capture all that we would want to say about this extract. For example:

- in L2, L's negative response is 'softened' by the words 'not really', and she then goes on to explain or justify why this response was given – all strategies for maximizing a generally cooperative posture;
- the phatic word 'umm' is used even in these typewritten dialogues, to signal that the speaker is still attentive, but needs to think;
- a number of responses to negotiations are not simply of the affirmative/negative kind, but communicate a *degree of confidence* on the part of the respondent (e.g. L6 " Ok I think, Umm. . .").

Negotiation Example 2

T31: ? Can I say something?
L32: yes
T33: That's quite a lot wrong, I'm afraid.
    D'you want to tell me about it in English?
L34: Not really
T35: Ah. What do you want to do then?
L36: Stop?
T37: Oh. Really? I'd quite like to talk through this one, and it isn't exactly all that ego-boosting for your Prolog morale so far is it?
L38: What Prolog morale?
T39: Oh, come on. You can do it. <<continues>>

The general structure is as follows.

T31: ? U1(negotiates(T T _).
L32: U2(responds(L U1 a)
T33: U3<<That's quite a lot wrong, I'm afraid.>>
    U4(negotiates(T L
    <that L explains their problems and problem solving for previous utterance>))
L34: U5(responds(L n U4)
T35: U6(negotiates(T L negotiates(L _ _)))
L36: U7(negotiates(L _ <"Stop?" – terminate dialogue>))
T37: U8(negotiates(T _ <continue, U4))
    U9<<It isn't exactly boosting for your Prolog morale so far is it?>>
L38: U10<<What Prolog morale?>>
T39: U11(negotiates(T L U4)
    U12<<You can do it.>>

Q1: What is negotiated in tutorial dialogues?

The principal propositions negotiated here are:

- that L explains and discusses her problem;
- that L negotiates another goal (there are other cases where negotiations can be nested, i.e. *x* negotiates that *y* negotiates that . . . As with beliefs, there must be some psychological limit to nesting);
- that they stop the dialogue;
- that they continue the dialogue (and that the original negotiation of T be accepted).

Q2: When does negotiation occur, and why?

Negotiation occurs here because T believes that L is not achieving their goal that she solve the problem. This *conflict* of belief (about the correct problem solution) and goal (that the problem be solved by L), leads to *demotivation* on the part of the student, which T then attempts to redress by *persuasion*. The initial conflict thus leads to further conflict concerning whether the dialogue should be pursued or not.

Q3: What interaction structures occur in negotiation ?

The propositional posture of CONFLICT is marked by an interruption of the socially preferred turn-taking structure: L responds negatively, and exchanges of negotiation and opposed counter-negotiation follow one after the other. This illustrates the important point that turn-taking structures may provide analytical evidence for cooperation or conflict attitudes, as described earlier (see Roschelle & Behrend in press).

T31: interrupts
     negotiates
L32: responds
T33: utterance
U4: negotiates
L34: responds
T35: negotiates
L36: negotiates
T37: negotiates

Q4: When negotiation occurs, why does it occur explicity or implicity?

All negotiation is explicit here, but nevertheless the first interruption/ negotiation is 'softened' – i.e. has an increased likelihood of being accepted – by being non-specific – 'Can I say *something*'. The situation of conflict is heightened by the exchange structure and the explicitness of the opposed negotiations.

Q5: What makes negotiation succeed or fail?

The teacher's initial negotiation succeeds in virtue of its non-specificity – less likely to directly conflict goals or beliefs – and its placement in the dialogue almost at the end of the student's (erroneous) problem-solving. We can imagine that an interruption in the middle of this process, and with greater specificity, would be less likely to be successful. The subsequent negotiations fail because the student is not *motivated* to pursue the proposed goals (see the analysis in Elsom-Cook 1990b). Subsequently in the dialogue, the CONFLICT situation is removed by the teacher, who succeeds in motivating the student sufficiently so that she is *persuaded* to choose a simpler subproblem to work on.

We have analysed a number of other negotiations in this corpus of dialogues. The general conclusions we would make, relevant to criticizing the model to be described later, are summarized as follows:

Q1 What is negotiated in tutorial dialogues?

1 problem solving goals and subgoals
   - negotiated from generality towards specificity and with increasing concreteness, thus minimizing possibility of direct conflict
   - acceptance of a goal implies a presumption of acceptance of subgoals unless there are contrary indications
   - conflict on a subgoal leads to negotiation of alternative subgoals before new goals
2 dialogue goals
   - stopping/continuing the dialogue, bringing the dialogue to an agreed *closing*
3 timing/planning of joint interaction goals
4 interaction style
5 level of difficulty of problems
6 speaker and negotiator roles
7 motivation
   - negotiating the speaker's perception of their own ability in problem-solving, i.e. their *metacognitive awareness* of their problem-solving ability.

It is clear that there are no *a priori* limits to what can be negotiated, and that this may greatly depend on the domain and other variables. We would hope that future research could identify general *empirical* limits. The kinds of features which may be negotiated may well include most aspects of control and metacognitive control of problem-solving, planning at the cognitive level, and interaction style, speakers, negotiators, topics, etc. at the dialogue level.

Q2 When and why does negotiation occur?

From the dialogues which we have analysed, negotiation occurs under the following circumstances :

INDIFFERENCE
no goals are currently agreed, because
● it is the start of the dialogue,
● a previously agreed subgoal has been achieved
CONFLICT
goals or beliefs are communicated which are understood to be in conflict because
● a previously agreed subgoal is perceived to have failed or be in the likely process of failing (by either speaker)
● a speaker no longer desires to pursue a previously agreed goal (often because of lack of motivation)
PERCEPTION AND UNDERSTANDING
    actions or stated beliefs are not *understood* by either participant to be in accordance with the previously agreed goal

Q3 What interaction structures occur in negotiation?

The propositional postures of COOPERATION and INDIFFERENCE are marked by socially preferred and expected turn-taking structures (Schegloff & Sacks 1973) – generally, speakers respond to previous negotiations, then re-negotiate and are responded to, with few interruptions. CONFLICT is almost always marked by a suspension of these expected structures – negotiations may follow unrelated previous negotiations, which are sometimes but not always responded to. In our analysis we have not been concerned to identify specific utterance types. This was because we prefer to analyse the general exchange structure together with higher-level goal and belief structures. Nevertheless, the types of adjacency pairs (Schegloff & Sacks 1973) and utterance types which occur are reasonably small in number:

    question/answer
    offer/acceptance/rejection
    utterance/acknowledgement
    elicitation/response
    request/response
    statement(belief,goal)
    explanation
    justification

Q4 When and why does negotiation occur explicity or implicity?

Negotiation occurs implicitly, or 'indirectly' when *speakers believe that the goal or belief they are negotiating may lead to conflict*. Speakers may communicate their own meta-cognitive beliefs as a means of implicit negotiation, thus inviting help or comment from the other speaker (usually the teacher in this case). A provisional answer as to when this may be the case is therefore as follows :

> goals may be negotiated implicitly when
>> either
>>> the execution of an action to achieve a jointly agreed goal is interrupted by either speaker
>>> or
>>>> the interrupting speaker believes that their utterance may conflict with a jointly agreed specific goal (e.g. 'solve problem p1') or general goal (e.g. 'that the student be motivated', 'that the student learn')
>>>> or
>>>>> the interrupted goal was previously agreed 'with difficulty' from a marked conflict, and may hence be highly probable to lead to further conflict
>>>>> or . . .

We would need to look extensively at other examples in order to verify and complete this analysis. A different but important phenomenon concerns the *level of specificity* of an explicit negotiation, which may be made deliberatively tentative and general so as to minimize the possibility of conflict, where this is thought to be likely.

Q5 What makes negotiation succeed or fail?

Speakers attempt (unconsciously) to ensure that their negotiations succeed by a variety of strategies designed to promote acceptance and minimize the chances of conflict, as follows:

> *avoidance of conflict*, relating to the timing and level of specificity of the negotiated goal,
>> *a gradual general-specific negotiation* from a position of INDIFFERENCE,
>> or by
> *resolution of conflict,* by proposing some other (sub)goal, or *persuasion* on the part of one speaker, often using *motivational means.*

The reason why negotiations fail depends on the nature of what is being negotiated. In the case of problem-solving goals, failure relates to the negotiation respondent's *meta-cognitive* assessment of their abilities to achieve the goal. In the case of failure to achieve a goal, the student may become strongly *demotivated*, and hence future similar negotiations may fail. This in turn may have effects on the success of negotiated dialogue goals, such as wanting to terminate the dialogue.

There are a number of features of negotiation phases observed in the dialogues which we are analysing which have not been discussed earlier. We summarize them as follows:

Justification/explanation

Speakers often justify or explain why they are negotiating a particular proposition at a given point in a dialogue. For example "Could we do something simplish, just to make me feel good?", or "Can you do something else in another window while I think about it?." They also often justify or explain in the case of negative responses: "No, not really. Like I said, I haven't looked at your program with the idea of extending it yet." Similarly, they sometimes ask for an explanation of the goal negotiated:

"T41: <...>
... why don't we take the case in which first_word instantiates its second arg to be a list of the ascii codes of the first word, then you don't need to much k about with "name".
○
L42: You mean I use "name" in defining first_word?
I don't seeeeee what you mean. . . ."

Motivating moves

An important number of utterances in these dialogues are concerned with motivation – 'Don't panic', 'Oh come on, you can do it', 'Super stuff', 'It's VERY EASY'. Formalizing the recognition of motivational states is a difficult but important problem which needs to be addressed. The importance of motivation in these dialogues has been analysed by Elsom-Cook (1990b).

We now describe the current state of our model for dialogue generation. In the final section of the chapter we describe some directions of further work towards incorporating some of these features into our model.

4   KANT: A MODEL FOR HIGH-LEVEL PROCESSES IN TUTORIAL INTERACTION

The KANT system (Baker 1989c) is a computational model for generation of structures associated with high-level tutorial interactions. A model of 'high-level' interaction (Kiss 1986, Elsom-Cook 1990b) consists of the specification of a set of representations for mental states of interlocutors and the processes which operate upon them to generate a set of dialogue structures. These representations include beliefs (concerning a domain of discourse, the beliefs of some other interlocutor, the previous dialogue which has occurred), their goals, intentions, preferences, . . . and representations of other mental states. By the 'structure' of dialogue, we mean the structure of 'turn taking' (Schegloff & Sacks 1973), the content of each utterance unit, as defined in terms of a set of *dialogue goals*, parametrized for the speaker, negotiator and topic and a set of constraints on *sequences* of utterance units. We have adopted the research approach of attempting to specify such a model at a 'high' level, which does not extend to the level of sentences in natural language (the system uses 'canned' text). There are two reasons for adopting this approach. The first is that since there are currently few existing models of dialogue *per se*, in comparison with discourse and text generation, a reasonable approach is to develop hypothetical models, which may then be adapted with respect to results of dialogue analyses and in combination with models for generation and understanding of natural language. The second is that in the context of computer-mediated dialogues in Intelligent Tutoring systems, we seek models which are sufficiently general to serve as the basis for *multimedia* dialogues, where 'utterances' may be performed in graphical as well as linguistic form (see Reichman 1986). Once high-level dialogue research has produced more complete models, it is clear that such an approach which assumes a clear separation between deciding what to say, and how it is said will have to be abandoned. The scope of our research is of course limited: it emphasizes the definition of a framework which situates negotiation phases within a model which incorporates mechanisms for deciding which parametrized dialogue goal to negotiate, and how to negotiate it, in relation with a mechanism for controlling dialogue focus (Grosz & Sidner 1986). In terms of ITS research, we aimed to define a model where each interlocutor (computer and human student) was given as great a degree of symmetrical freedom to pursue their goals as possible, in accordance with the views expressed in the ITS literature by Elsom-Cook (1984) and by Petrie-Brown (1989b).

4.1 Representing the 'dialogue state'

The fundamental representations of mental states of a dialogue interlocutor used in KANT were based on the notion of a 'dialogue state'. This was first defined by Power (1979) as:

". . . the situation which has arisen between two speakers as a result of their previous dialogue" (p. 131).

In human dialogues this 'pragmatic context' should include elements of the social situation, such as social roles and affective goals. In KANT we restrict this context to a memory of dialogue goals and parameters negotiated so far, and beliefs explicitly communicated in dialogue. A third component is the specific activation pattern resulting from dialogue in the interlocutors' working memory (to be discussed later), which controls focus of attention.

Dialogue goals

The dialogue goals represented in the system were specifically adapted to the knowledge domain which the dialogue model discussed, which were assumed to consist of *justified beliefs* rather than 'knowledge'. The original domain on which KANT was based was that of *analysis of musical phrase structures*, as will be seen in the example trace later in the chapter. Our previous research on developing cognitive models for understanding musical structures (Baker 1989a, 1989b) had shown that in this domain, human experts have incomplete and largely implicit justified beliefs concerning multiple possible structural analyses. In the system which we developed as a domain model for KANT, a frame-based parser derived multiple solutions for phrase boundary positions in tonal melodies, with associated musical features used in the recognition process. These were represented in the form of a set of justified beliefs concerning phrase boundaries, for use in KANT. Dialogue goals were therefore incorporated in KANT for stating and illustrating beliefs and their justifications, and for critiquing the beliefs and justifications which had already been stated in the dialogue (by either dialogue participant). These goals corresponded to those which had been described (Toulmin et al. 1979, Reichman 1985) for *critical arguments* (see Figure 9.1). Their representation formalism was based on existing research (Cohen & Perrault 1979, Levin & Moore 1977) in representing dialogue goals as planning operators, based on the general theory of language as rational action – 'speech acts' – in the pursuit of goals (Searle 1969). The major differences in our representation are that extra kinds of preconditions were included for constraints on dialogue focus, the operators were parametrized (for speaker and negotiator roles) in order to be adapted to interactive dialogue, and they included preconditions relating to negotiation of those goals. More importantly, the major difference between our model and previous ones lies in the procedural role which the goal operators play in dialogue generation. Goals are represented *hierarchically*, which enables us to model the general-to-specific negotiation of dialogue goals, described in our previous analyses. This hierarchy is accompanied by successive *concretization* in defining speaker and topic parameter values, on descending the goal tree. For example,the system may begin by negotiating that a particular concept be discussed, then that a claim be made about it, then that the student should make the claim, and so on.

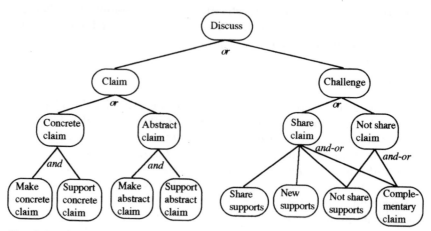

Fig. 9.1 Hierarchy of dialogue goals in the KANT system.

The and/or tree of goals is a fundamental representation in decision-making in KANT. It is searched top-down during the process of trying to find a relevant goal to be discussed. When the student has a 'negotiated turn', the same set of goals is available, with the exception of making an 'abstract claim', or general explanation. This goal is excluded in view of our concentration on high-level decision making mechanisms : since the system does not generate utterances down to the sentence level, neither can it analyse the meaning of sentences input by the student. At the highest level of the goal tree, a fundamental distinction is made between disjunctive 'claim' and 'challenge' goals. This corresponds generally to a distinction between stating something 'new' in the dialogue, related to the previous dialogue by local focus constraints, and a direct reference to a previously stated goal in the dialogue (e.g. critiquing a previous directly referred to claim).

Each dialogue goal has parameters for the current negotiator, speaker, concept and instance discussed (n,s,c,i), which are successively bound to specific values as the negotiation proceeds. The dialogue state preconditions consist of a logical expression into which current parameter values are substituted, and are evaluated with respect to the dialogue state. Negotiation preconditions state what needs to be negotiated and accepted for the dialogue actions associated to be performed. In this case there are no actions, since these are only attached to terminal nodes (see Figure 9.2). The operator lists its subgoals, and the effects of successful negotiation and performance of the dialogue action are propagated on the dialogue state by the 'negotiation effects'. These update the dialogue history with the instantiated negotiated goal, encode a representation of

```
dialogue move: CLAIM
parameters: (c inst n s)
dialogue_state_preconditions:
  ( (not (null c)) &
   ((null *dialogue_history*)
    OR
   ((in_focus? c (ltm_model s)) &
    (not (known? c (ltm_model (dialogue_participant  s)))) &
    (exists_ltm_trace? c (ltm_model s)))))))
negotiation_preconditions:
  ((negotiate s (goal= 'CLAIM)) & (negotiate s c)))
subgoals:
  (OR ((concrete_claim (c inst  s))
      (abstract_claim (c inst  s)))))
negotiation_effects:
  ((update_dialogue_history
   '((goal_name= 'CLAIM) (s= s) (c= c) (inst= inst)))))
action_effects: nil
actions: nil
```

Fig. 9.2 Example dialogue move 'CLAIM'.

the beliefs expressed in the action for each interlocutor and propagate activation through the belief network (according to the equations described in Anderson 1983).

Dialogue state preconditions refer to the dialogue history and the mental states of interlocutors. For example, a claim move is relevant if it is the beginning of the dialogue, the speaker has a memory representation for the concept to be communicated, and believes that the other interlocutor does not 'know' that concept. We have not addressed the philosophical and psychological problems associated with the distinction between knowledge and belief, nor concerning their acquisition. We simply assume that memory traces will be encoded in dialogue for concepts which are mentioned, which correspond to 'belief' in the way in which they are used in dialogue: beliefs are intensional objects which when communicated in dialogue, have to be justified, whose justifications can be critiqued, and which cannot serve as the basis of straightforward contradition of a previously stated belief.

Speakers' beliefs

The beliefs of each participant are represented as instances of concepts in a semantic network (Quillian 1969). Our model for memory encoding and retrieval during the course of dialogue is based on the ACT* model of

Anderson (1983). We assume that if a concept is mentioned then both interlocutors encode a working memory trace for it, which has a probability of forming a long-term memory representation with repetition. Retrieval from long-term memory is based on the phenomenon of *spreading activation* in semantic memory, from an input source. We have applied this feature of Anderson's theory to the definition of focus in dialogue (shown by the 'in_focus?' predicate in the example above). From the point of view of the system, when it attempts to satisfy *relevance* (Sperber & Wilson 1986) dialogue state preconditions for a dialogue move, it checks the current concept value with respect to its own working memory, being the traces with the highest activation level: if the concept is in working memory, then it is viewed as sufficiently in focus to satisfy this precondition, otherwise not. If no concept is proposed, then it selects the concept with the highest activation level, in order to find a parameter value which enables this precondition to be satisfied. When it is the student's turn to negotiate a dialogue goal, the system bases part of its decision as to whether to cooperate or not on checking its own representation of the activation level of that concept, thus judging its relative focus.

We have now discussed the basic data representations which need to be understood in order to describe the fundamental dialogue generation mechanisms of KANT.

4.2 Managing turn-taking in negotiation

At the highest level, a 'dialogue controller' program controls the alternation of negotiated turns between system and student. These do not necessarily correspond to speaker turns, since an interlocutor may negotiate that a dialogue goal be pursued by the other. Our model can accommodate this by specifying dialogue moves and their associated parametrized preconditions in a sufficiently general way so that a dialogue goal may be used with any combination of speaker and other parameter values (for example, n = system/s = system, n = student/s = system, for a claim goal). The dialogue controller incorporates a simplified version of the turn-taking mechanism described by Schegloff and Sacks (1973):

> "1. at least and no more than one party speaks at a time in a single conversation; and
> 2. speaker change recurs" (p. 293).

The turn-taking mechanisms in KANT are simpler than those which have been described for natural human conversations. They may be summarized as follows:

1 Speaker1 negotiates a goal;
2 Speaker2 responds with agreement or disagreement;
3 If speaker2 agrees, then speaker1 performs dialogue actions associated with the agreed goal;
4 When a dialogue action associated with a goal is performed by speaker1, speaker1 may self-select, and attempt to negotiate subgoals of the first goal (step 1). These may succeed, in which case associated dialogue actions are performed, or they may fail, in which case the negotiator role changes.
5 Depending on the degree to which speaker1 believes that speaker2 understands the subgoal to be negotiated, speaker1 may pursue a subgoal, generate a preannouncement, or negotiate it as in step 1. Upon assent to a preannouncement, dialogue actions of subgoals are performed.
6 If the speaker disagrees, then the negotiator role changes, and the disagreeing speaker takes a negotiated turn (goto step 1).

In Step 4 above, we can see that the mechanism is in fact recursive – Step 4 invokes Step 1. We shall see this mechanism in operation when we present an example dialogue generation trace produced by KANT, in Section 4.7 of this chapter. The simple turn-taking and negotiation mechanism described is on of the assumptions of our model which we shall consider with respect to negotiation phases which are analysed in Section 5.

4.3 Factors determining which dialogue move to negotiate

We now turn to the mechanisms which speakers use to decide which goal to attempt to negotiate, and how they decide whether to cooperate or not with a negotiated goal. The following are factors which are used in determining which goal to negotiate:

- the structure of the and/or decision tree of dialogue moves, which defines mutually exclusive alternatives, and conjunctive possibilities;
- satisfaction of dialogue state preconditions for the relevance of a dialogue move, with respect to the dialogue state;
- choice of alternative mutually relevant dialogue moves according to a set of educational preferences.

When either speaker converses, the dialogue move tree is searched in order to find a set of goals in the tree whose dialogue state preconditions are satisfied, and the negotiation of which is accepted. For each goal encountered, existing parameter values are substituted into the dialogue state preconditions expression, which is evaluated with respect to the dialogue state (factor 2). If it returns 'true', the goal is satisfied and can be negotiated, otherwise not. If alternative goals are both satisfied, then the set of educational preferences is applied in order to choose one (factor 3). Upon success, any attached dialogue actions are performed, and search continues below that goal. If none are satisfied, then the speaker 'can think of nothing [relevant, preferred] to say', and the other speaker is now the negotiator. The number of educational preferences required is related to the number of points where a choice may be made, i.e. the number of disjuctive branches. In the present goal tree, there are only two: discriminating between claim and challenge goals, and between abstract and concrete claims (other preferences are required for preferred parameter instantiations of these goals, as discussed later).

It is often the case that in evaluating a particular dialogue state precondition expression, parameter values are not already assigned. For this reason, the system may attempt to satisfy preconditions by *actively searching* for some appropriate value. Thus the evaluation process involves procedures which search for certain parameter values as well as intepreting the expression. For example, in the following precondition expression, the system may have to choose a value for s (speaker) and c (concept):

```
((in_focus? c (ltm_model s)) &
    ;; is the concept c in focus with respect to memory model for speaker s?
(not (known? c (ltm_model (dialogue_participant s)))))
    ;; is the concept c known with respect to memory model of other speaker?
```

This is done using a complex set of functions which choose the concept most in focus (activation level in working memory), and which prefer to select a concept which is 'not known' to the hearer (discussed later).

4.4 Educational preferences for discriminating dialogue goals

The preferences used are as follows:

Pref 1: 'Prefer to challenge an existing claim if relevant to do so, rather than making a new claim' (claim and challenge goals).

Pref 2: 'Prefer to make a concrete claim, if relevant to do so, rather than making an abstract claim' (concrete_claim and abstract_claim goals).

Pref 1 relates to the stable 'initiate-response-feedback' pattern observed by Sinclair and Coulthard (1975) in classroom educational dialogues: in effect it prefers to give feedback to a response rather than stating something new, thus making more connected dialogue. Pref 2 corresponds to concretization of a discussion, before discussing a concept in the abstract.

For determining a preferred speaker parameter value for a dialogue goal, a second kind of educational preference is used:

Pref 3: 'Prefer the student to be the speaker when the system is the negotiator' (choosing preferred s parameter value).

This is derived from the empirical analyses of classroom dialogues of Bellack et al. (1966), who found that the majority of teachers' 'moves' were elicitation, i.e. the teacher negotiating that the student should respond. If the precondition expression cannot be satisfied with the (preferred) student as speaker, then the system attempts to satisfy it with the system as speaker. In summary, for each predicate referred to in the dialogue state preconditions, there are both:

1 procedures which test its truth value under a given substitution with respect to the dialogue state;
2 a set of procedures which search the dialogue state for parameter values (for goal, concept, speaker, instance) under which the expression would evaluate to be true.

4.5 Performing dialogue actions

Once a dialogue goal has been satisfied as relevant, discriminated according to preferences, and negotiated as accepted, dialogue actions (if any) may be performed, and effects propagated on the dialogue state. Since we concentrated on describing a model for high-level decision processes in dialogue, the performance of dialogue actions in KANT involves generating a text template corresponding to communicating the concept and instance parameter values which have been satisfied as relevant and communicated for a goal, for a given speaker. In the case where the student is speaker, the system generates a summary of this, and asks the student to agree that this represents their negotiated goal. For each dialogue goal, the function 'INFORM' has the appropriate parameters which were negotiated. In addition, each concept node in the semantic network may have some explanatory text associated with it. For example, in performing the dialogue goal ((INFORM s c)) as part of an abstract claim, the system says:

"The following is an explanation of concept $<<c>>$: $<<$explanatory text generated$>>$."

In the case of a concrete claim, there will also be an instance parameter value, leading to:

"I am claiming that $<<i>>$ is an instance of concept $<<c>>$."

In the case of challenge subgoals, a repetition of the name of the goal which has been negotiated plays an important part in communication. For example, in the 'new_supports' subgoal, this corresponds to stating one or more justifications which the speaker also believes to apply to a previously stated instance. Therefore, the system generates a summary of what the goal is. For example :

"goal: new_supports = state a new justification for a previous claim about a concept",

communicates the sense of the 'standard' statement generated as for a concrete claim:

"I am claiming that $<<i>>$ is a justification of concept $<<c>>$."

and the fact that this claim is viewed as a new *support* to the previous one. Restating the goal definition thus corresponds to explicitly stating the dialogic or argumentative *relation* between dialogue goals (Ferrara 1985). In describing the negotiated turn-taking mechanism earlier, we stated that after a dialogue goal has been uttered, the speaker may self-select, and, under certain conditions, either state or negotiate subgoals of that goal. In accordance with the model of dialogue focus based on spreading activation encorporated in KANT, subgoals are explored in order of highest activation level. This also involves a recursive invocation of the turn-taking mechanism ('dialogue controller'), an algorithm for choosing the order of pursuit of subgoals, the generation of special metadialogue sequences called *preannouncements*, and tests for their applicability. Preannouncements (Levinson 1983) are sequences where speakers announce the general topic of what they are going to say before doing so, in circumstances where they are not sure of its 'newsworthiness'. For example, before someone says "England won against Mozambique at football last night", they may try to ensure that what they are going to say is not already known by saying ". . . about the match on

TV last night . . .", or "Did you see the match last night?", thus allowing the hearer to say "No, go on . . .", or alternatively "Yes, England won didn't they?". Since these sequences relate to the beliefs of one speaker about those of the other, we incorporate this feature using a the predicate 'known?', which is defined in terms of (theoretically uninteresting) values of the strength of a memory trace (*re* concept node in the semantic network), as follows :

- if a concept is 'known', then the system does not pursue it as a subgoal, and mentions this;
- if a concept is 'possibly known' then the system generates a preannouncement of the form 'I now want to go on and discuss the subconcept $<<c1>>$; is that ok?';
- if a concept is 'not known', then the system negotiates it as a subgoal.

When the student is the speaker, exactly the same dialogue generation mechanisms are used. The principal difference lies in the input and output to the program. In the case of the student as speaker, the system generates summaries of the responses (yes and no) to negotiation, of the beliefs and instances chosen, and presents the set of dialogue moves available at a given point in the goal tree for the student to choose.

4.6   Acceptance and refusal in negotiation

We finally need to say how a negotiator decides whether to accept a negotiated goal or not. The mechanism which we have adopted in the present version of KANT bases this decision on the same relevance preconditions which an interlocutor uses to decide which dialogue goal to pursue, i.e.:

an interlocutor $i1$ agrees to accept a negotiated dialogue goal if and only if the dialogue state precondition expression for that goal evaluates as satisfied with respect to the interlocutor's representation of the dialogue state when substituted with the negotiated parameter values and $i1$ as speaker.

In this sense, the speaker asks himself if, from his own point of view, the dialogue goal negotiated by the other is *minimally* relevant. Note that the restriction is not so strong as to demand that the goal be also *preferred*. Clearly, this is a considerable simplification, resulting from the fact that the dialogue system does not incorporate a notion of longer-term and higher-level goals. Our negotiation mechanism is also considerably simplified in that it could easily be modified to include further exchanges where the respondent does not accept a goal with some parameters, but then attempts to find values under which it would accept, which are then proposed in turn as a 'compromise' (see Sycara 1988, 1989). We did not incorporate such further sophistications into KANT at this stage, preferring to reserve them for a phase of evaluating the model with respect to dialogue transcripts.

4.7 Example dialogue trace generated by KANT

Finally, we discuss an example a dialogue trace generated by KANT, describing how it is generated. We restrict ourselves to a single example which illustrates most features. In the examples, typed input by the user is in *italics*, plain text is an output trace generated by KANT. The lines have been numbered (e.g. '9/') for reference in the commentary.

This is an example taken from the middle of a 'dialogue' with KANT, i.e. an interactive trace. There are two negotiated turns, each of which consists of a negotiation phase, followed by a dialogue action, which is recursively continued in the second negotiated turn. In the first turn, the student is the negotiator and the speaker, in the second the system is the negotiator and speaker, and challenges the claim made by the student in the first. The domain discussed is that of a set of justifications for the existence of musical phrase boundaries in an example melody, integrated into a semantic network representation.

1/My turn over . . . your move
2/Are you sure you want to continue the discussion? (y or n)
3/*y*
4/Please type who you want the SPEAKER to be . . .(student or system)
5/*student*
6/Please type in the concept you want to talk about (if you want a full list of possibilities, type 'show')
7/*phrase_boundary*
8/Please type in the instance position you want to talk about
9/*p10*
10/I will tell you if I agree to cooperate . . . Ok, I will cooperate
11/Please choose one but not both of the goals to pursue:
12/ CHALLENGE = make a challenge to a previous claim
13/ CLAIM = make a claim concerning a concept
14/*claim*
15/I will tell you if I agree to cooperate . . . Ok, I will cooperate
16/Please choose one but not both of the goals to pursue:
17/ CONCRETE_CLAIM = make a specific claim about a concept instance
18/ ABSTRACT_CLAIM = make a general explanatory claim about a concept
19/*concrete_claim*
20/I will tell you if I agree to cooperate . . . Ok, I will cooperate
21/Please choose a goal to pursue:

22/MAKE_INSTANCE_CLAIM = state a claim about an instance
23/SUPPORT_INSTANCE_CLAIM = state justifications for an instance claim
24/*make_instance_claim*
25/I will tell you if I agree to cooperate . . . Ok, I will cooperate
26/You are pursuing the dialogue goal MAKE_INSTANCE_CLAIM, with
27/PHRASE_BOUNDARY as a concept, and P10 as its instance. Please confirm or
disconfirm your intentions (y/n)
28/*y*
29/Ok, I'll remember that.
30/Please choose a goal to pursue:
31/SUPPORT_INSTANCE_CLAIM = state justifications for an instance claim
32/*support_instance_claim*
33/Please type in the justification(s) for the instance P10
34/*(CONTRAST PARALLELISM)*
35/I will tell you if I agree to cooperate . . . Ok, I will cooperate
36/You are pursuing the dialogue goal SUPPORT_INSTANCE_CLAIM, with
37/PHRASE_BOUNDARY as a concept, P10 as its instance, and (CONTRAST
PARALLELISM)
38/as the justifications. Please confirm or disconfirm your intentions (y/n)
39/*y*
40/Are you sure you want to continue the discussion? (y or n)
41/*y*
42/My move . . .
43/Do you accept that we pursue the dialogue goal CHALLENGE (== make a challenge
to a previous claim) (y/n?)
44/*y*
45/Do you accept that we discuss the concept PHRASE_BOUNDARY (y/n?)
46/*y*
47/Do you accept that we discuss the concept instance P10 (y/n?)
48/*y*
49/Do you accept that we pursue the dialogue goal CLAIM_SHARED (== agree with a
previous claim) (y or n?)
50/*y*
51/Iagree that P10 is an instance of the concept PHRASE_BOUNDARY
52/Do you accept that we pursue the dialogue goal AGREE_SUPPORTS (== agree with
some previously stated justification types) (y or n?)
53/*y*
54/AGREE_SUPPORTS is the dialogue goal currently being pursued with the justification
type(s) PARALLELISM.
55/I want to try to explain what I mean by the justification(s) PARALLELISM. Is that ok?
(y/n)
56/*n*
57/Ok, maybe we'll talk about PARALLELISM next time around. . .
58/Do you accept that we pursue the dialogue goal NEW_SUPPORTS (== state some
justifications which we not mentioned for previous instance claim) (y or n?)
59/*y*
60/NEW_SUPPORTS is the dialogue goal currently being pursued with
CHORD_PROGRESSION as the new support(s).
61/I want to try to explain what I mean by the justification(s) CHORD_PROGRESSION.
Is that ok? (y/n)
62/*n*
63/Ok, maybe we'll talk about CHORD_PROGRESSION next time around. . .

64/Do you accept that we pursue the dialogue goal DISAGREE_SUPPORTS (==
disagree with some previously stated justification types) (y/n?)
65/*y*
66/DISAGREE_SUPPORTS is the dialogue goal currently being pursued with CONTRAST
as the disagreed support(s).
67/I want to try to explain what I mean by the justification(s) CONTRAST. Is that ok? (y/
n)
68/*n*
69/Ok, maybe we'll talk about CONTRAST next time around. . .
70/My turn over . . . your move

Lines 1–35: Negotiation phase

> $n=$ student
> $s=$ student
> $c=$ phrase_boundary
> $i=$ p10

At 1/ the dialogue controller gives the negotiated turn to the student, the previous negotiator having been the system. At 2/ we have a 'transition relevance point' (Schegloff & Sacks 1973), where speaker roles may shift and either participant may choose to terminate the dialogue. From 4/ to 35/ the dialogue goal tree is searched top-down, and at each point parameters which are unbound are presented to the student with the choices available, as well as the choices of dialogue move at that point. At the beginning, the 'DISCUSS' move is satisfied provided that the memory representations of both participants are not equal. For the student, the s, c and i parameters are presented for choice. The system now substitutes the chosen parameter values into the preconditions of 'DISCUSS', which evaluate to 'true' and so the system agrees to cooperate. The student now chooses the 'CLAIM' move, for which a summary explanation is given (lines 11–14). Again the system substitutes the parameter values into preconditions, this time to give:

```
( (not (null 'PHRASE_BOUNDARY)) ;; there is a current concept value
    &
   ((null *dialogue_history*) ;; it is not the start of the dialogue
      OR
   ((in_focus? 'PHRASE_BOUNDARY (ltm_model 'SYSTEM)) ;; the concept is
sufficiently in focus
        &
   (not (known? 'PHRASE_BOUNDARY (ltm_model (dialogue_participant 'STUDENT))))
   ;; the student does not know the concept to be claimed
        &
(exists_ltm_trace? 'PHRASE_BOUNDARY (ltm_model 'STUDENT))))))
   ;; the student possesses a memory trace for the concept
```

The system evaluates this expression with respect to the dialogue state: the concept 'PHRASE_BOUNDARY' is found to have a high enough focus level in the system's representation of the student's memory, naturally, the student is found to possess a memory trace for the concept concerning which (s)he wants to make a claim, the node strength for this concept in the system's memory is found to have a strength sufficiently low so that it should decide to want to hear something about this concept, so it agrees to cooperate (line 15). A similar procedure takes place with respect to the proposed CONCRETE_CLAIM goal and its subgoals (conjunctive).

Lines 36–39: Dialogue action

The student performs the dialogue action in the form of agreeing to a summary of a statement generated by the system.

". . . You are pursuing the dialogue goal SUPPORT_INSTANCE _CLAIM, with 37/PHRASE_BOUNDARY as a concept, P10 as its instance, and (CONTRAST PARALLELISM) 38/as the justifications. Please confirm or disconfirm your intentions (y/n) 39/y"

This is followed by a similar procedure for the conjuctive 'SUP-PORT_INSTANCE_CLAIM' subgoal. After line 39/ is generated, the system performs negotiation and dialogue goal effects, which are to update the dialogue history and the memory models of each interlocutor. This involves 'PHRASE_BOUNDARY' becoming an input source of activation in both network representations, through which activation is spread, and increasing the appropriate node strength.

Lines 40–54: Negotiation phase

$n=$ system
$s=$ system
$c=$ phrase_boundary
$i=$ p10

At 40/ the argument controller passes a negotiated turn to the system. Both the claim and challenge goals are satisfied as relevant, but since a 'challengable' claim has been made, preference Pref1 operates to choose the challenge goal. The concept parameter is now bound to the concept referred to in the previous dialogue move (i.e. PHRASE_BOUNDARY of CLAIM move), from the dialogue history, together with the instance p10 to be challenged. Looking at its own memory representation and the supports claimed by the student in the previous turn, the system agrees with the previous support 'PARALLELISM', performing a dialogue action.

Lines 55–69: Dialogue action

At this point (line 55) the system decides that subconcepts of PARALLELISM are 'possibly known', and so generates a preannouncement in line 55. This is not accepted by the student, so the system continues to negotiate with other satisfiable subgoals of the CHALLENGE move. It states some NEW_SUPPORTS for the claim challenged which the student had not mentioned (line 60), then finally disagrees with the support CONTRAST for this claim (line 64). Again it attempts to pursue this dialogue action, which is refused by the student. After each of these actions, effects are propagated on the dialogue state as before. Finally, at line 69 the system has no futher satisfiable subgoals to negotiate, all subactions of dialogue actions have been refused, and its negotiated turn ends. At 70 the argument controller passes the negotiated turn to the student.

There are a number of features which we have not been able to show in this example (see Baker 1989c for further details) such as the system refusing to cooperate with negotiation, the system negotiating that the student should speak, the student negotiating that the system should speak, and so on. Nevertheless, we have illustrated the major features of KANT, which also apply in these other cases.

4.8   Some preliminary criticisms of KANT

We must emphasize that we are not claiming that the example which we have described would be suitable for 'real' use with students, and no effort has presently been made to develop an educationally suitable and robust interface. The example is *an interactive trace of the execution of a model for generation of tutorial dialogue*, incorporating a notion of dialogue focus and a negotiative style.

An immediate comment which may be made is that the negotiation phases are very lengthy: it would be possible to condense much of this into a single sentence, for example

"Do you accept to tell me where you think there is an instance of a phrase boundary?."

We did not adopt this approach initially because any such conjunction would require analysis into the 'finegrained' mechanism shown above in the case where this was not accepted – does the respondent disagree with who speaks, with the topic, . . . ? Furthermore, it is not clear that goals need always be negotiated, nor that they are always negotiated explicitly. The range of moves which can be performed with the present version of KANT is limited by the fact that there is no understanding of the student's utterances – propositions are simply compared and 'contrasted' – which is one effect of our initial hypothesis that dialogue mechanisms can be initially specified at a 'high' level. In general, the negotiation mechanism itself is too simple, and does not admit of interactive renegotiation on a given negotiated turn.

We now summarize some of the assumptions which we made in developing KANT, and some initial simplifications which we made for methodological reasons, as a focus for comparing the model with dialogue analysis results.

4.8.1 Assumptions of KANT

1 In tutorial dialogues, the topic and goals of dialogue are negotiated.
2 Negotiation of goals proceeds from higher level to lower level goals, with increasing concreteness.
3 When a goal is successfully negotiated, it is pursued by the agreed speaker.
4 After a negotiation initiated by a given speaker fails, the other speaker initiates a negotiation.
5 After a negotiated turn, either speaker may decide to terminate the dialogue.
6 After speakers have successfully negotiated and pursued a goal, they may negotiate its subgoals.
7 When negotiating the pursuit of subgoals after the higher level goal has been pursued, speakers may generate preannouncements depending on their knowledge of the other speaker's mental states.
8 A speaker cooperates with a negotiated goal if (s)he believes it to be relevant, otherwise not.
9 The propositional content of dialogue utterances is encoded in working memory.

4.8.2 Simplifications of KANT

1 Goals are (always) negotiated, and always negotiated explicitly.
2 A determinate set of dialogue goals (such as those used in KANT) are used within any given dialogue.

5 COMPARISON WITH DIALOGUE TRANSCRIPT ANALYSES

Our previous analyses of computer-mediated teaching dialogues have given us some analytical data with which to test the assumptions and initial simplifications which were made in KANT.

5.1 Negotiating goals

Evidence that negotiation forms an important part of educational dialogues is clearly evident from our analyses. As a rough measure, of the 83 exchanges (turns) in the example dialogue analysed here, approximately 46 are concerned with explicit or implicit negotiation. This dialogue was the second in a total series of 8, and so we would expect a greater degree of negotiation to be initially required in order to define general goals.

5.2 Generality and specificity of goals negotiated

There are a number of cases in which goals are negotiated from general to specific:

T1: I would greatly enjoy doing some PROLOG ...
   negotiates(T _ PROLOG)
T5: ... How about writing a predicate called second_word ...
   negotiates(T L <PROLOG(predicate second_word)>)
L8 ... I am wondering about strings
   negotiates(T L <PROLOG(predicate
second_word(strings))>)

Here we can see a process similar to the successive definition of negotiator, speaker and topic parameters, used in KANT. However, this example occurs at the very beginning of the dialogue, in order to define the general goals of the interaction. Later in the dialogue, these more general goals are assumed to be still in operation, so speaker and subtopic parameters are negotiated directly in a truncated form:

T27 ... why not warm up by defining first_word, which can (nearly) be done in one clause?
   negotiates(T L <PROLOG(predicate first_word)>)

This suggests that recognizable subgoals of an already agreed goal may

be negotiated assuming the higher-level goal to still hold, even if they are ,
not the current explicit focus. Our assumption of general-specific, and
successive negotiation of parameters was therefore too strong – KANT
needs to incorporate negotiation at this general level of successive
negotiation of parameters, and to subsequently be able to switch to a
smaller 'grain-size', to negotiate completely instantiated goals in a single
utterance (as discussed in the previous section).

5.3 Negotiation and dialogue actions

The distinction between negotiation phases and performance of the
agreed goal, is generally supported by analysis – it relates to a difference
between metacognitive and cognitive activity. For example:

> "T27 ... why not warm up by defining first_word, which can (nearly) be done in
> one clause?
>   [negotiation]
> L28: ok [response]
>   first_word([], []).
>   . . . .
>   [dialogue action]

Given the problem-solving domain in these dialogues, actions here
concern problem-solving in the domain, whereas in KANT actions
concerned communication of beliefs and their justifications. We can,
however, find dialogue actions which communicate belief:

> L8: Well, yeah, I am just wondering about strings and things ...
> T9: We discussed this last week.
> A string is really a list of ascii codes, yeah?"

In this example, the learner's utterance is interpreted as an implicit
request for information from the teacher.

5.4 Negotiation and turn-taking

This prediction is partially confirmed by the transcripts. For example:

> T1: I would greatly enjoy doing some prolog. Did you have something in mind?
>   **[negotiation]**
> L2: No, not really.
>   **[negative response]**
> Like I said I haven't really looked at your program with the idea of extending it yet.

Could we do something simplish, just to make me feel good?!
[negotiation]

This is equivalent in structure to the following extract from the KANT dialogue trace shown earlier:

(KANT OUTPUT TRACE)
67/I want to try to explain what I mean by the justification(s) CONTRAST. Is that ok? (y/n)
   [NEGOTIATION – system]
68/n
   [NEGATIVE RESPONSE – student]
69/Ok, maybe we'll talk about CONTRAST next time around. . .
70/My turn over . . . your move
71/Are you sure you want to continue the discussion? (y or n)
72/y
73/Please type who you want the SPEAKER to be . . .(student or system)
74/student
   [NEGOTIATION – student]

However, as we mentioned earlier, this 'normative' turn-taking sequence only applies in cases of INDIFFERENCE or COOPERA-TION, and breaks down in cases of CONFLICT, the paradigmatic case where negotiation is required. KANT therefore needs to be extended to incorporate elements of both structures, together with the required mechanisms for recognizing the appropriate propositional posture with which they are associated.

5.5   After a negotiated turn, either speaker may decide to terminate the dialogue

Attempted negotiation of the termination of the dialogue does occur (example 2 in Section 9.3 of this chapter), and therefore this needs to be provided as a possible choice to each speaker. However, we have also seen that *benevolence* cannot necessarily always be assumed – in KANT, we adopted the initial simplification that if the student wishes to terminate the dialogue, the system automatically consents, and *vice versa*. We therefore need to incorporate some elements of Galliers' (1989) analysis of conflict situations, in order to address the issue of when a speaker should agree to terminate, and when they would accept the negotiation of some alternative goal for which they have a preference. As Schegloff and Sacks (1973) argued, closings of conversations need to be *prepared* in order to be mutually acceptable, which includes the generation and careful timing of *preclosings*. Some aspects of conversation analysis applied to openings and closing of conversations have been incorporated as a 'grammar of adjacency pairs' in the advice system of Frohlich and Luff (1990). In the dialogues analysed, elements of preclosings can be seen in a shift from actual problem-solving and negotiation of its joint control, to a retrospective discussion for evaluating the student's performance:

> L75: Jesus christ I don't know why it took me so long. . .
> T76: Some days things like that are hard. Brains switch off . . .
> T78: You're warming up now. . .
> T80: Good. I don't think we can do much more at the moment. Shall I leave you with a problem to ponder, and we can talk about it some other day?

5.6 Negotiating subgoals

Speakers naturally extend their dialogue actions to subgoals which are strictly beyond the initially agreed goal, for example, in giving further information than is requested :

> L12: . . . If I did name("fish and chips", N). would I get N = [no, no, no, no, 32 no,no,no,32, no,no, etc]?
> ((question))
> T13: No, actually, you'd get an error.
> ((answer))
> The first argument has to be atomic and the second list.
> ((explanation/clarification))
> If you did
>   name(X, "fish and chips")
> you'd get X=fish and chips
> where the value of X is actually an ATOM, though it doesn't look like it.
> What I suspect you want is . . . . [etc.]
> ((explanation))

Notice that the teacher remains the speaker, and that the extra information is still of a 'reasonable turn length'. We may therefore hypothesize that if the teacher wished to continue on an extended discussion of some concept – e.g. atoms, etc. – that this *would* be negotiated, or that if the continued extra information required the other to speak, then this would also be negotiated. The lessons which we draw for KANT are therefore:

- subgoals may be negotiated if longer than the 'normal' length of a single turn, or if they require speaker change;
- otherwise, a speaker may extend their negotiated and agreed dialogue action without explicit negotiation.

We would require further empirical work in order to establish the precise extent to which turns may be extended by a speaker. The initial simplificiation of allowing a speaker to continue to negotiate subgoals of an action in a straightforward depth-first search manner must therefore also be modified. The question of how long a 'reasonable' turn is can probably be simply resolved by giving the student the possibility of *interrupting*. From the point of view of the system, however, we need further research before we could specify exactly when the system should interrupt the student. Given a certain educational philosophy which prefers the maximum of initiative to be taken by the student (see the educational preferences included in KANT), it is possible that this aspect should *not* be symmetrical for the system and student : we would want the student to be allowed to continue a turn as much as possible, provided the system recognizes that their actions are relevant to achieving the agreed goal. In fact we do find the teacher interrupting in this way, when he feels that the student is no longer performing actions to achieve the goal:

```
L28: . . . first_word([],[]).
first_word(A,B) :- name(C,A);
    hang on
first_word(([],[]).
first_word(A,B,) :- name[C|[D|E]],A);
D=32
That C should be a B
T29: Is that it?
L30: um
T31? can I say something?
((. . .))
```

5.7 Negotiating subgoals and preannouncements

Although preannouncements occur in everyday conversations, we have not observed their use in these dialogues, in the way in which they are incorporated in KANT. The extent to which this poses a problem for the model depends on our research goals. If we want to generate human-computer dialogues in ITS which are perceived as coherent by a learner, it is possible that the inclusion of preannouncements for negotiation of subgoals could improve user acceptability. Their use in everyday conversations is well established (Levinson 1983), even though we have not observed them in these example dialogues. For the present, the changes which need to be made to KANT with respect to negotiation of subgoals indicate that we should suppress their inclusion in KANT until their use can be better defined by analysis.

5.8 Relevance and cooperation with negotiated goals

We have not analysed cases where a speaker refuses to cooperate with a negotiated goal because it is not relevant. Conversely, all goals negotiated which *were* relevant to the previous goal were accepted. In KANT the notion of relevance combines topic-based focus, with speaker roles and dialogue goals, in a complex set of preconditions with respect to the dialogue state. We observed cases where the speaker does not accept such a combination, presumably in terms of their *preferences* :

> T1: I would greatly enjoy doing some Prolog. Did you have something in mind?
> (negotiates(T L negotiates(L_prolog))
> L2: No, not really.
> (responds(L n U2)).

Since KANT includes the use of (educational) preferences in choice of goals to pursue, it therefore should be extended beyond its present (relevance-based) benevolence (Galliers 1989) to incorporate more strict criteria for accepting the student's negotiated goals, using these preferences. Given the greater likelihood of conflict which would result, we need to extend the current mechanisms to resolve these conflicts. One way to do this would be to attempt to find a 'compromise' satisfaction of the dialogue goal which was close to that proposed by the student – for example, with a different speaker role – or else to attempt to defer the goal to later in the dialogue. In order to achieve this, we need to incorporate a representation of *preferences* and *commitments* (as described by Cohen & Levesque 1990, Galliers 1989) and a more explicit representation of temporal aspects of *deferred goals*. Conflicts arise mostly in the dialogues because the goals proposed concern the form of the dialogue itself – such as its termination – rather than its topic. The extent to which a speaker accepts such negotiated goals must relate to higher level persistent goals, or commitments (again, in Cohen and Levesque's terms) – such as 'that the student should complete the problem' – and the extent to which they are in direct conflict in these negotiations.

Other more fundamental aspects which need to be developed in KANT include a more sophisticated model of relevance (Sperber & Wilson 1986), and means for managing *conversational repair* (Good 1990). The following is an example of a misunderstanding leading to a repair sequence:

```
T23: ? Can I suggest?
second_word(A,Bno
L24: yes
T25: yes what? I'm confused.
L26: Yes, suggest.
T27: Oh. . .
```

5.9   Encoding utterances in dialogue

The simple memory encoding hypotheses used in KANT were consistent with the general theory of memory adopted (Anderson 1983), but clearly fail to distinguish a memory that some other speaker stated a belief from a belief which is genuinely *adopted by the hearer as their own*. This difficult problem will need to be addressed in the future in terms of recent AI theories of *belief revision* (see the collection of papers in Halpern 1986).

6   SUMMARY AND CONCLUSIONS

In this chapter we have explored the nature of negotiation, and attempted to establish the functions which it performs in teaching dialogues. We have analysed computer-mediated teaching dialogues in order to identify what may be negotiated, why negotiation occurs, and the interaction structures with which it is associated.This has provided us with an extensive research agenda of new features to incorporate in a first prototype computational model for intelligent teaching dialogues which includes negotiation mechanisms. With respect to existing work on negotiation, the distinctive contributions of KANT include the integration of negotiation mechanisms within a more general model for extended dialogue, rather than in a single exchange, and the extension of the problem of modelling negotiation in tutorial dialogues beyond conflict resolution situations. Major features to be modified in KANT include:

- changes to turn-taking mechanisms in negotiations, with respect to the propositional attitudes of conflict, indifference and cooperation;
- introduction of mechanisms for resolving conflict by the more principled representation of propositional postures, preferences and commitments;
- changes to the procedures used for negotiating dialogue subgoals;

- provision of mechanisms for interruption, including knowledge of when and how to interrupt whilst maintaining a cooperative posture.

We also described a number of other specific phenomena which the model needs to take into account, including the range of goals and beliefs which can be negotiated and explanation and justification of negotiated goals. Clearly, a number of difficult problems were not addressed previously, including belief revision (Harman 1986, Fagin & Halpern 1988), the formal representation of conflict and its resolution (Galliers 1989), and the representation of meta-cognitive awareness and reasoning. From our dialogue analyses, the negotiation of goals from more abstract and general to more concrete and specific, and the basic turn-taking mechanism were shown to be adequate at a first approximation.

As a phenomenon in interaction, negotiation is closely linked with *meta-cognitive awareness* of problem-solving abilities on the part of a speaker, as a prerequisite for negotiation of future cooperative control of joint dialogue goals. An important feature of meta-cognitive awareness is a speaker's affective attitude to towards the possibility of achieving goals, especially in conditions of apparent failure. When we consider the problem of how a teacher can successfully negotiate goals, therefore, the problems of understanding the affective and the motivational effects of utterances are particularly important. Progress for cognitive modelling in the area of affect (Donohew et al. 1988), the emotions (Ortony et al. 1988) and motivation (Weinhert & Kluwe 1987) is now at the stage where we may have reasonable hope of including such aspects in models for dialogue in Intelligent Tutoring Systems. Given the different *nature* of the goals and beliefs of teachers (and ITS) and learners, it is clear that negotiation in educational discourse fulfills the important functions of securing cooperativity and genuine *engagement* in the learning process on the part of the student, and the possibility of a joint construction of meaning.

In future research we plan to validate and refine KANT by a combination of approaches. In order to test the extent to which an extended version of KANT can successfully maintain a coherent and focussed dialogue, and use negotiation appropriately in interaction with a human student, we plan to develop a graphical interface to the system (which is implemented in Lisp), for 'pragmatic validation' with students.

ACKNOWLEDGEMENTS

The research concerning the first prototype of KANT was conducted at the Open University, Centre for Information Technology in Education, under the supervision of Mark Elsom-Cook. Thanks to him for guidance and encouragement, and for providing the dialogues analysed. My ideas have greatly benefitted from discussions with Andrée Tiberghien at CNRS-IRPEACS (Lyon).

10 A Discourse Repertoire for Negotiating Explanations

RACHEL RIMMERSHAW

*Department of Educational Research,
University of Lancaster, UK*

ABSTRACT

In this chapter the notion of negotiation is explored as it applies to interactions in 'natural' educational contexts, and with particular reference to the negotiation or coordination of explanations. The discussion is illustrated with examples from a variety of learning situations in which explanations are requested or volunteered. It deals with the question of what tutors and students could be negotiating *about*, and also with the repertoire of discourse moves by which explanations are negotiated in human dialogue (both spoken and written). This is followed by a brief consideration of the feasibility of making such a repertoire available in Intelligent Tutoring Systems. The main focus of the chapter, however, is on providing an analysis of the way explanations are negotiated between humans. Tutoring systems designers face the challenge of taking this understanding into account where possible.

INTRODUCTION

The idea of negotiation in educational interactions is not a new one. Students and teachers come to terms with each other over a range of issues, including the content of the curriculum, time spent, teaching styles, coursework and assignments, and so on. These negotiations can range from ones attempting to compromise between widely divergent aims ("We'll discuss AIDS at the end of the lesson if you're quiet now and copy the diagram of a bacteriophage on the board into your books"),

KNOWLEDGE NEGOTIATION
ISBN 0–12–509378–0

to ones in which the aims may be broadly similar but the possible means for achieving them need to be negotiated ("It's no good using the example of a vacuum cleaner to explain this concept, because I've never seen one"). The negotiations to be discussed in this chapter will be about both aims and means, but the examples and the implications are restricted to situations in which students are genuinely trying to learn something, whether or not that is what someone is trying to teach them.

In order to negotiate about *what* is to be discussed or explained, and in *what terms* (for what purpose), by means of *what kind of* devices, teachers and learners need to coordinate how they represent the topic to themselves, and the language they use for communicating that understanding. How this is done, and the extent to which it is genuinely done, may be a function of the power relations between the participants. Learning partners may come to coordinate their mutual knowledge (Shadbolt 1986), referring expressions (Garrod & Anderson 1987) and viewpoints (O'Malley et al. 1984), but where participants don't have equal status in the interaction the negotiation may sometimes be more apparent than real (Armstrong *et al.* 1991, Edwards & Mercer 1987).

These issues, both of the range of matters negotiations may be *about*, and of the extent to which lack of power may limit the value of such negotiations to students, will have important implications for their potential interactions with tutoring systems. They are taken up first, however, in the following section, in which explanatory dialogues in 'natural' educational settings are considered.

1   THE NEGOTIATION OF EXPLANATIONS IN TEACHING ENCOUNTERS

I have argued elsewhere (Rymaszewski & Beveridge 1989, Beveridge & Rimmershaw 1991) that the importation by philosophers of education (Ennis 1969, Green 1971, Swift 1961) of the perspectives on explanation common in the philosophy of science until the 1960s has been unhelpful.

In particular, these accounts of explanation in education have centred on distinguishing different *kinds* of explanation and the circumstances in which they are appropriate. However, whether they are looking at teachers' (Ennis, Green) or at learners' (Swift) explanations, they all treat explanations and their explananda as unproblematically objective. A good explanation is characterized as one which is 'complete' or of the type appropriate to the question that has been asked. This assumes that there is a straightforward relationship between explanation and explanandum which is independent of the agents involved in the explanation-giving interaction. The only scope for negotiation is for one party to ask for an omitted element of the explanation to be supplied, or to say that they wanted a developmental rather than a functional account, say.

I want to argue here that this conception of explanation giving is misconceived, and to suggest that an account of explanations in teaching and learning encounters must recognize their intersubjective nature. The work of Toulmin (1958) on argumentation shows that in getting someone else to believe a proposition people not only offer data in support of their claims, but also warrants and backing. A warrant is to persuade the receiver that the data is relevant to the claim and backing is a reason for accepting the warrant. These elements of an argument derive from the need to address different belief systems. Explanations must deal not only with the beliefs of the recipient, but their purposes as well. Whether or not it is explicitly acknowledged between the participants, the educational enterprise involves the coordination and accommodation of the long-term aims and short-term purposes of both teachers and learners. Mehan (1979) has shown how this mutual accommodation takes place in routine classroom procedures, in which the teacher, rather than simply transmitting the intended material to the students, must adapt it to the language and experiences offered by the students in their responses.

Bruner (1986) strongly emphasizes the negotiated nature of education, on the basis that learning is in most settings a communal activity, a sharing of the culture. He reminds us that most of our encounters with the world are indirect (mediated by language, for example), and claims that our puzzlements about what we encounter are dealt with by renegotiating meanings "in a manner that is concordant with what those around us believe" (p.122). It has long been recognized in psychology and philosophy that all our sense experience is processed or interpreted, and to the extent that that interpreted experience is communicable it is indeed common. That is not to say, however, that it is objective, and Bruner nicely captures the need for negotiation in educational encounters when he says "what is needed is a basis for discussing not simply the content of what is before one, but the possible stances one might take towards it" (p.129).

Armstrong et al. (1991) show how the different participants in another kind of interaction, where the role relationships are not reciprocal, may have different perceptions of what is being negotiated, and hence of what has been agreed. So at the end of an interview with parents an educational psychologist may believe they have negotiated a consensus about what would be best for the child they are discussing, while the parents may believe that what has been going on is the development of a mutual recognition of who has the power to decide.

The whole theme of Edwards and Mercer's recent book (Edwards & Mercer 1987) is the development through classroom interaction of a shared culture of understandings, or as they call it 'common knowledge'. One of their particular concerns is the extent to which the common knowledge developed by the pupils may be of a ritual rather than principled kind. This can be interpreted as the result of an ambiguity in the 'stance' towards knowledge conveyed by the teachers. The teachers in Edwards and Mercers' study espoused a relatively 'progressive' or 'discovery learning' approach. This manifested itself in the design of activities in which the (8–10 year old) pupils took an active part and had scope for making their own decisions, and also in the teachers' refusal simply to 'give the answers'. However, perhaps partly as a result of the teachers' reluctance to make explicit their aims to their pupils, the pupils' strategies could be recognized as the ones of 'sussing out' what the acceptable answers were; strategies familiar to us from the work of Sinclair and Coulthard (1975), Mehan (1979), and MacLure and French (1980). So the teachers' avowed intentions of developing their pupils' understandings, and self-reliance as learners, by getting them to reflect on their own experience, and to draw on it to frame new understandings, are undermined by their role in the interactions as arbiter and (more knowledgeable) guide. There appears to be a tension between the teachers' stance towards knowledge as needing to be 'owned' by the knower, and as a set of publicly accepted 'facts' and procedures. In principle these two stances are compatible, but only if the principles and methods for establishing and calling into question those facts and procedures are made available to the learner.

In drawing attention to the *idealized* conception of educational interactions as negotiation in Bruner's work, Edwards and Mercer neatly summarize the interpretation they put on the data they collected: "Our own depiction has been of a more compromised process, where the negotiation is a rather one-sided affair in which the teacher's role as authoritative bearer of the ready-made knowledge simply finds alternative, more subtle means of realising itself than the crudities of brute 'transmission'" (p.163).

In what circumstances then, one may ask, can knowledge be genuinely negotiated? I shall attempt to throw some light on this question by examining data from a range of sources and settings in which explanations could be said to be being negotiated. The negotiations vary in how successfully they are concluded, and in how openly they are conducted, and form the basis for the tentative specification of a discourse repertoire for negotiating explanations to be discussed in Section 4 on negotiating machinery, and reviewed from the intelligent tutoring systems perspective in Section 5.

To call something an explanation rather than a description tells nothing about what is said, but rather something about what the utterance means *to the interlocutors*. Indeed, as Sless (1981) points out, "what may be offered by an author as a description can be perceived as an explanation by an audience, and vice versa" (p.125). He suggests that the difference in stance towards what is talked about is that "whereas a description of something assumes it to be intelligible, an explanation assumes that in some respect the phenomenon is unintelligible" (p.123). The distinction could be rephrased in terms of my earlier discussion as one between drawing on, as opposed to constructing, common knowledge.

However in talking about 'things', 'phenomena', 'knowledge', there is a danger of persuading oneself that learning and explaining simply involve creating a match between two people's mental representations of some independently existing state of affairs. To render something *intelligible* invokes an audience who will make sense of it, and to successfully give an explanation depends as much on understanding the audience as it does on understanding the 'phenomenon'.

2   THE POTENTIAL BASES OF NEGOTIATION

I shall begin to illustrate this point by drawing on the correspondence in the Notes and Queries column which appears each Monday in *The Guardian* newspaper[1]. In this section of the paper, readers write in with responses to other readers' queries published in previous editions. The explanations offered are not negotiated, since although a number of replies may be published for any one query, and in some cases further letters are published challenging the explanations given, the person who asked the original question never (so far) makes a second contribution to the correspondence. What the analysis of these examples will show, however, is the *scope* for the negotiation of such explanations by revealing some of the potential bases for negotiation in explanatory dialogues. They include:

- the *kind of explanation* required (historical, functional, . . .)
- the *question concept* (i.e. what *exactly* is to be explained)
- the *assumptions* made by the questioners
      (usually facts or values implicit in the question)
- the *assumptions* made by the explainers
      e.g. assumptions about mutual knowledge
         assumptions about shared viewpoints
         assumptions about why the learner wants to know

---

[1] The data from Notes and Queries, published between 13.11.89 and 26.03.90, are reproduced with permission from *The Guardian*.

In the absence of any interactional or pragmatic context for the queries, respondents sometimes make quite diverging judgements as to how to meet the questioner's needs. To the following question, for example, four answers were published, each offering not just a different explanation, but a different *kind of explanation*:

Q. To, either out of ignorance or boldly and with malice aforethought, insert words into a verb's infinitive form is considered grammatically sinful. Why?

A1. Because the question has to be read twice to be understood.

A3. Lost for appropriate models, 18th century grammarians turned to Latin when a need was felt to regularise or standardise English. In Latin of course, it is not possible to split an infinitive – it's one word. Arbitrarily this "rule" was applied to English.

The first answer quoted offers an explanation of why the convention is reasonable, the second of its historical origins, and others (not quoted) offer bases for rejecting the rule. However, from these data we have no means of knowing what kind of explanation the questioner was looking for, or which of the answers best satisfied them. Clearly, if the questioner was hoping to learn from the explanation for the rule, for example, in what circumstances if any it does not apply, then the historical explanation is much less useful than the others. Conversely, if they wanted to know how such a perverse 'rule' ever came to be the convention then the historical explanation is probably the most useful.

Making judgements about what kind of explanation to offer is only one of the ways in which an explanation giver must take account of their audience. They also decide on the level of detail to give, which is also a very difficult judgement in the absence of feedback from the audience. This question:

Q. What happens to spiders washed down the plughole?

received two very succinct answers, where it was assumed that the ultimate fate of the spiders was what was in question:

A1. They drown, naturally. _ _ [polemic on fate of those who indulge in this barbaric practice] _ _[2].

---

[2] Where parts of the published text have been omitted, the omission is indicated by the marks _ _ _ _.

A2. Mine are strong: they crawl back up again.

The third answer interpreted 'what happens' as a request for an account of the process leading to this fate, and offered:

A3. _ _ [statement of source of information] _ _. The demonstration showed a large spider washed down a transparent drainpipe. As the water hit it, the spider curled up its legs trapping an air bubble between them. When the water stopped pouring down the pipe and the turbulence ceased, the spider was buoyed to the surface on its air bubble and able to climb back up the drain and out of the plughole. However, I imagine that a very small spider, faced by a prolonged rush of water might find the odds against him rather higher than his chances of survival. In which case the answer would be even simpler.

These different interpretations are in effect not merely different choices about how much detail to go into, but different judgements about what the *question concept* is (result or process). This is a frequently occurring source of miscoordination in explanatory dialogues, as I have suggested elsewhere (Rymaszewski 1987), and as is borne out by the large number of examples in these data. In some cases questions are phrased in such a way that there can be little doubt as to which of the potential question concepts they want an explanation to address:

Q. Does anyone ever win a whopping dirty great big prize after returning lucky numbers in a "No" envelope?
(The answer, it seems, is "Yes").

But more often there are a number of potential question concepts which explainers have to guess at if they can't negotiate directly with the questioner. In some cases respondents have exploited the range of possible question concepts for humorous purposes, by deliberately addressing an unlikely one. In the example that follows the unlikely concepts (A1: cat-scratching-garden; A2: neighbour's cat) are rendered unlikely on the basis of cultural knowledge about the questioner's probable motive. The non-humorous answers (e.g. A5) address this *assumed motive*, and may even signal that it is shared:

Q. How do you stop a neighbour's cat scratching up your garden?
A1. Concrete one or the other.
A2. Get a cat of your own: your cat will keep your neighbour's cat away and will do most of his or her own scratching.
A5. I am trying short pieces of holly in the ground.

In other cases it is less easy to impute a probable motive to the questioner. In the next example neither the 'straight' nor the 'humorous' answer draw on it. A2 relies for its humour on the unlikeliness that the questioner needed a definition (*assumed mutual knowledge*), and hence the unlikeliness of disc-is-round as the question concept. Unlikely, because it would be a deliberate violation of Grice's maxim of quantity (Grice 1975), for the questioner to introduce superfluous concepts (car, tax):

Q. Why are car tax discs round?

A1. They were made round to be waterproof in the days when they were fixed outside cars (and are still fixed on motorbikes). Before plastic was invented the only logical solution was a circular holder over which a circular glass cover in a metal frame could be screwed into a waterproof seal.

A2. I think the answer can be found in Collins' Concise English Dictionary, page 215: "Disc. Any flat, circular thing."

In some cases a humorous reply appears on the surface to offer no explanation at all, but this is to mistake the text for the explanation. The explanation is constructed from the text by the reader, and so this response may well serve as well as a more conventional account to meet the questioner's puzzlement:

Q. If sugar is bad for you, how come humming birds can eat nothing else?

A. Sugar is also bad for humming birds. Have you ever seen one with a full set of teeth?

Generally, however, people give explanations more cooperatively than this, and not only supply information from which they believe the learner can construct the explanation they are looking for but also rhetorically tune how they present it in a way they believe addresses the learner's purpose. So in the next example the last part of the explanation is tuned to the assumption the respondent has made about the circumstances which led the question to be posed (*assumed purpose*):

Q. Why is nail varnish removed from fingers and toes, even during minor operations unrelated to hands and feet?

A. _ _ _ _ , the single essential of anaesthesia is that the circulating blood should contain sufficient oxygen. The fingernail bed is a good place to see if the blood is pink with oxygenated haemoglobin, not the darker, purply-blue colour of haemoglobin without oxygen. _ _ _ _.

Thus when a modern pulse oximeter is to be used, nail varnish need not be removed.

However, not all operating theatres are so equipped, and if your anaesthetist does ask you to remove your nail varnish, it is because he is determined to make your anaesthetic safe.

Occasionally, much less well-founded assumptions about what motivated a question are made, and spontaneous explanations are offered, as in this case:

Q. Who allocates names to hurricanes?
A. The US Weather Bureau allocates names on a five year cycle, alternating male and female names from A to W. _ _ _ _ . Names given to particularly memorable storms have to be "retired", _ _ _ _ _ . Research shows that people identify much more closely with a named storm, and are far more willing to evacuate low-lying coasts as he/she approaches.

In this case, since the information about the consequences of naming a storm was not the focus of the initial question, questioner and respondent would have nothing to negotiate about, though of course if they had the opportunity for further interaction follow-up questions might well have been posed.

Another way explainers take the initiative is by challenging the *assumptions of common knowledge implicit* in the readers' questions, as in this example:

Q. Why do the British drive on the left and other countries on the right?
A3. Implicit in the question is the suggestion that Britain is alone in this particular practice. In fact, over 40 countries drive on the left.

or the *implicit values*, as in this one:

Q. Can any of your readers recommend a source of hard-wearing, non-leather boots? I know I am not the only vegetarian who has trouble finding suitable footwear.
A2. _ _ _ the decision not to wear animal skin does seem to be rather at odds with environmental considerations, particularly as most alternatives are made from non-renewable petroleum products.

This analysis of two-turn dialogues (question and reply) has demonstrated that in explanatory exchanges there is scope to negotiate about the kind of explanation required, about what exactly the locus of puzzlement or question-concept is, and about the assumptions made by the participants about knowledge, values, viewpoints and purposes. In the two sections which follow I shall investigate how these bases for negotiation are exploited in more extended explanatory interactions.

3 NEGOTIATIONS IN ACTION

Sarantinos et al. (1990) describe the natural dialogue style of the experts used in their research as 'active'. By this they mean that they not only answered novices' questions but also took the initiative of correcting their errors and mistaken assumptions and making suggestions when they were 'stuck'. On the basis of my argument in Section 1, and my aim of identifying a discourse repertoire in Section 4, I will be interested here in characterizing in much more detail not only explainers' actions but also those of the learners.

In order to see whether negotiations take place around the bases identified in Section 2 in practice, and what else, if anything, could be negotiated in explanatory dialogues, I examine here some rather more interactive explanatory exchanges. One basis (the *kind* of explanation required) was never negotiated over in the data I analysed, but all the others were. In addition two new negotiable features of explanations emerged – explanatory devices and explainer's or explanation's credibility. Negotiations of all these types are illustrated and discussed in this section. They reveal how learners manage to:

- get the right kind of explanatory *devices,*
- *assess the credibility* of explanations,
- define the *question concept,*
- check out *mutual knowledge,*
- change the *viewpoint,* and
- determine the *purpose* the explanations are to serve.

The sources I shall refer to include discussion from the BBC2 programmes 'The A–Z of Belief' [B][3], two holiday courses for adults (Improve Your Photography [P] and Absolute Beginners' Italian [I])[4], a collaborative group of academics and students [C][4], informal work-

---

[3] The data from 'The A–Z of Belief' is taken as near verbatim as possible from programmes produced by BBC Northern Ireland and broadcast between December 1989 and February 1990.

[4] Data reproduced with the permission of the participants.

related conversations between academics and secretarial staff [A][4] and Svartvik and Quirk's *Corpus of English Conversation* [E][5]. This range of sources has been chosen as it represents a range of social relationships between the explainers and the recipients of their explanations and a range of social settings in which the explanations are given. These relationships and settings are characterized in brief in the five paragraphs which follow.

The participants in 'The A–Z of Belief' [B] are young people with differing religious or political beliefs. In each programme one of them is responsible for explaining their particular belief system to the rest of the group. These discussions take place with the participants standing and moving around in a large empty warehouse or hall. There is no status or age gap between the explainers and the rest, and since the explainers are on their own, physically surrounded, and of a different persuasion to the others the atmosphere is sometimes even hostile or defensive. Typically, the explainer is not listened to deferentially but is bombarded with a lot of questions.

The participants on the holiday courses [P, I] are all adults between the ages of 17 and 70, with tutors aged about 30. The courses are voluntarily chosen and so the level of commitment and interest are generally high. Beginners' Italian is a classroom-based course in which the tutor (female), a native speaker of the language, uses a variety of styles including whole class, group and individual work based around video-recordings, worksheets and role-plays. Improve Your Photography also has a classroom component which is largely formal and didactic, followed by substantial periods of practical work in the field with informal interactions between the tutor (male) and individuals or small groups of students. The data to be discussed here and in the following section comes largely from these fieldwork sessions.

The collaborative discussions [C] took place at a semi-formal meeting of a research interest group to discuss the possible shape and contents of a proposed book. The participants (largely female) included university research and teaching staff, post-graduate and undergraduate students.

The talk between academic and secretarial staff [A] arose naturally in the course of administrative work on which they were engaged, and was captured by a tape-recorder left running in the secretary's office. The secretary was new not only to the job but to the type of institution in which she had come to work.

In the words of the editors, the specimens of conversation offered in the *Corpus of English Conversation* [E] are "intended to represent

---

[5] Data based on the prosodic transcription of conversations published in J. Svarvik & R. Quirk (eds.) (1980) *A Corpus of English Conversation*, Lund: Lund University Press.

spontaneous conversation among educated British speakers." The participants in the explanatory dialogues used for this study[6] were largely middle-aged and included university academics, primary and secondary school teachers, computer specialists, housewives, a doctor, a stockbroker, and a banker.

One respect in which most of these interactions are unlike the educational explanation-giving in classroom contexts is the high level of purposefulness of the 'learners', either in terms of interest or needing to get something done, or both. This choice of sources is not accidental. My arguments about the ways in which an intelligent tutoring system needs to take into account the viewpoints and purposes of its users in its explanation-giving are based on the assumption that such systems will be used purposefully by individuals. That is not to deny that purposeful learning takes place in classrooms, but to recognize that the one-to-many relationship between teacher and learners and the 'authoritative' status of the teacher in most classrooms makes it a relatively fruitless arena for the study of the genuine negotiation of explanations. Student questions are relatively rare in classroom discourse (Dillon 1982), and teachers have a repertoire of devices for not answering them when they do occur. Examples of this avoidance of addressing student needs or interests can be found in the lesson-based sources of data used here (P), (I), although in the data as a whole these cop-outs were relatively rare. The photography tutor said things like "I don't really want to go into it at this point" in response to questions when he was lecturing to the students in the first part of the lesson.

The most striking thing about the bases for negotiation which can be observed in this varied collection of data is that the one potential category identified in the previous section which *never* occurred, was that of the *kind* of explanation required. This is a particularly noteworthy finding, given the attention that has been paid to different kinds of explanations in both the educational and expert systems literatures. I shall comment on the implications for intelligent tutoring systems design in Section 5.

However, another category, which the analysis of Notes and Queries did not predict, was negotiation of the explanatory *devices* which were most useful to the learners. In the Italian class, getting a helpful domain of examples onto the tutor's agenda was 'negotiated' in a very subtle way over a number of teaching sessions. It began with one or two students calling out usages of the words they were learning which they recognized from a musical context. So in a lesson on adjectives of size, this exchange occurred:

---

[6] Data identified in texts S1.1, S1.7, S1.11, S1.13, S2.2, S2.9, S2.10, S3.5.

T.	Alto?	
Ss.	[translate in chorus]	
T.	Tall and high	
	Basso?	
Ss.	[chorus]	
T.	Short and low	
S1	Basso profundo	*Connects to known musical phrase*
T.	Below, on the left-hand side: Largo?	
Ss.	[chorus]	
T.	Wide, broad.	
S2	Like the lake.	*Connects to known tourist phrase*
T.	Like . . . like what, sorry?	
S2	Like a lake.	
T.	Like a lake? No that's "lago". Lake is "lago" without the "r". Larrrgo, is large, with an "r".	
S3.	It doesn't bear much resemblance to "largo" in music though, does it?	*Doubts connection to known musical phrase*
S4	No.	
T.	Yes, it *is* the same.	
S2	Wide.	
T.	It is the same, it's a *wide* movement, yes.	*Confirms musical connection*

The learners' strategies are to connect the new vocabulary to existing knowledge and the richest source of these connections for at least some of them is in musical terminology. At first the tutor does not exploit this resource, and sometimes appears not to recognize it, as in this case, where the context of a shop, that has been set up in the lesson, is maintained in her response to the student's offered phrase:

T.	Something else you might need, if you are pointing at articles, items in a shop: in alto	*Context of use supplied*
Ss.	Up.	
T.	Up there.	
	In basso.	*Introduces word*
Ss.	Down there.	
T.	Down there.	
	A sinistra.	
Ss.	To the left	
T.	A destra	
Ss.	To the right.	
S.	It fits of course with "basso profundo"	*Connects with known musical phrase*
T.	Basso profundo! Oh dear. That's very deep down. If they have a cellar, yes.	*Sticks to shopping scenario*

The students' next strategy is to make explicit the domain in which they are drawing connections:

T.	Il numero quattro e sotto il cavallo a dondolo.	*Gives model answer*
S.	[indecipherable]	
T.	under the horse.	
S.	sotto voce	*Connects to known musical phrase*
T.	Sotto che?	
S.	Oh sorry.	
T.	Sotto what?	
S.	Singing – sotto voce.	*Gives domain and repeats connection*
T.	Ah! sotto voce, yes, yes.	*Acknowledges*

And soon the tutor is spontaneously confirming the correctness of the learners' connections:

T.	"Mi fa vedere *quella*, per favore". Can I see *that* one please. "Si. Eccola."	*Reading from handout dialogue*
S.	Here it is..	*Translating*
T.	Here it is. Yes.	*Confirming*
S2.	Ecco la primavera	*Matching to words of known song.*
T.	[laughs] E bellissima.	*Accepting connection*

Eventually she begins to draw on the musical domain in examples herself, justifying a quotation from the Duke in Verdi's Rigoletto in this example by addressing it to one of the students with a declared interest in opera:

T.	And the question here that the shop assistant is asking is "le piace", "le piace questa?" Questo, questa (masculine, feminine). Quello, quella if you are pointing at something which is a bit further away. That one.	*Checking understanding of vocabulary and gender agreement from audio-tape dialogue*
S.	So you say, questo – this, quello – that.	*Checking translation*
T.	"Questa, quella per me pari sono", yes. You are the opera man. This and that.	*Offering example from domain of music*

So whilst no explicit negotiations were held about useful mnemonic devices, the students have managed to manoeuvre the tutor into giving them just that, and so the learners' needs are better taken account of in the later lessons of the course.

In addition to negotiations about devices, the other unanticipated issue around which discussions took place was *credibility*. It is not surprising that such interchanges were identified in the 'A to Z of Belief' discussions where the participants were of different persuasions and similar social status, but they also occured in more informal and less hostile family discussions (as in the example from the Corpus which follows), and even in the lesson-based data (as in the example from the photography class), where deference to the tutor was quite marked at times.

These questions of credibility seem to fall into two types. The first could be characterized as *testing the reliability of the explainer's knowledge*:

Q.	I've been there and it seems very materialistic to me. It's beautiful.
A.	What do you mean by "materialistic"? You keep saying it's materialistic.
Q.	What do *you* mean?
A.	Material means that which we accept to be real with the false idea that I am this body _ _ _ _ this world is a prison house, so the idea is not to live here comfortably, the idea is to get out.

Q.   What do *you* mean?   *Turns question back to A.*

In this example from the 'A to Z of Belief' a request for clarification seems to have a validating function. In turning A's request for a definition back to him, the questioner Q2 suggests that he is using the term in an unexpected way, and that he must justify his usage to her. In an informal family discussion about voting in a national referendum in the corpus data (following), no-one takes the role of expert, but all collaboratively explore the basis for B's judgement that a ballot paper with a tick is spoiled:

A.	Is it not, is it in a general election that it's a cross really ?	*Limit to rule suggested*
C.	Well I assume so otherwise they wouldn't have bothered to say something special for the referendum, the thing about	*Warrant for limit offered*
B.	but how can I, I've listened to 'cos I listened to every single referendum programme I've never heard anybody debating crosses and ticks	*Warrant for disbelief offered*
C/B	_ _ _ _ _	
A.	It is actually rather illogical to sort of em you know turn down	*Basis of doubt articulated*
C.	cross, yes and put no	*– And shared*
A.	turn down the sign that says, means "yes" and accept the sign that means "no" –	

In this case the credibility of the explanation is established through the provision of warrants for the beliefs expressed.

The second type of credibility issue could be characterized as *getting details in order to evaluate generalities*, as in this example from the 'A–Z of Belief'. Before the questioner will buy the claim that reformed Judaism is 'harder' than orthodox, they want details of what conforming to the code of social ethics would involve for the individual:

Q.	Is reformed Judaism not just an easy way at the Jewish life?	*Question*
A.	I actually think it's harder.	
Q.	Why is it harder?	*Request for explanation*
A.	Because central to reformed Judaism is a code of social ethics _ _ _	
Q.	Can you tell us what some of these ethics are?	*Request for details*

What is noteworthy in these examples of establishing credibility is that, with the exception of the collaborative discussion on voting, it is the learners or receivers of the explanations who tend to put this issue on the agenda and make moves in the dialogue which raise it.

The other categories identified from the analysis of Notes and Queries all occur quite frequently in these data. Negotiations about the *question concept*, or what exactly is to be explained, were particularly common in the Italian class:

S2	So you can use "fermata" for anything where you'd use "stop"? In most senses of the word "stop"?	*Asks how general a translation is*
T.	Yes, yes. Fermata is any kind of stop, yes.	
S3	If you wanted me to stop doing something.	*Asks for confirmatory example in a different grammatical category*
T.	If you want – if I want you to stop doing something I would say "Ferma ti". "Stop yourself". "Ferma ti".	

Here the follow up question ensures that the tutor's generalization applies to stop as a verb as well as a noun, and in the next example the student's follow-up moves ensure the tutor sees their question as being a 'what's the difference?' one:

T.	In cima alla scala. It's on top of the ladder.	
S2.	On top of – in cima?	*Checks data*
T.	In cima a.	*Corrects data*
	On the top of the mountain: in cima alla montagna.	*Gives further example*
S2.	It's not the same "on top of" as "sopra"?	*Specifies question concept more clearly*
T.	No because . . "sopra" is, it can be on something that is very low, and you're just on top of it, touching it; whereas "in cima" it implies it is something very high, very tall and you are on the very top.	*Addresses the redefined question concept*

In many cases the negotiation involves more explicitly referring back to earlier learning or even specific parts of the discourse in order to clarify the source of the puzzlement not only in the state of the learner's mental model but also in the relation of that model to the tutor's contribution to the discourse so far:

S.	When you buy the ticket – it says "andata e ritorno"	*Sets up scenario, reminds of learned phrase*
T.	Yes.	
S.	That means "going out and coming back".	*Checks understanding*
T.	Yes	
S.	We would say a single. They would say to us "single or return?".	*Gives British context equivalent*
T.	Yes. You would say "single or return". For us "andata" which means "going" or "andata e ritorno" which is "going and coming back".	*Confirms difference*
S.	You can't just say "ritorno"?	*Gets to the point of the question*
T.	No. If you say "ritorno" they – well? Would they understand? Mm. I don't know. Better say "andata e ritorno".	*Addresses probable pragmatic basis*

Having rechecked the earlier learning on which the question is based, the learner finally gets to the point of the question. This still leaves some interpretation about what the learner's purpose is for asking it, so the tutor's answer makes explicit the purposive context she assumes. In other words she takes the question to mean not 'Is it grammatically correct?' but 'Is it pragmatically correct? – Will it get you the right kind of ticket?', and signals this interpretation explicitly in her reply, thus giving the learner the possibility of telling her they had a different purpose in mind.

In the next example the learner makes much use of reference to particular episodes in previous lessons to get the tutor to understand the viewpoint of her question:

T.	Seicento cinquanta	*Answer (650)*
S.	When do they use the fifty and when do they use the half, because yesterday we had a two hundred and a half.	*Question*
T.	[puzzled]	
S.	On one of yesterday's we had two hundred and a half grams.	*Reminds of mutual knowledge and when it arose in the discourse*
T.	Oh. That was *grams*.	*Identifies distinguisher*
S.	Yes	
T.	Yes for grams you can have – half a kilogram is mezzokilo, or five hundred grams, cinquecento grammi	*Confirms earlier usage*

S.	But we also had two hundred grams and a half	*Restates problem to address with reference to learned phrase*
T.	Yes	
S.	Which I assumed was two hundred and fifty grams.	*Offers interpretation for checking*
T.	Yes, it was, but that's only for weight, only for grams. Whereas for lire, and anything else that you're counting, it's just cinquanta, cinquecento and so on.	*Confirms interpretation, and makes basis of distinction explicit.*

Many of the negotiations in these data can be seen as ones involving the construction or coordination of mutual knowledge.

In this example from the photography class new knowledge is being constructed by the student on the basis of what the tutor has told him, but this process must take account of his existing mental model of the domain. So he gets the tutor to give him a 'worked example' of the refined version of the rule they have been given, and follows it by a check on whether this new understanding is still consistent with a previously held understanding:

T.	*But* there's a catch to this. If your subject is the same size in any lens, at the same aperture, the depth of field will be identical, at all times.	*States proviso to rule*
S.	So if you fill the frame-	*Prepares to check application*
T.	If you fill the frame-	*Accepts application parameters*
S.	no matter what the size is	
T.	No matter what the focal length of the lens is. If I take a head and shoulders picture: now if I take that with a 35mm I get very close	*Reformulates more precisely Takes over specification of example*
S.	Yeh.	*Accepts*
T.	Fill the frame. Depth of field will be x to y. If I step back, take a 200mm lens, fill the frame exactly the same proportions, same aperture, depth of field will be exactly the same.	*Goes through how rule applies to the particular case.*
S.	Yeh but what they call em wide angle distortion, like if you went there, the nose is like three times as large as it really is.	*Checks understanding of limits of 'same' rule*
T.	That's right, yes.	*Confirms*
S.	Now you don't get that with the longer lens from further back.	*Continues check*

In the next case, from the Italian class, new knowledge is also being constructed, but in the process a great deal of coordination of prior mutual knowledge takes place as a basis for discussing analogies. The tutor has referred to the items on sale at a tabaccaio (cigarettes, matches, salt) as monopoly goods:

S.	It's the idea of a monopoly which is alien to us.	*Explains surprise*
T.	Oh. That's alien to you. Em. So your cigarettes don't go through . .	*Checks own beliefs*
S.	There's no monopoly.	*Confirms*
S.	Although it's rather like our pubs, isn't it? I mean if we have a pub they have to sell certain beers don't they.	*Offers alternative example*
T.	Yes. In a way yes. That's probably the most similar concept _ _ _	*Makes analogy explicit*
	and also you can't buy *stamps* anywhere else, so you know, the	*Continues account*
S.	You can *now*.	*Challenges statement*
T.	Well no, but in *Italy* you can't. They are just, they are supplied by the central organization, by the monopoly. In each big town there is the monopoly. You can *only* get them from there.	*Corrects assumption about domain and continues account*
S.	Is it a private, not a state thing?	*Checks understanding, (shaken by reference to 'each town'?)*
T.	Oh it's a state thing, yes. State, yes, yes. State. State monopoly. _ _ _ _	*Disconfirms emphatically*
S.	So you can't buy stamps in a post office?	*Checks understanding*
T.	Oh yes, you can buy stamps in a post office yes. Em, but you wouldn't go to buy stamps in a post office for the simple reason that _ _ [long omission] _ _. But yes, that's the only other place you can buy stamps. You couldn't buy it in normal shops, as you do here, you couldn't go to a W H Smith and buy . . .	
S.	*We* can't.	*Disconfirms distinction*
T.	You can go to W H Smith's. Yes.	*Reasserts it*
S.	W H Smiths sells . .	*Doubts assertion*
T.	Yes, W H Smith sells stamps. Yes!	*Confirms it*

In this long example expressions of surprise and mismatches in beliefs are the catalysts for considerable comparison of existing knowledge about analogies from the British context (more familiar to the students, but less familiar to the tutor) as a basis for learning new facts about what you can buy in an Italian tabaccaio.

In the photography fieldwork sessions, referring expressions needed to be coordinated. This often took the form of matching up verbal formulations with practical actions, like turning the aperture ring or shutter-speed dial:

T.	So you close down the shutter speed by four stops.	*Verbal instruction*
S.	That way?	*Spatial translation*
T.	Yes	
S.	To a thousand?	*Numerical corroboration*

In the research interest group's discussions [not quoted] a coordination of beliefs is negotiated largely by means of reformulation moves. The negotiation is very much focussed on the meaning of particular forms of words (co-author, collaboration, participatory research). In the process of negotiating a coordinated interpretation of the referring expressions, some reformulations are accepted as preserving the group's meanings and others rejected as distorting them or reclassified as related but different.

In more unequal situations the verbal formulations needed to be coordinated between tutor and learner too, as in this case where the tutor suspects the learner is using 'exposure latitude' inappropriately:

B.	Er, how many stops could your colour film actually have of latitude?	*Question*
T.	Usually one stop under exposure and three stops over.	*Answer*
B.	That's as much as it'll take?	*Expresses surprise*
T.	Yes	*Confirms*
B.	So you've only got a latitude of about four stops?	*Reformulates answer to check understanding*
T.	Well that's, no, no, you're talking about contrast ratio aren't you?	*Checks terminology*
B.	Er, I think so. Well like how much would be –, before it sort of whites out the sky, say, so how bright a sky could you have and how dark a shadow?	*Offers own definition*
T.	Yes, you're talking about contrast ratio there. That's actually not more than about four or five stops.	*Confirms definition and answer in B's terms*
B.	Ah.	*Accepts*

In the next example roles are partly reversed, as the tutor is admiring a student's equipment. Again, however, it is the tutor who recognizes when something needs to be explained, as he did in the previous case, treating the student's hesitation in replying as a signal that a definition of parallax is needed:

T.	How does it cope with parallax then?	*Question*
S.	Er . . .	*Confusion implied*
T.	Parallax is the difference between what you see through the viewfinder and where the lens actually is.	*Explain question term*

In this final example of negotiating mutual knowledge, from the Corpus data, a misapprehension is corrected by means of an explanation which makes reference to assumed mutual prior knowledge about sailors, scurvy and citrus fruit. The assumption of mutual knowledge is signalled by the question tags 'didn't they?', 'would they?', giving an opening to C to confirm or deny they have it.

C.	I thought it was vitamin C
A.	But the nutrition, no that's scurvy
C.	No I thought vitamin C was the sun vitamin
A.	No, no all the sailors used to get scurvy didn't they which is vitamin C and oranges
C.	But I thought
A.	If it had been the sun I mean the sailors wouldn't have got it would they // cos there's plenty of sun
C.	But I thought that the vitamin that oranges supplied you with was the vitamin that the sun supplied you with
B.	No

It is interesting in this example that in spite of A's several references to what is intended to be helpful prior knowledge, C's every turn throughout this exchange began with 'I thought', indicating that it is the particular bits of knowledge underpinning *his* misconception that must be addressed for him to be satisfied. This underlines the point that for explanations to be effective, learners must be able to get their needs taken into account.

As well as mutual knowledge, *shared viewpoints* on the explanandum may need to be negotiated. The previous example can be seen as one in which the learner has managed to change the viewpoint from that of which vitamin deficiency is associated with which set of symptoms to that of which vitamin is associated with which source. In this next case, again from the Corpus data, the sources of surprise are signalled as shared by both parties, by at least three means: repetition of the key phrase by the learner, the use of the word 'curiously' by the explainer, and the cutting short of the other's contributions by both participants:

A.	. . . so the stockbroker hasn't in that sense got the incentive to write to people	*Explaining*
B.	Hasn't got the incentive	*Repeats key phrase*
A.	No he hasn't curiously enough	*signals surprise justified*
B.	I would have thought that he had because	
A.	No but they haven't because they	*Doesn't wait for specification*
B.	Barclays get their money whether they advise the chap to do anything or not but you only get your money if	*Completes answer himself*
A.	Yes, I know but you see it's very expensive running this system	*Addresses new surprise*

One way in which learners put their viewpoints onto the agenda is by using explanatory exchanges for *testing hypotheses*. In this example from data source A, D (a secretary) maintains her viewpoint in the discussion (where 'doctors' and 'professors' fit into the academic hierarchy) through a succession of inferences and hypotheses which she offers for testing. Whatever explanation E offers, D responds by generating an inference based on the current state of the mental model she is constructing:

D.	When people come to be a professor, have they to take extra examinations from a doctor?	*Yes/no question*
E.	No. No, that's the highest examination there is, doctor.	*Offers information which addresses likely gap in knowledge on basis of question*
D.	So a doctor's higher than a professor.	*Checks inference*
E.	No, no. "Professor" is, ahha,–	*Rejects, and starts definition*
D.	And what's –	
E.	– the "Doctor" reflects the fact that you've got a particular qual-, you can't be a doctor without a certain qualification.	*Restarts with definition of different term*
	Right?	*Offers turn to D. if needed*
E.	Whereas people's *titles*, whereas "professor" is a title of a sort of status, which isn't anything to do with an exam, like getting a certain level of- I mean it is a recognition of your academic standing.	*Makes distinction*
D.	Is it because they've been doing it for so long?	*Offers new hypothesis*
E.	No it's not automatic, no.	*Rejects it*
D.	Oh.	
E.	So it's like a recognition of your good work and all the rest of it.	*Reformulates own explanation*
D.	Oh, I see	
E.	But it's like a job title rather than a qualification, do you see what I mean?	*Checks distinction appreciated*
D.	Yeh	
E.	It's like the difference between "secretary", "personal assistant", blah, blah, blah. They're not qualifications they're jobs.	*Offers analogy in terms of known prior knowledge of D.*
D.	So they could say to you, after x amount of years, and you'd transfer to a different position	*Offers revised understanding, as example, for checking*
E.	Yes	*Confirms*
D.	As professor.	*More precise*
E.	Right. _ _ _ _ _ _	*Reconfirms*

In a conversation in the Corpus data (not quoted) one person takes over the questioning from another in order to get her viewpoint addressed. The conversation has been predominantly A, a doctor, telling about his *viva voce* examination in medicine when this listener moves the topic from 'how A answered the question in the exam' to 'how come people in countries with plenty of sunshine are vulnerable to rickets'.

Although she doesn't get a satisfactory explanation in fact, she does succeed in changing the focus of A's remarks. An explainer may persist in offering explanations from a particular viewpoint, however. In explaining to his friends how two projectors are useful for showing multireel films without a break, a speaker in the Corpus data (not quoted) keeps on referring to the speed of the film through the projector (e.g. 'they go surprisingly slowly really'). However, neither questioner appears to acknowledge these references (unless non-verbally), probably because their contributions to the dialogue indicate that the focus of their interest is not in 'how can the projectionist time it right', but in 'how are the film and projectors set up to enable it'. So while they never reject the explainer's responses by actually saying 'that's not the point' or 'that's not what's puzzling us', they manage to get their viewpoint addressed by persevering with a series of questions until they have got the information they need to clarify the part of their mental model which was fuzzy.

The final category of negotiable elements identified was the *learner's purpose*. In these natural explanations we can see both tellers and learners making moves which are related to the issue of why the learner wants to know.

The first sub-category therefore is of *spontaneous inferences to purpose by the tutor*. This can be illustrated by an excerpt from a stockbroker's explanation of his trade, from the Corpus data. The learner (B) has set up his question, but the explainer does not simply answer 'yes' or 'no'. He infers that the purpose of B's question almost certainly was not simply to know whether the firm had received a proposition of the kind he describes, but to know whether they would accept such a proposition. So whilst also addressing another interpretation (whether they are allowed to), he addresses this assumed purpose in his answer:

B.	Do clients ever say look Mr. Chatwick let me give you five hundred pounds or something?
A.	Yes
B.	and instead of you ringing me up all the time
A.	Yes
B.	I will take this as merely gambling money and you play it and don't just have commission but let me give you ten percent or something. Are you allowed to do this?
A.	We have a – not quite under those terms, well we would be allowed to do it but I don't think we would. . . .

The photography tutor sometimes explicity referred to the purpose explanations offered by himself or the students might serve: "that may not be what you want to do". The Italian tutor also shows herself to be quite sensitive to the sources of students' questions – picking up in one case for example that the student needs to know because they are mapping the new Italian vocabulary onto their existing French one:

S   What is the word for "closed" then?
T.   Oh. Closed. Chiuso. No it's not "ferme".
       Fermata is bus-stop. If you want to say "closed
       door": "porta chiusa".

The second sub-category of negotiating about purposes can be characterized as learners *getting their own experience or needs taken into account*. The photography class afforded several examples of this. Towards the end of a long exchange, S2 and S3 make the origin of their questions in practical problems they have experienced quite clear, though in this case the tutor's responses take no account of them:

S2	I put one of these films through _ _ [describes wrong exposure or development] _ _ and I sent it back to them, I got the result back the other day. It was exactly the same.	*Poses relevant problem from own experience*
S3	Well I had a similar experience. I was about to ask you do these printing machines adjust for every individual frame or do they check the first frame and then run the reel off at the same setting?	*Poses question to check out own explanation of problem phenomenon*
T.	No they don't, they adjust for each one.	*Supplies disconfirming information*
S3	Cos I had a film which started with a night one, and the rest were completely overdeveloped.	*Explains basis of hypothesis*
T.	They're set up to cope with holiday snaps, basically.	*Closes interaction [by use of intonation] with explanation that doesn't address problem*

In the next example, the student (S3 again) starts the interaction with a statement of what he has done and ends it by double checking that the tutor has reasoned towards the intended objective:

S.	Now *I* got that totally wrong . . . because we were . . . I wanted *you* and so . . . I exposed, em, I took, took down two stops at 5.6	*Claims problem. Gives account of actions*
T.	Right	*Acknowledges account or approves actions*
S.	For you. But the camera said I was two stops over-exposed.	*Identifies source of puzzlement (expectations not met)*
T.	Yes, it would.	*Implies expectations wrong*
S.	Because it was reading that.	*Offers tentative explanation*

T.	Because the camera's metering off the whole of the background . . . Yeh. So it's quite correct.	*Reformulates explanation more explicitly and endorses it*
S.	It'll do what I wanted it to?	*Checks implication*
T.	You've got a perfectly exposed subject.	*Confirms*

In this section I have analysed negotiations in action in 'natural' explanatory dialogues. This analysis has revealed a number of features which could be significant for ITS design. They include the fact that in natural explanation dialogues learners have the power to:

- get the right kind of explanatory *devices*
    - by requesting examples, demonstrations, etc.
    - by trying out their own analogies, examples, etc.
- assess the *credibility* of explanations
    - in terms of their own and the explainer's confidence in the explanation and related knowledge
    - by getting definitions, backing, warrants
- define the *question concept*
    - by referring back in the discourse
    - by refining the question
- check out *mutual knowledge*
    - by stating their own beliefs, and
    - offering their own formulations
- change the *viewpoint*
    - by rejecting the explainer's offered viewpoint
    - by offering hypotheses and
    - by offering alternative explanations
- determine the *purpose*
    - by stating problems

and also that tutors are able to:

- use different kinds of explanatory *device*
    - e.g. examples from different domains, analogies, applications, worked examples, demonstrations
- justify *confidence* in their explanations
    - by offering definitions, backing, warrants
- address different *question concepts*
    - by interpreting multiply ambiguous questions
    - by keeping track of the history of a query in the discourse
- check on *mutual knowledge*

by monitoring the reception of examples or analogies
by recognizing learners' reformulations
by recognizing learners' statements of belief
- share *viewpoints*
by evaluating learners' hypotheses
by interpreting learners' alternative explanations
- address the learner's *purpose*
by inferring and/or asking why they want to know

In the hope of providing further insights to tutoring systems designers, I propose to look at the same data in a slightly different way in the next section, in which I shall attempt to classify the moves in the repertoires of the two parties to these explanatory encounters, as a basis for considering the dialogue machinery through which a computer-based tutor might negotiate explanations with a learner.

4   NEGOTIATING MACHINERY

From the data studied, including the interactions discussed in the previous section, it is possible to identify a range of moves which learners and tutors make in coordinating their contributions to an explanatory exchange. Learners' moves can be seen as fulfilling three major functions – controlling the interaction, representing their needs and purposes to the explainer, and constructing and comparing mental models. Tutors' moves can also be seen as falling into three groups – controlling the interaction, taking account of the learner's needs and purposes, and establishing the explainer's viewpoint. This categorization reflects the nature of the relationships between explainer and explainee, fluctuating between cooperation and conflict according to the degree to which the two agents are in agreement either about the aim of the dialogue or the means for achieving it.

In view of the discussion on pages 243–244 it is necessary to examine dialogues from a range of social contexts in order to tease out the influence of explainer's power on the types of negotiating moves made by learners. What is clear from the examples set out below is that certain kinds of move more commonly occur in some sources of data than others.

For example, learners' controlling moves are much more frequent in the 'A to Z of Belief' data than in any of the other sources, where the status of the explainer was closest to that of the learners. By contrast in the photography class, where the tutor's expert status was established by an hour's formal lesson before the practical work, students made virtually no controlling moves, other than asking questions, and registered their needs by means of moves in which they tell of their own experience, but not by ones in which they demand different answers, or different explanatory devices. In both these contexts learners were often left dissatisfied, but for different reasons. In the case of the photography class the tutor often used his power to decline to answer a question or address an alternative viewpoint posed by a student. In the 'A to Z of Belief' discussions learners were more often dissatisfied with the warrants or other bases of credibility offered by the explainers, even though far more moves of this kind were made in these discussions.

On the next pages I offer examples of the moves identified. Where the nature of the move is signalled by a recognizable lexical device I have highlighted the device in bold type.

Learners' moves:

1. *Moves for controlling the interaction*

Determining the topic or changing the focus
    What I want to get at is, is why this *particular* chant (B – Nishiren Shoshu)
    That's all very well, but what about . . . (B – Pentecostal)
Returning to an earlier starting point
    You were telling us a long complicated story about (E, p.329 – women dentists)
    Sorry, I know I keep going back to it (B – Wicca)
Clarifying the rhetorical force of an explanation
    And how does this tie in with . . . (E, p.331 – women dentists)
    What's that got to do with what I just said? (B – Mormon)

2. *Moves for representing their needs and purposes to the explainer*

Asking for a different presentation of the explanation
    I'm sorry, I'm such a linear thinker (C)
    This has gone over my head, it's all really technical, all we want to know is (B – Nishiren Shoshu)
    Can you be more specific – what do you mean they're almost the same? (B – Wicca)
    Don't answer "Read the scripture" again please. (B – Pentecostal)
Asking for devices which will meet current needs
    Could you give us a demonstration. (B – Nishiren Shoshu)
    Can you give us some instances? (B – Nishiren Shoshu)
    When you say . . . **can you be more** specific about . . .
        because if they're different from other religions then it does matter whether we're following your cult or not (B – Krishna)
Suggesting or rejecting domains for analogies and exemplification
    Singing – sotto voce (I)

Although it's rather like our pubs isn't it? (I)
Well we never went to school dental officers so I wouldn't have
   known (E, p.330 – women dentists)
Registering surprise and puzzlement
   I thought it was vitamin *C* was the sun vitamin (E, p.598 – rickets)
   I am surprised actually cos I thought (E, p.618 – voting)
   I can imagine . . . but (E, p.330 – women dentists)
   I'm sure there was (E, p.330 – women dentists)
   It's the idea of a monopoly which is alien to us (I)
   A statement that . . . seems to belie the whole idea which *I* have. (B
      – Krishna)
   That's as much as it'll take? (P)
   What even in the National – ? (E, p.331 – women dentists)
Registering personal applicability of explanandum
   It'll do what I wanted it to? (P)
   So if I put it on my 24 (P)
   That's what I was worried about (C)
   So my DX coating's an advantage for that one I should think (P)
   May I ask what goes into that paper, because I have to advise a
      couple of people who are doing it. (E, p.34 – exam)

3. *Moves for constructing and comparing mental models*

Checking agreement of mental models by stating own beliefs
   I think isn't vitamin D the vitamin you get from the sun? (E, p.597 –
      rickets)
   But the women wear veils and everything **don't they**? (E, p.598 –
      rickets)
   Which **I assumed** was 250 grams (I)
   No, but she lived here for twenty years (E, p.330 – women dentists)
   It doesn't bear much resemblance to "largo" in music though **does it**?
      (I)
Clarifying ambiguous referents
   Is it she who won't do the allowing or he? (E, p.281 – ladders)
   On your part or on the clients' part? (E, p.435 - stockbroking)
   You mean there's a mark on the *film*? (E, p.198 – projection)
Requesting definitions and specifications
   What specifically does the sun god do? (B – Wicca)
   Can you tell us what some of these ethics are? (B – Judaism)
Checking the scope of application of a statement
   And for them too you don't make any charge aside from
      commission? (E, p.433 – stockbroking)
   Are all pagans vegetarian? (B – Wicca)

So you can use "fermata" for anything where you'd use "stop"?
In most senses of the word "stop"? (I)
Checking construction of mental model by restating explanation
So that's the physical thing you're doing. (B – Nishiren Shoshu)
You mean they're both running at the same time? (E, p.199 –
projection)
Do you mean they've got the same pictures on the tail end of one
through the beginning of another? (E, p.199 – projection)
*Checking agreement of mental models by generating new output for
matching*
So a doctor's higher than a professor. (A)
So you've only got a latitude of about four stops (P)
Establishing the significance of matches and mismatches
It seems to me that what you're talking about is exactly the same
thing (E, p.607 – surgery)
I think that contradicts with your belief that life is sacred (B – Wicca)
I don't know if it's worth saying, but I took you as meaning for
example . . . (C)
Is reformed Judaism then not just an easy way at the Jewish life? (B
– Judaism)
Surely that's a weak form of pacifism (B – Judaism)
Checking the reliability of the explainer's model
How do you know your gods exist? (B – Wicca)
So we only have your personal testimony that the Bible is correct. (B
– Pentecostal)
Why is it you're not giving us any rational arguments? (B – Krishna)

Tutors' moves:

1. *Controlling the interaction*

Establishing the right to speak and the order of topics
Let me finish (B – Pentecostal)
Let me explain salvation first and then I'll come to that (B –
Pentecostal)

2. *Taking account of the learner's needs and purposes*

Confirming the question concept or rhetorical force of the question
The pronunciation? (I)
What I'm trying to find out is the relevance of that question (B –
Pentecostal)
Yes, you're talking about contrast ratio there (P)
Requesting definitions and specifications
I don't understand **what you mean by** . . . (B – Nishiren Shoshu)

What do you mean by materialistic? You keep saying it's materialistic.(B – Krishna)

Addressing the learner's prior knowledge
You think it's weird because you've been brought up with a certain set of values (B – Krishna)
It's like secretary, personal assistant – they're not qualifications they're jobs (A)
"Questa, quella per me pari sono" yes, you are the opera man. (I)
Oh. That's alien to you. So your cigarettes don't . . .(I)
I think Hogarth drew some pictures of people with bow legs **didn't he**, kids? (E, p.597–598 – rickets)

Signalling mutual knowledge or surprise
No he hasn't **curiously** enough (E, p.431 – stockbroking)
Remember why should she 'cos she hasn't . . . .(E, p.330 – women dentists)
Ah, that's another one, . . .(C)

Addressing learner's purpose
That may not be what you want to do (P)
Better say "I want" (I)

3. *Establishing the explainer's viewpoint*

Checking the reception of the explanation
But it's like a job title rather than a qualification, do you see **what I mean**? (A)

Reformulating explanation
What I'm saying is chanting brings out positive potential (B – Nishiren Shoshu)

Qualifying scope of explanation
We would be allowed to do it, **but** I don't think we would (E, p.434 – stockbroking)
Yes that's . . .**though**; it's not . . .(P)
But there's a catch to this (P)
Yes, it was, **but** that's only for grams **whereas** for . . .it's. . .(I)

Offering explanatory devices
"Stretto" means narrow. So you have **for example** "Lo stretto di Messina". (I)
Unfortunately I can't talk about the North East of England but **I can talk about** my own situation and what I understand (B – Pentecostal)

Reformulating learners' explanations
Because the camera's metering off the whole of the background, yeh. (P)

There's this whole notion of . . . in which . . .
      so it looks like what you're talking about falls within this area (C)
Accepting or rejecting learner's formulation
      That's right, yes (P)

I have suggested throughout this chapter that the power relations between explainer and learner will influence how (and indeed if) explanations are negotiated. A relatively powerless learner may find it impossible to perform some negotiating functions, or alternatively may have to resort to different classes of move to fulfil the function in question. This is not simply a matter of degrees of politeness however. Even in the least deferential of these encounters, the 'A to Z of Belief' programmes, where questioners were prepared to say bluntly "I find that ridiculous" or "Don't answer . . . again", there are plenty of examples of questioners softening their moves with polite introductions like "Sorry, I know I keep going back to it" or "I'm sorry to push the point but it's really bugging me."

I have already offered an example of how learners in the Italian class managed to manipulate the tutor into giving them the kind of examples they found helpful, without explicitly demanding them. However, although some of the functions to do with representing their needs to the explainer were indirectly fulfilled in this way by students in the two lesson-based sources of data, there are other functions which it appears they were hardly able to perform. It is notable, for example, that as well as making no moves for controlling the interaction they also made no evaluative moves such as ones 'establishing the significance' of the current state of the explanation or 'checking the reliability of the explainer's model', whereas people in more equal relationships with the explainer did.

This issue of learners' power is clearly an important one. The disabling of certain learners' moves in unequal relationships often prevents them from getting explanations which meet their needs. It is of concern, therefore, whether new generations of tutoring systems can succeed in giving learners more power in the interactions they allow.

Of course, for effective negotiation of explanations tutors' reciprocal power is also important. A learner's power to put their needs and purposes on the agenda is of no value unless the tutor can address those needs. While the range of moves tutors make in these data is smaller than that of the learners, many of them fulfil just this function.

The aim of the final section of this chapter will be to consider in broad terms the implications of the way explanations are negotiated, in these natural dialogues, for improving the explanation facilities of intelligent tutoring systems. More specific techniques of ITS design and knowledge representation which might tackle some of these points are discussed in other chapters (e.g. Chapter 9). See also Evertsz and Elsom-Cook (1990).

5   NEGOTIATING EXPLANATIONS IN INTELLIGENT TUTORING SYSTEMS

In the previous two sections I have demonstrated that learners are very active in getting the explanations they want, and appear to have an even larger range of moves in their negotiating repertoire than 'tutors' do. It would be desirable, therefore, having identified the most important types of move, to make as many of them as possible available to learners using intelligent tutoring systems.

At the end of Section 3 on negotiations in action, I suggested that both learners and teachers use their moves in natural interactions to fulfil functions concerning credibility, question concepts, mutual knowledge, viewpoint, devices and purpose.

The issue of credibility has been offered as an explanation for the low take-up of expert system consulting programs in the commercial world. Professionals are not likely to act confidently on the basis of advice for which no satisfactory rationale is given. Similarly, learners cannot be expected to update or revise their knowledge without some basis of confidence that it is appropriate to do so. To this end they need to be able to get definitions for terms which seem to refer to different things in their own mental representations and those of the explainer (program). They need to be offered backing for explanations in terms of causal and other model-based relationships, rather than traces of activated heuristic rules. And they need to be able to get warrants of the credibility of these explanations, definitions, and backing.

It is clear that first generation expert systems are unable to support the moves needed by a tutor to fulfil these functions. Indeed, the need to provide credible, and so effective, explanations and not simply efficient problem solving performance is an important motive in the development of second generation systems incorporating causal or model-based representations.

The move towards giving expert system programs deeper knowledge is an important means of addressing credibility issues, but it is not enough in itself to support some of the other components of the negotiating machinery that this study has suggested teachers and learners need. If users of expert systems and ITSs are to find explanations effective and useful then their purposes must be addressed by them.

Although it was notable that the kind of explanation offered never seemed to be the subject of negotiations in the interactions studied here, the analysis of Notes and Queries showed that this was indeed a potential area of miscoordination between the two parties. It may be that the task-based nature of the 'lesson' dialogues (P, I) and the mutual understanding of the dialogue's history in the less formal ones (B, E, C, A) led to generally accurate assessments of the learner's purpose, and hence the kind of explanation that would address it. There is some suspicion that students in the photography class might sometimes have been looking for a different kind of explanation than the one they got, but the power relations between them and the tutor meant that they were not prepared to say "No, that's not what I wanted to know." Their strategy for getting their own purposes addressed was often to pose problems from their own experience (either of doing the fieldwork task, or of photographic activities prior to coming on the course). It may be unreasonably difficult to provide an ITS with the capability of inferring learners' purposes from the dialogue history, and even more so to represent those purposes in a way which enables the program to generate appropriate explanations of different kinds (deductive, historical, functional, probabilistic). However, giving learners the power to request them requires less: that the program has its knowledge represented in such a way that alternative kinds of explanation can be generated, and that both have a vocabulary for talking about them. Allowing learners to get their own purposes on the agenda by posing their own problems would clearly be an important aim for the design of tutoring systems with negotiable explanations. Whether the explanations generated in the course of solving those problems would satisfy them would depend on how negotiable they were, not only in terms of the kinds of explanation that can be offered but also in terms of the other negotiating points identified in this study: viewpoints and question concepts, mutual knowledge and explanatory devices.

At first sight the most problematic of these would seem to be mutual knowledge. In natural dialogues learners check out mutual knowledge by stating their own beliefs about the topic, and by offering their own formulations of the understanding they already have, or are tentatively coming to. Tutors do so by monitoring the reception of the examples and analogies they use which are based on assumed mutual knowledge, and by interpreting and evaluating learners' statements of belief and their reformulations of the explanations they have been given. The subtleties of linguistic representation that are so central to the process of formulation and reformulation mean that incorporating this element of the negotiating repertoire in an intelligent tutoring system is at present and may always be for the realms of science fiction.

However, it is noticeable that relatively few of the negotiating moves, identified in Section 4 on negotiating machinery, are recognizable by linguistic features (highlighted in bold in my examples). Of the few that are linguistically signalled, many ('but', 'so') are highly ambiguous. Our ability to recognize what functions they fulfil in the negotiation of an explanation is not based on the sophistication of our natural language processing skills. Rather, it is founded on our ability to interpret communicative purposes on the basis of our assumptions about the pragmatic basis of conversational moves. So the identification of a repertoire of moves in this research offers a starting point for the development of a communication interface for tutoring systems which is (as graphical interfaces are) pragmatically rather than linguistically based.

Designers may wonder how feasible it would be to take account of learners' needs to specify the question concept and change the viewpoint if necessary. The tutor's function of interpreting multiply ambiguous questions, and addressing more than one interpretation, implies multiple representations of the domain knowledge, as I suggested earlier. Their function of keeping track of the history of a query in the discourse, in order to model the learner's purpose or discover exactly what it is they want to know, implies a sophisticated plan recognition capability. But again it seems that there may be more scope for developing the repertoire of moves that *learners* can make (referring back in the discourse, refining questions with 'rather than . . .' clauses, offering hypotheses, offering alternative explanations). The utility of allowing these kinds of moves of course depends largely on the ways in which the system can respond to them. A key capability that would seem to be necessary is that of creating alternative representations on the fly in consultation with the learner (for example, by means of a knowledge engineering facility for the learner's use) in order to interpret respecified questions, evaluate learners' hypotheses or critique their alternative explanations.

Getting the right kind of explanatory devices implies that an intelligent tutoring system must be able to respond to requests for examples, demonstrations, analogies, applications to a case and so on. In the familiar domains of programming, or algebra, some of this repertoire is already available, and worked examples or demonstrations may be relatively straightforwardly generated from the expert system rule base. But while running the rules over data input by the student who is trying an application to a case (cf. "So if I put it on my 24[mm lens]". (P)) may be a simple requirement to fulfil, generating analogies would seem much more problematic. It is for human explainers too, in some respects. The photography tutor's use of an analogy about forcing a low gear on an automatic car was a fairly long shot given the small proportion of people in Britain who are familiar with driving automatics. Since analogies are by definition from different domains from the to-be-explained phenomena, they are particularly unlikely to be generated by a domain-specific tutoring system. What would seem to be more useful to learners in this area would be the possibility of checking out analogies suggested by their own mental model-building. The implication of wanting to give learners this sort of move in their repertoire is again that the discourse component of an ITS have a knowledge engineering capability itself. That is to say, in order to evaluate an analogy offered by a student the program would have to be able to elicit information from the student which it could use to construct a representation of the relevant features of the analogy for comparison.

CONCLUSION

This study has shown that although the negotiation of explanations may be a very compromised process even in many natural explanation-giving contexts, tutors, and more particularly learners, have a large and subtle range of negotiating machinery for achieving their intersubjective ends. The translation of some of this repertoire to the interactions between learners and intelligent tutoring systems presents interesting challenges to software designers. It seems that expanding the range of moves available, to learners in particular, may significantly increase the utility of the explanations they receive. Increasing the learner's power and providing the right kinds of knowledge representation to underpin the system's response to these new kinds of move is the challenge this research poses to the designers of the next generations of tutoring systems.

11 Sharing the Interface

MARK ELSOM-COOK

Institute of Educational Technology
The Open University, Milton Keynes, UK

1 INTRODUCTION

Successful negotiation of a teaching interaction requires that the participants have a common ground of mutual understanding around which to negotiate. In this chapter we will explore the sorts of information which need to be present in a shared model if a learner is to negotiate effectively with a teaching system. The process of negotiation will only be discussed peripherally, since the main focus is on the knowledge which must be present for the process to take place at all.

We will commence with a brief discussion of the guided discovery approach to tutoring, and show how this necessarily implies a negotiated interaction. By examining the difficulties of establishing such a negotiation we will identify a variety of levels at which a shared understanding must be constructed. Different forms of negotiation may utilize information from different levels. Following this discussion, the issues raised here will then be illustrated with two simple examples.

2 GUIDED DISCOVERY TUTORING

The philosophical standpoint which forms the basis for the guided discovery approach is that knowledge communication is not an appropriate paradigm for education. Knowledge communication is taken to describe a methodology in which a learner is considered to be a receptacle which has some knowledge missing. The role of the teacher in this approach is to transfer knowledge from her own head into that of the learner. There have been a number of educational objections to such an approach. In the first place, the teacher's own conception of the domain may not correspond to the structure which the student already has in

KNOWLEDGE NEGOTIATION
ISBN 0–12–509378–0

place, and consequently it may not be possible for the student to identify the relationship between her existing knowledge and the new knowledge which is being offered to her. This leads to the problem of 'inert ideas' (Whitehead 1932) which exist in the student's head and can be regurgitated, but which can not necessarily be applied by the student because they are not integrated with her existing conceptions, and hence may not be accessible to her reasoning mechanisms. To some extent this objection can be overcome by assuming that the teacher engages in some analysis of the cognitive state of the student, and restructures the knowledge which is being transferred to the student such that it fits better with the pre-existing structures. Alternatively, the teacher may find it necessary to restructure the knowledge which is already in the student's head in order to fit with new material. Even making this allowance, however, the student is still seen as an object to which the teacher does something, whereas in fact, the student probably has a better understanding of what is inside her head than the teacher does. The dividing line between a system where the tutor adapts material based on inference about the student's state, and a system where the adaptation of material is negotiated is not always clear. A mechanism of implicit negotiation lies between the two.

A second problem with the communication model is that it does not actively engage the learner. Human beings are active learners, in the sense that they construct and test theories of the domain in which they are operating. By becoming actively involved in the learning process, the learner can integrate new experiences into her existing models, and can construct explanations which justify her beliefs. The effects of this active participation are partly motivational, but it has also been shown that such engagement leads to better retention of learnt material.

A proposed alternative to the knowledge communication approach is the use of discovery learning (e.g. Papert 1980). The underlying assumption here is that, in an 'appropriate' environment, the learner will construct theories and learn about a domain without actively being taught. Child-centred approaches to education have started from this position, but the term 'appropriate' raises many difficulties. Different environments support different conceptions of a domain, and to ensure the learner constructs an effective model requires that the environment be structured very carefully. Essentially, this is a form of indirect teaching, because the environment will necessarily be structured by the teacher (or creator?) with particular educational objectives in mind. There is the additional problem that it is not clear that all things can be learnt in this way (or at least, learnt in a reasonable time). Learning science by discovery, for example, would require a student to repeat the history of scientific discovery, including making the same errors. For many students this would be impossible, and certainly could become extremely demotivating.

Guided discovery (Elsom-Cook 1990a) is based upon a combination of these approaches. It regards the student as an active constructor of theories who is engaging in learning within an environment, but there is also a tutor present with knowledge of the domain about which the student is learning. This tutor can provide varying degrees of direction for the student, facilitating more effective learning and maintaining motivation. The student centred nature of the system is satisfied by the requirement that the tutor can never be directive without the agreement of the student, and by utilizing a 'decreasing intervention' strategy in which the tutor tries to make itself unnecessary as the student gains more experience. These requirements clearly require a facility for negotiation to take place between tutor and student, since the locus of control may vary and the content and form of the teaching must be agreed between the participants.

An intelligent tutoring system constructed in the guided discovery manner must consist of a tutor and a learning environment. For the present it will be assumed that the environment also resides within the computer, since the problems implied by the computer trying to interact with an external environment are much broader than those arising from an internal environment, although the educational issues are similar in both cases. Suchman (1987) examined an intelligent help system in which the 'environment' was external to the computer. In this study the target domain was a photocopier, and Suchman identified a number of problems which arose because the computer and user did not have equal access to this environment. The computer could 'see' things (such as the internal state of the machine) which were not visible to the user. Similarly, the user perceived parts of the system (such as a paper feed tray improperly fitted) which were not accessible to the computer. Consequently, misunderstanding of terminology and the referents of particular phrases arose. This in turn led to failures of communication and consequent failures in learning.

In a previous paper (Elsom-Cook 1990a), I stated that the learner and tutor in a guided discovery situation must have equal access to the environment. They must be able to 'see' the same things, and have the same range of actions upon the environment available to them (see Figure 11.1). It might be assumed that placing the environment within the computer, such that the machine had access to all aspects of it, and then restricting that access to only those parts which can be seen by the user would solve this problem. This is not the case, however. The problem is similar to one that arises in interface design generally: the user's model of the system may not agree with the designer's model of the system (as

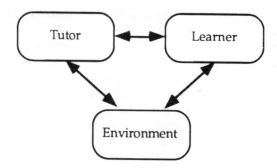

Fig. 11.1 Symmetry of communication in Guided Discovery.

embodied in the interface). In current computers it is necessary for the user to adapt her model to fit that of the designer. In doing this, she receives no assistance from the system. In keeping with the guided disovery approach, we wish to provide the student with assistance in developing a model of that environment. This will involve negotiation about the environment (and the interface) between system and student. The purpose of this paper is to clarify the sorts of information that are required in order for such negotiation to take place.

It is also important to note that the learning environment may require the learner to develop two distinct models. The environment approach is based upon the idea that interacting with the environment will enable the learner to construct a model of the domain embodied in that environment. To this end, the designer attempts to make the workings of the environment itself transparent to the user, imposing no additional learning overhead. This goal is unlikely to be achieved in reality, so there is a second model which is, effectively, a model of the mechanics of the interface. A simple example of this would be in a system such as the Alternate Reality Kit (Smith 1986) which is for learning about physics. All the objects in the system respond to physical laws, and hence the domain model is concerned with physics and applies across the system. However, because it is necessary to distinguish operating on an object from manipulating the behaviour of that object there is an extra distinction required. An example would be that pressing a button needs to be a different activity from moving that button to a different place in the system. This is achieved by the use of multiple mouse keys – a technique which has no meaning in the domain – and hence requires a small model of the interface.

A key assumption of the approach presented in the following section is that interaction between human and computer is not oriented around commands and responses. This imperative model is appropriate for some forms of interaction, but clearly is not suited to negotiated interaction or to a teaching situation. Furthermore, it is assumed that the intention of a particular communicative act may not correspond to the surface form, and may not be explicitly represented within that act. In current computer systems, a communication is normally a self-contained entity in which all the information is explicitly represented. A move towards more natural interaction with a computer necessarily implies getting closer to human-human forms of communication, and hence to allowing implicit communication of both the intention and the content of certain utterances. For this reason, the representation described here is intended to be a step towards a model based upon research into the nature of human dialogue. This work does not necessarily require that the computer understands natural language, but it does imply that certain structures of day to day conversation must be supported by the representation. Further discussion of dialogue modelling and it's application to tutoring systems can be found in Baker (this volume), Elsom-Cook (1990b, 1991), Blandford (1990) and Petrie-Brown (1989).

3 LEVELS OF REPRESENTATION

In seeking to establish the basis for a communication between the computer and tutor, we need to establish the different levels at which agreement (or disagreement) about the communication can occur. This enables us to examine the mechanisms which might occur at each level, and to identify the forms of misunderstanding which might arise. Since we are trying to achieve a deeper level of understanding than simply agreeing a surface form of a communicative act, we will identify the different levels of representation of the communication by analogy with a communicative act between two human beings.

The goal of supporting knowledge negotiation implies that we are attempting to achieve a symmetry between the computer and user in terms of what they are able to express and the roles that they are able to take in the interaction. We attempt to capture this here by ensuring that each of the levels of description which we present may exist in the head of each agent in the dialogue. There is, however, an intrinsic asymmetry when it comes to representing and reasoning about the dialogue. This arises because any given agent has a privileged access to its own internal state. It can access its own beliefs, but it can only have beliefs about the beliefs of the other agent. This uncertainty means that the agent's representation of its own perception and of that of the other agent are necessarily different. In discussing representation, we have therefore taken the perspective of the machine, and discuss primarily how the

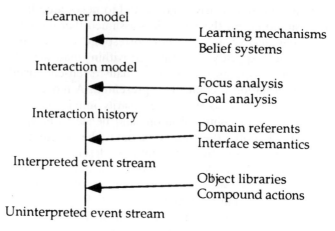

Fig. 11.2   Information levels in the interaction.

machine might represent the different levels. How the student is represented is discussed in terms of the machine's representation of the student, rather than the student's own representation. The issue of representing the other agent's representation (at whatever level) is a task for the highest level of this analysis, and will be discussed in Section 3.5.

The model proposed here consists of five levels of information. Each level can be described as an abstraction over the previous level, and it is not necessary for a level to refer to anything other than the one immediately beneath it. The proposed levels are summarized in Figure 11.2, together with the additional information that is needed to make the transformation between the levels. The two highest levels (the learner model and the dialogue model) will only be briefly sketched in this paper, since both are active areas of research. The major focus of this chapter is on the form and purpose of the lowest three levels. It is also worth noting that there is a continuum of negotiability of information at the different levels. Level 1 essentially corresponds to the raw data of the outside world, and is hence non-negotiable: the learner has to adapt to the machine's view. As we move up the levels, however, the negotiability of description increases, and by the highest level we are essentially at the opposite extreme, where the machine is adapting to the student.

3.1   Level 1 – The uninterpreted event stream

We will begin by assuming that there are a set of communication channels between the computer and the user. These channels can be one way, or two way. Most current interfaces use only one way communication channels. A keyboard, for example, is a one way communication channel from the user to the computer, while the screen is a one way channel from the computer to the user. An example of a two way channel might be a sound board which allows the user to speak to the machine and the machine to speak to the user. More complex interface devices, such as an airdrum or dataglove, may still be represented as a communication channel in this sense. Some caution is required in identifying the directionality of an interface channel. For example, it might be thought that a touch screen constitutes a two-way channel. This is only the case if the channel is symmetrical between the computer and the user. A touch screen is only bi-directional if everything which can be seen on the screen can be touched, and any event which can be generated by the computer on that screen can also be generated by the user. Normally, only some of the things on the screen can be touched, and only some behaviours can be generated by the user. In this case, we have two one-directional channels, but there is a relationship between them. This relationship requires interpretation, however, so it is not at the same level as the communication that we are discussing at present, but at level 2.

We will refer to this first level as an uninterpreted event stream. Each event has an initiator (computer or user), a time of occurence, and some descriptive data associated with it. This is the only interpretation that occurs at this level. It is assumed that computer and user can agree on when something happened and who did it. We do not allow events such as "click at icon#3", since this requires an agreement as to what the icon is (which is on an output channel) and hence requires construction of a shared belief in order to create the interpretation. An example of an event description at level 1 might be:

```
agent: user
channel: mouse port
time: t5
data: 23,17,1
```

In some sense, we can see this level of communication as similar to that arising between two agents exchanging written communication in a language that they do not understand and a script that they do not understand. The agents can agree on when a certain piece of writing occured, and can agree on the appearance of the marks on the paper, but are not able to understand what the marks mean, or even parse them into distinct symbols.

In fact, we can identify a small difference in representation at this point, since computer and user may not describe the same data in exactly the same way. A computer may know that a mouse pointer is at screen coordinates 23,21, for example, but a learner may just have this encoded as a rough area of screen.

3.1.1 Errors at level 1

At the first level, there are few misunderstandings which can arise between the participants in the interaction. We can basically identify errors of attention, resulting in one participant being unaware of events of which the other participant is aware, and errors of memory, resulting in a participant forgetting a part of the event stream of which they were previously aware. Each of these errors can be applied to any combination of the four parts of an event description. In terms of our analogy with language, an agent can forget who wrote something, when they wrote it, or what the appearance of the thing which was written was. They can, of course, forget all three and believe that the event never happened. The errors of attention can be important in a computer interface. With multiple channels of communication, the user cannot necessarily attend to them all simultaneously. Even with a single channel, such as the screen, the user may fail to see something happen because her attention was elsewhere on the screen. This sort of error is independent of any understanding of the event. If, for example, the computer indicated that the disk was full by flashing a disk-shaped picture in the top left hand corner of the screen, the user might misunderstand it for various reasons. It may be that the symbol is not immediately salient – the interpretation is not obvious. This form of error does not reside within the level which we are currently discussing. At the current level the user could only misunderstand the action in the sense that she failed to see the symbol at all because her attention was elsewhere. Alternatively, she could see it, start to do something else, and forget that she had seen it. This would also be an error of communication at the first level. Another example of a memory error would be remembering that you had to type a control sequence to carry out some task, but forgetting exactly which control character was used.

It is important to enumerate the errors at this level, since they will result in errorful models being constructed at higher levels in the representation.

3.2 Level 2 – Interpreted event stream

The second level of representation of the interaction involves creating a basic interpretation of the event stream. This result of this interpretation is similar to what is traditionally called an 'event stream' in an operating system, in that each event is an encoding describing a particular action and objects upon which that action was performed. No interpretation of the 'meaning' of the event is carried out, however. The interpretation involves resolving each element of the uninterpreted event stream into a new description consisting of an action taken from a library of actions, and a set of objects taken from a library of objects. Although we choose to refer to these entities as libraries, it does not imply that they are a finite, fixed collection of objects. The items may be generated from some deeper model. Examples of such generation are given in Section 4. Nevertheless, from the point of view of identifying differences, it is convenient to refer to these components as libraries.

The interpretation of the event stream introduces ambiguity, in that the two agents may be in possession of different libraries which they are attempting to use to construct the interpretation. The computer must use a model of the interface which has been explicitly given to it by a designer. The learner does not possess such a representation. Indeed, one of the tasks facing the learner is to construct a model at this level. This involves recognizing the actions and objects which occur on the stream. Let us consider the simple example which follows:

```
agent: user
channel: mouse port
time: t5
action: mousedown
objects: quit-icon
```

This description corresponds to the user pressing the mouse button down on an icon called quit. The interpretation which has taken place to derive this from the previous level is to identify the primitive action mouse-down, and to convert a coordinate where this action occured into a reference to a specific object in the environment. Given that the computer has a representation of the designer's model of the interface, this description can be derived unambiguously by the machine. This is not the case for the user, however. The user may not be aware of the vocabulary of available actions. For example, different systems may be sensitive to a mouse press on an object (possibly with more than one button), to the mouse cursor entering an object, to a mouse cursor leaving an object, etc. This repertoire of possible actions must be learnt if the computer and user are to construct a shared model. This means that, as far as representing the other agent's model of the interface is concerned, one agent must allow for ambiguity in the representation. The computer may know that the user clicked on the quit icon, but the user may be unaware that she has done this, or that 'quit' was an icon. The possible errors arising are discussed further below.

Another important thing to notice about the example given above is that the description of the event on the mouse channel involves reference to an object which is (presumably) on the 'screen' channel. Part of the process of interpretation at this level is to identify the connections between the different communication channels. Note that we are only concerned with the direct links between channels at this level. For example, in a drawing program, one might select an item in the drawing and click on a menu entry called 'delete'. This action of deleting ultimately refers to the selected object. At level 2 of the representation, however, we are not aware of this. Our concern is to establish a link between the action mouse-click and the object 'delete'. This is, again, unambiguous for the computer which is interpreting the situation in terms of the designer's model. The relationship between channels (i.e. what channel can refer to objects in what other channel) can be specified unambiguously to the system. For the user, however, the link between the channels need not be obvious. An example might be the case in which a keypress (such as F1) has a referent such as 'the previous object on the auditory input channel' (it might, for example, mean, 'remember the previous sound').

It is not too difficult for the user and computer to establish an agreement that a particular action has occured. In current interfaces, most actions are discrete, and hence can clearly be identified as having happened or not. The problem of interpretation becomes more complex when we are referring to compound actions made up of several primitive events. We can group arbitrary sub-strings of actions into higher level items which have a different semantic role from their components. Examples of this are double-clicking the mouse, or dragging an object between two locations. This can be a source of discrepancy in the representations of computer and user, since these actions may need to be learnt. It is not clear to a new user that 'double-click' is a meaningful entity. There is also a source of ambiguity at this level in that the existence of a particular sub-sequence does not guarantee that it corresponds to a particular complex action. Pressing the mouse-down, moving it and releasing it may be a dragging action, but for non-draggable objects it may not be an action at all. Note that at this level we do not know whether a subsequence has a meaning: it could be a totally arbitrary sunstring. Whether these sub-sequences are meaningful depends of the semantics of the interface as described by level 3.

A much greater problem exists in establishing mutual agreement about what constitutes an 'object'. If we simply consider the screen, how can a user know to what an action with the mouse refers? From level 1, we have decided that the participants can effectively agree on the marks on the paper. In terms of the screen this consists of reaching agreement as to what the colour of each individual pixel is. Any higher level of description than this involves interpretation. In terms of our analogy with writing, the problem is for our agents to agree on where individual symbols, or words, begin and end – although this still does not involve agreement about what the symbols mean. So long as there is agreement between the set of known objects of computer and user, the description problem is the same as that which occurs more generally in event streams. If there is a discrepancy, then establishing agreement about what constitutes an object leads us into difficulties, since we need, at some level, to solve the problem of machine perception if the machine is to be made aware of the learner's perception of an object. There are intermediate positions, however, in which the learner can indicate a region of screen considered to be an entity.

In effect, this second level is a lexical analysis of the events. The actions and objects are elements of a lexicon provided to the computer by the designer, and the problems which arise at this level are concerned with reaching mutual agreement on the lexicon being used.

3.2.1 Errors at level 2

As has been briefly mentioned above, we can identify three basic causes of misunderstandings arising between the computer and learner at this level. The main one is due to the differences in the libraries of the two agents. We would expect that the difference in libraries can be explained by the presence of items in one library which are absent in another. This is not sufficient, however, because while the computer's library is fixed at this level, that of the learner is changing dynamically. We would certainly expect that the learner initially has a different (and probably smaller) library than the machine from which to construct the interpretation. It is necessary to remember, however, that humans are systems which actively construct knowledge, and that perceiving an event for which she doesn't have a description is likely to result in the learner constructing a representation of that event. Relating the learner's constructed representation to the system's representation is an area which a machine may not be able to carry out automatically, and which becomes an area for negotiation between the agents.

An example of a difference in lexicon can arise from a statement such as 'Open the Apple menu' (on a Macintosh). Users may construct the idea of a menu header as being a piece of text which responds to mouse-down, and hence look for the word 'Apple' somewhere in the system. In fact, this menu is the only one in the basic system for which the header is graphical, so a user with the model above would fail to establish the referent. In this case, rather than using a fixed library of objects, the description of menu headers in general can generate an infinite library of such items. The fact that this library does not include the graphical menu header places this error in the category of absent items mentioned above.

There may be similar problems of lexical difference in resolving actions. The use of key modifiers, such as control, may not be apparent to a user, and hence she will not be able to parse such actions at this level of description.

A second major source of error arises from the attempts to establish referents between streams. A user may be aware of performing an action on a certain stream, and aware of the existence of objects on a stream to which she is referring, but may be unaware of the mechanism by which the referent of the action is established. An example of this would be the distinction between a mouse cursor and a text insertion point. A user may begin typing, expecting the text to appear where the cursor is, when it actually appears at the insertion point. This is quite a common misconception, but at this level of analysis all we can say is that there is a mismatch in resolving the referent of the typing action.

3.3   Level 3 – Interaction history

In the first two levels we have been concerned with recognizing the symbols which constitute the communication. There has been no attempt to interpret those symbols as having communicative intent. The third level of analysis is concerned with identifying such an intent. Effectively, we are dividing the actions of computer and user up into utterances. Each of these utterances may be composed of many events, and they go beyond the previous levels in that they establish referents in the domain of discourse (as opposed to the actions and objects of the interface itself). The analysis does not seek to establish a 'deep' meaning for the utterance, but is more like an analysis of surface form. A simple example of an utterance at this level might be:

```
agent: user
time: t6
event: quit
```

In this case, the term 'quit' no longer refers to an item in the interface, but is a command associated with that item. It is in the domain of discourse underlying the interface. The same representation at level 3 would also arise if the user had selected 'exit' from a file menu, or typed 'goodbye', or pressed 'escape'. There are many possible ways that the interface could permit the user to express the desire to leave a program. Each of these resolves to the same description at level three because it is essentially a request for the same behaviour from the system. In this sense, level 3 can be regarded as an operational semantics for the interface.

A more sophisticated example can be demonstrated with the use of 'drag'. At level 2 of analysis, we may have descriptions as follows:

agent: user	agent: user	agent: user
channel: mouse port	channel: mouse port	channel: mouse port
time: t5	time: t5	time: t5
action: drag	action: drag	action: drag
objects: my-icon trashcan	objects: my-icon disc-icon	objects: my-icon print-icon

These three descriptions are essentially the same at level 2. Each is based on a group of five level 1 actions, but the differences between those groups is reflected only in the different target object of the drag action at level 2. It must also be emphasized that 'drag' is still a meaningless symbol giving a name to a sequence of actions. It may have no meaningful semantic interpretation. The analysis of these actions at the third level involves reaching an interpretation in terms of the mechanisms of the system, and hence requires the 'utterance' to be interpreted in context. In the case given above, we are essentially representing the idea that the action 'drag' in the interface has three different semantic interpretations. In the case above, these would appear at level 3 as:

agent: user	agent: user	agent: user
time: t5	time: t5	time: t5
action: delete	action: copy	action: print
objects: my-file	objects: my-file	objects: my-file

Alternative ways of doing the same thing (such as printing by selecting the object and choosing control-P) would resolve to the same level 3 description. It is also important to notice that at this level the different communication channels have been eliminated from the description. Indeed, there is no reference to the interface at all. An interaction description may combine behaviour on any number of streams.

The generation of this layer from the previous one can be achieved (in the designer's terms) by providing a grammar that connects the levels. For the user, this is a difficult transformation, and can give rise to a wide variety of errors, which will be discussed in the next section.

3.3.1   Errors at level 3

In creating a description at level 3, the user (and computer) are making a mapping from the utterance to the communicative form of that utterance (which is not necessarily the communicative intent). At this level, the model is dealing, for the first time, with entities which are not explicitly represented in the interaction. There is, for example, no concrete object corresponding to the action of copying something. The development of this mapping is the first level at which there is real scope for negotiation about the interaction. The primary source of errors is from failing to make the appropriate connection between the interface and the 'world' it represents.

In the case of actions, there may be unitary actions (such as clicking on quit) or compound ones (such as drag). These actions can be arbitrarily complex, including multiple arguments and constraints on the properties of those arguments and the relationships between them. In a drawing package, for example, an action such as 'fill' might require selecting an object in the drawing area, selecting a fill pattern, and pressing a 'fill' icon. At the interface level, we can regard pressing the fill icon as the action. However, within the domain of reference, we have not successfully made an utterance regarding that action unless the other actions have also been carried out. Equally, if the object selected is a bitmap rather than a geometric object, the command 'fill' is meaningless. In these cases we have a discrepancy between the intended utterance and the actual utterance. This requires negotiation about the communicative intent of the action sequence if the problem is to be resolved. Clearly, in addition to this failure to construct a meaningful utterance, there is the possibility of constructing a meaningful utterance with the wrong meaning. An example of this would be the difference between 'copy' and 'duplicate' in a standard Macintosh graphics package. Although they are clearly distinguised in the interface, many users expect the 'copy' action in the interface to resolve to the 'duplicate' action in the underlying system.

Turning to objects in the underlying domain, there is a similar problem with relating them to objects in the interface. There need not be a one-to-one mapping, and objects in the underlying domain need not have any form of direct representation in the interface. If we consider the example of wanting to delete all files whose names end with the string '.bak', then at the interface we are likely to issue a command such as 'rm *.bak'. The interface object which is the string must be resolved to a reference to all the files in this directory. If a user has happened to call her backup files '.back' then the referents will be resolved erroneously, or fail to be resolved at all.

3.4   Level 4 – Interaction model

As was mentioned earlier, the underlying assumption behind the approach outlined here is that we are moving towards a model of communication between computer and user which is similar to the sorts of interaction which occur between human agents. The three levels that we have described so far are concerned with producing complete time sequences describing the whole interaction. Clearly, human agents do not conduct their interaction based upon this sort of infinite memory. The fourth level of analysis therefore abstracts from the dialogue history to produce a representation of those events which need to be taken immediately into account when generating and understanding utterances. Previous papers (e.g. Elsom-Cook 1985, Elsom-Cook 1990b) have outlined the form of dialogue model which is proposed as part of the Guided Discovery approach, but we will briefly explain the way in which that model relates specifically to the interface levels discussed here.

The major components of the dialogue model are concerned with the focus of the interaction, and the goals of the interaction, at a given time. The focus of interaction represents the immediate focus of communication, and this is divided into the current explicit focus and one or more implicit foci. The focus model also contains a representation of things which have been a previous focus and can be referred back to. The approach taken is based upon the use of focus spaces (Grosz 1978, Reichman 1978). A focus space describes a particular topic as it has been used in a given context. Active focus spaces are those which are currently in focus, while open focus spaces are those which have been active recently, but can be referred to or become active again. This approach was developed for human dialogue, but has also been applied to human computer interaction with a windowing system (Reichmann 1986).

The component of the dialogue model concerned with goals represents those goals which the participants are pursuing through the dialogue. The participants may have goals of their own, which are not embodied in the dialogue, but these are not part of this level of description. We assume that the only goals represented in the dialogue model are those which have been mutually agreed by the participants. This agreement may either be explicit or implicit. It is reasonably straighforward to model goals which have been explicitly mutually agreed (as was done, for example, in KANT (Baker 1990)), but with goals that have been implicitly agreed, it is possible for one participant to believe that a goal has been mutually agreed when the other participant does not believe this to be the case. There are still serious theoretical problems raised by this issue (for example, see Smith 1982). In essence, it is the case that neither participant can be aware of an absolute mutual knowledge. Instead, each participant can only have access to their belief about what the mutual knowledge is, and this relies upon that participant having a representation of the other participant's beliefs about the mutual knowledge. This can become a recursive structure. For the present we will focus on goals which have been mutually agreed explicitly.

This model is a representation of the current state of the dialogue, and hence moves away from the strongly time-dependent structures of the earlier levels of analysis.

3.5   Level 5 – Learner model

The final level constitutes constructing a model of the belief structures of the learner. This involves integrating an abstraction of the dialogue model with previous knowledge about the learner. It is at this level that we capture beliefs about the beliefs of the other agent, and hence can identify the highest level of difference between the knowledge states of the agents for which negotiation is necessary. As was mentioned earlier, this level involves an intrinsic asymmetry. We may try and approach a symmetric interaction, but ultimately any agent can only have actual knowledge of its own internal state. The mechanisms for reasoning from this representation will therefore be different for an agent when it is reasoning about it's own behaviour, or the behaviour of another agent.

This level of the model is where most research on student modelling has focussed, and hence the internal structure of the level is still a topic of further research. From the perspective of this paper, we are assuming the use of a technique for combining belief systems, uncertainty and machine learning, called Belief-based bounded user modelling (Elsom-Cook 1990c).

4   A SIMPLE EXAMPLE – TEXT EDITOR PROBLEMS

We will provide a concrete example of the way that the levels described above apply to a real piece of software by considering a well known bug in the usage of the editor ED. This is a line oriented editor in which commands are issued as a single character, possible modified by an integer expressing the number of times that the command is to be repeated. For example, the command 'i' indicates that a line should be inserted before the current one, while the command 'a' indicates that a line should be appended after the current one. The well known bug arises with moving up and down a text file. The user discovers that to move up five lines, the correct command to issue is:

5u

If the user is then asked to move down five lines. The common response to this is to type:

5d

This command actually deletes five lines. The correct command to have issued would have been 5n (n for next). It is clear that this error is an easy one to make, and that it is due to a difference between the designer's model of the system and that of the user. Let us examine how this could be captured in our current representation.

At level 1 there is no difference between the event streams as perceived by the user and the computer. This is also true at level 2 (if we assume that the user can read the alphabet). At this level, the computer and user are in agreement that the symbols 5 and *d* have been typed, and can also agree that the *d* is the object to which the 5 is to be applied. This simply relies on the libraries having sufficient commonality to share the notion that single characters or integers are acceptable. It may be that the user has a different library since she may not know all the commands in the system, but we will assume that the library in this case is simply the full set of letters, and hence is a superset of the computer library.

The problem arises at level 3 of the analysis. Here, the interpretation is dependent on the designer's model (in the case of the computer) or the learner's previous model (in the case of the user). We can assume that the designer's model includes a specific set of mappings such as:

I(nsert)
A(ppend)
D(elete)
U(p)
N(ext)

The user's model at this level presumably includes some previously learnt commands, and, we might assume, some mapping of opposites as follows:

Up-Down
Previous-Next
Left-Right

These opposites are used to generate library items in the way that was discussed earlier. We can see that in this case, the computer and user can construct different entries in the interaction history as follows:

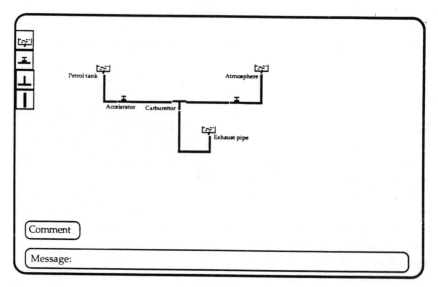

Fig. 11.3 A fluid flow learning environment.

Computer	*User*
agent: user	agent: user
channel: keyboard	channel: keyboard
time: t7	time: t7
event: Delete 5 lines	event: Down 5 lines

Note that this discrepancy only occurs at level 3 (and above) of the analysis. At level 2, both agents are in agreement that what happened was that the command '5*d*' was typed. Once the discrepancy has arisen at this level, it will be propogated to higher levels. We will always be able to trace the source of the problem back to this level, though. It is not being claimed here that the process of identifying the way in which the user might apply their model to this level is simple. Indeed, as indicated above, it may be very complex and it is a source for further work. The claim is simply that this is the appropriate level of the representation sequence for this type of error to occur.

5   AN EDUCATION EXAMPLE: FLUID FLOW

The previous example showed how the models described here might be applied to an issue concerned with the interface. To give a clearer idea of the application of these models in an educational setting, we will now show the use of these models within a simple educational system.

The system which we will discuss is illustrated in Figure 11.3. It is a simple system which allows the computer and user to discuss fluid flow within hydraulic-type systems. The central area is a drawing space in which either the computer or the learner can draw out a flow diagram. This diagram is made up of the components in the palette on the left-hand side of the screen. In effect, there are reservoirs, valves, joins and pipes. At the bottom of the screen are a 'comment' button, which allows the user to ask the computer to comment on a particular diagram, and a message box in which the computer can ask the user to make similar criticisms.

We will assume that the problem facing the learner is to discover how the flow of petrol and air around an internal combustion engine operates. For this domain, we have provided a fixed vocabulary of names (such as carburetor) on the right-hand side. The task is therefore to correctly construct a diagram of the flow, and correctly label it. The anticipated result is something like that shown in drawing area of Figure 11.3. Learning takes place by a mutual critiqueing process, and the critiqueing is communicated by one agent modifying the diagrams hypothesized by the other. We will discuss what must be represented at each of the levels of description outlined in Section 3, before going on to explain how those levels might be used in a teaching interaction.

If we ignore the possibility of typed input, this example has only two communication channels: the mouse and the screen. At the first level, therefore, the representation of uninterpreted events is straightforward. Input events can only be simple mouse behaviours, while output events (to the screen) only consist of drawing an object chosen from a fixed set at some point on the screen.

At the level of the interpreted event stream, the basic events to be supported are mousedown and mouseup events, as well as the drawing of objects on the screen. This interface is interesting in that there are two sorts of objects. One class of objects correspond to the icons which are always present on the screen. These can be unambiguously represented (as far as the computer is concerned) by a library describing the objects which the designer feels are primitive in the interface, although the interpretation of these objects by the student must be established. The second class of objects is those which are present in the diagram drawn by either agent. These objects are not built into the interface, so both the learner and the computer must establish what these objects are and where they are located.

The interaction history relies heavily on the establishment of a common vocabulary of objects at level 2. At this level we have a fixed vocabulary of actions (in the computer interpretation). This vocabulary divides into two categories. The first category consists of the simple action of selecting various objects. The second category is the interpretation in terms of creating, moving and deleting objects. There is an additional level of complexity in that creating a pipe has a deeper interpretation as connecting two other objects. This involves recognizing internal graphical structure of the objects such as reservoirs, so that the user and computer can agree where the connection points are. This is a specific case of a more general problem, which is the recognition of relationships between objects in the system.

The interaction model in this instance is quite clearly defined. At any time the constructed objects in the diagram form the main body of things to which reference can be made. The objects, at this level, are not graphical, but are the actual entities in a car engine, such as a carburretor, and the connections in the diagram correspond to statements about the domain of discourse, such as stating that petrol flows from the fuel tank to the carburettor. These constitute the objects of the focus space. The dialogue goals are concerned with expressing information about fluid flow in car engines.

The student modelling component concerns creating a representation of the student's belief about the behaviour of engines. No other aspects of the communication need to be considered for this example.

Let us now examine a simple interaction between student and system. We will assume that two objects have been created: one is a reservoir which has been named 'fuel tank' and the other is a valve which has been named 'carburretor'. What we wish to establish is the way in which the different levels of knowledge are applied in order to arrive at the interpretation in the learner model corresponding to a student belief that fuel flows from the fuel tank to the carburretor. This belief in the learner model would appear as follows:

believes(learner, flows(petrol, from(fuel tank), to(carburretor)), ())

The final argument here (which corresponds to the reason why the student holds the belief) is empty. This is because the student has simply stated the belief, and the computer has no idea why she holds the belief.

At the level of the uninterpreted event stream, this communication corresponds to six events. Four of these are events on the mouse stream, and two are events on the screen. Although they are not interpreted as such at this level, we can basically describe them as, clicking on the 'pipe' icon, which then inverts, clicking on the output node of the reservoir, and an input node of the valve, and the corresponding appearance of a line between the two upon the screen. For variety, we will assume that the click to select the pipe icon involved both a mousedown and a mouseup, while the click on the starting point of the pipe must be a mousedown, and that at the ending point must be a mouse up. Bearing in mind the form of description given in Appendix 1, this can be represented as follows:

initiator	channel	time	data
user	mouse	t1	. . .
user	mouse	t2	. . .
computer	screen	t3	. . .
user	mouse	t4	. . .
user	mouse	t5	. . .
computer	screen	t6	. . .

We have not bothered to provide the actual form of the data in this example, since this will be system dependent. It should also be noted that, although we have picked out these six events as corresponding to a particular high-level communication, this is not apparent at this level of analysis, and the actions shown above would be part of a larger event stream. The problem of identifying this subset is dealt with at higher levels of analysis. We have also simplified the situation by ignoring the large number of events which will occur between those given above, which correspond to movements of the mouse. We will assume that the computer and user are in agreement about what happened at this level of analysis, since the issues raised by a discussion of misinterpretation at this level are not particularly interesting.

Moving to the second level of analysis, we must identify the events and objects to which they refer. The first three events can be interpreted from the fixed library of events and objects incorporated into the designer's model. These will appear as follows:

initiator	channel	time	action	object
user	mouse	t1	mousedown	pipe icon
user	mouse	t2	mouseup	pipe icon
computer	screen	t3	invert	pipe icon

There are several points to note about this description. Firstly, it so happens that in this case the mousedown event is irrelevant to the behaviour, in that it is the mouseup to which the icon responds. This can lead to a difference in interpretation of what has happened between the computer and user, since the user will never be able to do a mouseup without first doing a mousedown. It is also the case that we have used the term 'invert' as a shorthand for capturing a description of the values of the pixels in a certain area, but this may not be a salient description to the user, and hence may require the establishment of some agreement. More significantly, all these events refer to a common object called the 'pipe icon'. The computer can recognize this from its existing library, but the

learner may not recognize this as a single object, nor know how to refer
to it. This will also have to be agreed between the agents. The final three
events of this description can be analysed into several levels of interface
description. At the simplest level we have three distinct actions:

initiator	channel	time	action	object
user	mouse	t4	mousedown	reservoir#1
user	mouse	t5	mouseup	valve#2
computer	screen	t6	drawline	line#3

In this case the most difficult area on which to establish agreement is
the three dynamically created objects which are referred to in these
actions, since they were created on the screen stream. This is particularly
true of the line, since it only comes into existence *after* this set of actions
on the mouse channel has been completed. We have again used the term
'drawline' to refer to a set of pixel values which may need to be agreed
with the user. A further complication in this case is that the mousedown
and mouseup actions actually refer not to the whole object, but to a
particular part of it: the output port or input port in this case. To support
this requires that we recognize not just individual objects in the interface,
but hierarchical relationships between these objects. Clicking on
reservoir#1 will result in a different behaviour to clicking on the output
port which is a subpart of it.

This analysis is at the level that we have described as primitive interface
events. As was discussed earlier, we can group sequences of events into
single entities, although at this level there is no reason to assume that the
grouping has any semantic interpretation. For convenience, however, we
will assume that we have happend to introduce a 'drag' operation. This
would result in t4 and t5 being combined into a single event:

initiator	channel	time	action	object
user	mouse	t4–5	drag	reservoir#1 valve#2

This analysis can go further, since the dragging action can be
interpreted as the creation of a link between the two entities. This
interpretation would connect the events between t4 and t6 into a single
entity. This interpretation of the dragging action relies, however, on the
system being aware of the context in which the action occured (i.e. which
palette item was selected), and hence this analysis must take place at the
level of the interaction history, which interprets the meaning of the events
in the context of a particular application.

We now move on to analysis at the level of the interaction history. The
major change at this level is that actions and referents now refer to the
domain of discourse, rather than their representations in the interface.

Events at t1 to t3 resolve into a selection of the pipe mode. The reference to channels on which the information was communicated is no longer necessary, but the user and event is. As described above, the assumption at this level is that each communicative act can be reduced to a single action applied to zero or more objects:

initiator	time	action	object
user	t1–3	select	pipe-mode
user	t4–5	link	fuel tank. .carburretor

The first three levels are sufficient to take us from simple actions to utterances in a domain other than that of the interface objects, and hence are a source of those errors which can be discussed without referring to specific domain knowledge (other than the syntax of possible utterances in the domain).

6 DISCREPANCIES BETWEEN THE AGENTS

At level 1, the possible errors are those due to lack of attention or loss of memory, which are unlikely to occur in an interface which is this simple. At level 2, the errors in action can be to do with resolving the active objects in the interface, but the primitive actions are fairly straight-forward. At the third level, the action of creating an object (such as a valve) may give rise to errors with regard to establishing the screen location for the new object. Similarly, moving an object is a dragging motion which may not be familiar to the user. The most likely source of error is in creating a pipe, since this has a complex syntax if it is to be a meaningful utterance. The pipe must be created between pre-existing objects, and from output port to input port.

It is at this last level that we can begin to see discrepancies which could potentially be resolved by negotiation. If, for example, the learner preferred to make connections from an output port to an input port, such a change could be discussed (and implemented) by a computer which had this level of knowledge of its own interface. Equally, we can see that the agents could agree to create a new interface object which could be used to specify the direction. Given the fixed underlying behaviour of the system, knowledge of the sort described here could make the whole interface negotiable. From the HCI perspective it is debatable whether this is a good idea, but from the educational perspective such a facility permits construction of interactive systems whose structure for com-munication reflects the structures of a specific learner.

7 CONCLUSIONS

In this paper we have outlined a set of levels of analysis which can be applied to an interaction between a learner and a computer. The purpose of defining these levels has been to provide a first step towards identifying the variety of sources of information which must be considered if we are to move closer to a genuinely symmetric interaction between a computer and a user. Achieving this symmetry is seen as a prerequisite for genuinely negotiated learning interactions.

Each of the levels captures a simple representation of the sorts of description, and the sorts of misunderstanding which can arise at that level. There remain a number of major research problems to be tackled before such an interface model can be applied to real educational systems. In particular, the problems associated with agreeing on the perception of a visual object, and coping with dynamic behaviour of the system have not been tackled at the three lowest levels of description. The higher levels are open problem areas. The intention of this paper has been to present a framework upon which those higher levels can sit.

APPENDIX – LEVEL DESCRIPTION SYNTAX

The syntax for describing the first three levels is given in this appendix. It is only illustrative. In particular, categories such as object, action and channel may be extended arbitrarily to support different interfaces. The language used for the first three levels is an extension of that which was applied in the DOMINIE tutoring system (Elsom-Cook & Spensley 1988). The language for level 4 is an extension of the dialogue model in ECAL (Elsom-Cook & O'Malley 1990). The language for level 5 is a subset of that proposed for belief-based bounded user modelling (Elsom-Cook 1990).

Level 1 – Uninterpreted event stream
    ues ::= uevent*
    uevent ::= initiator channel time data
    initiator ::= **computer** | **user**
    channel ::= **keyboard** | **screen**| **mouseport** | **serialline** | **soundboard** . . .
    time ::= integer
    data ::= anything!

Level 2 – Interpreted event stream
    ies ::= ievent*
    ievent ::= initiator channel time eventdesc

eventdesc ::= action interfaceobject*
action ::= **keypress** | **mousedown** | **mouseup** | **drawobject** . . .

Level 3 – Interaction history
ih ::= utterance*
utterance ::= initiator time domain-action domain-object*

12 Program Visualization and Knowledge Negotiation: Some Proposals for Visual Techniques in Tutorial Dialogue as Applied to Concurrent Logic Languages

MIKE BRAYSHAW[1]

Human Cognition Research Laboratory,
The Open University, Milton Keynes, MK7 6AA, UK

ABSTRACT

In this chapter we will explore the notion of using program visualization techniques as a medium for information sharing between programmer and machine. The focus will be novice programmers and pedagogically motivated programming environments. We will discuss the possibilities that visual based dialogue might have and suggest ways that this technique could be integrated into a more traditional ITS. The discussion will focus on the domain of parallel logic programming languages and argue that visual representations provide an excellent platform for describing those types of concurrent behaviour. Commonly occurring misconceptions will be discussed and visual alleviation of these problems proposed. An agent architecture to implement some of these ideas will be outlined. However, in order to achieve true knowledge negotiation, the communication needs to be a two way process. Although we can hard wire the machine to produce a specific visualization, we will end on a note of caution about some of the practical problems that face the design of a true, visually based, mixed initiative system.

[1] This work is currently supported by a MRC/SERC/ESRC UK Joint Research Council Grant #89/CS31, the support of which is gratefully acknowledged.

KNOWLEDGE NEGOTIATION
ISBN 0–12–509378–0

1 INTRODUCTION

Logic programming already has a reputation for being somewhat problematic to learn (e.g. Taylor 1987, Fung et al. 1990). As Gilmore and Green (1989) have pointed out, this may be because the languages are largely devoid of explicit surface features to guide comprehension. Calls to system keywords (e.g. explicit call to things like *for* or *while* statements) are not present. Thus, understanding these languages requires a sound working knowledge of both the search/inference processes and the pattern matching that they use, in order to infer the program behaviour. For novices these models are either absent or not well developed. It is therefore no surprise that they flounder. Acquiring a model of this type is a significant task in its own right: a PARLOG or Prolog virtual machine is a more difficult concept to grasp than simply looking up the syntax of a *for* statement in the programming manual. In this paper we will look at potential ways to address this problem, and in particular look at how we could use visual techniques in an interactive dialogue, within the ITS domain.

In an attempt to overcome some of the difficulties novices face when learning logic programming, we proposed a visual account of Prolog which emphasized a clean, clear, and consistent account of the execution of Prolog (Eisenstadt & Brayshaw 1988, 1990). The hope was that by presenting an explicit model of the virtual machine (in graphical form) from the outset, many novice misconceptions could be anticipated and learning accelerated. This work is continuing in the attempt to produce an environment for experts that allows them a greater repertoire of graphical representation techniques (Brayshaw 1991a, b, c), both for Prolog and PARLOG. In this paper we will discuss how this approach can be generalized to provide a visual dialogue that could form the basis of knowledge negotiation between a machine agency and a user. This will involve a discussion of both program visualization and knowledge negotiation, leading to a section on ways to integrate the two approaches for tutoring.

The paper will be structured as follows. First, we will give our definition of *knowledge negotiation* and map out the way in which the contents of this paper relate to it. Then we will introduce program visualization and explain why it is an important concept that software designers should take on board. Subsequently some examples both from within the logic programming world and more generally, will be presented to show the utility of this approach, emphasizing its use for novices and teaching. Following this we will argue that implicit within many of these systems has been a form of (passive) knowledge negotiation between user and machine, and discuss ways that this can be explored and expanded upon. The notion of passive negotiation, where the user interacts with a passive machine, is contrasted with active negotiation where both the machine and the user can take the initiative and take part in an interactive visual dialogue. The two approaches will be contrasted on the basis of the amount of AI required to achieve more intelligent (*active*) negotiation. Implementation issues and the design of a dialogue agent capable of producing such intelligent interaction will be elaborated upon. Finally, we conclude with a discussion about the wider role of program visualization within Intelligent Tutoring Systems, exploring possible ways of integrating graphical based approaches into an ITS, noting problems, and proposing a hybrid solution path.

2 KNOWLEDGE NEGOTIATION

Moyse (1989) has proposed the term *knowledge negotiation* to cover a variety of issues raised by using multiple models to tutor a particular domain. A strict epistemic interpretation of the use of the word *knowledge* should be avoided. In a strict sense, knowledge is something you either know about the world or you don't. The only thing that could be negotiated about the world are beliefs, goals, and meta-cognitive knowledge such as 'I know that I know'. What is meant by the term in this case is a much looser label to describe the information flow that takes place between the user and the tutor. In this sense, knowledge can be thought of as the beliefs of the agents involved in the interaction. When we adopt a particular model of the domain (= viewpoint), we adopt a series of beliefs about that domain. By adopting and using different viewpoints, we can *negotiate* these beliefs (knowledge) to find mutual stances.

There seem to be two essential themes to the idea of knowledge negotiation. The first is the idea of multiple models of a domain, and the second is the use of these models within the context of a dialogue which attempts to agree upon mutual goals, topics, and viewpoints to use in the tutorial setting. Stated briefly, it is argued that domains are frequently many faceted, and any one view only captures a part of the whole. In any domain we can have a series of different descriptive, metaphorical, and analogical models. In some sense we can think of all these models as being equally true: which best reflects the current needs depends upon the explanatory requirements of the situation, and this itself will be dependent upon the beliefs of the user. Given that we have these multiple options available, the negotiation aspect is applied when we decide which view to use. Moyse's argument is that the best tutorial models to adopt are a matter for negotiation between student and machine. Thus a viewpoint is not imposed but mutually adopted by the student and the teacher, with the intention of maximizing mutual benefit. Indeed, the claim in its strongest form would be that the very use of models in this flexible manner necessarily implies a degree of knowledge negotiation between the participating agents. This claim appears to be too strong. We regard negotiation as a dialogue task. It is possible to have negotiation about a single model and its contents in terms of arguing about beliefs held about a particular model. Multiple models may be needed for some forms of negotiation, but such models do not result in negotiation simply through being used.

Moyse's arguments suggest it is possible to obtain a better overall model of the domain by using multiple viewpoints. It is also noted that using a single view has the disadvantage of showing a limited, rigid model, and this inflexiblility can lead to problems. Using different models for tutoring requires the user to integrate beliefs across views, and engage in reasoning about their reasoning (often called meta-cognitive reasoning). Clearly, this can also lead to problems, but if successful, its proponents would claim, can lead to a better understanding for the student.

Elsewhere, we have argued (Brayshaw 1990, 1991a, b, c) for the importance of using different visualizations of software for expert programmers as well as novices. To summarize the argument, the claim is that both in terms of the information needed to assist the problem solving processes of the user and the basic physical properties of the notations employed, different visualizations are required. What is the optimum visualization may be task, user and program specific, reflecting who is doing what and how. This argument led to the proposal to use several default visualizations in order to enhance the descriptive vocabulary of the software. Parallel to this is the development of tools to let the user define their own visualizations. As a result, experts can define viewports that best fit their own particular circumstances and needs. We will discuss how this approach can be applied to helping novices, within the context of knowledge negotiation, and then make some suggestions about how this can help introduce true negotiation into the dialogue.

We will take Moyse's definition as a starting point. Moyse (1989) points to five questions concerning how to use and develop knowledge negotiation. We will first attempt to answer these questions below, in order to try to clarify how knowledge negotiation could be applied in the context of software environments. Based on this discussion we will make a case for program visualization as a way of achieving these goals, before taking up the central ideas of multiple models and their use in a flexible dialogue. The titles of the following sections each correspond to one of Moyse's questions.

2.1 What viewpoints should be tutored?

Clearly, this is ultimately an empirical question, and highly domain dependent. It raises other questions such as how we should go about evaluating a viewpoint. Further, given any viewpoint, and any student's current set of beliefs, what is the mapping between the two, and what should we do *even* if we know what this mapping is? Simply deciding to incorporate extra viewpoints doesn't solve anything. It is still necessary to decide how to use them. This seems to argue for the central rôle of dialogue in negotiation, with multiple viewpoints playing a supporting part.

Even without empirical evidence, it is possible to present some initial hypotheses about the structure and use of viewpoints within a software tutoring system. Viewpoints can be linked with possible dialogue rôles that they can play. They can be thought of as visual articulations of some larger dialogue component. For example, if we want to talk (either the user or the machine) about the concept of data-flow, then we want an appropriate model on which to base the dialogue. The visualization should present the concept explicitly and unambiguously, and related to the appropriate control regime embodied in this viewpoint. In Sections 4 and 5 a series of different graphical visualizations, each appropriate for different topics, will be presented. In addition we will attempt to show a principled mapping between topics and visualizations. If we have recognized a misconception on the part of the user, we could link the use of possible visualization techniques to the removal of particular sort of bug. It should be noted that visualizations can't be presented standalone: it is necessary to decide how visual models are integrated alongside other tutorial dialogue (i.e. the user is likely to be confused if shown a new visual model unless some context about what its trying to achieve is present).

2.2 How is the student to know when to apply them?

As was mentioned in the introduction to this section, this chapter talks about the concept of negotiation and viewpoints as being an interactive and reciprocal interaction. From this perspective, question 2.2 should really be stated as 'How is either agent to determine which model to use?'. The question is thus being generalized to consider the negotiated interaction between two autonomous agents, adopting no prejudice as to their implementation. This position ignores questions about the possible performance of AI systems given current technology. Requiring an agent to know what is the appropriate viewpoint for the machine to adopt (and attempt to get the user to adopt), means that the machine has a significant level of intelligence. For example, it needs to be able to model the student, have its own beliefs, and suggest proposed actions.

2.3 What specific advantages accrue from tutoring one or more views?

This question is partially answered in the introduction and in Section 3. To be pessimistic for a moment, we need to be clear of the extent to which multiple models create problems as well as solving them. Presenting different stories to the user can be potentially confusing if the user doesn't spot the mapping between the representations in the viewpoints. Obviously, making these mappings explicit and flagging particularly important correlations can help this to some degree. For programming, the approach taken in Brayshaw (1990, 1991a, b) is to allow multiple views of a single execution model. The execution story, i.e. the model of the virtual machine under discussion, doesn't change. We just see different perspectives of the same machine, each emphasizing different aspects or information. The kernel of all these representations remains the same. This is an important point. The hope is that we get the advantages outlined for multiple models without the handicaps of confusing the user by introducing conflicting/disparate descriptive accounts.

2.4 To what extent can the system establish and work with the students own model of the domain: can and should tutoring be related to the student's previous experience?

It is not our intention to enter a discussion on the advantages and disadvantages of student modelling at this point. Instead we will talk about the user's existing knowledge and models. In particular we will consider how we can use this knowledge, and problems associated with its use, in the context of teaching software.

The comments here are restricted to teaching logic programming. In other domains where there is prior or background knowledge, then clearly an argument can be made to support the exploitation of that knowledge. In logic programming we follow the argument proposed in (Eisenstadt & Brayshaw 1988b, 1991) that we should attempt to impose mental hygiene on the user and foster only one execution model. If the user has a different model of the virtual machine, then it is not clear that it is always a good idea to encourage it (although this must depend on the precise model to some degree). There are few search models (for example) for Prolog, which are not going to lead to problems when the user comes to generalize them. It seems to be the case that models adopted for short term expediency, can often lead to long term grief.

A common ploy is to introduce Prolog as a simple database search language. A typical example is often a family lineage exercise (Prolog's equivalent of the print 'hello world' program!). So the novice enters a large database of facts, e.g.:

```
parent_of(william,charles).
parent_of(william, diana).
parent_of(charles, elizabeth).
parent_of(charles, phillip).
........ etc
```

Ormerod (1986) demonstrated empirically that people attempt to solve this type of problem by using what appeared to be their knowledge of the real world rather than their knowledge of the language and the actual program they have typed. In other words, by bringing in extra domain knowledge about the world, the learning process was not helped. If all the symbols the student met where *foo1* through to *foo‹N›*, then it would be obvious that we are just using symbols and pattern matching. However, the artificial nature of the example would probably also affect the users badly, and certainly convey no practical application of the techniques they are being asked to learn. The appropriate solution probably lies somewhere between the two extremes. Scenarios where the example is real enough, but the syntactic nature of many of the operations of the language are also communicated, may well be appropriate direction. The important aspect of this for knowledge negotiation is that when we talk about AI languages and inferencing we must be careful about over generalisations of real world knowledge, based on perfectly sensible (but incorrect) similarities of surface features.

To emphasize this point, there are notable differences between conventional style languages and logic languages, and encouraging any mapping can cause problems. We noted earlier the lack of keywords or explicit control constructs (excepting the guard, and's, or's, and set and series operations in PARLOG) mean that languages contain different concepts and operate differently. The logic languages lack the *do*, *for*, *while*, and *until* style control structures and rely almost totally on recursion. Consequently, there is a limit to what information could be mapped across from existing languages and a real danger that errors could be introduced. For example, consider variable assignment in the following three statements:

```
n = n * 10     /* C style arithmetic variable assignment */
SECONDS := SECONDS + 1     { PASCAL style }
(setf *value* (+ *value* 1))        ;;; LISP style
```

Generalizing from =, :=, and *setf* and with the knowledge that arithmetic variable assignment in Prolog or PARLOG is *is* might produce the following error:

```
X is X + 1.
```

This is logically wrong, though an eminently sensible generalization. A specific example will show us why. Suppose X is bound to 3, then the above line actually means *3 is 3 + 1*, which is obviously wrong. The correct version being:

```
New_variable is X + 1.
```

This type of error is often observed (e.g. White 1987). It is necessary to be very careful regarding when and how to use existing knowledge in tutoring logic languages, because of the danger of over-generalization and misapplication when bringing in real world knowledge. Indeed, Ross (1988) in his Prolog book, explicit flags those parts where the concepts embodied in Prolog are at variance with other languages, so as to avoid this type of confusion.

To conclude, we are cautious about the use of existing knowledge, and believe in trying to impress on the user a good working model of the machine, rather than allowing them to foster their own, possibly erroneous, model. It is not helpful to allow the user to develop their own idiosyncratic model with all the potential bugs and lack of generalization that follows. The very artificial 'naturalness' of these high-level languages means that there is a danger of people over-generalizing and believing that the machine in some senses 'understands' and has a degree of 'common sense' which clearly it doesn't. All this argues for careful choice of examples to avoid encouraging dangerous assumptions, often based on sound prior experience, on the part of the user.

We have discussed knowledge negotiation and how some of the ideas relate to teaching software. In the next section we will do the same thing for Program Visualization, before moving on to discussing the use of the two systems together.

3   PROGRAM VISUALIZATION FOR TUTORING

So far we have talked about the needs for a dialogue agent that can negotiate with a student and decide, based on mutual decision making, what to do next and what model to adopt. But what type of dialogue acts are we going to require of the tutor? Can these acts include ones that incorporate a visualization component? Not only can visualizations be used to make a point by the dialogue agent, but they are particularly important in their own right since they have different properties to conventional dialogue. The nature of their explanations can be different, they are interactive, and provide miniature environments that can be explored. Indeed, if the user can present and run their own code, they can be used as miniature software laboratories to play and experiment with code and ideas. Thus they significantly broaden the repertoire of possible responses by the machine and allow the dialogue agent to set up interactive learning environments to teach various points or argue their case. Thus the visualizations can be thought of as an extended and special type of dialogue, which has special properties, that we can seek to build into our idea of negotiation.

If we first design an interface, then that will allow us to see how the user interacts with the system and the type of functionality we require. In other words, interface requirements provide a way of determining how much 'intelligence' we need to put into our ITSs (i.e. we can assess our performance requirements based on the desired external behaviour). Taking this further, as Eisenstadt (1989) points out, new techniques, like visualization, may radically change the way we think and teach. In the context of teaching programming the entire structure of the tutor might be radically altered. The more things become intuitive and self-apparent to the user, the less needs to be tutored and explained. The more the student can interact with the interface and find their own way, the less intelligent guidance is required from the machine. As Eisenstadt notes "the role of visualization techniques for teaching programming may prove to be more effective than theories of student-modelling, cognitive 'plans', and automatic program debugging" (p. 100). Visual dialogue has properties of its own. Not only can the visualization convey a simple message about something, but the user can interact with that visualization. In other words, a visual utterance can be further explored and queried, allowing the user to explore and clarify their beliefs as though in further stages of conventional dialogue. The next section will describe visualization in more detail.

3.1 Program visualization

Program visualization is an attempt to broaden and enhance the communication channel between user and machine by expanding the media that are used. This is not merely a technological fix. Using graphics for the sake of it is not necessarily going to solve anything. Instead the claim is that graphical representations provide a new platform which broadens and enriches the descriptions and explanations within the dialogue between user and machine. In particular, the combination of text and graphics provides an enhanced series of properties for a medium in which to talk about software and its behaviour. Some of these possible enhancements are detailed below:

- Large amounts of information can be dealt with, yet the display kept orderly and navigable.
- Structural and organisation properties of the on screen displays can be used to aid accessibility and manipulation. Thus things like associations between objects in the program, or mutual dependencies, implicit within the code, can be made apparent to the user.
- Different graphical techniques have different properties. Some display techniques are better than others for dealing with certain types of data or information. We can look to use the full power of these graphical techniques in order to optimize the methods of information presentation.
- Dynamic or transient behaviours can be caught and replayed via animations. We can report from our own experiences (e.g. Eisenstadt & Brayshaw 1988) how useful it is for experts, let alone novices, to have a replay facility, enabling them to wind the program backwards and forwards, so as to truly understand the dynamics of the program's behaviour.
- Abstract concepts, like a virtual machine, can be mapped into a concrete realization, namely the visual model of the machine that you present to the user. Specific concepts can be graphically modelled to provide pertinent cognitive hooks (e.g. after Papert 1980). Thus the novice can be presented with a clear and consistent visual story of the machines' workings by a tangible physical rendering (e.g. see Eisenstadt 1988 for an example of a multi-media study pack based on a visual virtual machine).
- Visualizations are physical things with surrounding tools and thus can

be used interactively. Hence the user's dialogue with them is not restricted to that of quiescent observer, but permits them to be an active explorer and manipulator.

- Once you have a visual model of the machine, you can use it both to build second order tools to facilitate its use (e.g. the replay facilities we talked about above) and as the basis for communicating with the user. A tutoring system, using its knowledge of the user and of the graphical arsenal at its disposal, can now consider whether, in a particular set of circumstances, the visual medium is the best dialogue device with which to talk to the user. Likewise, the user can explore the possible information space about the program's behaviour by considering different visualizations of it. Indeed, if the user has a graphical palette, they then can describe desirable behaviours of a program to the machine and the machine can fabricate the program. This technique is called *visual programming* and has already been proposed and developed elsewhere in the educational context (e.g. VIP (Kenyon 1988) and Gunkara Sun Systems 1988).

Having talked about program visualization in general we will now take an example of it and see how we could use it in an education context, and how parts could be used within a dialogue component.

4 VISUALIZING THE EXECUTION OF PARLOG PROGRAMS

In this section we will discuss different models of PARLOG execution. For a full description of PARLOG, see either Gregory (1987) or Conlon (1989); here we shall only give a very brief flavour of the language. In brief, PARLOG is a language in which parts of the program are executed in parallel with one another. The language consists of logic statements which can be thought of as rules, with additional knowledge about the world stored in a database of facts. Programs work by using the rules and facts to prove goals. A rule can solve a goal if it can break the goal down into subgoals and find rules and facts to prove these subgoals. The search process involves both AND and OR-parallel search. Each rule can have an extra synchronization mechanism, called a guard. When there are many different rules that could solve a particular goal, all the guards to these different rules are tested in parallel to find the first to pass. The rule whose guard wins this *guard race* is the one chosen to try and prove the goal. All the others are discarded. Brayshaw (1990a) contains a full description of this mechanism and a visual model of PARLOG's execution.

PARLOG provides an interesting test case for the use of program

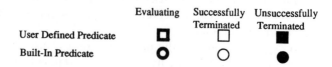

Fig. 12.1 The nodes indicate process state and outcome.

visualization, not only to try and generalize our own earlier work on visualizing Prolog (Eisenstadt & Brayshaw 1986, 1987, 1988, Brayshaw & Eisenstadt 1988, 1990), but also to deal with special dynamics of parallelism and associated problems like *starvation* and *deadlock* (Ringwood 1988 provides a discussion of some of these problems). The basics of the model we will present here are built around the concept of a node representing a process, the shading of the node indicating the process state. These nodes are used consistently in all the representational formalisms, being augmented in different contexts to reveal different aspects of the execution history. Figure 12.1 shows the basic representation: note also how we distinguish between user and system defined code.

We can distinguish four separate types of view, each of which has a different perspective. These views will be presented in the abstract, since the discussion will be focussed on the information bearing load of these representations, rather than on the intricacies of concurrent logic programming. Each of these different representation techniques can be thought of as being a potential dialogue mechanism, depending upon what is being taught. Each shows a program's execution from a particular perspective. In each, certain types of behaviour are emphasized and made explicit at the expense of other information. Depending upon the tutorial context, a selection can be made by the dialogue agent as to which representation best fits with the information the agent is attempting to convey. In some contexts, the agent may conclude that more than one representational device should be used. Indeed, one of the techniques to show fine grained information can be arbitrarily interleaved within other representations to allow hybrids views best suited to a particular context.

An important caveat which should be made at this point is that all the representations we employ here contain the same model of the virtual machine and have embodied within them the same execution story. We have discussed earlier in the paper, and in Eisenstadt and Brayshaw (1988, in press) why we think this is particularly important. It is a common (and convenient) practice when teaching to change the description of the thing you are trying to teach, depending upon the particular context, and to better fit the ideas that you are trying to convey. In the context of an interpreted programming language like PARLOG or Prolog, the thing which you change is frequently the description of the virtual machine. In the context of logic programming, Bundy et al. (1986) suggested that adopting different accounts of program execution can be the cause of possible student confusion. Paxton and Turner (1984) showed that novices prefer more sparsely featured and rigid systems which focus on one view of execution. Rajan (1990) generalized this to propose a maxim of *non-proliferation of views* for novices, concentrating on only one view and only spreading to new views once the basics are soundly in place. We have considerable sympathy for this view. Proliferation of views for its own sake doesn't seem to be very sensible. Hence it is necessary to be very careful when you introduce novices to new views. It may be better to choose a single model and stick with it until the user is able to properly appreciate the added perspectives and insights that may flow from using multiple models or viewpoints. The very rigidity that may result from a single, myopic viewpoint, may also be its biggest virtue when we consider novices. For this reason, we have adopted a standard execution model, taken from Conlon's excellent description of the language (Conlon 1989) and stuck to this throughout. Also, initially we would concentrate on just once viewpoint, that of AND/OR trees, until the user is ready to move on. However, as we have already mentioned, all the viewpoints adopt a model of the machine that is consistent, although they may shown the same process in different lights. All that changes in our viewpoints is the perspectives on the virtual machine, not the model of the virtual machine itself.

Returning to our four representational devices, we shall go through them in turn. The first and kernel device we use is the AND/OR tree. The tree is a very good model of control and temporal synchronization. An abstract example is shown in Figure 12.2.

This view gives us two informative models of the program. Firstly, the nodes in the diagram show call/callee relations in the program. Thus the top-most node in the tree is the main process. Its relation to sub-processes can be seen from the structure of the tree. On the left we see the basic notation we use, conjoined goals are shown as *ANDs* and can be distinguished from *ORs* by the conjunction bar linking arcs in the tree. The disjunctions are shown in the choice of which clause to use, in items called guards. Guards are special tests which determine which clause to use in order to solve a problem, and these guards literally race to be the first to succeed and thus commit to a given solution path. Guards can be distinguished by using characteristic line stippling. Once the processes commit to one particular choice, the successful guard changes to a broader hashed line style to distinguish it from the surrounding

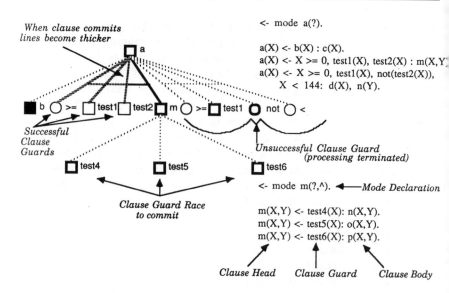

When clause commits
lines become thicker

<- mode a(?).

a(X) <- b(X) : c(X).
a(X) <- X >= 0, test1(X), test2(X) : m(X,Y)
a(X) <- X >= 0, test1(X), not(test2(X)),
            X < 144: d(X), n(Y).

Successful
Clause
Guards

Unsuccessful Clause Guard
(processing terminated)

Clause Guard Race
to commit

<- mode m(?,^). ◄——Mode Declaration

m(X,Y) <- test4(X): n(X,Y).
m(X,Y) <- test5(X): o(X,Y).
m(X,Y) <- test6(X): p(X,Y).

Clause Head   Clause Guard   Clause Body

Fig. 12.2 An example of a tree based account of PARLOG.

unsuccessful ones (which are left in whatever state they were in when the commitment took place). The fact that one of the clause guards is shown as being successful necessarily implies that the others have not been. When a clause commits they are shown in whatever state they were in when they were terminated, as this can be informative about how and why a particular process failed/successfully committed at a particular point.

The trees show us two main things. Firstly, the execution structure of the program. We can see who calls what and when. A second important thing that we can get from these trees is a model of the dynamics of the execution. One of the main advantages of these representations are their ability to capture the dynamics of program execution in an intelligible manner that could be used as a basis of a model to teach novices. We shall discuss this in greater detail later.

A second representational technique allows us to take a closer look at the execution of individual nodes. That is, it represents a step down to a finer grain size of detail. An individual node can be embellished, as shown in Figure 12.3.

The new finer level view shows the clause head matching and unification process. The overall state of the process is shown in the large icon on the left. The notation is the same as we have see before. The top text line shows the overall goal, the bottom line the matching clause head. The number of the clause that is chosen as a result of the guard

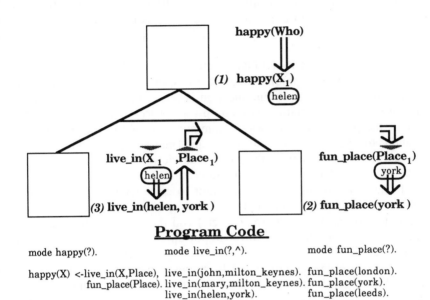

Program Code

mode happy(?).   mode live_in(?,^).   mode fun_place(?).

happy(X) <-live_in(X,Place),   live_in(john,milton_keynes).   fun_place(london).
          fun_place(Place).   live_in(mary,milton_keynes).   fun_place(york).
                               live_in(helen,york).   fun_place(leeds).

Fig. 12.3 A second representational technique, showing a much finer level of detail of an individual process node. The code that is being traced is shown to the left. The simple example computes that fact that you are happy if you live in a place that is fun.

race is shown to its left. Data-flow is indicated by the arrows. Notice the additional horizontal lines that indicate how the pattern-matcher parsed certain terms. This model is describe in full in Eisenstadt and Brayshaw (1989). In addition, for the PARLOG version of this account notice the additional arrows at the top of the diagram, used to depict mode declarations. The mode declarations (whether an argument is input or output) are shown by the shaded arrows above the goal. These correspond to the modes of the respective arguments. ▼ indicates input, and ▲ output.

These fine grained visualizations present us with a way of recounting different information about the program. Information about unification, clause head matching, and data-flow, can be conveyed using this representation. Notice, however, that the large node on the left is the same as those found in the tree representation. Thus we can arbitrarily interleave this more fine grained information with the coarser one that we saw using the basic tree representations. Thus we can produce hybrid representations that combine both the advantages of tree representations, with the extra fine grained information of the close-up view. Brayshaw (1990) describes this in more detail, and explains how these fine-grained views can be expanded to give a similar fine grained account of the guard race process.

We have noted that PARLOG execution can be thought of as a series of processes inter-communicating. If we want to consider behaviours where the inter-process communication is the central focus of attention, we can use a representation with an upfront process based model. In this model, the process and the way it communicates with other processes is brought to the centre of the stage and made explicit. Thus control information, clearly seen in the tree based views, is obscured in order to make the view of inter-process communication the most important one. A good reason for doing this is if we want to consider PARLOG as being similar to an Object Oriented Programming language. The communication between the processes (the objects) and the data-flow between them (the messages), is then of central importance. An example is given in Figure 12.4.

Processes are again represented by nodes, as in the other representations. However, in this view they are linked by the communication channels between them. In PARLOG, data is passed around using variables. Processes can carry out a two way communication by incrementally adding to the binding of a variable. In these views this information can be shown. The actual data that is communicated is shown on the arcs linking the nodes. As the execution of the program develops the information flow between the processes is shown on the arcs. If this flow is incremental in nature, the dynamics are preserved, so that we can see how the overall message is constructed over time. Also notice that the

---

Fig. 12.4 The third representational formalism, emphasizing the processes and the communication that takes place between them. The example illustrates a very simple eco-system. Rain falls, producing standing water, which then evaporates producing water vapour. This water paper condenses, resulting in new rain. An example program is shown on the left. Processes are used to model the four interacting components. Each component is mutually dependant on the other. This then tells the *landstate* processes about the rain. *Landstate* now notes that the land is wet and passing it to the *evaporate* processes. *Evaporate* process now sends water vapour to the *condense* process. *Condense* produces water vapour, which in turn is sent back to the *rain* process, producing more rain, and the cycle repeats. This message passing between processes is shown by the variables. In the bottom diagram, we see the message passing between the processes. On the links between the processes, we see the dataflow. At the point in the diagram, the very first production of *watervapour* is being communicated to the *condense* process. Notice that the variable $CondensedVapour_1$ is unbound showing that this process has not yet sent the news of any condensed vapour to the *rain* process to produce new rain.

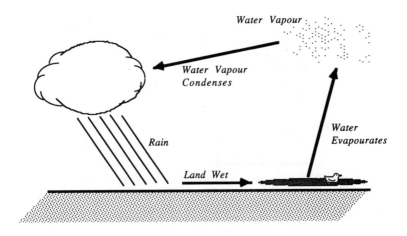

Rain Cycle: Rain causes water to lie on the land.   This water subsequently evapourates, producing water vapour in the air.   This water vapour condenses and more precipitation results

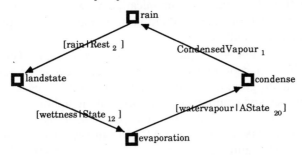

/* define eco-system */

```
rain_cycle(Startstate) <-   /* Startstate is the initial state of the world */
  rain(Startstate,CondensedVapour,Rain),  /* start state causes rain */
  landstate(Rain,LandWet),  /* the land gets wet from the rain */
  evaporation(LandWet,WaterVapour),  /* the dampness evapourates to produce water vapour */
  condense(WaterVapour,CondensedVapour).   /* condensed water is now passed back
                                      to the rain processes and the loop continues */
```

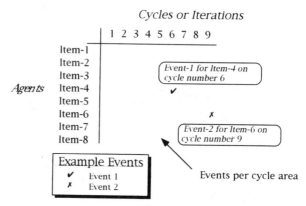

Cycles or Iterations

(model adapted from Domingue, 1988; Domingue and Eisenstadt, 1989)

Fig. 12.5 A generic model of a cycle chart (after Domingue & Eisenstadt 1989).

variable notation and how we use it is consistent with our more fine grained model. As a result, we can also embed the fine-grained information within the process communication view, providing a hybrid that combines clause head selection and pattern matching with processes communication and dataflow.

A final representation we employ is called a *cycle graph*. The aim of this is to attempt to capture clearly and explicitly cyclic or repetitive behaviours of the program and capture them on a cycle by cycle basis for subsequent analysis and comparison. The original metaphor can be found in Domingue and Eisenstadt (1989), a full treatment in its application to Prolog in Brayshaw (1991), and for PARLOG in Brayshaw (1990a). An example is given in Figure 12.5.

In this model, cycles are represented along the top-axis of a graph, and the individual agents whose actions are to be monitored on these cycles are shown down the left-hand-side. When an event occurs involving a particular agent on a particular cycle, this is shown by an icon drawn at the intersection point of the agent and cycle number on the graph. Multiple events per cycle can be shown by modification or super-imposition of the icon(s).

In addition to the basic representational capabilities of the visualiza-tions we have discussed, we have also emphasized the need for these visualizations to be dynamic in order to capture the behaviour of the program. I believe that this is of critical importance when trying to understand the behaviour of programs that execute in parallel. The approach taken here aims to provide additional support for depicting this type of behaviour. We can use these visualizations to produce a *movie show* depicting the program's execution. The metaphor we use (e.g. see Eisenstadt & Brayshaw 1988, Brayshaw & Eisenstadt in press) is that of a replay panel. This attempts to provide the full functionality of a home video recorder for interrogating the trace. The user can thus interrogate the visualization watching the evolving dynamics in front of them, and by experimenting with the visualization, winding it forward or backwards, at the chosen speed, in order to fully understand the dynamic behaviour of the program.

The *replay panel* technique is common to all the representations we shall look at here. One of the main claims for using visualizations in order to teach novices logic languages is their ability to capture the dynamics of the system. In order to understand the execution of languages like PARLOG, the novice has to get their head around the concurrent execution of the processes in the program. We have already noted that the clause guards race in parallel. We can use the dynamic visualizations to capture this race, showing the competing guards and the degree of their satisfaction. Another important type of dynamics in PARLOG is process suspension. Extra tests can be placed upon goals which make pre-conditions before this process is allowed to run. If these preconditions are not met, then that process becomes suspended. Again we can show this visually. Notice the lines under certain nodes in Figure 12.5. These indicate suspended nodes, i.e. processes awaiting some further event before they can carry on their evaluation. This type of behaviour is of further interest because it might be indicative of problems in the program, and a reason why it is not working. These problems are often termed *starvation* and *deadlock* (see Ringwood 1988 for a fuller discussion). In simple terms, a process suffers *starvation* if it is waiting on some event which never happens, and thus it is starved of the input it requires, and as a result, the program fails to perform as expected. Another synchronization problem is program *deadlock*. In deadlock, every processes is waiting on some other process. This mutual dependence means that the program literally gets stuck, it can go no further because each process is waiting for something else happening. However, nothing else will happen, because all the other processes are suspended waiting for somebody else. Again we can try and explain these dynamics by showing a visualization with the appropriate animations placed on it. It is my intuitive belief that animated visualizations provide a suitable medium to display and foster an understanding of the underlying execution dynamics. Hence the claim that visual models provide a good media for a tutorial dialogue between teacher and student. The next problem is, however, deciding which visualizations to use to tutor what concept and, given that the student runs into problems, which errors on the part of the student are best treated by what means. In the next section we will try and present some hints about how we might be able to point to a mapping between a dialogue message we wished to portray and the corresponding option of a visual dialogue.

5 VISUAL DIALOGUES: MATCHING VISUALIZATION AND TUTORIAL TASK

In this section we will try and list the relationship between the various representational techniques and the dialogue acts they could portray. For each of the techniques we will split this up into two sections, focussing on the representational strengths of the individual representations, and their possible uses in a tutorial dialogue.

5.1 AND/OR trees

5.1.1 Representational strengths

Dynamics: showing the changing behaviour of the program. The AND-parallel concurrency can be seen *in action*, as different nodes simultaneously execute in different parts of the tree. Suspension will lead to parts of the tree 'freezing' for a period.

Program Synchronization: some parts of the program are dependant on others before they execute. We can see globally the results of this type of dependency, and see how some parts of the program are dependant upon the actions of others.

Calling Structure of the Program: the AND/OR tree shows the calling structure of the program as it is executed.

Guard Race: the OR-Parallel race to commit is shown. Individual nodes that are part of the guard can be seen to be competing with one another in the race to satisfy these constraints.

Effects of the Commit: when the guard commits the effects are shown. Abandoned processes in failed guards can be investigated.

5.1.2 Misconceptions

Flow of Control: any misconceptions about the flow of control could be helped by these views. Correct models can be demonstrated, and novice errors compared with suitable demonstrations. Deadlock and Starvation can also be seen in the way they cause various parts of the trace to 'lock up', or in the most fatal form, cause the whole program to come to a complete standstill.

Execution Models: the execution model we are trying to teach is embodied within the dynamics of the trace, hence these traces can be used to show the correct behaviour of the program and used to debug the students erroneous one.

Search: the search routines of the system, including both the AND-parallel and OR-Parallel behaviour can be demonstrated. Errors about how the clauses are searched, what happens, the difference between AND and OR-parallel search, and the consequent lack of effect of ordering in the database, can all be tackled in this way.

Erroneous Guard Behaviour: again, because of the explict model, any false notions about guard behaviour can be compared with the correct behaviour and debugged. Among the errors that might be address here include those concerning when, why, and what effect commitment (= one particular guard succeeding) has on a process.

5.2   Fine grained views

5.2.1   Representational strengths

Unification: unification is shown, indicating how the data is parsed and what matches with what. This not only helps us get a better understanding of unification, but also helps to explain the behaviour of things like operators.

Clause Head Matching: all the OR-Parallel clause head matching searches can be shown. This allows us to see why a particular head matches.

Data-flow: arrows indicate clearly the data-flow.

Causes of Suspension: suspension can be identified whether it is caused by a mode declaration, or because of a condition of a guard. Although the AND/OR Tree will show this for the guard, the fine-grained view is required to show the action of the mode declarations.

5.2.2   Misconceptions

Fine Grained Models of Execution: unification, data-flow, mode declarations and the like are all shown in very great detail. The claim is that any misunderstanding about the fine-grained operations of the interpreter could be helped by using these close-up views; examples would include

(i) when to re-name variables, and why this is important to avoid name clashes;
(ii) how unification works, what can match with what, and what can't;
(iii) the effects of commitment on variable binding, the data-flow implications of this binding of output arguments, and the effects on other parts of the OR-Parallel search being undertaken at that point.

5.3   Process communication

5.3.1   Representational strengths

Dynamic Data Interaction: it shows who is talking to whom and when.

Interdependency of Processes: the interdependency of the processes can be shown by watching the actions of the process (e.g. whether they are suspended) and communication between them.

Spotting important events in the program: since we can choose which nodes to use, we can specifically wait for certain events to occur between particular processes. We can thus set up views that directly focus on specific events in the program and target the tracing of them.

5.3.2   Misconceptions

Clearly, these views are very good at linking the actions of processes and data, so any problems associated with these topics could be thus tackled. Further, we noted earlier that we could view PARLOG as similar to an object-oriented language. We could thus use these views to enforce these additional models of PARLOG execution. Possible uses include:

(i) any error involving the influence of one process upon another by the action of passing data;
(ii) the dynamic interaction of processes;
(iii) the *producer/consumer* relationship between processes, i.e. where two process operate as mutual data provider and data consumer. For example, where one process attempts to implement a generator function, and another a test. Misconceptions about how to implement this or the metaphor more generally;
(iv) other high level metaphors involving synchronization. For example, consider the following:

. . . ,a(Stream1,Stream2), b(Stream2,Stream1), . . .

a and *b* are mutually dependant upon each other. *a*'s output on stream *Stream1* is sent to *b*. Each time *b* gets a new input from *a*, it produces a new output on *Stream2* which it hands back to *a*. When *a* receives this new value it then produces a new value which it then hands on to *b* and the cycle repeats. This is actually a version of the *producer/consumer* cliché we saw in (iii). The difference is that the producer *a* only produces a value when asked to. This is what is know as a *lazy* producer, as opposed to an *eager* producer, since it needs this type of prompting. Again, we can use the process communication view precisely to tell the story about this type of higher level cliché.

5.4 Cyclic behaviour

5.4.1 Representational strengths

These are more abstract representations than the others. When a program is carrying out some repetitive behaviour, such views are appropriate. In other words, these views can often be quite high level, and can be used to discuss some of the higher-level behaviours of the program.

5.4.2 Misconceptions

When the behaviour of the program can be conceptualized in this manner, then this type of behaviour can be pointed out so as to help the user grasp what is going on. Particular uses include:

(i) *Guard races*. The result of a guard race can be viewed for the individual clauses involved, and for all the occurrences when this goal is evaluated.

(ii) *Showing other higher-order repetitive behaviours of the program*. These need not necessarily map onto the lower dynamics of PARLOG, but instead tell the story of higher levels of repetitive behaviour in the algorithm, rather than purely in terms of the underlying implementation.

There are also a large number of combinations of these views that could be presented together. Continuing themes like data-flow, dynamics, synchronization occur in all the types of representation, and thus the different techniques could be used to compliment each other. Suppose we want to talk about how data-flow and synchronization effect each other. We could use a combination of an AND/OR Tree to show synchronization and dynamics, together with fine-grained and process communication views to show how the dynamics and data-flow views interact, and the resulting overall behaviour of the system. Indeed one of the features of this style of approach is the use of several of these pictures all together, to show and emphasize different aspect of the virtual machine, allowing users to build an overall view of the program, whilst showing the interaction between various sub-components of the machine.

Clearly there is a extra issue. It is all very well saying that a particular technique could be used to remove a given misconception, but that's not saying anything about how to recognize the misconceptions in the first place. This is a major research issue in its own right (e.g. see Fung 1989). There is no space to discuss this issue further here.

6   KNOWLEDGE NEGOTIATION AND PROGRAM VISUALIZATION

So far we have talked about program visualization which uses multiple views. This is not really knowledge negotiation according to our earlier definition. In knowledge negotiation, we said, two active agents interact. In the systems we have discussed this far, however, one of the agents, the machine, has acted in a passive manner, merely being the purveyor of information (albeit in multiple viewports) asked of it by the user.

To have genuine knowledge negotiation requires the user and the machine to negotiate a mutual stand, for both parties to proffer information at their own initiative, and for there to be some form of dialogue about that information. The next obvious question is what type of system could achieve this type of proficiency and could we build one? A related question is whether we have to posit the architecture of a full-fledged intelligent agent or whether something less powerful will do. Thirdly, we have to consider the issue of dialogue. We wish to argue that when we are talking about the dialogue between machine and user, in the programming domain, we can choose to use program visualization in order to augment the expressiveness of the dialogue agent, and to explore its articulatory rôle.

In order to have true negotiation, so that the two agents can be sensitive and responsive to each other, the systems must be aware of the others actions and capable of conditionally responding. It is therefore just possible to consider some type of branching-CAL system being so responsive, and being able to provide conditional responses, using its canned repertoire. Taking as a starting point a system like BALSA

(Brown & Sedgewick 1985, Brown 1987), the courseware designer could build a series of BALSA style animations and fit them within the frames of the CAL-style system. Remedial tutelage might then be provided by alternative or more fine grained visualizations. However, the critical thing that is missing from these interactions is the collective decision making implicit in negotiation.

An agent that could provide a more truly negotiation-based approach would require a model of the outside world (and thereby a model of the agent(s) they were conversing with), a model of their own beliefs and desires (goals), and a dialogue model to guide the flow and structure of the interaction. It is in the latter area that we will try and link the ideas of program visualization within a knowledge negotiation style scenario.

6.1 An agent based model of tutorial dialogue

We have previously noted some basic requirements of a dialogue capable of knowledge negotiation and specifically the types of rôle visualizations might play. In order to suggest how this might take place, the next step is to develop a possible architecture. In order to do this we will introduce a dialogue agent, and attempt to demonstrate how an intelligent architecture such as this agent might implement some of these ideas. The crucial concept in this agent is the notion that the agent needs to have some evaluatory mechanism, so that attitutes to situations and actions can be ascertained. This is essential for negotiation: only when the agent can assess what it feels about the actions of others and correspondingly evaluate its own potential actions can we have the type of interactive flexibility and adaptability to implement negotiation. The agent must be able to gauge (a) what it feels about the current situation (e.g. does it agree with what the user proposes or does it want to contest it), and (b) how it can differentiate between the options available (how should it go about negotiating and what should it say next). In the discussion we will focus not only on flexibility, but on how you might use this interactive capability to implement the necessary dynamics for negotiation. The discussion here is heavily influenced by the agent theory proposed by Kiss (1988), and parts of the ensuing model are borrowed from it. A good account of other possible applications of agent theory to the design of an intelligent tutor can be found in both Blandford (1989) and Baker (this volume).

As we noted earlier, we see essentially three things that can be negotiated, beliefs (cognitive attitudes), goals, or meta-cognitive knowledge. In a tutorial dialogue, the negotiation process is essentially one of trying to find mutual goals of the dialogue or to negotiate about different beliefs concerning what to do next, which viewpoint to use or the behaviour of a program. Clearly, when the goals and beliefs of both interacting agents are very similar, there is less need for negotiation. More interesting cases occur when the stated desire of the two agents conflict, and either a mutually agreed compromise has to be reached, where one agent gives up their position and adopts that of the other, or a stalemate results. Galliers (1988) presents a formal theory of such intra-agent conflict, based on an extension of the logic of intentions of Cohen and Levesque (1987).

Another model of conflict occurs in the work on argumentation by Stutt (1989). Stutt attempts to develop a model of argumentation, and then apply this model to an argument support system within the domain of archaeology. Warrant and counter-warrant can be interrogated in a graphical environment, so that the user can explore the others' beliefs. Multiple views of a domain are implicitly present in the knowledge base of the system, so in some sense, we can think of a form of passive negotiation taking place, as we search the information space of our arguing partner.

Let us now consider what would be required of agents for them to be in a position to negotiate. We assume at this point two agents (one presumably human) which both have a base set of beliefs about the world and a series of goals that they wish to achieve. In the educational context, beliefs are things that are held about the domain and goals may represent longer term considerations, e.g. about the purpose or eventual outcome of the interaction. Based upon these the agents can both propose actions regarding what they wish to do. When the action proposals of the two are not in conflict, they can simply be executed. When they are in conflict, there must be some type of compromise or agreement reached between the two conflicting agents: this can be characterized as a process of negotiation. In order to make this possible, we will characterize each agent as follows. An agent must be aware of its beliefs and goals given a certain situation, and able to propose actions based upon them. Likewise, it must be able to conjecture about the goals and beliefs of the other agent. Each agent can respond to a conflict situation with action proposals that are intended to bring about a change in the perceived state of the other agent. Typically, these might be a dialogue act that attempts to change the beliefs or goals of the other agent. Again these actions can be evaluated by the same function as before to see which action has consequences that best suit the needs of the proposing agent. When we have chosen an action we can look to see what effects this action has had on the other agent. If a conflict still exists, we can iterate again. Thus the model consists of the following steps: analyse the current situation using an evaluation function, decide if a conflict exists and you need to negotiate. If no conflict exists, then both agents can carry out their actions (this will be the case when the teaching agent wants to teach the student and the student wants to listen, but a conflict will exist when the teacher wants to teach a specific item in their next action, and the student wants to change topics). If a conflict exists, we have to propose some other actions to overcome the conflict. These other actions can likewise be evaluated according to the same evaluation function previously employed. Finally, we can choose some action and iterate.

Figure 12.6 will help give an overview of what is suggested. The three critical parts of the model are the evaluation function, conflict detection and resolution, and the actions and visualizations. We will deal with each in turn below. The diagram shows the principle structure. Note the general algorithm the dialogue agent uses. Whether trying to decide how to respond to the current situation or to the proposed (conflicting) actions of the agent, the dialogue agent proposes possible actions, then applies an evaluation function to choose which is the best of these actions; either to propose, or to execute.

6.2   An evaluating function

The basic model we wish to propose is based upon and adapted from Kiss (1988). In this paper Kiss proposes some of the basic properties of an agent system. In this system, the agent is hierarchically organized, featuring more specialized sub-agencies as we descend the hierarchy, involving an increase in power brought about by the specialization, with a corresponding loss of generality. A key concept is the use of a preference mechansim. This mechanism allows the agent to optimize its actions according to the constraints of the different 'goals' or 'values' of the agent.

The term 'goals' needs some qualification. As Kiss points out, these can be both states that the agent can achieve (the conventional sense of goals), or other 'states' which the agent cannot achieve, yet which will nonetheless have the same type of positive influencing effect (i.e. a state an agent believes it to be desirable to be in, but which is either unachievable, or impossible given the other constraints imposed by satisfying the competing desires of the agent). In Kiss (1990) they are talked about instead as *attractors* or *repellers*. Attractors are states the agent believes are desirable and it tries to achieve. Some it can achieve (e.g. conventional goals), others it cannot (but still draw the agent

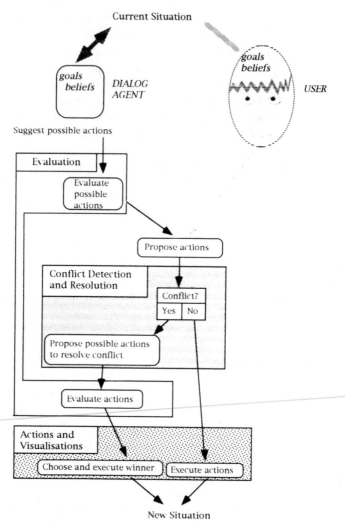

Fig. 12.6

towards it). We shall use this latter terminology to describe the teleological states that the agent tries to achieve. Put simply, these attractors and repellers form the basis of the evaluation mechanism by which the users responses are evaluated, and subsequent actions chosen.

This model has been applied to HCI in Kiss et al. (1988). In these scenarios, agent theory is discussed embedded within an operating system. Thus the system has values (attractor states) like tidyness, security, reliability, locatability, descriptiveness, and compactness. Given an action on the part of the user of the system, it is evaluated according to the values of the agent before it is carried out. If the action conflicts with the attractor states of the agent, then the agent can enter into a dialogue with the user. This dialogue can either simply check that the user really means what they say (and possibly point out the repercussions of their action) or may go as far as denying the user their wishes.

Such a system is well suited to carry out the type of negotiation under discussion here. By considering the desires of the agent, we can build a system that can negotiate beliefs and 'goals' with the user. If the user does anything that conflicts with the desires of the agent, the agent can enter into a dialogue with the user in order to negotiate a compromise that achieves the highest level of satisfaction of the attractors of both the agent and the user.

Applying this framework to evaluating what to do, we assume that the agent has a series of actions that it could take. These actions can be proposed if their preconditions match the current world state or solve a conflict situation. Given any action, we can evaluate how good that action is for the agent by gauging how well the consequences of our actions fit in with the goals of the agents. In Kiss and Brayshaw (1989) a numerical weighting algorithm was used to determine which states the agent found most desirable. Thus given a set of actions, we can order that set of options by seeing which actions move us nearer our (weighted) optimal states. Using a state-space metaphor (and assuming all goals states, in this instance, can be represented in this search space), if we are at point P, we will prefer state-space operators (actions) that move us to a point P', such that P' is closer to our desired goal states.

6.3 Conflict detection and resolution

As a result of looking at and evaluating the current situation, the dialogue agent proposes some action. The user may also wish to propose an action. This may not always be the case if the machine is driving the dialogue: the user may be happy letting the tutor get on with the job. However, the user may want to change what they are doing, or may disagree with a change or use of viewpoint which has just been proposed by the other agent. If the user disagrees with these actions, he or she can subsequently propose his or her own actions. For example, the tutor may decide to change topic or switch viewpoint. The tutor can then execute that action, e.g. with the utterance "Let's stop doing this, and instead consider a new scenario . . .". Looking at the new situation, the student may wish to object ("No, I still don't understand what we've just been doing"). This will result in two possible action proposals, to start tutoring a new item (based on the decision to change topics on the last cycle) and to deal with the students objections. The agent must now spot that either the proposed actions or the consequences of proposed actions (for example, the agent could propose to continue on a topic, the user to change) contradict each other.

Once a contradiction has been spotted, the agent can try and find a way round it. One approach is to seek a compromise action plan. The alternative is to try and change the mind of the dialogue partner. Given that the agent has model of the goals, knowledge, and beliefs of the student, it may be able to make hypotheses about which of these beliefs underpin the proposed action proposal. If it can identify those beliefs, it can then look at its own available actions and try to find one of these actions which might cause the student to revise her beliefs. This could be done in several ways. Firstly, it may be that certain beliefs are erroneous and misplaced. This can include things like misconceptions which we can be predictive about and attach actions to directly tackle and revise them, when we detect them. Other cases may not be so simple (for example, the user may wish to change topic because they do not feel that they are getting sufficient out of the current exercises). In these cases, the agent might be able to change the attitude of the student if it can correctly model the justifications behind her conclusions. It can then look to see which of its actions are able to contradict the justifications of the student and lead to belief revision. This method is basically the same as that for performing argument of Stutt (1989) where we model the process of argument/negotiation as the challenging of the warrant (justifications) of the person we are conversing with, in an attempt to persuade them that their position should be revised. The student can, of course, do the same thing. If they can show the tutor why an action in the current situation is not valid, then that action proposal can be dropped. This can be achieved by the user telling the tutor (in this model this could be done by asserting in the current situation) new information, such that the tutor would now find actions no longer acceptable proposals.

Given that we have a series of action proposals on the part of the tutor, we can use the same evaluation mechanism as before to decide between them.

If the machine tutor cannot find a way out of the conflict, there are several things that could happen next. One is that it could try and identify sub-parts of the two actions proposals which are not in conflict and execute them. The idea behind this is that if you are in an impasse now, if you do something (which may not itself solve the conflict), then the result will be a new state, and it may just be that the conflict does not exist in this state. It might be the case that this new state resolves the deadlock or that actions are now preferred which do not lead to deadlock. If the worst comes to the worst, then one will must prevail over another. If you can't persuade the other agent to change its mind, then you must just let one agent (e.g. the student) have its own way.

6.4 Actions and visualizations

Actions can have visualizations built into them. Thus not only can an action propose to tutor something, it can propose to tutor it in some particular manner using a visualization. Since these visualizations are then associated with action proposals this means that they can also be the subject of the evaluation function. This proposed framework would let us make several possible suggestions for visual methods of dialogue, and the evaluation function would have to assess which one it thought best fitted the requirements of the user. The consequence of this is that visualizations are just treated like any other action/dialogue proposal, yet the agent (via the evaluation function) has a measured way of deciding when it is best to use them.

7 THE DYNAMICS OF VISUAL DIALOGUE

We have now discussed how we could go about implementing some of these ideas. In this final section we will discuss what these visual dialogues might look like and some of the potential problems and difficulties. We will attempt to claim that visualizations can have an important role to play in the machine agent/student dialogue. However, their role is essentially complimentary to the arsenal of the dialogue agent. There are also cases where it would be inappropriate to use the types of visualizations we have been talking about. Program visualization attempts to make the behaviour of programs more accessible and easier to understand and change. Therefore its sets its limits on its own scope as a dialogue device: namely programs and their behaviour. Dialogue that doesn't address itself to this area is unlikely to be amenable to this style of treatment. For example, in an ITS that employed knowledge negotiation, the goals and the specific contents of the interaction can be open ended. Thus we can imagine a student negotiating their own curriculum in the sense of wanting help on areas they don't yet know or are not confident in, but skipping areas where they already have competence. Such a dialogue need not necessarily even be at the level of

any particular programming language or implementation route. A request
to *'Teach me how to write a program to say "hello world"'* is far removed
from the level of the language or solution technique. The proffered study
is also much dependent upon the machine's model of the student, i.e. do
they want a discussion of a *write* statement, or do they instead want a
discussion of AI techniques for natural language generation. Although we
might want to produce a visual language someday, so that this dialogue
could be carried out in a visual manner, this is far beyond the scope of
this paper. It is also debatable as to when visual languages of this sort
would help and when they would hinder. It may be that in this case they
would offer no improvement over natural language, and quite the
converse, might prove cumbersome to use.

We have already argued that good visual models should be used to
encourage a good mental model of the virtual machine, and this in turn
could be used to cut down or remove misconceptions on the part of the
user. Consider the following: suppose that we have a misconception
about something like unification in clause head matching. We could
choose to show a visualization together with appropriate dialogue in
order to tutor the student. Indeed we are not limited to a single
visualization: we could use two or more together. In the unification
scenario, one possibility is to show a fine grained model of the unification
process. As the models can be animated, a step-by-step run-through of
the process could be given, with an accompanying commentary. Indeed,
there is no reason why only a single visualization should be used. We can
imagine using multiple visualizations in order to tutor different aspects of
the same issue. If we were to consider a novice error about flow-of-
control and variable binding then we could use different views to show
this. Consider Figure 12.7

Both of these pictures show the same view. They can also be
temporally synchronized. The one on the left shows the clause head
selection process 'close up'. The one on the right shows the process and
how it communicates with other processes. Thus playing the two
processes through, we can see on the left, the data-flow and process
communication. This in turn will effect the clause head selection process.
In the example above, we can see on the right a fine-grained view of the
clause head selection process. Recall that the small arrows over the
variable names indicate mode declarations (i.e. required direction of
dataflow). The figure on the left shows a close-up view of *live_in*. We can
see that all three clauses are being attempted in parallel. Clauses one and
two do not match, since *helen* cannot be matched with *john* or *mary*.
Clause three can, however, match, as we will see shortly. Turning to the
process communication view, we can see that *happy* communicates with
live_in which in turn communicates with *fun_place*. Data is shown on the

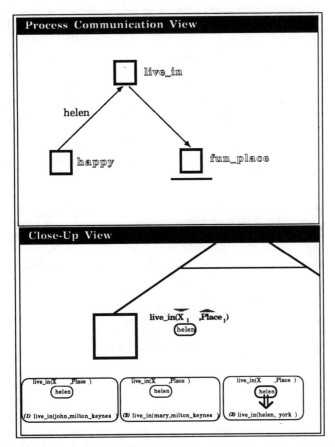

Fig. 12.7 Example of using two complimentary figures, each showing different aspects of the execution processes. The two views can be yoked together, with the same temporal synchronization, so that different aspects of the models can be emphasized. (The example is the same as the one we first saw in Fig. 12.4.)

links between the processes. As we can see, *happy* has sent the process *live_in* the binding *helen*. There has been no communication between *fun_place* and *live_in*, hence the link is shown to be blank. Notice also that *fun_place* is suspended, as indicated by the line underneath the node.

In Figure 12.8, *live_in's* variables are now bound and the clause head matching processes has finished. As a result, the value *york* is communicated to *fun_place*. Consequently, all the processes have succeeded, and this is shown by the node shading. In both views we can see the final successful outcome: as a result of *live_in* passing *fun_place* the value *york* it was no longer suspended, and the process succeeded. Although we have skipped a few steps here, the important point should

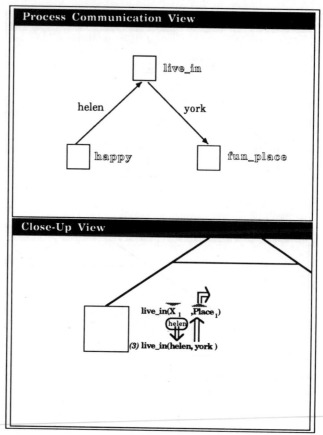

Fig. 12.8 The same program as in the previous figure, only viewed a few evaluation steps later.

be clear. We can use these views, and their dynamic properties, to create tutorial dialogues with the novice. In the case we were talking about earlier, presenting different views with accompanying commentary, we can seek to both tutor and debug the novice. In the last two figures, we can see how we can explain the clause head selection process, *and* show how this is dependent on other processes. By presenting a more total picture and relating different views together, the hope is that a better understanding of program evaluation can be gained, and incorrect models more quickly rectified.

So far we have talked about using visualizations as an adjunct in the negotiation process, in support of normal dialogue. We could hypothesize a scenario where we use just graphic dialogue. Thus the user could talk about the program in graphical terms to the system, and the ITS in its turn could present its part of the dialogue again visually. That is, we could not only use program visualization techniques to communicate information about the program, but we could also use visual programming in order to allow the user to tell the ITS about the program they wished to develop, and how they thought it would work.

Interestingly, if the user was also able to animate these visualizations themselves, could derive a very good model of the user's perception of the control processes, i.e. the fine grained animations produced by the novice would tell us in great detail about what the user thought was going on, because it makes them make explicit their own control rules for the execution process. In principle it may be possible to derive the source code from the animation the user produces, and find its actual behaviour, i.e. from the calling structure, name, number of arguments, and variable names, we might be able to re-construct the code (i.e. that the user incorrectly animates the program execution, may not necessary be fatal to the process of re-constructing the desired code. Even if formally this might be hard, some heuristic short-cuts could still provide the necessary means of doing this). Comparing the ITS re-construction with the one simulated by the user, we should be able to clearly ascertain the errors and present the correct animation, pointing out the differences and discussing the points of diversion.

To allow the user to visually program these types of visualizations, we can imagine producing a graphics editor. This editor could contain a graphics palette (e.g. after MacPaint^{TM} or MacDraw^{TM}) and a frame by frame animator (e.g. after VideoWorks^{TM}). The user can draw the animation by using the graphics sprites on the left hand tool-panel. In order to produce an animation, the new frame option on the replay panel would produce a new frame in the animation, derived initially from a copy of the preceding frame. The graphics tool-panel can then be used to update the next image. We can have a separate editor for each of the visualizations, with different sprites on the graphics package as appropriate. An example using the process control view is given in Figure 12.9.

In Figure 12.9 we see a hypothetical visual programming interface. On the left-hand-side we see a tools palette. Each of these tools correspond with common sprites in the particular representation chosen. In this case the sprites are nodes and interconnecting data-flow, plus text to annotate these graphics. At the bottom is a replay panel, with an extra tool to add an additional frame to the animation. This tool would enable the user to build their own visualization and animations, by producing a new frame, which is a copy of the preceding frame. In this manner animations can be built up by incrementally editing individual frames.

Although the above scenario is technically possible, there are drawbacks. Specifying, in a frame by frame approach, specifying the

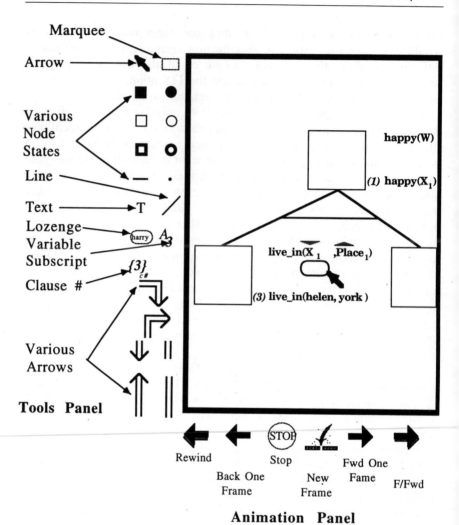

Animation   Panel

Fig. 12.9   Hypothetical graphics editor to implement a visual programming style
interface.

behaviour of the program is very labour intensive. It is also very error
prone. Even if you are a logic programming expert, the artistic effort of
specifying each frame at the level of detail required, is a major task. If
you are a novice, then the processes is even harder. What the interaction
between learning the notation, the editor, and the graphic environment
is, is an open question. Detail that is useful if it can be generated
automatically, is awkward if you have to specify it yourself by hand. The
bottom-line is that *what makes a good program visualization doesn't*

necessarily make a good visual programming language. Information that is advantageous in one view may be cluttersome or too sparse from a different usage perspective. For example, levels of detail that can be omitted in program visualization in order not to clutter up the display, may be essential in visual programming to fully specify the program. This can result in over-elaborate displays. The visualizations that we have presented here have been designed with explanatory purposes first in mind. The ease of drawing them is not an issue, because it is the job of the programmer to generate the visualization. Hence drawing effort is not an issue, explanatory power is. We remain to be convinced if you can produce visualizations that are easy to draw. I have to admit to being slightly sceptical about the prospects for visual programming. It seems that the level of detail that is required to write a program is best specified in text, where things like control and data-flow are implicit within the grammar of the language. If this control and data-flow information has to be specified by hand, a system of this sort places an extra burden on the programmer, without clear benefits. Yet explicit control and data-flow information is precisely the type of information that you might require from a program visualization. In other words, there may be conflicting goals between program visualization and visual programming in the sense that program visualization optimizes for the best explanatory representation. Visual programming optimizes for programmability, so the result may not always be the best for illustrative purposes. There may be a middle path. In ITS systems, there is a good argument to be made for maximising the explanatory nature of the representations used, bearing in mind that other dialogue could be implemented via other means. However, there is a hybrid scenario which might allow us to mix both program visualization and visual programming techniques which we will describe next.

Instead of writing the whole of the program themselves, via visual programming, the system could instead present computer generated visualizations, with various parts omitted or left ambiguous, and require the user to graphically fill out the missing parts. This technique has been used in textbooks (e.g see Eisenstadt 1988), where detailed diagrams of Prolog execution were presented with things like variable binding missing. The exercise was to fill in the missing parts. In an ITS scenario, graphical exercises could be presented in a similar manner. Given an example program, and an example query to evaluate, a visualization could be produced in an environment like the editor we saw earlier, but with part of the visualization deliberately missed out. It is thus the job of the user to go away and fill out these missing parts using the tools from the palette of the graphical editor, and the tool panel, as required.

However, we could also go further. Instead of just filling out missing information, the user could be required to specify extra data-flow information, or to further animate the program (a 'what happens next?' style question). This is made easier than in the pure visual programming scenario, because the user has less to draw, but still carries out a visual interaction with the ITS. Thus if the ITS wanted to focus on control issues and test the users understanding of various parts of the evaluation process, the machine could produce a program trace, and stop it at some critical moment. The exercise would then be to ask the student to animate it from that point. If the animation task is presented at a sufficiently fine level of detail, then the machine should be able to gain a fairly good model of what the novice thinks is going on, by looking at how they describe the process in the ensuing frames of animation. For more advanced students, such fine level animation might not be appropriate (since we could assume more competence on their part, and a better model of the virtual machine), and we could tutor at a much coarser grain size of analysis. A couple of examples may serve to illustrate this point (see Figure 12.10).

Figure 12.10 shows two possible graded exercises, the first simpler than the second. The program and snapshot is exactly the same as that in Figure 12.8. In the first example what has been omitted is the value of one of the variables, which the user has to specify. They can do this by using the text tool from the palette on the right. In the second, all the data-flow information is missing and the user must specify this by hand. Again the necessary icons are present on the right-hand palette. The action of the users is essentially visual programming, however, because half the solution is presented, the effort needed to do this is much reduced. Such a hybrid approach, which tries to maximize the pay-off of visual techniques against pragmatism and ease of use of the system, may well be the best way to go in the future.

8 CONCLUSIONS

In conclusion, we have tried to have a first pass attempt at mapping out the space of visual knowledge negotiation techniques and presenting some of the problems raised in realizing them in practice. The paper has attempted to address the following points:

- What are the issues involved in using knowledge negotiation for teaching software?
- How does knowledge negotiation relate to the use of multiple viewpoints on a domain?

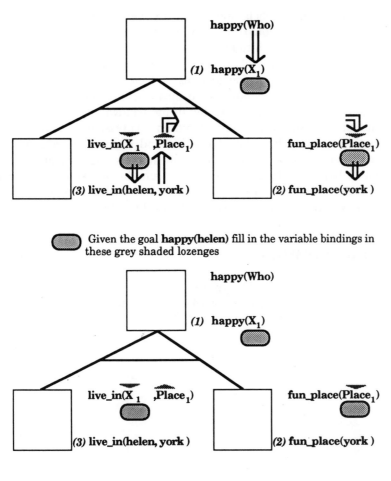

Given the goal **happy(helen)** fill in the variable bindings in these grey shaded lozenges

Given the goal **happy(helen)** fill in the variable bindings in these grey shaded lozenges and using arrows, indicate the data-flow.

Fig. 12.10 A hybrid approach to visual interaction, the two diagrams are deliberately unfinished. It is the task of the user to fill in the blanks.

- What contributions could visual styles of dialogue have in knowledge negotiation? Where would they fit in and how would they work?
- What are the practical and implementational repercussions?

Some of the answers to the questions posed are, ultimately, empirical. How best to balance a dialogue between graphical and natural language;

when and where to use each; and what is the best method in a particular set of circumstances, would need to be determined. At points in the paper I have attempted intuitive guesses at these problems, but these would need to be tested. Likewise, I have ignored many problems that are common to most tutoring systems. I have interpreted knowledge negotiation fairly broadly, not just to mean negotiation about the core curriculum, but to mean a broadening of the bandwidth between teacher and student, in order to maximize freedom, expression and information exchange, leading to both belief revision and learning. I have tried to point to where I think visual dialogue techniques might fit into such a dialogue. I hope that in doing so I have been able to sketch the overall feel of such a system, and how it might work; enabling us to see what *visual knowledge negotiation* might actually look like.

ACKNOWLEDGEMENTS

MacPaint^{TM} and MacDraw^{TM} are trademarks of Apple Computers, Inc. VideoWorks^{TM} is a trademark of MacroMind, Inc.

References

Adler, M.R., Alvah, B.D., Weihmayer, R. & Worrest, W. (1988). Conflict-resolution Strategies for Nonhierarchical Distributed Agents. In *Distributed Artificial Intelligence: Volume II*. London: Pitman Publishing.

Allen, J. (1987). *Natural Language Understanding*. Menlo Park: Benjamin/Cummings.

Allen, J., Perrault, C.R. (1980). Analyzing Intention in Utterances. *Artificial Intelligence* 15: pp. 143–178.

Alpay, L. (1988). Medical Problem-Solving and Intelligent Tutoring Systems: Proposed Research Directions. CITE Research report no. 47, The Open University, U.K.

Alpay, L. (1989a). Developmental User Models. *Interactive Learning International* 5: pp. 79–86.

Alpay, L. (1989b). Acquisition of Reasoning Strategies in Medical Diagnosis. CITE Research report no. 81, The Open University, U.K.

Alpay, L. (1990). Investigating the development of Reasoning Strategies in Medical Diagnosis: A report on an Empirical Study. CITE Research report no. 102, The Open University, U.K.

Amarel, S. (1968). On representations of problems of reasoning about actions. In D. Michie (ed.), *Machine Intelligence 3*. Edinburgh: Edinburgh University Press.

Anderson, J.R. (1983). *The Architecture Of Cognition*. Cambridge, Mass.: Harvard University Press.

Anderson, J.R., Kosslyn, S.M., eds. (1984). *Tutorials In Learning And Memory*. New York: W.H. Freeman.

Anderson, J.R., Boyle, C.F., Yost, G. (1985). The Geometry Tutor. *Proceedings of the Ninth International Joint Conference on Artificial Intelligence*, Los Angeles.

Armstrong, D., Galloway, D., Tomlinson, S. (1991). Decision-making in psychologists' professional interviews. *Educational Psychology in Practice* 7, pp. 82–87

Baker, M.J. (1989a). An artificial intelligence approach to musical grouping analysis. *Contemporary Music Review* 3(1): pp. 43–68.

Baker, M.J. (1989b). A computational approach to modeling musical grouping structure. *Contemporary Music Review* 4(1): pp. 311–325.

Baker, M.J. (1989c). Negotiated Tutoring; An Approach to Interaction in Intelligent Tutoring Systems. Unpublished Ph.D. thesis, Open University, Milton Keynes, U.K.

Baker, M.J. (1989d). A Model for Tutorial Dialogues Based on Critical

Argument. In D. Bierman, J. Breuker, J. Sandberg (eds.), *Artificial Intelligence and Education*. Amsterdam: IOS Publishers.

Baker, M.J. (1990). Arguing with the tutor. In Elsom-Cook, M.T. (ed.), *Guided Discovery Tutoring*. London: Paul Chapman

Baker, M.J. (1991). The Influence of Dialogue Processes on Students' Collaborative Generation of Explanations for Simple Physical Phenomena. *Proceedings of the International Conference on the Learning Sciences*, Evanston, Illinois.

Baker, M.J. (1992). Modelling negotiation in intelligent teaching dialogues (this volume). In R. Moyse, M.T. Elsom-Cook (eds.), *Knowledge Negotiation*. London: Academic Press.

Ballim, A., Wilks, Y., Barnden, J. (1988). Belief ascription, metaphor, and intensional identification. Technical Report MCCS-88-138, Computing Research Laboratory, New Mexico State University.

Baroody, A.J., Gannon, K.E. (1984). The development of the commutativity principle and economical addition strategies. *Cognition and Instruction* 1(3): pp. 321–339.

Bellack, A.A., Kliebard, H.M., Hyman, R.T., Smith, F.L. (1966). *The Language of the Classroom*. Columbia University: Teachers College Press.

Bennett, N. (1976). *Teaching Styles and Pupil Progress*. London: Open Books.

Beveridge, M., Rimmershaw, R.E. (1991). Teaching and Tutoring Systems: Explanatory Dialogues in Context. In P.M. Goodyear (ed) *Teaching Knowledge and Intelligent Tutoring*. Norwood, N.J.: Ablex.

Bhuiyan, S., Greer, J., McCalla, G. (1989). Mental Models of Recursion in Computer Programming. *Conference on Knowledge-Based Computer Systems*, Bombay, India.

Blandford, A. (1990). A Model for the Generation of Tutorial Dialogue. Technical Report 121, Centre for Information Technology in Education, The Open University, U.K.

Blandford, A. (1991). Design, Decisions and Dialogue, Unpublished PhD thesis, Institute of Educational Technology, Open University, Milton Keynes, U.K.

Bliss, J., Ogborne, J. (1989). Tools for exploratory learning. *Journal of Computer Assisted Learning* 5: pp. 37–50.

Bloom, B.S. (1956). *Taxonomy of Educational Objectives, Handbook I: Cognitive Domain*. New York: David McKay Company Inc.

Bobrow, D., (ed). (1984). *Qualitative Reasoning about Physical Systems*. Amsterdam: North Holland.

Bobrow, D.G., Collins, A.M. (1975). *Representation and Understanding*. New York: Academic Press.

Bond, A.H., Glaser, L. (1988). *Distributed Artificial Intelligence*. San Mateo, CA: Morgan Kaufmann.

Bourne, J. Bourne, J., Cantwell, J., Kawamura, K., Kinzer, C., Li, X., De Brock, L., Jiang, J., Vargas, J., Miyasaka, N. et al. (1988). Intelligent CAI in

Engineering: knowledge representation strategies to facilitate model-based reasoning. *International Journal of Intelligent Systems* 3: pp. 213–228.

Brayshaw, M. (in preperation a). Integrating procedural, declarative, and knowledge-based techniques for debugging in logic programming.

Brayshaw, M. (in preperation b). Programming by example as an aid to user defined program visualisations.

Brayshaw, M. (1990a). Visual Models of PARLOG Execution. Submitted to *Journal of Visual Languages and Computing*. Also available as Technical Report 64, Human Cognition Research Laboratory, The Open University, U.K.

Brayshaw, M. (1990b). Visualising Cyclic Behaviour in Prolog. Submitted to *Human Computer Interaction*.

Brayshaw, M. (1991a). An Architecture for Visualisating the Execution of Parallel Logic Programs. *Proceedings of International Joint Conference on Artificial Intelligence*, Sydney, Australia

Brayshaw, M. (1991b). Visualising Cyclic Behaviour in Prolog. Submitted for publication

Brayshaw, M. (1991c). Information Management and the Information Space: Issues in the design of Software Monitoring Systems. Submitted for publication.

Brayshaw, M., Eisenstadt, M. (1988). Adding Data and Procedural Abstraction to the Transparent Prolog Machine. In R.A. Kowalski and K.A. Bowen (eds.), *Logic Programming*, Cambridge, MA: MIT Press.

Brayshaw, M., Eisenstadt, M. (in press). A Practical Graphical Prolog Tracer. *International Journal of Man-Machine Studies*.

Brecht (Wasson), B.J. (1990). Deciding the focus of instruction: Content Planning for Intelligent Tutoring Systems. Ph.D. thesis, University of Saskatchewan, Canada.

Brecht (Wasson), B.J., McCalla, G., Greer, J., Jones, M. (1989). Planning the Content of Instruction. In D. Bierman, J. Breuker, J. Sandberg (eds.), *Artificial Intelligence and Education*. Amsterdam: IOS Publishers.

Briars, D., Siegler, R. (1984). A featural analysis of preschoolers' counting knowledge. *Developmental Psychology* 20: pp. 607–618.

Brna, P., Bundy, A., Pain, H., Lynch, L. (1987). Programming tools for Prolog environments. In J. Hallam & C. Mellish (eds.), *Advances in Artificial Intelligence*. Chichester: John Wiley.

Brown, J.S. (1985). Process versus product : a perspective on tools for communal and informal electronic learning. *Journal of Educational Computing Research* 1(2): pp. 179–201.

Brown, J.S. (1990). Toward a new epistemology for learning. In C. Frasson & G. Gauthier (eds.), *Intelligent tutoring systems: At the Crossroads of Artificial Intelligence and Education*. Norwood, NJ: Ablex.

Brown, J., Burton, R. (1975). Multiple representations of knowledge for tutorial reasoning. In D. Bobrow & A. Collins (eds.), *Representation and Understanding*. New York: Academic Press.

Brown, J.S., Burton, R.R. (1978). Diagnostic models for procedural bugs in basic mathematical skills. *Cognitive Science* 2: pp. 155–191.

Brown, J.S., Burton, R.R. (1982). An investigation of computer coaching for informal learning activities. In D. Sleeman, J.S. Brown (eds.), *Intelligent Tutoring Systems*. New York: Academic Press.

Brown, J. S., Burton, R. R., de Kleer, J. (1982). Pedagogical, natural language, and Knowledge engineering techniques in SOPHIE I, II, and III. In Sleeman, D. H., Brown, J. S. (eds.). *Intelligent Tutoring Systems*. London: Academic Press.

Brown, J.S., Collins, A., Duguid, P. (1989). Situated Cognition and the Culture of Learning. *Educational Researcher* 18(1): pp. 32–42.

Brown, J. S., Rubinstein, R., Burton, R. R., (1976). Reactive learning environment for computer-assisted electronics instruction. BBN Report 3314, Bolt, Beranek and Newman Inc., Cambridge, MA.

Brown, M.H., Sedgewick R. (1985). Techniques for Algorithm Animation. *IEEE Software* 2(1): pp. 28–39.

Brown, M.H. (1987). *Algorithm Animation*. MIT Press, Cambridge, MA.

Bruce, B., Newman, D. (1978). Interacting plans. *Cognitive Science* 2: pp. 195–233.

Bruner, J. S. (1986). *Actual Minds, Possible Worlds*. Harvard University Press: London.

Bundy, A., Pain, H., Brna, P., Lynch, L. (1985). A proposed Prolog story. D.A.I. Research Paper no. 283, University of Edinburgh, Edinburgh, U.K.

Carbonell, J.R. (1970). AI in CAI: an artificial intelligence approach to computer-assisted instruction. *IEEE Transactions on Man-Machine Systems* 11(4): pp. 190–202.

Carbonell, J.R. (1981). Politics. In R. Schank, C. Riesbeck (eds.), *Inside Computer Understanding*. Hillsdale, NJ: Lawrence Earlbaum.

Carley, K. (1986). Knowledge acquisition as a social phenomenon. *Instructional Science* 14: pp. 381–438.

Carpenter, T.P., Moser, J.M. (1983). The acquisition of addition and subtraction concepts. In R. Lesh, M. Landau (eds.), *Acquisition of Mathematics Concepts and Processes*. New York: Academic Press.

Carr, B. (1977). Wusor-II: a computer-aided instruction program with student modeling capabilities. AI Lab. Memo. 417, (Logo Memo. 45). MIT, Cambridge, MA.

Clancey, W.J. (1979). Tutoring rules for guiding a case method dialogue. *International Journal of Man Machine Studies* 11: pp. 24–49.

Clancey W.J. (1983). The Epistemology of a Rule-Based expert System – a Framework for Explanation. *Artificial Intelligence* 20(3).

Clancey, W.J. (1987). *Knowledge-Based Tutoring: the GUIDON Project*. Cambridge, MA.: MIT Press.

Clancey, W.J., Shortliffe, E.H. (eds.) (1984). *Medical Artificial Intelligence: The First Decade.* Reading, MA.: Addison-Wesley.

Cohen, P.R. (1978). On knowing what to say: planning speech acts. Ph.D. thesis, University of Toronto, Canada

Cohen, P., Levesque, H. (1980). Speech acts and the recognition of shared plans. *Proceedings of the 3rd Biennial Conference of the Canadian Society for Computational Studies of Intelligence,* Victoria, BC.

Cohen, P.R., Levesque, H.J. (1990). Intention is Choice with Commitment. *Artificial Intelligence* 42(2-3): pp. 213–261.

Cohen, P.R., Perrault, R. (1979). Elements of a Plan-Based Theory of Speech Acts. *Cognitive Science* 3: pp. 177–212.

Cohn, A.G. (1989). Approaches to qualitative reasoning. *Artificial Intelligence Review* 3: pp. 177–232.

Collins, A., Brown, J.S. (1988). The Computer as a Tool for Learning through Reflection. In H. Mandl, A. Lesgold (eds.), *Learning Issues for Intelligent Tutoring Systems.* New York: Springer-Verlag.

Collins, A., Stevens, A.L. (1983). A Cognitive Theory of Inquiry Teaching. In C.M. Reigeluth (ed.), *Instructional-Design Theories and Models: An Overview of their Current Status.* Hillsdale, NJ: Lawrence Erlbaum.

Conlon, T. (1989). *Programming in PARLOG.* Wokingham, U.K.: Addison-Wesley

Costa, E., Duchenoy, S., Kodratoff, Y. (1988). A resolution based method for discovering students' misconceptions. In J. A. Self (ed.), *Artificial Intelligence and Human Learning.* London: Chapman and Hall.

Cowan, J. (1986). Are we neglecting real analytical skills in engineering education? *European Journal of Engineering Education.*11(1).

Davis, R., Smith, R.G. (1983). Negotiation as a metaphor for distributed problem solving. *Artificial Intelligence* 20: pp. 63–109.

Derry, S.J. (1990). Flexible Cognitive Tools for Problem Solving Instruction. Paper presented at *Computers as Cognitive Tools* (AERA symposium), Boston, MA.

Devi, R. (1990). Acquisition of commutativity and associativity. *Proceedings of the British Society for Research into Learning Mathematics,* Thames Polytechnic, London.

Dillenbourg, P., Self, J. (in press). Designing Human-Computer Collaborative Learning. In C.E. O'Malley (ed.), *Computer Supported Collaborative Learning.* Springer-Verlag, Heidelberg

Dillon, J.T. (1982). The effect of questions in education and other enterprises. *Journal of Curriculum Studies* 14: pp. 127–152

Domingue, J. (1988). TRI: The Graphical Rule Interpreter, In N.Shadbolt (ed.) *Research and Development in Expert Systems VII.* Cambridge University Press, Cambridge, U.K.

Domingue, J., Eisenstadt, M. (1989). A New Metaphor for the Graphical

Explanation of Forward Chainging Rule Execution, *Proceedings of International Joint Conference on Artificial Intelligence* (IJCAI-89), Detroit, MI.

Donohew, L., Sypher, H.E., Higgins, E.T. (1988). *Communication, Social Cognition and Affect*. Hillsdale, NJ: Lawrence Erlbaum.

Douglas, S.A. (1991). Detecting and repairing tutoring failures. In P. Goodyear (ed.), *Teaching Knowledge and Intelligent Tutoring*. Norwood, NJ: Ablex.

du Boulay B., O'Shea T., Monk J. (1981). The black box inside the glass box: presenting computing concepts to novices. *International Journal of Man-Machine Studies* 14: pp. 237–249.

Durfee, E.H., Lesser, V.R. (1989). Negotiating task decomposition and allocation using partial global planning. In L. Gasser, M.N. Huhns (eds.), *Distributed Artificial Intelligence II*. San Mateo: Morgan Kaufmann.

Edwards, D., Mercer, N. (1987) *Common Knowledge*. London: Methuen.

Eisenstadt, M. (1985). Tracing and debugging Prolog programmes by retrospective zooming. HCRL Technical Report no. 17, The Open University, Milton Keynes, U.K.

Eisenstadt, M. (ed.). (1988). *Intensive Prolog*. Associate Student Central Office (Course PD622), The Open University, Milton Keynes, U.K.: Open University Press

Eisenstadt, M. (1989). (AI in (Education in AI)): What does 'domain visualisation' have to offer ITS?, Invited Paper in D. Bierman, J. Breuker, J. Sandberg (eds.), *Artificial Intelligence and Education: Synthesis and Reflection: Proceedings of the 4th. International Conference on AI and Edutcation*, 24–26 May 1989, Amsterdam, The Netherlands, pp. 100., IOS, Amsterdam.

Eisenstadt, M., Brayshaw, M. (1986). The Transparent Prolog Machine (TPM), *Technical Report No. 21, Human Cognition Research Laboratory*, The Open University, Milton Keynes, U.K.

Eisenstadt, M., Brayshaw, M. (1987). Graphical debugging with the Transparent Prolog Machine (TPM). *Proceedings of the Tenth International Joint Conference on Artificial Intelligence (IJCAI-87)*. Los Angeles: Morgan Kaufmann.

Eisenstadt, M., Brayshaw, M. (1988). The Transparent Prolog Machine (TPM): an execution model and graphical debugger for logic programming. *Journal of Logic Programming* 5(4): pp. 1–66

Eisenstadt, M., Brayshaw, M. (1989a). An integrated textbook, video, and software environment for novice and expert Prolog programmers. In E. Soloway, J. Spohrer (eds.), *Studying the Novice Programmer*. Hillsdale, NJ: Lawrence Erlbaum.

Eisenstadt, M., Brayshaw, M. (1989b). AORTA Diagrams as an aid to Visualising the execution of Prolog Programs. In A. Kilgour, R. Earnshaw (eds.), *Graphics Tools for Software Engineers*. Cambridge University Press, Cambridge, U.K.

Elsom-Cook, M. T. (1984). Design considerations of an intelligent tutoring system for programming languages. PhD thesis, Warwick University, U.K.

Elsom-Cook, M. T. (1985). Towards a framework for human-computer discourse.

In P. Johnson, S. Cook (eds.), *People and Computers: Designing the Interface*. Cambridge University Press, Cambridge, U.K.

Elsom-Cook, M. T. (ed.) (1990a). *Guided Discovery Tutoring: A Framework for ICAI Research*. London: Paul Chapman Publishing.

Elsom-Cook, M.T. (1990b). Analysis of a Tutorial Dialogue. In M. Elsom-Cook (ed.), *Guided Discovery Tutoring: A Framework for ICAI Research*. London: Paul Chapman Publishing.

Elsom-Cook, M. T. (1990c). Belief-based bounded user modelling. In *Proceedings of Delta and Beyond Conference*, Den Haag, November.

Elsom-Cook, M.T. (1991). Dialogue and teaching styles. In P. Goodyear (ed.), *Teaching Knowledge and Intelligent Tutoring*. New York: Ablex.

Elsom-Cook, M. T., O'Malley, C. E. (1990). ECAL: Bridging the gap between CAL and Intelligent Tutoring Systems. *Computers and Education*. 15 (3): pp. 69–83

Elsom-Cook, M. T., Spensley, F. (1988). Knowledge representation in a tutoring system for procedural skills, Technical report no. 36, Centre for Information Technology and Education, Open University, Milton Keynes, U.K.

Elstein, A.S., Shulman, L.S., Sprafka, S.A. (1978). *Medical Problem Solving: An Analysis of Clinical Reasoning*. Cambridge, MA: Harvard University Press.

Engelmore, R., Morgan, A., (eds.) (1988). *Blackboard Systems*. London: Addison-Wesley.

Ennis, R.H. (1969). *Logic in Teaching*. Englewood Cliffs, NJ: Prentice Hall.

Evertsz, R., Hennessy, S., Devi, R. (1988). GADL: A Graphical Interface for Mental Arithmetic Algorithms. CITE Report No. 49, The Open University, Milton Keynes, U.K.

Evertsz, R., Elsom-Cook, M. (1990). Generating critical problems in student modelling. In M. Elsom-Cook (ed.), *Guided Discovery Tutoring*, London: Paul Chapman Publishing.

Fagin, R., Halpern, J.Y. (1987). Belief, awareness, and limited reasoning. *Artificial Intelligence* 34: pp. 39–76.

Feltovitch, P.J., Johnson, P.E., Moller, J.H., Swanson, D.B. (1984). LCS: The role and development of medical knowledge in diagnostic expertise. In W.J. Clancey, E.H. Shortliffe (eds.), *Medical Artificial Intelligence: The First Decade*. Reading, MA: Addison-Wesley.

Ferrara, A. (1985). Pragmatics. In T.A. Van Dijk (ed.), *Handbook of Discourse Analysis, Vol. 2*. London: Academic Press.

Frederiksen, J.R., White, B.Y. (1988). Intelligent learning environments for science education. *Proceedings of Conference on Intelligent Tutoring Systems*, Montreal, Canada.

Frolich, D., Luff, P. (1990). Applying the Technology of Conversation to the Technology for Conversation. In P. Luff, N. Gilbert, D. Frohlich (eds.), *Computers and Conversation*. London: Academic Press.

Fung, P. (1989). An Application of Formal Semantics to Student Modelling: an investigation in the domain of teaching Prolog. *CITE Ph.D. Theses #5*, Institute of Education Technology, The Open University, Milton Keynes, U.K.

Fung, P., du Boulay, J.M.B., Elsom-Cook, M.T. (1987). An initial taxonomy of novices' misconceptions of the Prolog interpreter. CAL Research Group Technical Report no. 69, IET, The Open University, Milton Keynes, U.K.

Fung, P., Brayshaw, M., duBoulay, J.M.B., Elsom-Cook, M.T. (1991). A Taxonomy of Novices misconceptions about backtracking. *Instructional Science*, 19 (4/5): pp. 311–337.

Furnham, A. (1988). *Lay Theories: Everyday Understanding of Problems in the Social Sciences*. Oxford: Pergamon.

Fuson, K.C., Hall, J.W. (1983). The acquisition of early number word meanings: a conceptual analysis and review. In H.P. Ginsburg (ed.), *The Development of Mathematical Thinking*. London: Academic Press.

Gale, J., Marsden, P. (1983). *Medical Diagnosis From Students to Clinicians*. Oxford, U.K. Oxford University Press.

Galliers, J.R. (1989). A Theoretical Framework for Computer Models of Cooperative Dialogue, Acknowledging Multi-Agent Conflict. Unpublished PhD thesis, *Technical Report No. 51*, Human Cognition Research Laboratory, The Open University, Milton Keynes, U.K.

Garrod, S., Anderson, A. (1987). Saying what you mean in dialogue: a study in conceptual and semantic coordination. *Cognition* 27: pp. 181–218.

Gelman, R. (1977). How young children reason about small numbers. In N.J. Castellan, D.P. Pisoni, G. R. Potts et al. (eds.), *Cognitive Theory, vol. 2*. Hillsdale, NJ: Lawrence Erlbaum.

Gelman, R., Gallistel, C.R. (1978). *The Child's Understanding of Number*. Cambridge, MA: Harvard University Press.

Gelman, R., Meck, E. (1983). Preschoolers counting: Principle before skill. *Cognition* 13: pp. 343–359.

Gelman, R., Meck, E. (1987). The notion of principle: the case of counting. In J. Hiebert (ed.), *Conceptual and Procedural Knowledge: the Case of Mathematics*. Hillsdale, NJ: Lawrence Erlbaum.

Genesereth, M.R., Nilsson, N.J. (1987). *Logical Foundations of Artificial Intelligence*. Los Altos: Morgan Kaufmann.

Gentner, D. (1983). Structure mapping: a theoretical framework for analogy. *Cognitive Science* 7: pp. 155–170.

Gilbert, J., Watts, M. (1983). Concepts, misconceptions and alternative conceptions: changing perspectives in science education. *Studies in Science Education* 10: pp. 61–98.

Gilmore, D.J., Green, T.R.G. (1988). Programming plans and programming expertise. *Quarterly Journal of Experimental Psychology* 40A: pp. 423–442

Gilmore, D., Self, J. (1988). The application of machine learning to intelligent tutoring systems. In J. Self (ed.), *Artificial Intelligence and Human Learning*. New York: Chapman and Hall.

Goldstein I.P. (1978). The genetic graph: a representation for the evolution of procedural knowledge. *Proceedings of the Second Annual Conference of the Canadian Society for Computational Studies of Intelligence*, Toronto, Canada, pp. 100–106.

Goldstein I.P. (1979). The genetic graph: a representation for the evolution of procedural knowledge. *International Journal of Man-machine Studies* 11:. pp. 51–77. Reprinted in D. H. Sleeman, J. S. Brown (eds.) (1982), *Intelligent Tutoring Systems*. London: Academic Press.

Good, D. (1990). Repair and Cooperation in Conversation. In P. Luff, N. Gilbert, D. Frohlich (eds.), *Computers and Conversation*. London: Academic Press.

Goodyear, P., (ed.) (1991). *Teaching Knowledge and Intelligent Tutoring*. Norwood, NJ: Ablex.

Green, T.F. (1971). *The Activities of Teaching*. New York: McGraw-Hill

Greeno, J.G., Riley, M.S., Gelman, R. (1984). Conceptual competence and children's counting. *Cognitive Psychology* 16: pp. 94–153.

Greer, J.E., Mark, M.A., McCalla, G.I. (1989). Incorporating Granularity-Based Recognition into SCENT. In D. Bierman, J. Breuker, J. Sandberg (eds.), *Artificial Intelligence and Education*. Amsterdam: IOS Publishers.

Greer, J.E., McCalla, G.I. (1989). A Computational Framework for Granularity and its Application to Educational Diagnosis. *Proceedings of the International Joint Conference on Artificial Intelligence*, Detroit, MI.

Gregory, S. (1987). *Parallel Logic Programming in PARLOG: The Language and its Implementation*. Wokingham, U.K.: Addison-Wesley.

Grice, H. (1975). Logic and conversation. In P.Cole, J.L.Morgan (eds.), *Syntax and Semantics, Vol. 3: Speech Acts*. London: Academic Press.

Grosz B.J. (1978). Focus-spaces: a Representation of the Focus of Attention in a Dialog. In D.E. Walker (ed.), *Understanding Spoken Language*. New York: North-Holland.

Grosz, B.J., Sidner, C. (1986). Attention, Intentions and the Structure of Discourse. *Computational Linguistics* 12(3): pp. 175–204.

Gunkara Sun Systems Limited (1988). *PROGRAPH: Programming in Pictures*, personal demonstration.

Hage, J., Meeker, B. (1988). *Social Causality*. Winchester, MA: Allen & Unwin.

Halpern, J. (ed.) (1986). *Theoretical Aspects of Reasoning about Knowledge*. Los Altos, CA: Morgan Kaufmann.

Hendrix, G. (1975). Expanding the utility of semantic networks through partitioning. *Proceedings of the International Joint Conference on Artificial Intelligence*, Tbilisi, Georgia, USSR.

Hennessy, S. (1986). The role of conceptual knowledge in the acquisition of arithmetic algorithms. Unpublished Phd thesis, University of London, U.K.

Hennessy, S. (1990). Why bugs are not enough. In M. Elsom-Cook (ed.), *Guided Discovery Tutoring: a Framework for ICAI Research*. London: Paul Chapman Publishing.

Hewitt, C. (1986). Offices are open systems. *ACM Transactions on Office Information Systems* 4: pp. 271–286.

Hintikka, J. (1971). Semantics for propositional attitudes. In L. Linsky (ed.), *Reference and Modality*. London: Oxford University Press.

Hollan, J.D., Hutchins, E.L., Weitzman, L. (1984). STEAMER: an interactive inspectable simulation-based training system. *AI Magazine* 5(2): pp. 15–27.

Hudlicka, E. (1988). Construction and use of a causal model for diagnosis. *International Journal of Intelligent Systems* 7: pp. 315–349.

Huhns, M.N., Stephens, L.M., Lenat, D.B. (1988). Cooperation for DAI through common-sense knowledge. Technical Report ACA-AI-060-88, MCC, Austin, TX.

Iwasaki, Y., Simon, H. (1986). Causality in device behaviour. *Artificial Intelligence* 29: pp. 3–32.

Jonnaert, P. (1988). Le raisonnement spontanné des élèves au service des didactiques des mathématiques et des sciences expérimentales à l'école fondamentale. Projet de thèse de doctorat Université de Mons. Belgique.

Kahn, K.M. (1989). Objects – A fresh look. Research paper, Xerox Palo Alto Research Centre, Palo Alto, CA.

Kamsteeg, P., Bierman, D. (1988). An object-oriented prolog and its use in a simulated laboratory for physics. *Proceedings of the 2nd European Seminar on ITS*, Le Mans, France.

Keat, R., Urry, J. (1975). *Social Theory as Science*. London: Routledge and Kegan Paul.

Kiss, G. (1986). High-Level Dialogue in Man-Machine Interaction. A Survey Commissioned by the Alvey Directorate, Human Cognition Research Laboratory, The Open University, Milton Keynes, U.K.

Kiss, G.R. (1988). Some Aspects of Agent Theory. *Technical Report No. 43, Human Cognition Research Laboratory*, The Open University, Milton Keynes, U.K.

Kiss, G.R. (in press). Autonomous Agents, AI, and Chaos Theory. In S. Wilson and J.A. Meyer (eds.), *Simulation of Adaptive Behaviour: From Animals to Animats*. Cambridge, MA: MIT Press.

Kiss, G.R., Brayshaw, M.C. (1989). A report on the axiological demo software. *Alvey High-Level Dialogue in MMI Project Report, Report Number HLD/WP/ OU/GRK, MB/4,*

Kiss, G.R., Clark, M., Hopkins, C., Cliffe, N., McTear, M. (1988). A progress report on specifying the first exemplar: Axiological Attitudes in Dialog Agents. *Report on Milestone 2 of the High-Level Dialogue in MMI Project. Report No: HLD/RE/TEAM/1.*

Klahr, D., Langley, P., Neches, R. (eds.) (1987). *Production System Models of Learning and Development.* Cambridge, MA: MIT Press.

de Kleer, J. (1986). An assumption-based TMS. *Artificial Intelligence* 28: pp. 127–162.

de Kleer, J., Brown, J. (1984). A qualitative physics based on confluences. *Artificial Intelligence* 24: pp. 7–83.

de Kleer, J., Brown, J. (1986). Theories of causal ordering. *Artificial Intelligence* 29: pp. 33–61.

Konolige, K. (1984). A deduction model of belief and its logics. Ph.D. thesis, Stanford University, CA.

Kornfeld, W.A., Hewitt, C. (1981). The scientific community metaphor. *IEEE Transactions on Systems, Man and Cybernetics* 11: pp. 24–33.

Kripke, S. (1963). Semantical analysis of modal logic. *Zeitschrift fur Mathematische Logik und Grundlagen der Mathematik* 9: pp. 67–96.

Kripke, S. (1971). Semantical considerations on modal logic. In L. Linsky (ed.), *Reference and Modality.* London: Oxford University Press.

Langley, P., Ohlsson, S., Sage, S. (1984). Machine learning approach to student modelling. Technical report CMU-RI-TR-84-7, Robotics Institute, Carnegie-Mellon University, Pittsburgh, PN.

Langley, P., Simon, H., Bradshaw, G. & Zytkow, J. (1987). *Scientific Discovery: Computational Explorations of the Creative Process.* Cambridge, MA: MIT Press.

Langoltz, C.P., Fagan, L.M., Tu, S.W., Sikic, B.I., Shortliffe, E.H. (1987). A Therapy Planning Architecture That Combines Decision Theory and Artificial Intelligence Techniques. *Computers and Biomedical Research* 20: pp. 279–303.

Larkin J.H., McDermott J., Simon D.P., Simon H.A. (1980). Expert and novice performance in solving Physics Problems. *Science* 208: pp. 1335–1342.

Laurillard, D. (1990). The pedagogical limitations of generative student models. In M. Elsom-Cook (ed.), *Guided Discovery Tutoring: A Framework for ICAI Research.* London: Paul Chapman Publishing.

Lave, J. (1988). *Cognition in Practice.* Cambridge, U.K.: Cambridge University Press.

Lenat, D. (1983). Theory formation by heuristic search. *Artificial Intelligence* 21: pp. 31–59.

Lesgold, A.M. (1984). Acquiring expertise. In J.R. Anderson, S.M. Kosslyn (eds.), *Tutorials In Learning And Memory.* New York: W.H. Freeman.

Lesgold A. (1988). Toward a theory of curriculum for use in designing intelligent instructional systems. In H. Mandl, A. Lesgold (eds.), *Learning Issues for Intelligent Tutoring Systems.* Berlin: Springer-Verlag.

Leventhal, L.M., Instone, K. (1988). Becoming an Expert: The process of acquiring expertise among highly novice computer scientists (Pilot and Proposal). Research Report. Department of Computer Science, Bowling Green University, USA.

Levesque, H. (1984). A logic of implicit and explicit belief. *Proceedings of the National Conference on Artificial Intelligence*. Los Altos: Morgan Kaufmann.

Levesque, H. (1986). Making believers out of computers. *Artificial Intelligence* 30: pp. 81–108.

Levin, J.A., Moore, J.A. (1977). Dialogue-Games: Metacommunication Structures for Natural Language Interaction. *Cognitive Science* 1(4): pp. 395–420.

Levinson, S.C. (1983). *Pragmatics*. Cambridge, U.K.: Cambridge University Press.

Lochhead, J. (1985). Teaching Analytic Reasoning Skills Through Pair Problem Solving. In J.W. Segal, S.F. Chipman, R. Glaser (eds.), *Thinking and Learning Skills. Volume 1: Relating Instruction to Research*. Hillsdale, NJ: Lawrence Erlbaum.

Luff, P., Gilbert, N., Frohlich, D. (1990). *Computers and Conversation*. London: Academic Press.

MacLure, M., French, P. (1980). Routes to right answers: on pupils' strategies for answering teachers' questions. In P.Woods (ed.), *Pupil Strategies*. London: Croom Helm.

McCalla, G., Bunt, R., Harms, J. (1986). The Design of the SCENT Automated Advisor. *Computational Intelligence* 2(2): pp. 76–92.

McCalla, G.I., Greer, J.E., the SCENT Research Team (1990). SCENT-3: An Architecture for Intelligent Advising in Problem Solving Domains. In C. Frasson , G. Gauthier (eds.), *Intelligent Tutoring Systems: At the Crossroads of Artificial Intelligence and Education*. Norwood, NJ: Ablex.

McCarthy, J., Hayes, P. (1969). Some philosophical problems from the standpoint of artificial intelligence. In B. Meltzer, D. Michie (eds.), *Machine Intelligence 4*. Edinburgh, U.K.: Edinburgh University Press.

Martins, J.P., Shapiro, S.C. (1988). A model for belief revision. *Artificial Intelligence* 35: pp. 25–79.

Mehan, H. (1979) *Learning Lessons: Social Organisation in the Classroom*. Cambridge, MA: Harvard University Press.

Michalski, R.S., Carbonell, J.G., Mitchell, T.M. (1983). *Machine Learning*. Palo Alto, CA: Tioga Publishing Co.

Miller, P.B. (1975). Strategy Selection in Medical Diagnosis. Master Dissertation, MAC TR-153, MIT, Cambridge, MA.

Miller, R.A., Massarie, F.E. (1989). Use of the Quick Medical Reference (QMR) program as a tool for medical education. *Methods of Information in Medicine* 28: pp. 340–345.

Minsky, M. (1981). A Framework for representing knowledge. In J. Haugeland (ed.), *Mind Design*. Cambridge, MA: MIT Press.

Minsky, M. (1987). *The Society of Mind*. London: Heinneman.

Moore, R.C. (1977). Reasoning about knowledge and action. *Proceedings of the International Joint Conference on Artificial Intelligence*, pp. 223–227.

Moyse, R. (1989). Knowledge Negotiation Implies Multiple Viewpoints. In D. Bierman, J. Breuker, J. Sandberg (eds.), *Artificial Intelligence and Education*. Amsterdam: IOS Publishers.

Moyse, R. (1990). Multiple Viewpoints for Tutoring Systems. Unpublished PhD. thesis, Institute of Educational Technology, The Open University, Milton Keynes, U.K.

Moyse, R. (1991). Multiple viewpoints imply Knowledge Negotiation. *Interactive Learning International* 7(1): pp. 21–37.

Moyse, R., Elsom-Cook, M.T. (1992). Knowledge negotiation: An introduction (this volume) In R. Moyse, M.T. Elsom-Cook (eds.), *Knowledge Negotiation*. London: Academic Press.

Ohlsson, S., Rees, E. (1988). An information processing analysis of the function of conceptual understanding in the learning of arithmetic procedures. Tech. report no. KUL-88-03, Pittsburgh, PN.

O'Malley, C.E. (1989). Graphical Interfaces for Guided Discovery Learning: Problems for Student Modelling. Paper given at the NATO Advanced Research Workshop on Guided Discovery Tutoring, Italy.

O'Malley, C. E. (1990). Interface issues for guided discovery learning environments. In Elsom-Cook, M.T. (ed.), *Guided Discovery Tutoring*. London: Paul Chapman

O'Malley, C.E., Draper, S.W., Riley, M.S. (1984). Constructive interaction: a method for studying computer-user interaction. In B.Shackel (ed.), *Interact '84 First Conference on Human-Computer Interaction*, Amsterdam: North Holland.

Ortony, A., Clore, G.L., Collins, A. (1988). *The Cognitive Structure of Emotions*. Cambridge, U.K.: Cambridge University Press.

O'Shea T., Smith R. B. (1987). Understanding Physics by violating the laws of nature: Experiments with the Alternate Reality Kit. *Proceedings of the Conference on Computer-Assisted Learning*, (CAL'87), University of Strathclyde.

Pain, H, Bundy, A. (1987). What stories should we tell novice Prolog programmers. In R. Hawley (ed.), *Artificial Intelligence Programming Environments*. New York: John Wiley.

Papert, S. (1980). *Mindstorms*. Harvester: Brighton.

Patel, V.L., Frederiken, C.L. (1984). Cognitive processes in comprehension and knowledge acquisition by medical students and physicians. In H.G. Schmidt, M.L. DeVoder (eds.), *Tutorials in Problem Based Learning*. Assen, Holland: Van Gorcum.

Paxton, A.L.,Turner, E.J. (1984). The application of human factor to the needs of the novice computer users. *International Journal of Man-Machine Studies*. 20: pp. 137–156.

Perkinson, H.J. (1984). *Learning from our Mistakes*. Greenwood: Westport.

Petrie-Brown, A. (1989a). Discourse and Dialogue: Concepts in Intelligent Tutoring Interactions. *Journal of Artificial Intelligence in Education* 1(2): pp. 21–29.

Petrie-Brown, A. (1989b). Intelligent Tutoring Dialogue: The structures of an interaction. In D. Bierman, J. Breuker, J. Sandberg (eds.), *Artificial Intelligence and Education*. Amsterdam: IOS Publishers.

Petrie-Brown, A. (1990). Freedom of speech: The concepts of guidance and dialogue in Intelligent tutoring. In Elsom-Cook, M.T. (ed.), *Guided Discovery Tutoring*. London: Paul Chapman.

Power, R. (1979).The organisation of purposeful dialogues. *Linguistics* 17: pp. 107–152.

Quillian, M.R. (1969). Semantic Memory. In M. Minsky (ed.), *Semantic Information Processing*. Cambridge MA: MIT Press.

Rajan, T.M. (1990). Principles for the design of dynamic tracing environments for novice programmers. *Instructional Science*. 19 (4/5): pp. 377–406.

Ramsden, P., Whelan, G., Cooper, D. (1988). Some Phenomena of Medical Students' Diagnostic Problem-Solving. *Medical Education* 22: pp. 799–809.

Reichman, R. (1978). Conversational Coherency, *Cognitive Science*. 2 (4): pp. 283–327.

Reichman, R. (1985). *Getting Computers to Talk Like You and Me*. Cambridge, MA: MIT Press.

Reichman, R. (1986). Communication paradigms for a window system. In D.A. Norman, S.W. Draper (eds.), *User Centered System Design: New Perspectives in Human-Computer Interaction*. Hillsdale, NJ: Lawrence Erlbaum.

Reimann, P. (1989). REFRACT: a microworld for refraction phenomena. Technical Report 49, Psychological Institute, University of Freiburg, Germany.

Resnick, L.B. (1980). The role of invention in the development of mathematical competence. In R.H. Kluwe, H. Spada (eds.), *Developmental Models of Thinking*. New York: Academic Press.

Resnick, L.B. (1983). A developmental theory of number understanding. In H.P. Ginsburg (ed.), *The development of mathematical thinking*. London: Academic Press.

Resnick, L. (1989). Mutual scaffolding in collaborative reasoning. Paper given at *3rd European Conference for Research on Learning and Instruction*, Madrid, Spain.

Richard, J.F. (1990). *Les Activités Mentales*. Paris: Armand Colin Editeur.

Ringwood, G.A. (1988). PARLOG86 and the Dining Logicians. *Communications of the ACM* 31(1): pp. 10–25.

Roschelle, J. (1990). Designing for Conversations. Paper presented at the *AAAI Symposium on Knowledge-Based Environments for Learning and Teaching*, Stanford, CA.

Roschelle, J., Behrend, S.D. (in press). The Construction of Shared Knowledge in Collaborative Problem Solving. In C. O'Malley (ed.), *Computer Supported Collaborative Learning*. Heidelberg: Springer Verlag.

Rulifson, J.F., Derksen, J.A., Waldinger, R.J. (1972). QA4: a Procedural calculus for intuitive reasoning. Tech Note 73, SRI AI Centre, Stanford University, CA.

Rymaszewski, R.H. (1987). Negotiating Cooperative and Effective Explanations. *CeRCLe Technical Report No. 39*, University of Lancaster Centre for Research on Computers and Learning, Lancaster, U.K.

Rymaszewski, R.H., Beveridge, M. (1989). Explanation for tutoring systems: some lessons from classroom learning. Paper presented at the *3rd European Conference on Learning and Instruction*, Madrid, Spain.

Sarantinos, E., Johnson, P., Johnson H. (1990). Theoretical, empirical and computational approaches to explanation dialogues. Paper presented at the *AI in the User Interface Colloquium*, IEE, April 27 1990.

Schank, R. (1982). *Dynamic Memory*. Cambridge, U.K.: Cambridge University Press.

Schegloff, E.A., Sacks, H. (1973). Opening up Closings. *Semiotica* 8(4): pp. 289–327.

Schmidt, C.F., Sridharan, N.S., Goodson, J.L. (1978). The plan recognition problem. *Artificial Intelligence* 11: pp. 45–83.

Schmidt, H.G., Devolder, M.L., (eds.) (1984). *Tutorials in Problem Based Learning*. Assen, Holland: Van Gorcum.

Schofield, J.W., Evans-Rhodes, D., Huber, B.R. (in press). Artificial Intelligence in the Classroom: The Impact of a Computer-Based Tutor on Teachers and Students. *Social Science Computer Review*.

Schubuaueur-Leoni, M.L., Bell, N. (1987). Pupil's representations in Didactic Interactions. Paper presented at the *2nd European Conference for Research on Learning and Instruction*, Tübingen, Germany.

Schutz, A. (1963). Concept and theory formation in the social sciences. In M. Natanson (ed.), *Philosophy of the Social Sciences*. New York: Random House.

Searle, J. (1969). *Speech Acts: An Essay in the Philosophy of Language*. Cambridge, U.K.: Cambridge University Press.

Self, J.A. (1988a). The use of belief systems for student modelling. Paper given at *The European Congress on Artificial Intelligence and Training*, Lille, France.

Self, J.A. (1988b). Knowledge, belief and user-modelling. In T. O'Shea, V. Sgurev (eds.), *Artificial Intelligence III: Methodology, Systems, Applications*. Amsterdam: Elsevier Science Publications.

Self, J. (1988c). Bypassing the intractable problem of student modelling. *Proceedings of ITS-88*, Montreal, Canada.

Self, J.A. (1989). The Case for Formalising Student Models (and Intelligent Tutoring Systems generally). Paper given at the *4th.Conference on Artificial Intelligence and Education*, Amsterdam, Netherlands.

Self, J.A. (1990). Theoretical foundations for intelligent tutoring systems. *Journal of Artificial Intelligence in Education* 1(4): pp. 3–14

Self, J.A. (1992). Computational Viewpoints (this volume). In R. Moyse, M.T. Elsom-Cook (eds.), *Knowledge Negotiation*. London: Academic Press.

di Sessa, A. (1982). Unlearning Aristotelian physics: a study of knowledge based learning. *Cognitive Science* 6: pp. 37–75.

di Sessa, A. (1986). Models of Computation. In D.A. Norman, S.W. Draper (eds.), *User Centered System Design: New Perspectives in Human-Computer Interaction.* Hillsdale, NJ: Lawrence Erlbaum.

Shadbolt, N. (1986). Discourse strategies. Paper presented at the *1st Alvey KBS Club Explanations Workshop,* University of Surrey, Guildford, March 1986.

Shoham, Y. (1988). *Reasoning about Change.* Cambridge, MA: MIT Press.

Shortliffe E. H, (1976). *Computer-based Medical Consultations: MYCIN.* New York: Elsevier.

Sinclair, J., Coulthard, R.M. (1975). *Towards and Analysis of Discourse: The English Used by Teachers and Pupils.* London: Oxford University Press.

Sless, D. (1981). *Visual Communication.* London: Croom Helm.

Smith, N. V. (ed.) (1982). *Mutual Knowledge.* Academic Press: London.

Smith, R.B. (1986). The Alternate Reality Kit: An animated environment for creating interactive simulations. *Proceedings of the 1986 IEEE Computer Society Workshop on Visual Languages,* Dallas, TX: pp. 99–106.

Soloway, E.M., Johnson, W.L. (1984). Remembrance of blunders past: a retrospective on the development of PROUST. *Proceedings of the Sixth Cognitive Science Society Conference,* Boulder, CO: p. 57.

Sperber, D., Wilson, D. (1986). *Relevance: Communication and Cognition.* Oxford: Basil Blackwell.

Stevens, A. L., Collins, A. (1980). Multiple conceptual models of a complex system. In R. E. Snow, P. Federico, W. E. Montague (eds.), *Aptitude Learning and Instruction Volume 2: Cognitive Process Analyses of Learning and Problem Solving.* Hillsdale, NJ: Lawrence Erlbaum.

Stevens, A.L., Collins, A., Goldin, S. (1979). Misconceptions in Students' Understanding. *International Journal of Man-Machine Studies* 11: pp. 145–156. (Reprinted in D. Sleeman, J.S. Brown, (eds.) (1982), *Intelligent Tutoring Systems.* London: Academic Press).

Stevens A.L., Roberts B. (1983). Quantitative and Qualitative Simulations in Computer Based Training. *Journal of Computer-Based Instruction* 10(1): pp. 16–19.

Strawson, P.F. (1971). Intention and convention in speech acts. In J.R. Searle (ed.), *The Philosophy of Language.* London: Oxford University Press.

Suchman, L.A. (1985). Plans and Situated Actions: The Problem of Human-Machine Communication. Xerox Parc Technical Report P85-00005, Xerox Corporation, Palo Alto Research Centers, CA, U.S.A.

Suchman, L. (1987). *Plans and Situated Actions: The Problem of Human-Machine Communication.* Cambridge, U.K.: Cambridge University Press.

Swift, L.F. (1961). Explanation. In R.H. Ennis, B.O. Smith (eds.), *Language and Concepts in Education.* Chicago: Rand McNally.

Sycara, K. (1988). Resolving Goal Conflicts via Negotiation. *Proceedings of the AAAI-88 Conference*, St. Paul, Minnesota.

Sycara, K. (1989). Multiagent compromise via negotiation. In L. Gasser, M.N. Huhns (eds.), *Distributed Artificial Intelligence II*. London: Pittman.

Taylor, J. (1984). Why novices will find learning Prolog hard. *Procedings of the European Conference on Artificial Intelligence (ECAI-84)*, Pisa, Italy.

Taylor, J. (1988). Programming in Prolog: an in-depth study of problems for beginners learning to program in Prolog. Cognitive Science Research Paper no. 111, School of Cognitive and Computing Sciences, University of Sussex, U.K.

Thomas, D. (1979). *Naturalism and Social Science: a Post-Empiricist Philosophy of Social Science*. Cambridge, U.K.: Cambridge University Press.

Thomson, A. (1989). Hooks and the Nature of Discovery Learning. Paper presented at the NATO Advanced Research Workshop on Guided Discovery Tutoring, Italy.

Tiberghien, G. (1986). Context and Cognition: Introduction. *Cahiers de Psychologie Cognitive* 6(2): pp. 105–119.

Toulmin, S.E. (1958) *The Uses of Argument*. Cambridge, U.K.: Cambridge University Press.

Toulmin, S., Rieke, R., Janik, A. (1979). *An Introduction to Reasoning*. New York: Macmillan Publishing Co.

VanLehn, K. (1988). Towards a theory of impasse-driven learning. In H. Mandl, A. Lesgold (eds.), *Learning Issues for Intelligent Tutoring Systems*. New York: Springer-Verlag.

Voss, J. (1988). Problem solving and reasoning in ill-structured domains. In C. Antaki (ed.), *Analysing Everyday Explanation*. London: Sage.

Voss, J., Greene, T., Post, T., Penner, B. (1983). Problem solving skill in the social sciences. *The Psychology of Learning and Motivation* 17: pp. 165–213.

Vygotsky, L.S. (1978). Mind in Society: The Development of Higher Psychological Processes. In M. Cole, V. John-Steiner, S. Scribner, E. Souberman (eds.), Cambridge, MA: Harvard University Press.

Weinert, F.E., Kluwe, R.H., (eds.) (1987). *Metacognition, Motivation and Understanding*. Hillsdale NJ: Lawrence Erlbaum.

Wellman, H.M. (1985). The Child's Theory of Mind: The Development of Conceptions of Cognition. In S.R. Yussen (ed.), *The Growth of Reflection in Children*. Madison, WI: Academic Press.

Wenger, E. (1987). *Artificial Intelligence and Tutoring Systems: Computational and Cognitive Approaches to the Communication of Knowledge*. Los Altos: Morgan Kaufmann.

Wertsch, J.V. (1985). Adult-Child Interaction as a Source of Self-Regulation in Children. In S.R. Yussen (ed.), *The Growth of Reflection in Children*. Madison, WI: Academic Press.

White, B.Y., Frederiksen, J.R. (1986). Intelligent tutoring systems based upon qualitative model evolutions. *Proceedings of the Fifth National Conference on Artificial Intelligence*, Philadelphia, PN.

White, R, (1987). Effects of Pascal upon the learning of Prolog – an initial study. *Unpublished Research Report*, Department of Artificial Intelligence, University of Edinburgh, U.K.

Whitehead, A. N. (1932). *The Aims of Education*. Benn: London.

Wilensky, R. (1983). *Planning and Understanding: A Computational Approach to Human Reasoning*. Reading, MA: Addison-Wesley.

Wilson, S., Shulman, L., Richart, A. (1987). 150 ways of knowing: representations of knowledge in teaching. In J. Calderhead (ed.), *Exploring Teachers Thinking*. Cassell: London.

Winch, P. (1958). *The Idea of a Social Science and its Relation to Philosophy*. London: Routledge and Kegan Paul.

Winne, P. H. (forthcoming). Motivation and Teaching. In H. Waxman, H. Walburg (eds.), *Effective Teaching: Current Research*. Berkley, CA: McCutchan.

Winograd, T., Flores, F. (1986). *Understanding Computers and Cognition*. Norwood, NJ: Ablex.

Young, R., O'Shea, T. (1981). Errors in children's subtraction. *Cognitive Science* 5: pp. 153–177.

Young, R.M. (1983). Surrogates and Mappings: Two Kinds of Conceptual Models for Interactive Devices. In D. Gentner, D.L. Stevens (eds.), *Mental Models*. Hillsdale, NJ: Lawrence Erlbaum.

Young, R.M., Simon, T. (1987). Planning in the context of human-computer interaction. In D. Diaper, R. Winder (eds.), *People and Computers III*. Cambridge, U.K.: Cambridge University Press.

Index